SCHAUM'S®
outlines

French
Grammar

—————— Seventh Edition

Mary E. Coffman Crocker

French Editor and Consultant
Toronto, Ontario

Schaum's Outline Series

New York   Chicago   San Francisco   Athens   London   Madrid
Mexico City   Milan   New Delhi   Singapore   Sydney   Toronto

MARY E. COFFMAN CROCKER is a French editor, author, and consultant in Toronto, Ontario. She was previously Senior Editor, French as a Second Language, Copp Clark Pitman, Toronto, Ontario; Directrice des Éditions, Langes Secondes, Centre Éducatif et Culturel, Montréal, Québec; and Sponsoring Editor, Foreign Language Department, McGraw-Hill Book Company, New York, New York. She is also the author of *Schaum's Outline of French Vocabulary*, Fourth Edition and a biographee in *Who's Who of American Women*, Ninth Edition.

1 2 3 4 5 6 7 8 9   LOV   23 22 21 20 19 18

ISBN   978-1-260-12095-0
MHID   1-260-12095-3

e-ISBN 978-1-260-12096-7
e-MHID   1-260-12096-1

PREFACE

This review book has been designed and developed in order to facilitate the study of French grammar. The book is divided into nine chapters. Each one concentrates on the basic problem areas of the language: nouns and articles; adjectives and adverbs; prepositions; numbers, dates, and time; verbs; interrogatives; negatives; pronouns; and special meanings of certain verbs.

Each grammatical or structural point is introduced by a simple explanation in English. The explanation is further clarified by many concrete examples. It is recommended that you first read the explanation and then study the illustrative examples. You should then write out the answers to the exercises that follow. You should rewrite the entire sentence in fill-in-the-blank exercises even though only one or two words are required. It is recommended that you correct yourself immediately before proceeding to the next exercise. An answer key appears at the end of the book.

Many of the exercises involve authentic, meaningful contexts and practical, real-life situations to which students can relate. Some of the exercises will require you to understand meaning as well as form in order to successfully complete them. Other exercises provide for openended and personalized answers. These exercises will help you develop proficiency in French and prepare for communicative activities in your classroom.

One of the most difficult and tedious tasks in acquiring a second language is learning the many forms that exist in the language, whether they are noun, adjective, or verb forms. In *Schaum's Outline of French Grammar*, all forms have been logically grouped in order to make their acquisition as simple as possible and also to minimize what at first appear to be irregularities. In many texts, the verbs *courir*, *rire*, *rompre*, and *conclure* are treated as separate irregular verbs in the present tense. You will note, however, that these verbs have a lot in common. The same endings as those for regular **-re** verbs are added to the infinitive stem except in the third person singular:

courir—il court, je cours, tu cours, nous cour**ons**, vous cour**ez**, ils cour**ent**
rire—il rit, je ris, tu ris, nous ri**ons**, vous ri**ez**, ils ri**ent**
rompre—il rompt, je romps, tu romps, nous romp**ons**, vous romp**ez**, ils romp**ent**
conclure—il conclut, je conclus, tu conclus, nous conclu**ons**, vous conclu**ez**, ils conclu**ent**

This can be done with many verbs in all tenses. Making such groupings will greatly facilitate your task of mastering the many forms.

Schaum's Outline of French Grammar can be used as a review text, as a companion to any basic text, or as a reference book. In order to reinforce each point you are learning in your basic text, you may wish to get additional practice by doing the clear, logically organized exercises provided throughout this book. Each chapter contains review exercises. These sections are indicated by the gray bar in the outer margin.

See the inside ad to find directions on downloading a companion audio recording. Based on selected material (page 389) from the answer key, you can use this recording to practice your French comprehension and pronunciation skills.

New to this edition are French typographical rules.

For a review of vocabulary organized by topic, see *Schaum's Outline of French Vocabulary*.

MARY E. COFFMAN CROCKER

Spelling Reforms

Although the Académie française has recently recommended spelling reforms, they are not widely implemented so the changes are not applied in the body of this book and in most textbooks. The Académie considers both the old and the new forms correct. Following are some of the new rules.

The circumflex (^) is no longer obligatory on the letters **i** and **u** except when the missing accent could be confused for another word

New	Old
maitresse	**maîtresse**
paraitre	**paraître**

But:

il croît (*it grows*), not to be confused with **il croit** (*he believes*)
mûr (*ripe*), not to be confused with **mur** (*wall*)

All compound numbers can now be hyphenated.

New	Old
vingt-et-un	vingt et un
quatre-cent-quarante-deux	quatre cent quarante-deux

With verbs that have the letter **é** in the next to the last syllable of the infinitive, the **é** becomes **è** in the future and conditional tenses.

Infinitive: **préférer**

New	Old
Future: **je préfèrerai**	**je préférerai**

Conditional:

Je préfèrerais	**je préférerais**

The agreement of the past participle of **laisser** when followed by an infinitive is now optional.

Old	New
Il nous a laissé(e)s partir.	**Il nous a laissé partir.**

CONTENTS

CHAPTER 1   *Nouns and Articles*   *1*

Gender and the Definite Article   1
    Singular Forms.

Gender Identification by Word Endings   2

Nouns Indicating Occupations, Nationalities, Relationships and
Domestic Animals   3

Words with Different Meanings in Masculine and
Feminine Forms   4

Plural Forms of Nouns   4
    Regular Plurals. Nouns Ending in *-s*, *-x* or *-z*. Nouns Ending in *-au*,
    -eau, *-eu* or *-œu*. Nouns Ending in *-ou*. Nouns Ending in *-al*. Nouns
    Ending in *-ail*. Irregular Plurals.

Singular or Plural   7

Compound Nouns   8

Special Uses of the Definite Article   9
    With General or Abstract Nouns. With Titles. With Languages and
    Academic Subjects. With Days of the Week, Seasons, Dates and Time
    Expressions. With Names of Continents, Countries, Provinces, Regions,
    Islands, Mountains and Rivers. With Weights and Measures. With Parts
    of the Body or Clothing.

Omission of the Definite Article   14

Contractions of the Definite Article   14

The Indefinite Article   16

Omission of the Indefinite Article   16
    After the Verb *être*. Other Omissions of the Indefinite Article.

The Partitive Article   18

The Partitive Article Versus the Definite and Indefinite Articles   19

Exceptions to the Rule for Using the Partitive Article   19
    When the Sentence is Negative. When an Adjective Precedes a Noun in
    the Plural. After Expressions of Quantity and Expressions with *de*.

CHAPTER 2   *Adjectives and Adverbs*   **24**

Formation of the Feminine of Adjectives   24
Regular Forms. Adjectives Ending in a Vowel, Pronounced Consonant or
Mute -*e*. Adjectives Ending in -*el*, -*eil*, -*il*, -*en*, -*on*, -*et* and -*s*. Adjectives
Ending in -*er*. Adjectives Ending in -*x*. Adjectives Ending in -*eur*.
Adjectives Ending in -*f*. Adjectives Ending in -*c*. Irregular Adjectives. The
Adjectives *beau, nouveau, vieux*.

Plural of Adjectives   31
Regular Forms. Adjectives Ending in -*s* or -*x*. Adjectives Ending in -*eu* or
-*eau*. Adjectives Ending in -*al*.

Agreement Problems of Certain Adjectives   33
Adjectives of Color.

Compound Adjectives   35

Position of Adjectives   36

Adjectives That Change Meaning According to Position   39

Formation of Adverbs   41
Regular Forms. Adverbs Formed from Adjectives Ending in a Vowel.
Adverbs Ending in -*ément*. Adverbs Ending in -*amment* and -*emment*.
Irregular Adverbs.

Position of Adverbs   46

Comparison of Adjectives and Adverbs   47
Regular Comparisons. Comparative Followed by a Noun.

Superlative of Adjectives and Adverbs   49

Irregular Comparatives and Superlatives   50
Adjectives without Comparative and Superlative Forms. Useful Phrases
with Comparatives and Superlatives.

Possessive Adjectives   54
Use of the Definite Article as a Possessive. With *on, personne,
tout le monde*. With *chacun*.

Demonstrative Adjectives   58

Indefinite Adjectives   59

CHAPTER 3   *Prepositions*   **70**

Uses of Certain Prepositions   70

Prepositions to Indicate Location or Direction
to or from a Place   71
À, de, dans, en, chez.

Prepositions with Geographical Names   73
À. En. Au. Dans. De.

Prepositions with Modes of Transportation   76

Prepositions with Expressions of Time   77
À, at. *Dans, en*, in. *Avant*, before and *après*, after.

Prepositions Used to Join Two Nouns   79
To Indicate Function or to Join a Noun that Modifies Another Noun. To
Mean *with*. To Introduce the Material from Which an Object is Made.

CONTENTS

Prepositions of Cause 80

Prepositions After Indefinite Pronouns 80

Prepositions in Adverbial Clauses of Manner 81

Prepositions to Introduce an Infinitive Depending on
a Noun or Adjective 82
To Indicate Function, Result or Tendency. After Expressions of
Duration, Length of Time and Position of the Body.

CHAPTER 4   ***Numbers, Dates, Time***   **88**

Numbers 88
Cardinal Numbers. Ordinal Numbers. Collective Numbers. Fractions.
Arithmetical Operations. Dimensions.

Dates 94

Time 95

CHAPTER 5   ***Verbs***   **98**

Moods and Tenses 98

Subject Personal Pronouns 99

The Present Tense 99
First Conjugation Verbs. Verbs Beginning with a Vowel. Verbs with
Spelling Changes: Verbs ending in *-cer* and *-ger*; Verbs with *-é-* in the
infinitive; Verbs with *-e-* in the infinitive; Verbs with *-yer* in the infinitive.
Second Conjugation Verbs. Third Conjugation Verbs. Irregular Verbs:
Verbs like *ouvrir*; Verbs like *courir, rire, rompre, conclure*; *Battre* and
mettre; Verbs like *partir*; *Vaincre*; Verbs like *connaître*; *Plaire* and *se taire*.
Verbs with Infinitives Ending in *-ire*: *Lire, dire, conduire, traduire*; *Écrire,
vivre, suivre*; *Croire, voir* and *mourir*; Verbs like *craindre, peindre, joindre*;
Verbs like *prendre*; *Venir* and *tenir*; *Acquérir* and *conquérir*; *Pouvoir,
vouloir, pleuvoir*; *Boire, devoir, recevoir*; *Avoir*; *Être*; *Aller*; *Faire*; *Savoir*;
Valoir and *falloir*. Special Uses of the Present Tense: *Depuis, il y a . . . que,
voilà . . . que*, and *ça fait . . . que* plus the present tense; *Venir de* plus the
infinitive.

Reflexive / Pronominal Verbs 132
S'asseoir. Reflexive Verbs with Parts of the Body. Reflexive versus Non-
reflexive Verbs. Reflexive Verbs in the Infinitive.

Imperatives 137
Affirmative Imperatives. The Affirmative Imperative of Reflexive
Verbs. The Negative Imperative. The Negative Imperative of Reflexive
Verbs.

The Present Participle 140
Formation. Use.

The Imperfect Tense 142
Regular Forms. Verbs with Spelling Changes. *Être*.

Uses of the Imperfect Tense 144
Continuing or Habitual Action. With Verbs Denoting Mental Activity or
Conditions. Descriptions in the Past. *Si* and the Imperfect Tense. *Depuis,*

il y avait... que, voilà... que, ça faisait... que and the Imperfect Tense. *Venir de* in the Imperfect Tense.

The Conversational Past Tense (*Passé Composé*) of Verbs Conjugated with *Avoir* 148
The *Passé Composé* of -er Verbs. The *Passé Composé* of -ir Verbs. The *Passé Composé* of -re Verbs. Irregular Past Participles: Past participle ending in -é; Past participle ending in -i, -is, -it; Past participle ending in -ait; Past participles ending in -u; Past participles ending in -ert; Past participle of verbs ending in -indre. Agreement of the Past Participle with Verbs Conjugated with *avoir*.

The *Passé Composé* of Verbs Conjugated with *Être* 156
Monter, *descendre*, *sortir*, *entrer*, *rentrer* with *être* and *avoir* in the *Passé Composé*. *Passer* with *être* and *avoir* in the *Passé Composé*. The *Passé Composé* of Reflexive Verbs. Agreement of the Past Participle with Reflexive Pronouns.

Uses of the *Passé Composé* 160
Present Perfect. Past Action. Differences between the *Passé Composé* and the Imperfect Tense: Specific action versus habitual or continuing action; With *souvent*, *parfois*, *quelquefois*; Specific action versus ongoing action; Events versus background; Verbs with different meanings in the imperfect and *passé composé*.

The Literary Past Tense (*Passé Simple*) 168
The *Passé Simple* of -er Verbs. The *Passé Simple* of -ir and -re Verbs. Irregular Verbs Building the *Passé Simple* upon the Past Participle: Verbs with past participles ending in -i; Verbs with past participles ending in -i plus a consonant; Verbs with past participles ending in -u. Irregular Verbs not Building the *Passé Simple* upon the Past Participle.

The Future 173
Aller with an Infinitive. Regular Forms of the Future Tense. Verbs Using the Third Person Singular Form of the Present Tense as the Future Stem: Verbs ending in -yer; Verbs with -e- in the infinitive. Verbs with Irregular Future Stems. Special Uses of the Future Tense: After certain conjunctions; After *penser que*, *savoir que*, *espérer que*, *ne pas savoir si* and in indirect discourse; To express probability.

The Conditional 182
Formation of the Present Conditional. Uses of the Conditional: To express the idea *would*; After certain conjunctions; To soften a request, command or desire; To express possibility or unsure action; In indirect discourse.

Compound Tenses 186
Pluperfect Tense (*Plus-que-parfait*). Future Perfect Tense (*Futur Antérieur*). Past Conditional (*Passé du Conditionnel*). The Past Anterior (*Passé Antérieur*) and the *Passé Surcomposé*.

Si Clauses 193

The Subjunctive Mood 195

Present Subjunctive 195
Regular Forms. Spelling Changes in the Present Subjunctive. Verbs with Internal Vowel Changes in the Present Subjunctive: Verbs with -é- in the infinitive; Verbs with -e- in the infinitive; *Prendre*, *tenir*, *venir*. Verbs with Variable Bases in the Present Subjunctive. Verbs with Irregular Bases in the Present Subjunctive. Uses of the Subjunctive: Subjunctive in noun clauses; Subjunctive with impersonal expressions that express opinion or emotions; Subjunctive with expressions of doubt; Subjunctive with

CONTENTS

subordinate conjunctions; Subjunctive as an imperative; Subjunctive after an affirmation. Subjunctive in relative clauses: Indefinite antecedent; After *rien, personne, quelqu'un*; With the superlative and *seul, unique*. Subjunctive after indefinite words such as *si... que, quelque... que, quel... que, qui que...*, etc. Avoiding the Subjunctive.

The Past Subjunctive   213

The Imperfect Subjunctive   215
  Use of the Imperfect Subjunctive.

The Pluperfect Subjunctive   217
  Use of the Pluperfect Subjunctive.

Si Clauses in the Subjunctive   218

Sequence of Tenses in Indirect Discourse   218
  Indirect Discourse in Sentences with an Interrogative Word. Interrogative
  Pronouns in Indirect Discourse. Inversion of the Subject in Indirect
  Discourse.

Uses of the Infinitive   221
  After Prepositions. As a Noun. As an Imperative. In an Interrogative
  Phrase Expressing Deliberation. In an Exclamatory Phrase. *Faire* in
  Causative Construction. *Laisser* and Verbs of Perception plus the
  Infinitive. The Use of the Prepositions *à* and *de* before an Infinitive.

Passive Voice   230
  Forms of the Passive Voice. True Passive with *être*. The Passive Voice
  with *se*.

CHAPTER 6 **Interrogative Words and Constructions**   **232**

Forming Questions   232
Interrogative Forms by Inversion—Simple Tenses   233
Interrogative Forms by Inversion—Compound Tenses   234
Interrogative Adverbs and Adverbial Expressions   235
Interrogative Pronouns   236
Qu'est-ce que c'est? Qu'est-ce que?   238
Interrogative Adjective *Quel*   238
Interrogative Pronoun *Lequel*   239

CHAPTER 7 **Negative Words and Constructions**   **242**

Negation of Simple Tenses   242
Negation of Compound Tenses   243
The Negative Interrogative   244
Si in Answer to a Negative Question   245
Omission of *Pas*   245
Negation of the Infinitive   245
Negative Words and Phrases   246

CHAPTER 8 **Pronouns** **252**

Subject Pronouns   252
Direct Object Pronouns   253
  Le, la, l', les. Special Use of the Pronoun *le*.
Direct and Indirect Object Pronouns   255
  Me, te, nous, vous.
Indirect Object Pronouns   256
  Lui, leur.
The Pronoun *Y*   257
The Pronoun *En*   258
Double Object Pronouns   259
Position of Object Pronouns   260
  With Conjugated Verbs. With an Infinitive. With Infinitive Constructions:
  Causative *faire* (*faire faire*), *laisser* and Verbs of Perception. With
  Affirmative Commands.
Reflexive Pronouns   265
Disjunctive Pronouns   266
Possessive Pronouns   268
Demonstrative Pronouns   270
Indefinite Demonstrative Pronouns   271
  Ce, ceci, cela (*ça*).
Relative Pronouns   272
  Qui who, which, that. *Que* whom, which, that. *Ce qui* and *ce que*. Relative
  Pronouns with Prepositions Other than de: Qui, lequel. Où. Relative
  Pronouns with the Preposition *de*: *Dont, duquel. Quoi, ce dont.*
Indefinite Pronouns   279

CHAPTER 9 **Special Meanings of Certain Verbs** **285**

Expressions with *Aller*   285
Expressions with *Avoir*   286
Expressions with *Être*   287
Expressions with *Faire*   288
Special Uses of Other Verbs   289
  *Devoir, pouvoir, savoir, vouloir. Habiter, demeurer, vivre. Jouer, jouer à,
  jouer de. Manquer, manquer à, manquer de. Penser à, penser de. Partir,
  sortir, s'en aller, laisser, quitter. Passer, se passer, se passer de. Plaire.
  Se rappeler, se souvenir de. Servir, se servir de. Savoir versus connaître.
  Venir de.*

Answers to Exercises **298**

Verb Charts **369**

French Typographical Rules **379**

Index **383**

Companion Audio Recording **389**

CHAPTER 1

Nouns and Articles

Gender and the Definite Article

Singular Forms

All French nouns, unlike English nouns, have a gender. Every noun is either masculine or feminine. Nouns that refer specifically to males (people or animals), such as *father*, *son*, etc., are masculine. Those that refer to females (people or animals), such as *mother, daughter,* etc., are feminine. For most other nouns, gender is usually arbitrary and must be memorized.

The definite article (*the*) that accompanies masculine nouns is **le. La** accompanies feminine nouns. **L'** is used before masculine or feminine nouns beginning with a vowel or silent **h.**

Masculine		*Feminine*	
le garçon	*boy*	la fille	*girl*
le frère	*brother*	la sœur	*sister*
le père	*father*	la mère	*mother*
le chien	*dog*	la chienne	*dog*
le chat	*cat*	la chatte	*cat*
le musée	*museum*	la plage	*beach*
le marché	*market*	la boutique	*shop*
le salon	*living room*	la chambre	*bedroom*
l'ami	*(male) friend*	l'amie	*(female) friend*
l'homme	*man*	l'épée	*sword*
l'ordinateur	*computer*	l'école	*school*

But:

le héros	*hero*
le haricot	*bean*
le hors-d'œuvre	*hors d'œuvre, canapé*

1

1. Complete the following with the correct form of the definite article **le, la** or **l'**.

1. _Le_ garçon joue avec _la_ chatte dans _le_ salon.
2. _Le_ père prépare _le_ dîner à _la_ maison.
3. _Le_ professeur enseigne _l'_ histoire, _l'_ anglais, _la_ géographie et _la_ philosophie.
4. _L'_ arbre est plus grand que _la_ fleur.
5. _La_ chienne joue avec _le_ chat sur _la_ plage.
6. _L'_ artiste dessine _le_ portrait.
7. _L'_ ami de Pierre joue avec _la_ sœur de Marie.
8. _La_ sœur regarde _la_ statue dans _le_ musée.
9. _L'_ enfant aime _le_ bifteck et _le_ fromage.
10. _La_ mère laisse _la_ lettre sur _le_ bureau.

Gender Identification by Word Endings

Nouns ending in **-sion, -tion, -aison, -ance, -ence, -té, -ude, -ale, -ole, -ie** and **-ure** are usually feminine.

la version	*translation*
la nation	*nation*
la terminaison	*ending*
la connaissance	*knowledge*
la patience	*patience*
la beauté	*beauty*
la certitude	*certainty*
la plénitude	*plenitude*
la cathédrale	*cathedral*
la photographie	*photography*
la philosophie	*philosophy*
la parole	*word*
la culture	*culture*
la facture	*bill*

Nouns ending in **-asme, -isme, -eau, -ment** and **-acle** are usually masculine.

l'enthousiasme	*enthusiasm*
le sarcasme	*sarcasm*
le classicisme	*classicism*
le couteau	*knife*
l'enseignement	*teaching, education*
le gouvernement	*government*
le spectacle	*show, performance*

2. Complete the following sentences with the definite article **le, la** or **l'**. For each word beginning with a vowel, indicate whether it is masculine or feminine by writing **l'(f.)** or **l'(m.)**.

1. _La_ prononciation et _la_ (f.) intonation sont importantes dans _l'_ étude des langues.
2. Elle étudie _le_ classicisme, _le_ romantisme, _le_ symbolisme et _la_ civilisation française.
3. Ils admirent _la_ beauté de _la_ peinture.
4. Elle étudie _l'_ impressionisme et _la_ culture française.
5. Dès _la_ naissance, il faut surveiller _la_ nourriture du bébé.

6. _La_ sarcasme sera évident dans _le_ spectacle de ce soir.
7. _La_ multitude exprime _la_ certitude.
8. _Le_ parlement est dans _le_ bâtiment en face.
9. Elle étudie _la_ philosophie.

Nouns Indicating Occupations, Nationalities, Relationships and Domestic Animals

Nouns indicating professions, trades, nationalities, relationships and domestic animals have both masculine and feminine forms.

Occupations[1]

Masculine		Feminine	
le président	*president*	**la présidente**	*president*
l'avocat	*lawyer*	**l'avocate**	*lawyer*
le chanteur	*singer*	**la chanteuse**	*singer*
le danseur	*dancer*	**la danseuse**	*dancer*
le vendeur	*salesman*	**la vendeuse**	*saleswoman*
l'informaticien	*data processor*	**l'informaticienne**	*data processor*
le directeur	*head, director*	**la directrice**	*head, director*

But:

le médecin	*doctor*	**la femme médecin**	*doctor*
l'écrivain	*writer*	**la femme écrivain**	*writer*
le professeur	*teacher*	**la femme professeur**	*teacher*

Nationalities

le Français	*Frenchman*	**la Française**	*Frenchwoman*
l'Anglais	*Englishman*	**l'Anglaise**	*Englishwoman*

Relationships

le cousin	*(male) cousin*	**la cousine**	*(female) cousin*

Animals

le chien	*dog*	**la chienne**	*bitch*
le chat	*(male) cat*	**la chatte**	*(female) cat*

3. Complete the following sentences with the correct word and article.

1. _Le professeur_ Pierre Letarte enseigne à l'école Brébœuf.
2. Anne est la fille de Madame Dupont. Pierre est le fils de la sœur de Madame Dupont. Anne est _la cousine_ de Pierre.
3. _L'informaticienne_ Marie Pierron travaille avec les ordinateurs.
4. _L'Anglais_ Peter Smith habite l'Angleterre.
5. _La danseuse_ Simone Leclerc danse avec le Ballet national.
6. Pierre donne beaucoup à manger à ses animaux; donc, _la chatte_ de Pierre est grosse.

---

[1] In Québec many former masculine nouns have been given feminine forms, but despite attempts to do the same in France, they are not widely accepted. In French, the word **femme** is added to many masculine nouns to show that the person is female when there is no acceptable feminine form.

Words with Different Meanings in Masculine and Feminine Forms

The following pairs of words have different meanings for masculine and feminine forms.

Masculine		Feminine	
l'aide	helper	l'aide	help
le critique	critic	la critique	criticism
le guide	guide	la guide	reins (of a horse)
le livre	book	la livre	pound
le manche	handle	la manche	sleeve
le mode	method, mode	la mode	fashion
le moule	mold	la moule	mussel
l'office	office, duty	l'office	pantry
le page	page-boy	la page	page (of a book)
le pendule	pendulum	la pendule	clock
le poêle	stove	la poêle	frying pan
le poste	job	la poste	post office
le somme	nap	la somme	sum
le tour	turn, walk around	la tour	tower
le vase	vase	la vase	mud
le voile	veil	la voile	sail

4. Complete the following sentences with the correct form of the definite article **le** or **la**.

1. _____ critique fait _____ critique du roman.
2. On a offert _____ poste à _____ poste à M. Dupont.
3. On a fait _____ tour de _____ tour Eiffel.
4. _____ voile que la veuve porte est noir. _____ voile du bateau est jaune.
5. _____ guide explique comment tenir _____ guide du cheval.
6. Les pommes coûtent 3,50 € _____ kilo.
7. _____ mode détermine l'habit de l'homme.
8. L'homme se chauffe devant _____ poêle. Il met le bacon dans _____ poêle.
9. _____ manche de cette robe est déchirée. _____ manche de cette poêle est cassé.
10. Ne cassez pas _____ vase!

Plural Forms of Nouns

Regular Plurals

Most nouns are made plural by adding **s** to the singular forms. **Les** is the definite article accompanying all plural nouns. Note the liaison between **les** and a word beginning with a vowel.

Masculine		Feminine	
Singular	*Plural*	*Singular*	*Plural*
le garçon	les garçons	la fille	les filles
le livre	les livres	la table	les tables
l'ami	les amis	l'amie	les amies

Nouns Ending in -*s*, -*x* or -*z*

Nouns ending in -**s**, -**x** or -**z** are alike in both the singular and plural forms.

Singular		*Plural*
le bras	*arm*	**les bras**
la fois	*time*	**les fois**
le vers	*verse*	**les vers**
le prix	*price*	**les prix**
la voix	*voice*	**les voix**
le nez	*nose*	**les nez**

Nouns Ending in -*au*, -*eau*, -*eu* or -*œu*

Nouns ending in -**au**, -**eau**, -**eu** or -**œu** add **x** to form the plural.

Singular		*Plural*
le noyau	*pit (of a fruit)*	**les noyaux**
le bateau	*boat*	**les bateaux**
le château	*castle*	**les châteaux**
la peau	*skin*	**les peaux**
le feu	*fire*	**les feux**
le jeu	*game*	**les jeux**
le vœu	*wish*	**les vœux**

Exceptions:

le landau	*carriage*	**les landaus**
le pneu	*tire*	**les pneus**

Nouns Ending in -*ou*

Nouns ending in -**ou** generally add **s** to form the plural.

Singular		*Plural*
le clou	*nail*	**les clous**
le sou	*penny*	**les sous**
le trou	*hole*	**les trous**

Some nouns ending in -**ou** add **x** to form the plural.

Singular		*Plural*
le bijou	*jewel*	**les bijoux**
le caillou	*stone*	**les cailloux**
le chou	*cabbage*	**les choux**
le genou	*knee*	**les genoux**
le hibou	*owl*	**les hiboux**
le joujou	*toy*	**les joujoux**
le pou	*flea, louse*	**les poux**

Nouns Ending in -al

Many nouns ending in **-al** in the singular change **-al** to **-aux** to form the plural.

Singular		Plural
l'animal	animal	les animaux
le cheval	horse	les chevaux
l'hôpital	hospital	les hôpitaux
le journal	newspaper	les journaux

Exceptions:

le bal	ball, dance	les bals
le carnaval	carnival	les carnavals
le festival	festival	les festivals

Nouns Ending in -ail

Many nouns ending in **-ail** add **s** to form the plural.

le chandail	sweater	les chandails
le détail	detail	les détails
l'éventail	fan	les éventails

Exceptions:

le bail	lease	les baux
le travail	work	les travaux
le vitrail	stained glass window	les vitraux

Irregular Plurals

l'aïeul	ancestor	les aïeux
le bonhomme	old fellow	les bonshommes
le ciel	sky	les cieux
le gentilhomme	gentleman	les gentilshommes
l'œil	eye	les yeux
monsieur	Mr.	messieurs
madame	Mrs.	mesdames
mademoiselle	Miss	mesdemoiselles

Family names do not add **s** to form the plural.

les Dupont	the Duponts

5. Complete the following with the correct form of the indicated noun.

1. Les _tables_ sont petites.   *table*
2. J'aime beaucoup les _vers_ de Baudelaire.   *vers*
3. Ne mange pas les _noyaux_, ma petite.   *noyau*
4. As-tu des _sous_ ?   *sou*
5. Le chien est couvert de _poux_.   *pou*
6. J'adore les _festivals_.   *festival*
7. _Messieurs_, _mesdames_ et _mesdemoiselles_, écoutez bien.   *Monsieur, madame, mademoiselle*
8. Frottez-vous les _genoux_.   *genou*
9. Les _feux_ de forêt sont destructifs.   *feu*

10. Les _amis_ sont gentils. *ami*
11. Le Martien a deux _nez_. *nez*
12. Faites des _vœux_ pour le retour du beau ciel bleu. *vœu*
13. Les éléphants sont de grands _animals_. *animal*
14. Regarde les jolis _vitraux_ de l'église. *vitrail*
15. J'aime beaucoup manger les _choux_. *chou*
16. Il fait très chaud. Voici des _éventail_. *éventail*

6. Rewrite the following, changing all nouns to the plural. Make any other necessary changes.

1. La loi est juste. *Les lois sont justes* 42/44
2. La voix est jolie. *Les voix sont jolies*
3. Regardez le feu! *Regardez les feux*
4. Le trou est grand. *Les trous sont grands*
5. Le repas est bon. *Les repas sont bons*
6. Le journal explique le travail. *Les journaux expliquent le travail*
7. L'école est moderne. *Les écoles sont modernes*
8. Le château est joli. *Les châteaux sont jolis*
9. Le détail du dessin sur le chandail est magnifique. *Les détails du dessin sont magnifiques*
10. Le prix est élevé. *Les prix sont élevés*
11. Le jeu est amusant. *Les jeux sont amusants*
12. Voilà le clou. *Voilà les clous*
13. Le bijou est joli. *Les bijoux sont jolis*
14. Le caillou est petit. *Les cailloux sont petits*
15. Le bateau est grand. *Les bateaux sont grands*
16. Le musée est grand. *Les musées sont grands*
17. L'œil est grand. *Les yeux sont grands*
18. Le cheval est l'animal que vous aimez. *Les chevaux sont les animaux que vous aimez*
19. Monsieur, regardez la peinture. *Mr. regardez les peintures*
20. Le bal a lieu samedi. *Les bals ont lieu samedi*
21. Le gentilhomme est grand. *Les gentilshommes sont grands*
22. Voici un bonhomme de neige. *Voici un bonshommes de neige*

7. Rewrite the following, changing the nouns to the singular. Make all necessary changes.

1. Les rois habitent dans les châteaux.
2. Les nez sont grands.
3. Les joujoux sont intéressants.
4. Les carnavals sont amusants.
5. Les cieux sont bleus.
6. Les amis sont aimables.
7. Les peaux de vison sont chères.
8. Les journaux sont intéressants.
9. Les aïeux sont célèbres.
10. Les yeux sont bruns.
11. Les bras sont forts.
12. Les clous sont longs.
13. Les vitraux sont jolis.
14. Les vœux sont compréhensibles.
15. Les chandails sont chauds.
16. Les hiboux sont noirs.
17. Les voix des chanteurs sont jolies.
18. Les jeux de cartes sont intéressants.

Singular or Plural

Some nouns that are usually plural in English are <u>singular in French</u>.

Singular	*Plural*
le bétail	*cattle*
la famille	*family*
la police	*police*

Some nouns that are always singular in English are plural in French.

les fiançailles	*engagement*
les funérailles	*funeral*
les nouvelles	*news*
les honoraires	*fee*

8. Complete the following with the correct from of the definite article.

1. _____ *Les* funérailles pour M. Dupont auront lieu lundi prochain.
2. _____ *Les* nouvelles à la télé sont à six heures du soir.
3. _____ *Les* honoraires de votre comptable augmenteront cette année.
4. _____ *La* police va arrêter le criminel.

Compound Nouns

The plural of compound nouns is irregular.

1. If formed with two nouns in apposition, with a noun and an adjective, or with two adjectives, an **s** or **x** is added to both parts to form the plural.

Singular		*Plural*
le beau-frère	*brother-in-law*	**les beaux-frères**
la belle-sœur	*sister-in-law*	**les belles-sœurs**
le chou-fleur	*cauliflower*	**les choux-fleurs**
le coffre-fort	*safe*	**les coffres-forts**
la grand-mère	*grandmother*	**les grands-mères**
le grand-père	*grandfather*	**les grands-pères**
le wagon-restaurant	*dining car*	**les wagons-restaurants**

2. If the compound noun is formed by a noun and its complement, only the first part is plural.

Singular		*Plural*
l'arc-en-ciel	*rainbow*	**les arcs-en-ciel**
le chef-d'œuvre	*masterpiece*	**les chefs-d'œuvre**
le timbre-poste	*stamp*	**les timbres-poste**

3. In rare cases, **s** is added only to the last part.

Singular		*Plural*
le pique-nique	*picnic*	**les pique-niques**

4. If the compound noun is formed by an invariable word plus a noun, only the noun is made plural.

Singular		*Plural*
l'avant-coureur	*forerunner, precursor*	**les avant-coureurs**
le bien-pensant	*right-thinking, orthodox person*	**les bien-pensants**

5. If the compound noun is formed by a verb and its complement, both parts are invariable. The plural is the same as the singular.

Singular		*Plural*
l'abat-jour	*lampshade*	**les abat-jour**
le gratte-ciel	*skyscraper*	**les gratte-ciel**
le pare-brise	*windshield*	**les pare-brise**
le passe-partout	*passkey*	**les passe-partout**
le réveille-matin	*alarm clock*	**les réveille-matin**

But:

le cure-dent	*toothpick*	**les cure-dents**
le couvre-lit	*bedspread*	**les couvre-lits**
le tire-bouchon	*corkscrew*	**les tire-bouchons**

6. Other compound nouns that are the same in the singular and in the plural are as follows.

Singular		*Plural*
l'après-midi	*afternoon*	**les après-midi**
le hors-d'œuvre	*canapé, hors d'œuvre*	**les hors-d'œuvre**
le tête-à-tête	*private talk*	**les tête-à-tête**

9. Rewrite the following sentences, putting the nouns in the plural.

1. L'après-midi le grand-père dort.
2. Le réveille-matin sonne à huit heures du matin.
3. La grand-mère met le chou-fleur dans le panier pour le pique-nique.
4. Il lit le chef-d'œuvre de Racine.
5. Il y a un gratte-ciel à New York.
6. Le timbre-poste est dans le coffre-fort.
7. Il faut nettoyer le pare-brise.
8. Pour ouvrir la bouteille de vin, prenez un tire-bouchon.
9. Le beau-frère mange le hors-d'œuvre.
10. La belle-sœur aime l'arc-en-ciel.

Special Uses of the Definite Article

With General or Abstract Nouns

Unlike English usage, in French the definite article must be used with all abstract nouns or nouns used in a general sense. Compare the French and English in the following examples.

L'homme est mortel.
Man is mortal.
Il aime les bananes.
He likes bananas.
La biologie est une science.
Biology is a science.

L'amour est divin.
Love is divine.
Les cigarettes ne sont pas bonnes pour la santé.
Cigarettes are not good for the health.

The definite article is used when infinitives and adjectives are used as abstract nouns.

Le rire est bon pour la santé mentale.
Laughter is good for mental health.
Le tragique de l'histoire c'est que l'accident n'était pas inévitable.
The tragic aspect of the story is that the accident was not inevitable.
L'essentiel c'est de bien travailler.
The essential thing is to work well.

10. Complete the following with the appropriate definite article.

1. _Les_ Français sont fiers.
2. _La_ vie est dure.
3. _La_ patience est une vertu.
4. _Les_ chiens sont des animaux domestiques.
5. _Les_ diamants sont des bijoux.
6. _Les_ bananes sont des fruits.
7. _L'_ automne est une saison.
8. _Le_ charbon est noir.
9. Il aime _les_ pommes frites.
10. Il n'aime pas _les_ épinards.
11. _La_ biologie est une science.
12. _Les_ femmes d'aujourd'hui sont conscientes de leurs droits.
13. _L'_ essentiel c'est de bien écouter avant de répondre.

With Titles

When talking about someone, the definite article must be used with titles. The article is omitted, however, in direct address.

Le docteur Martin est dentiste.
Doctor Martin is a dentist.

But:

Bonjour, docteur Martin.
Hello, Doctor Martin.

Le général Pierron est arrivé.
General Pierron has arrived.

But:

Comment allez-vous, général Pierron?
How are you, General Pierron?

The article is never used with **monsieur, madame** and **mademoiselle** in direct address.

Monsieur Le Blanc vient.
Mr. Le Blanc is coming.
Comment allez-vous, Madame Le Blanc?
How are you, Mrs. Le Blanc?

In formal address, the article is used before the title.

Bonjour, madame la présidente.

11. Complete the following with the appropriate definite article, when it is necessary.

9/10

1. _Le_ docteur Merlier est un grand homme.
2. _Le_ comte de Deauville est ici.
3. Bonjour, _____ professeur Le Blanc.
4. _____ Mademoiselle Pierron habite à Roanne.
5. Où allez-vous, _____ Monsieur Péneau?
6. Savez-vous qui est ~~la~~ Madame Leclerc?
7. Comment allez-vous, _____ Madame Mercier?
8. Bonjour, monsieur _le_ président.
9. _Le_ capitaine Andrieu va faire un discours.
10. _Le_ présidente préside l'assemblée.

With Languages and Academic Subjects

The definite article is used with languages unless the name of the language immediately follows the verb **parler** or the prepositions **de** or **en**.

> **Le français est une belle langue.**
> *French is a beautiful language.*
> **J'étudie le français et l'anglais.**
> *I study French and English.*
> **Je parle très bien (le) français.**
> *I speak French very well.*
>
> *But:*
>
> **Je parle français.**
> *I speak French.*
> **J'ai un livre de français.**
> *I have a French textbook.*
> **Ce livre est écrit en français.**
> *This book is written in French.*

The definite article is also used with academic subjects.

> **J'étudie l'histoire et les mathématiques.**
> *I study history and mathematics.*

12. Complete the following with the definite article, when it is necessary.

7/7

1. Parlez-vous _____ français?
2. Il parle très couramment _le_ français.
3. J'apprends _la_ biologie.
4. _La_ russe est une langue difficile.
5. Est-ce que c'est un livre de _____ russe?
6. Elle lui écrit en _____ allemand.
7. Dites-vous cela en _____ anglais?

With Days of the Week, Seasons, Dates and Time Expressions

The definite article is used with days of the week to indicate habitual occurrence. The definite article has the meaning of *every* or *on*. The definite article accompanying the days of the week is masculine.

> **J'ai ma classe de français le lundi.**
> *I have my French class on Mondays (every Monday).*
> **Le dimanche, je ne travaille pas.**
> *On Sunday(s) I don't work.*

The definite article is omitted when talking about a <u>particular day</u>.

Je suis allé au cinéma lundi.
I went to the movies (on) Monday.
Je viendrai vous voir samedi.
I will come to see you (on) Saturday.
Dimanche est le dernier jour de la semaine.
Sunday is the last day of the week.

The definite article has the meaning of *in the* when used with parts of the day.

Le matin, je vais à l'église.
In the morning, I go to church.
L'après-midi, je vais à la plage.
In the afternoon, I go to the beach.
Le soir, je vais au cinéma.
In the evening, I go to the movies.

The definite article is used with seasons when discussing the season in a general sense.

L'été est une saison agréable.
Summer is a nice season.
L'hiver est une saison froide.
Winter is a cold season.

But:

Je vais à la plage en été.
I go to the beach in summer.
Je fais du ski en hiver.
I ski in winter.
les robes d'hiver
winter dresses

The definite article is used with dates.

Le 15 septembre, les classes recommencent.
On the 15th of September (September 15) classes resume.
Il sera ici le 10 août.
He will be here on the 10th of August (August 10).

13. Complete the following with the definite article, when it is necessary.

1. _____ Mercredi est le troisième jour de la semaine.
2. Je vais toujours au cinéma _(le)_ samedi.
3. _l'_ automne est ma saison favorite.
4. Il n'y a pas de classes _____ dimanche.
5. Il fait beau en __l'__ automne.
6. Mes vacances commencent _le_ vendredi.
7. J'ai mon cours de philosophie _(le)_ lundi.
8. Je suis allé au musée _le_ samedi dernier.
9. Il vous verra _le_ mercredi prochain.
10. _le_ 2 juin je pars en vacances.
11. Il viendra _le_ 15 octobre.
12. Je pourrais vous voir _le_ matin ou __l'__ après-midi.

14. Answer the following questions.

1. Quel jour est-ce aujourd'hui? *C'est aujourd'est lundi*
2. Demain, c'est quel jour? *Demain est Mard*
3. Quel est ton jour préféré? *Mon jour préféré est le le samedi*

4. Quels jours vas-tu au cours? *Je vais au cours le lundi, le mardi, le mercredi etc.*
5. Quel jour fais-tu les courses? *Je fait les courses le samedi*
6. Quels sont les jours de la fin de semaine? *Les jours de la fin de semaine sont samedi et...*
7. Quand vas-tu au cinéma? *Je vais au cinéma le samedi*
8. Quels jours as-tu ton cours de français? *J'ai mon cours de français le lundi, le mardi etc.*

With Names of Continents, Countries, Provinces, Regions, Islands, Mountains and Rivers

The definite article is used with names of continents, countries, provinces, regions, islands, mountains and rivers.

La France n'est pas un grand pays.
France is not a large country.
La Bretagne est pittoresque.
Brittany is picturesque.
L'Amérique du Nord est un vaste continent.
North America is a vast continent.
La Corse est une île méditerranéenne.
Corsica is a Mediterranean island.
Les Pyrénées sont entre la France et l'Espagne.
The Pyrenees are between France and Spain.

But:

Je vais en France.
I am going to France.
l'histoire de France
the history of France

No article is used with unmodified names of cities, but articles are used when the name of the city is modified.

Paris est une belle ville.
Paris is a beautiful city.
J'aime la vieille Paris.
I love the old Paris.

15. Complete the following with the appropriate definite article, when necessary.

10/10

1. _La_ Seine est le fleuve qui divise Paris.
2. _L'_ Europe est très diverse.
3. _Les_ Laurentides sont des montagnes du Québec.
4. _Le_ Midi est le sud de la France.
5. Je vais en _—_ France en été.
6. _La_ Corse est une île française.
7. Il traverse _le_ lac Ontario.
8. _L'_ Amérique du Sud est un vaste continent.
9. Voilà _l'_ Avignon du passé.
10. Je vais à _____ Strasbourg.

With Weights and Measures

The definite article is used with expressions of quantity when used in conjunction with a price to indicate *per*.

Les tomates coûtent 2,25 € (deux euros vingt-cinq centimes) le kilo.
Tomatoes cost 2.25 € (two euros, twenty-five centimes) a (per) kilogram.

Les œufs coûtent 2,64 € (deux euros, soixante-quatre centimes) la douzaine.
Eggs cost 2.64 € (two euros, sixty-four centimes) a dozen

16. Complete the following with the correct form of the definite article.

1. _____ pommes coûtent **1,25 €** (un euro vingt-cinq centimes) _____ livre.
2. J'ai payé 2 € (deux euros) _____ kilo.
3. _____ oranges coûtent 1,25 € (un euro vingt-cinq centimes) _____ douzaine.
4. _____ lait coûte 0,94 € (quatre-vingt-quatorze centimes) _____ litre.

With Parts of the Body or Clothing

The definite article is used instead of the possessive adjective with parts of the body or clothing, in order to avoid ambiguity.

Il se lave les mains.
He washes his hands.
Il s'en va, les mains dans les poches.
He goes away with his hands in his pockets.

17. Complete the following sentences with the appropriate definite article.

1. Il se brosse _____ dents.
2. Il est rentré, _____ chemise déchirée.
3. Il s'est cassé _____ jambe
4. Il a mal à _____ tête.
5. Elle se lave _____ cheveux.

Omission of the Definite Article

The definite article is not used before nouns in apposition.

Paris, capitale de la France, est une ville très belle.
Paris, the capital of France, is a very beautiful city.

The definite article is not used after **avec** or **sans** when used with an abstract noun.

Il travaille avec passion.
He works with passion.
Elle travaille sans passion.
She works without passion.

The definite article is not used when the preposition **de** introduces a noun that modifies another noun.

C'est mon livre de mathématiques.
It's my mathematics book.
Il porte une cravate de soie.
He wears a silk tie.

18. Complete the following with the correct article when necessary.

1. La danseuse danse avec _____ passion.
2. Dakar, _____ capitale du Sénégal, est une ville intéressante.
3. Elle porte une belle robe _____ soie.
4. _____ coton et _____ lin sont des tissus légers.

Contractions of the Definite Article

The definite article contracts with **à** (*to, at*) and **de** (*from, about, of*) in the following way:

à + le = au
à + les = aux

à + **la** do not contract
à + **l'** do not contract

Je vais **au musée**.	*I am going to the museum.*
Je parle **aux garçons**.	*I am speaking to the boys.*
Je parle **aux élèves**.	*I am speaking to the pupils.*
Je vais **à la pharmacie**.	*I am going to the pharmacy.*
Je parle **à l'étudiant**.	*I am speaking to the student.*
J'arrive **à l'hôpital**.	*I am arriving at the hospital.*

de + **le** = **du**
de + **les** = **des**
de + **la** do not contract
de + **l'** do not contract

Je parle **du garçon**.	*I am speaking about the boy.*
Je parle **des garçons**.	*I am speaking about the boys.*
Je parle **des étudiants**.	*I am speaking about the students.*
Je parle **de la fille**.	*I am speaking about the girl.*
Je parle **de l'élève**.	*I am speaking about the student.*
Quel est le nom **du livre**?	*What is the name of the book?*

Note the liaison between **aux** and **des** and a noun that begins with a vowel.

Je parle **aux élèves**.
Je parle **des étudiants**.

19. Complete the following mini-dialogues with the appropriate contractions of the definite article.

10/16

1. —Pierre va *au* restaurant.
   —Quel est le nom *du* restaurant?
   —C'est le restaurant *Chez Robert*.
2. —Anne va *à la* plage.
   —Quel est le nom *de la* plage?
   —C'est la plage Jones.
3. —André va *à l'* aéroport.
   —Quel est le nom *de l'* aéroport?
   —C'est l'aéroport Charles de Gaulle.
4. —Anne va *à la* bibliothèque.
   —Quel est le nom *de la* bibliothèque et qu'est-ce qu'elle y fait?
   —C'est la bibliothèque Mercier et elle lit des livres *aux* enfants.
   —Quels sont les noms *des* enfants?
   —Ce sont Anne, Marie, Claire, David, Jean et Pierre.

20. Answer the following questions choosing from the list below.

la boulangerie	la confiserie	la bibliothèque	les musées
le cinéma	le théâtre	la boucherie	la crémerie
la pharmacie	le stade	la pâtisserie	

Où va-t-on pour acheter du pain?
On va à la boulangerie pour acheter du pain.

1. Où va-t-on pour regarder un film? *au cinéma*
2. Où va-t-on pour acheter des bonbons? *à la confiserie*

3. Où va-t-on pour acheter du lait? *à la crémerie,*
4. Où va-t-on pour regarder des peintures? *aux musées*
5. Où va-t-on pour acheter de la viande? *la boucherie*
6. Où va-t-on pour regarder un match de football? *au stade*
7. Où va-t-on pour acheter des gâteaux? *la patisserie*
8. Où va-t-on pour acheter des cachets d'aspirine? *la pharmacie*
9. Où va-t-on pour regarder un spectacle? *au théâtre*
10. Où va-t-on pour lire des livres? *à la bibliothèque*

The Indefinite Article

The indefinite articles (*a, an*) in French are **un** for masculine nouns and **une** for feminine nouns. The plural is **des** (*some, any*). Note the liaison between **des** and a word beginning with a vowel.

Masculine		*Feminine*	
Singular	*Plural*	*Singular*	*Plural*
un livre	**des livres**	**une peinture**	**des peintures**
un garçon	**des garçons**	**une fille**	**des filles**
un élève	**des_élèves**	**une élève**	**des_élèves**
un ami	**des_amis**	**une amie**	**des_amies**

Some nouns have two genders.

Masculine		*Feminine*	
un élève	*a student (male)*	**une élève**	*a student (female)*
un artiste	*an artist*	**une artiste**	*an artist*
un enfant	*a child*	**une enfant**	*a child*

21. Complete the following with the correct form of the indefinite article **un, une** or **des** to show what the people wear in various locations and situations.

1. À la plage, je porte ___un___ maillot de bain, ___un___ chapeau de paille et ___des___ lunettes de soleil.
2. Au lit, elle porte ___un___ pyjama ou ___une___ chemise de nuit.
3. Au bureau, il porte ___une___ chemise, ___un___ costume, ___une___ cravate et ___des___ chaussures.
4. Au bal, Marie porte ___une___ jolie robe du soir et ___des___ bijoux et Jean porte ___un___ habit de cérémonie.
5. Quand il pleut, on porte ___un___ imperméable et ___un___ parapluie.
6. En hiver, on porte ___un___ manteau, ___un___ foulard, ___un___ chapeau, ___des___ gants et ___des___ bottes.
7. Dans le jardin, il porte ___un___ jean et ___un___ tricot.
8. Au restaurant, elle porte ___une___ jupe, ___une___ blouse et ___un___ gilet.

Omission of the Indefinite Article

After the Verb *être*

Unlike English, the indefinite article is omitted after the verb **être** (*to be*) when the verb is followed by an unmodified noun indicating nationality, religion or profession.

Elle est médecin.
She is a doctor.

Il est catholique.
He is a Catholic.
Elle est canadienne.
She is a Canadian.

When **c'est** is used instead of **il est,** the indefinite article is used.

C'est un Français.
He is a Frenchman.
C'est un avocat.
He's a lawyer.

The indefinite article is also used when the noun that follows the verb **être** is modified.

Victor Hugo est un auteur célèbre.
Victor Hugo is a famous author.
Victor Hugo est un auteur que tous les Français connaissent.
Victor Hugo is an author whom all French people know.

22. What are the classmates doing ten years after graduation? Complete the following sentences with the appropriate indefinite article, when it is necessary.

1. Pierre est _____ chimiste. C'est __un__ chimiste célèbre.
2. Anne est _____ avocate.
3. C'est ~~une~~ biologiste. __un__
4. Lucille est __une__ rédactrice qui voyage partout dans le monde.
5. Georges est _____ ingénieur.
6. Solange est _____ journaliste.
7. André est __un__ professeur exigeant.
8. Jean est __un__ avocat célèbre.

Other Omissions of the Indefinite Article

The indefinite article is not used:

1. after **quel** (*what a*):

Quelle belle vue!
What a beautiful view!

2. before nouns in apposition:

Paris, ville ancienne, est la capitale de la France.
Paris, an ancient city, is the capital of France.

3. after a noun that is a complement of another noun:

une robe de soie
a silk dress
un professeur d'histoire
a history professor

4. after the preposition **sans:**

Il travaille sans argent.
He works without money.

5. after **avec** when used with abstract nouns:

Travaillez avec soin.
Work with care.

But:

Travaillez avec des amis.
Work with some friends.

6. after **ni. . . ni:**

Il n'a ni argent ni pain.
He has neither money nor bread.

23. Complete the following with the indefinite article, when it is necessary.

6/8

1. Quel _____ garçon!
2. *Le Cid,* ~~une~~ pièce de Corneille, est très célèbre.
3. *Les Misérables* est __un__ roman de Victor Hugo.

4. Il achète une bague en ~~d'~~ _une_ or.
5. Écoutez avec _____ enthousiasme.
6. Il travaille avec __des__ copains.
7. Il reste sans _____ argent.
8. Il n'a ni _____ père ni _____ mère.

The Partitive Article

In English we use the words *some* or *any* or no article with nouns that cannot be counted, such as milk, coffee and tea. In French the partitive is used with these nouns and the partitive article cannot be omitted. The partitive is expressed by **de** plus the definite article. Note that **de plus le = du and de plus les = des.** The partitive articles are:

	Singular	Plural
Masculine	**du**	**des**
Feminine	**de la**	**des**
Masculine or feminine before a vowel	**de l'**	**des**

Study the following:

J'ai **de la soupe.**	*I have some soup.*
Elle veut **du sucre.**	*She wants some sugar.*
Il boit **de l'eau.**	*He is drinking (some) water.*
Voulez-vous **des oranges?**	*Do you want any oranges?*
Nous avons **des livres.**	*We have some books.*

Note that in general the partitive article is used in the singular. The plural **des** is the same as the plural indefinite article.

24. What does John eat and drink for each meal? Complete the following sentences with the appropriate form of the partitive.

16/18

Au petit déjeuner, il mange __du__ pain, __de la__ confiture, __des__ œufs brouillés ou __des__
                                  (1)   (2)   (3)   (4)
crêpes avec __du__ sirop d'érable. Il boit ~~de la~~ jus d'orange et __du__ café avec __du__ sucre et
              (5)   (6)   (7)   (8)
__de la__ crème.
  (9)
Au déjeuner, il mange __de la__ soupe et __de la__ salade. Il boit __du__ lait.
                        (10)   (11)   (12)
Au dîner, il mange __du__ rosbif ou ~~de la~~ __du__ poulet, __des__ légumes et __du__ riz. Il boit __de l'__
                     (13)   (14)   (15)   (16)   (17)
eau minérale et __du__ vin.
                  (18)

The Partitive Article Versus the Definite and Indefinite Articles

The definite article is used with nouns in a general sense. The partitive is used with an undetermined quantity of a noncountable item.

> Il aime **le café.**
> *He likes coffee. (all coffee)*
> Il boit **du café.**
> *He drinks coffee. (some coffee)*

With nouns that can be counted, such as bananas (one banana), or items used in the plural (some bananas), the indefinite article is used.

> Je voudrais **une poire.**
> Je voudrais acheter **des tomates** et **des bananes.**

Certain nouns can be count or noncount nouns depending on the way in which they are used. The definite, indefinite or partitive article can be used depending on the meaning.

> Voici **le gâteau.**
> *Here is the cake. (the cake I bought yesterday)*
> Voici **un gâteau.**
> *Here is a cake. (a whole cake).*
> Voici **du gâteau.**
> *Here is some cake. (part of the cake, a piece of cake)*

25. Say that Pierre likes the following foods and drinks and is ordering them from a menu in a restaurant. Follow the model.

    le fromage
    Il aime beaucoup le fromage et il va prendre du fromage maintenant.

    1. l'eau minérale   4. la salade
    2. la soupe aux pois   5. le pain italien
    3. les artichauts   6. le thé

26. Complete the following conversations in a restaurant with the definite, indefinite or partitive article.

    1. —Aimez-vous _le_ pâté?
       —Il y a _du_ pâté sur le menu?
       —Oui, il y a _du_ pâté français sur le menu. _le_ pâté français est délicieux.
    2. —_la_ glace ici est délicieuse. J'aime beaucoup _la_ glace. Je préfère _le_ glace au chocolat à _la_ glace à la vanille. Donc, je vais prendre _la_ glace au chocolat.
    3. —Regarde _le_ gâteau. C'est _le_ fameux gâteau qu'on fait à la pâtisserie Leclerc. C'est _un_ gâteau formidable. Vas-y! Prends _du_ gâteau.
    4. —Il y a _du_ fromage sur le menu?
       —Oui, je vais prendre _du_ roquefort. J'aime _le_ roquefort. Le roquefort est _le un_ fromage français.

Exceptions to the Rule for Using the Partitive Article

When the Sentence is Negative

Normally, in negative sentences, the partitive article is replaced by **de.** Study the following. Note that **de** becomes **d'** before a word beginning with a vowel.

Affirmative	*Negative*
J'ai du pain.	**Je n'ai pas de pain.**
I have some bread.	*I don't have any bread.*
J'ai une robe.	**Je n'ai pas de robe.**
I have a dress.	*I don't have a dress.*
J'ai des livres.	**Je n'ai pas de livres.**
I have some books.	*I don't have any books.*
J'ai des amies.	**Je n'ai pas d'amies.**
I have some friends.	*I have no friends.*

If the sentence implies an affirmative idea or if you want to emphasize the noun, you may use the partitive article in negative sentences.

> **N'avez-vous pas de la famille ici?**
> *Don't you have any family here?*
> **Je n'ai pas du respect pour lui, mais du mépris.**
> *I don't have any respect for him, rather scorn.*

27. Rewrite the following sentences in the negative.

1. Il a du courage.
2. Il y a de la soupe.
3. J'ai des bonbons.
4. Je bois de l'eau.
5. Elle fume des cigarettes.

When an Adjective Precedes a Noun in the Plural

When an adjective precedes a noun in the plural, the partitive article becomes **de**.

Singular	*Plural*
J'ai un bon livre.	**J'ai de bons livres.**
But:	
J'ai un livre intéressant.	**J'ai des livres intéressants.**

When an adjective and noun are very closely related, they are treated as one single noun and the partitive article is used.

des jeunes filles	*girls*
des jeunes gens	*young people*
des petits pains	*rolls*
des petits pois	*peas*

28. Rewrite the following sentences, putting the nouns in the plural.

1. Il y a une belle peinture ici.
2. Nous lisons un livre intéressant.
3. C'est une grande ville.
4. Elle mange un petit pain.
5. C'est une jeune fille.
6. J'ai une grande armoire.

After Expressions of Quantity and Expressions with *de*

The partitive becomes **de** after expressions of quantity such as the following:

assez	*enough*	**une boîte**	*a box*
beaucoup	*a lot*	**une bouteille**	*a bottle*

peu	*a little*		un verre	*a glass*
trop	*too much*		une tasse	*a cup*
tant	*so many, as many*		un kilo	*a kilogram*
autant	*as much, so much*		un litre	*a liter*
moins	*less*		une livre	*a pound*
			une douzaine	*a dozen*
			un morceau	*a piece*
			une tranche	*a slice*

Elle veut **de l'**eau.	*But:*	Elle veut **un peu d'**eau.
She wants some water.		*She wants a little water.*
Il a **des** livres.	*But:*	Il a **beaucoup de** livres.
He has some books.		*He has many books.*
Je bois **du** vin.	*But:*	Je bois **un verre de** vin.
I am drinking some wine.		*I am drinking a glass of wine.*

La plupart (*most*) and **bien** (*many*) are exceptions to this rule.

La plupart du temps, je travaille.	**Bien des** fois, il fait des fautes.
Most of the time, I work.	*Many times, he makes mistakes.*

After expressions using **de**, such as **avoir besoin de** (*to need*), **avoir envie de** (*to desire to want*), **se passer de** (*to get along without*), there is no partitive.

J'ai **de l'**argent.	*But:*	J'ai **besoin d'**argent.
I have some money.		*I need some money.*

Plusieurs (*several*) and **quelques** (*a few*) do not require the partitive. Study the following:

J'ai **beaucoup de** livres.	*But:*	J'ai **plusieurs** livres.
I have many books.		*I have several books.*
J'ai **assez de** livres.	*But:*	J'ai **quelques** livres.
I have enough books.		*I have some books.*

In expressions of quantity **de** cannot be used before a pronoun. **D'entre** is usually used.

plusieurs **d'entre eux**	*several of them*
quelques-uns **d'entre nous**	*some of us*

29. Complete the following sentences with the correct form of the partitive, when necessary.

1. Je voudrais un verre ___d'___ eau.
2. Elle a beaucoup ___d'___ amis.
3. Elle ne peut pas se passer ___de___ nourriture.
4. Il y a plusieurs ___X___ églises ici.
5. Elle achète une douzaine ___de___ pommes.
6. Il a quelques ___X d'___ amis.
7. Bien ___des X___ gens aiment le cinéma.
8. Donne-moi une tranche ___de___ pain.
9. Il mange trop ___de X___ bonbons.
10. Nous avons besoin ___d'___ argent.
11. Elle achète une livre ___de___ beurre.
12. La plupart ___du___ temps, j'ai raison.

Review

30. Complete the following sentences with the appropriate definite article or contraction.

17/23

1. _Le_ père travaille _au_ bureau.
2. C'est _un_ ami de Pierre. _l'_
3. _La_ qualité vaut mieux que _la_ quantité.
4. _Les_ romans sont dans _la_ bibliothèque.
5. _La_ patience est une vertu.
6. _La_ connaissance _des_ langues est utile.
7. _La_ femme achète des timbres _à la_ poste.
8. _l'_ homme se chauffe devant _le_ poêle. _le_
9. C'est _un_ livre _du_ professeur.
10. _Les_ enfants vont _à l'_ école.
11. Ne donnez pas _les_ bonbons _aux_ enfants.
12. _Les_ héros _de l'_ histoire se lave _les_ mains.
    _Le_   _de l'_

31. Rewrite the following sentences, changing the nouns to the plural. Make all other necessary changes.

1. Le repas est bon.
2. Le cheval est un animal.
3. J'aime le carnaval.
4. Ouvrez l'œil.
5. Le bateau est petit.
6. Le prix du clou n'est pas cher.
7. Le chou est dans le trou.
8. L'eau entoure le château.
9. Le jeu est intéressant.
10. L'après-midi, il prépare le hors-d'œuvre et le chou-fleur pour le pique-nique.
11. Monsieur, ne prenez pas ce bijou.
12. Le grand-père va acheter un abat-jour.

32. Tell what the people in various professions do. Complete the following with the correct form of the definite or indefinite article when necessary.

20/24

1. Madame Leclerc est ~~une~~ chirurgienne. C'est _une_ chirurgienne célèbre. Elle aide _une_ patiente qui s'est cassé _la_ jambe. _Les_ chirurgiens font _le_ travail délicat. Ils travaillent avec _le_ soin.
2. Madame Dupont est ~~une~~ journaliste. Elle utilise _un_ micro-ordinateur dans son travail. Quelle _∅_ journaliste! C'est _une_ journaliste qui écrit bien.
3. Marie est ~~une~~ biologiste. Elle travaille dans _un_ laboratoire avec _un_ microscope. _La_ biologie est _une_ science intéressante.
4. Monsieur Fournier est _un_ professeur à l'école secondaire. C'est _un_ professeur dynamique. Il enseigne _l'_ anglais. Il parle _l'_ anglais, mais il comprend ~~le~~ _le_ français et ~~le~~ russe. Il donne ses cours _le_ lundi, _le_ mercredi et _le_ vendredi. J'ai surtout aimé son cours _—_ lundi dernier.
   _le_

33. Monsieur Leclerc is doing the shopping. Show where he goes and what he buys. Complete the following sentences with the definite, indefinite or partitive articles and the contraction of the definite article when necessary.

1. _à la_ crémerie, il achète _de la_ crème, _du_ beurre, _du_ lait, _une_ douzaine _des_ œufs et _du_ fromage. Il aime _le_ brie. C'est _un_ fromage délicieux.
2. Il sort _de la_ crémerie et il va _à la_ boucherie où il achète _de la_ viande: _du_ bifteck, _du_ veau et _∅_ agneau.
3. _à la_ charcuterie, il achète un kilo _de_ porc et six tranches _de_ jambon. _Le_ porc coûte 10,30 € _le_ kilo et _le_ jambon coûte 3,25 €.

4. _au_ supermarché, il achète dix bouteilles _d'_eau minérale, quelques _des_ tomates, _de les_ petits pois, _du_ farine, _des_ sel, _du_ poivre et _de la_ moutarde. Il n'y a pas _d'_oranges; donc il achète _des_ pommes.

5. Maintenant, il a assez _de_ provisions et il peut rentrer chez lui. Ah! Il a oublié d'acheter _du_ café et il n'y a pas _de_ café chez lui. Donc, il s'arrête _à l'_épicerie pour acheter un peu _de_ café. Il achète aussi _de la_ glace parce que _la_ glace dans cette épicerie est délicieuse. Il achète _une_ glace à la vanille pour lui, et _une_ glace au chocolat pour sa femme. Il doit attendre un peu, car bien _des_ gens font la queue pour acheter _de la_ glace.

34. Answer the following questions, using **le, la, l', les,** a contraction of the article with **à** or **de,** a partitive or a preposition.

Qu'est-ce qu'il regarde? *le livre / professeur*
Il regarde le livre du professeur.

1. Qu'est-ce qu'il attend? *arrivée / professeur*
2. Qu'est-ce qu'il entend? *cris / enfant*
3. À qui parle-t-il? *ami / Jean*
4. Qu'est-ce qu'elle aime? *voix / chanteur*
5. Qu'est-ce qu'il cherche? *jouets / enfants*
6. Où va-t-il? *supermarché / village*
7. Qu'est-ce qu'il aime? *vitrail / église*
8. Qu'est-ce qu'il regarde? *peintures / musée*
9. Où veut-elle aller? *bibliothèque / ville*
10. Qu'est-ce qu'il achète? *sucre / gâteaux / glace*

35. Answer the following personalized questions.

1. Qu'est-ce que tu manges d'habitude au petit déjeuner? au déjeuner? au dîner?
2. Quand tu fais les courses au supermarché, qu'est-ce que tu achètes?
3. Quels sports aimes-tu?
4. Qu'est-ce que tu portes quand tu vas aux cours? au théâtre? à une noce?
5. Qu'est-ce que tu as dans ta chambre?
6. Quelles matières aimes-tu?
7. Quels jours as-tu ton cours de français?
8. Quel est ton jour préféré?
9. Quel jour est-ce aujourd'hui?
10. Quel jour est-ce demain?

36. Complete the following.

1. J'aime _____ et je mange souvent _____.
2. Je n'aime pas _____ et je ne mange pas _____.
3. J'aime _____ et je bois souvent _____.
4. Je n'aime pas _____ et je ne bois pas _____.
5. J'achète _____ à l'épicerie.
6. J'achète _____ au grand magasin.
7. Je vais _____ pour acheter _____.
8. Dans ma ville, il y a _____.

CHAPTER 2

Adjectives and Adverbs

Formation of the Feminine of Adjectives

Regular Forms

Every adjective must agree in number and gender with the noun it modifies. Most adjectives add **-e** to the masculine form to form the feminine. The final consonant sound is heard in the feminine form but not in the masculine form.

Masculine	Feminine
Il est **grand**.	Elle est **grande**.

Below is a list of common regular adjectives. The adjectives with an asterisk end in an **n** sound in the feminine in spoken French but have a nasalized ending in the masculine. Note that when proper nouns in French are adjectives, they are not capitalized.

Masculine	Feminine	
*américain	américaine	*American*
amusant	amusante	*amusing*
anglais	anglaise	*English*
chaud	chaude	*warm*
content	contente	*happy, contented*
court	courte	*short*
droit	droite	*right, straight*
étonnant	étonnante	*astonishing*
fort	forte	*strong*

français	française	*French*
froid	froide	*cold*
grand	grande	*tall, big*
gris	grise	*gray*
haut	haute	*high, tall*
*humain	humaine	*human*
intelligent	intelligente	*intelligent*
intéressant	intéressante	*interesting*
laid	laide	*ugly*
lent	lente	*slow*
lourd	lourde	*heavy*
mauvais	mauvaise	*bad*
méchant	méchante	*bad, naughty*
parfait	parfaite	*perfect*
petit	petite	*small, little*
*plein	pleine	*full*
*prochain	prochaine	*next*
puissant	puissante	*powerful*
sourd	sourde	*deaf*

Adjectives Ending in a Vowel, Pronounced Consonant or Mute -*e*

Some adjectives sound the same in the masculine and feminine forms. If an adjective ends in a vowel or pronounced consonant (**r** or **l**), the feminine is formed by adding **-e**. Below is a list of the most common of these adjectives.

Masculine	*Feminine*	
bleu	bleue	*blue*
compliqué	compliquée	*complicated*
désolé	désolée	*sorry*
fatigué	fatiguée	*tired*
gai	gaie	*gay*
joli	jolie	*pretty*
poli	polie	*polite*
clair	claire	*clear*
dur	dure	*hard*
égal	égale	*equal*
noir	noire	*black*
sûr	sûre	*sure*

Il est **fatigué.**
Elle est **fatiguée.**

If the adjective ends in a mute **-e**, the oral and written forms are the same for both the masculine and the feminine forms. Below is a list of some of the most common of these adjectives.

Masculine	*Feminine*	
agréable	agréable	*nice, pleasant*
calme	calme	*calm*
célèbre	célèbre	*famous*

désagréable	désagréable	*disagreeable, unpleasant*
difficile	difficile	*difficult*
facile	facile	*easy*
fantastique	fantastique	*fantastic, wonderful*
formidable	formidable	*fantastic, wonderful*
gauche	gauche	*left*
honnête	honnête	*honest*
jaune	jaune	*yellow*
jeune	jeune	*young*
large	large	*wide*
libre	libre	*free*
magnifique	magnifique	*magnificent*
malade	malade	*sick*
mince	mince	*thin*
moderne	moderne	*modern*
nécessaire	nécessaire	*necessary*
pauvre	pauvre	*poor*
populaire	populaire	*popular*
rapide	rapide	*rapid*
riche	riche	*rich*
sale	sale	*dirty*

1. Follow the model.

Comment est la fille? *petit*
La fille est petite.

1. Comment est l'idée? *mauvais*
2. Comment est la cathédrale? *grand*
3. Comment est la tour? *haut*
4. Comment est la cuisine? *parfait*
5. Comment est la sorcière? *laid*
6. Comment est la peinture? *joli*
7. Comment est la femme? *honnête*
8. Comment est la chemise? *rouge*
9. Comment est la pierre? *dur*
10. Comment est la réponse? *clair*

2. Complete the following with the appropriate form of the indicated adjective.

1. Le temps est _____. *mauvais*
2. Cette fille est _____. *français*
3. L'écrivain est _____. *grand*
4. L'homme est _____. *poli*
5. Le charbon est _____. *noir*
6. Le vieillard est _____. *faible*
7. La robe est _____. *noir*
8. La pièce est _____. *fantastique*
9. Le film est _____. *formidable*
10. La situation est _____. *compliqué*

3. Rewrite the following paragraph changing **Pierre** to **Marie**.

Pierre est français. Il est très jeune et très petit. Il n'est pas grand. Il est agréable et amusant. Et, il est très poli aussi.

Adjectives Ending in *-el, -eil, -il, -en, -on, -et* and *-s*

Adjectives ending in **-el -eil, -il, -en, -on, -et,** and some ending in **-s** double the final consonant before adding **-e.**

Masculine	*Feminine*	
cruel	**cruelle**	*cruel*
pareil	**pareille**	*similar*
gentil	**gentille**	*nice*

ancien	ancienne	*ancient, old*
parisien	parisienne	*Parisian*
bon	bonne	*good*
breton	bretonne	*Breton*
muet	muette	*silent*
net	nette	*clean*
bas	basse	*low*
épais	épaisse	*thick*
gras	grasse	*greasy*
las	lasse	*tired*
gros	grosse	*big, fat*

Some other adjectives that double the final consonant to form the feminine are:

Masculine	*Feminine*	
nul	nulle	*no*
paysan	paysanne	*peasant*
sot	sotte	*stupid*
tel	telle	*such a, so*

Some adjectives ending in **-et** change **-et** to **-ète** to form the feminine.

Masculine	*Feminine*	
complet	complète	*complete*
concret	concrète	*concrete*
discret	discrète	*discreet*
indiscret	indiscrète	*indiscreet*
inquiet	inquiète	*worried*
secret	secrète	*secret*

Exception:

prêt	prête	*ready*

Adjectives Ending in *-er*

Adjectives ending in **-er** change **-er** to **-ère** to form the feminine.

Masculine	*Feminine*	
amer	amère	*bitter*
cher	chère	*expensive, dear*
dernier	dernière	*last*
entier	entière	*entire*
étranger	étrangère	*foreign*
fier	fière	*proud*
léger	légère	*light*
premier	première	*first*

4. Complete the following with the appropriate form of the indicated adjective.

1. La sorcière est _____. *cruel*
2. La femme est _____. *parisien*
3. La pièce est _____. *bon*
4. Cette dame est _____ de naissance. *muet*
5. La sauce est _____. *épais*

   6. Sa réponse était _____.   *discret*
   7. La jeune fille est _____ à partir.   *prêt*
   8. La fille est _____.   *sot*
   9. La peinture est _____.   *cher*
  10. Cette dame est _____ de sa langue.   *fier*

5. Follow the model.

> **La fille est cruelle.**   *Le garçon*
> **Le garçon est cruel.**

   1. La pièce est sensationnelle.   *Le film*
   2. Le monument est ancien.   *La peinture*
   3. Cette boîte est grosse.   *Ce paquet*
   4. Cet étudiant est las.   *Cette étudiante*
   5. Ce mot est secret.   *Cette histoire*
   6. La femme est inquiète.   *L'homme*
   7. Monsieur Le Blanc est étranger.   *Madame Leclerc*
   8. Marie est première en math.   *Pierre*
   9. Ce mot est pareil.   *Cette phrase*

Adjectives Ending in -*x*

Most adjectives ending in **-x** change **-x** to **-se** to form the feminine.

Masculine	*Feminine*	
amoureux	**amoureuse**	*in love*
courageux	**courageuse**	*courageous*
curieux	**curieuse**	*curious*
ennuyeux	**ennuyeuse**	*boring*
furieux	**furieuse**	*furious*
heureux	**heureuse**	*happy*
jaloux	**jalouse**	*jealous*
merveilleux	**merveilleuse**	*marvelous*
peureux	**peureuse**	*fearful*
sérieux	**sérieuse**	*serious*

Exceptions:

doux	**douce**	*sweet*
faux	**fausse**	*false*
roux	**rousse**	*reddish brown*

Adjectives Ending in -*eur*

Adjectives ending in **-eur** form the feminine by changing **-eur** to **-euse** if the adjective is derived from a verb. Otherwise the feminine ends in **-rice**.

Masculine	*Feminine*	
flatteur	**flatteuse**	*flattering*
menteur	**menteuse**	*lying*
moqueur	**moqueuse**	*mocking*
trompeur	**trompeuse**	*deceitful, deceptive*
conservateur	**conservatrice**	*conservative*

créateur	**créatrice**	*creative*
protecteur	**protectrice**	*protecting*

Exceptions:

antérieur	**antérieure**	*anterior*
extérieur	**extérieure**	*exterior*
inférieur	**inférieure**	*inferior*
intérieur	**intérieure**	*interior*
majeur	**majeure**	*major*
meilleur	**meilleure**	*better, best*
mineur	**mineure**	*minor*
postérieur	**postérieure**	*posterior*
supérieur	**supérieure**	*superior*

6. Complete the following with the correct form of the indicated adjective.

1. La fille est _____. *heureux*
2. Son attitude est _____. *sérieux*
3. L'homme est _____. *furieux*
4. Le miel est _____. *doux*
5. La chanson est _____. *doux*
6. La chevelure est _____. *roux*
7. La réponse est _____. *faux*
8. La fille est _____. *menteur*
9. La loi est _____. *protecteur*
10. C'est la _____ chose. *meilleur*
11. C'est une femme _____. *créateur*
12. C'est la cause _____. *majeur*

Adjectives Ending in -*f*

Adjectives ending in **-f** in the masculine change **-f** to **-ve** to form the feminine.

Masculine	*Feminine*	
actif	**active**	*active*
attentif	**attentive**	*attentive*
bref	**brève**	*brief*
destructif	**destructive**	*destructive*
neuf	**neuve**	*new*
sportif	**sportive**	*athletic*
vif	**vive**	*alive, lively*

Note the grave accent on **brève**.

Adjectives Ending in -*c*

Adjectives ending in **-c** change **-c** to **-che** to form the feminine.

Masculine	*Feminine*	
blanc	**blanche**	*white*
franc	**franche**	*frank*
sec	**sèche**	*dry*

Note the grave accent on **sèche**.

Exceptions:

grec	**grecque**	*Greek*
public	**publique**	*public*

7. Complete the following with the correct form of one of the adjectives listed below.

blanc ✓	grec ✓	bref ✓
franc	neuf ✓	sec ✓
public ✓	attentif ✓	sportif ✓

9/9

1. La fille fait beaucoup d'attention en classe. Elle est _attentive_.
2. Cette robe n'est pas vieille. Elle est _neuve_.
3. Le garçon joue aux sports. Il est _sportif_.
4. Sa réponse n'était pas longue. Elle était _brève_.
5. La nappe n'est pas noire. Elle est _blanche_.
6. L'homme dit ce qu'il pense. Il est _franc_.
7. La robe n'est pas mouillée. Elle est _sèche_.
8. L'actrice vient de la Grèce. Elle est _grecque_.
9. Tout le monde a le droit de fréquenter cette place. C'est une place _publique_.

Irregular Adjectives

Some adjectives are completely irregular in the feminine.

Masculine	Feminine	
aigu	**aiguë**	*sharp*
ambigu	**ambiguë**	*ambiguous*
bénin	**bénigne**	*benign*
long	**longue**	*long*
favori	**favorite**	*favorite*
malin	**maligne**	*sly*
frais	**fraîche**	*fresh*

6/6

8. Complete the following with the appropriate form of the indicated adjective.

1. L'aiguille est _aiguë_. aigu
2. La robe est _longue_. long
3. C'est ma chemise _favorite_. favori
4. C'est une enfant _maligne_. malin
5. C'est un enfant _malin_. malin
6. La viande est _fraîche_. frais

The Adjectives *beau, nouveau, vieux*

The adjectives **beau, nouveau** and **vieux** have three forms. They have a special masculine singular form before words beginning with a vowel or silent **h.**

Masculine before a consonant	Masculine before a vowel	Feminine	
beau	**bel**	**belle**	*beautiful, handsome*
nouveau	**nouvel**	**nouvelle**	*new*
vieux	**vieil**	**vieille**	*old*

Two other adjectives that have special masculine singular forms are:

fou	**fol**	**folle**	*crazy*
mou	**mol**	**molle**	*soft*

Note that the masculine form before a vowel and the feminine form sound alike. When the masculine adjective follows a word beginning with a vowel, the regular masculine form is used.

C'est un **beau** garçon.
C'est un **bel** homme.   *But:* Cet homme est **beau.**
C'est une **belle** femme.

C'est un **nouveau** livre.
C'est un **nouvel** appartement.   *But:* Cet appartement est **nouveau.**
C'est une **nouvelle** maison.

C'est un **vieux** livre.
C'est un **vieil** écrivain.   *But:* Cet écrivain est **vieux.**
C'est une **vieille** statue.

9. Complete the following with the correct form of the indicated adjective.

1. C'est un *nouveau* livre. *nouveau*
2. C'est une *belle* histoire. *beau*
3. C'est un *vieil* homme. *vieux*
4. C'est une *nouvelle* peinture. *nouveau*
5. C'est un *nouvel* ami. *nouveau*
6. C'est un *vieux* tableau. *vieux*
7. C'est une *belle* robe. *beau*
8. C'est une *vieille* dame. *vieux*
9. C'est un *belle* artiste. *beau* *bel*
10. C'est un *beau* garçon. *beau*
11. Cet artiste est *belle*. *beau* *bel*
12. Cet arbre est *vieux*. *vieux*
13. Cet ami est *nouveau*. *nouveau*

Plural of Adjectives

Regular Forms

Most adjectives form the plural by adding **-s** to the singular form.

Masculine		*Feminine*	
Singular	*Plural*	*Singular*	*Plural*
petit	**petits**	**petite**	**petites**
grand	**grands**	**grande**	**grandes**

Le garçon est **grand.**   La fille est **petite.**
The boy is tall.   *The girl is small.*
Les garçons sont **grands.**   Les filles sont **petites.**
The boys are tall.   *The girls are small.*

Adjectives Ending in *-s* or *-x*

Adjectives ending in **-s** or **-x** are the same in the masculine singular and plural forms.

Singular	*Plural*
frais	**frais**
gros	**gros**
heureux	**heureux**

un garçon **heureux**	des garçons **heureux**
a happy boy	*some happy boys*
un fruit **frais**	des fruits **frais**
a fresh fruit	*some fresh fruit*

The feminine plural is regular.

Singular	*Plural*
fraîche	**fraîches**
grosse	**grosses**
heureuse	**heureuses**

une pièce **merveilleuse**	des pièces **merveilleuses**
a marvelous play	*some marvelous plays*

Adjectives Ending in -*eu* or -*eau*

Adjectives ending in **-eu** or **-eau** add **-x** to form the plural.

Singular	*Plural*
hébreu	**hébreux**
beau	**beaux**
nouveau	**nouveaux**

Le livre est **beau.**	Les livres sont **beaux.**
The book is beautiful.	*The books are beautiful.*

Exception:

bleu	**bleus**

The feminine plural is regular.

Singular	*Plural*
belle	**belles**
nouvelle	**nouvelles**
bleue	**bleues**

La peinture est **belle.**	Les peintures sont **belles.**
The painting is beautiful.	*The paintings are beautiful.*

Adjectives Ending in -*al*

Adjectives ending in **-al** change **-al** to **-aux** to form the masculine plural.

Singular	*Plural*
légal	**légaux**
loyal	**loyaux**
médiéval	**médiévaux**
royal	**royaux**

L'ami est **loyal.**	Les amis sont **loyaux.**
The friend is loyal.	*The friends are loyal.*

Exceptions:

banal	**banals**
fatal	**fatals**
final	**finals**
natal	**natals**
naval	**navals**

The feminine plural is regular.

Singular	*Plural*
loyale	**loyales**
fatale	**fatales**

La loi est **légale**.   Les lois sont **légales**.
The law is legal.   *The laws are legal.*

10. Rewrite the following sentences in the plural.

1. Le film est incroyable.
2. Le film est merveilleux.
3. La robe est bleue.
4. La note est mauvaise.
5. La loi est légale.
6. Le château est beau.
7. Le chandail est bleu.
8. L'homme est gros.
9. Le coup est fatal.
10. La maison est nouvelle.
11. La tomate est parfaite.
12. Le mot est final.

11. Complete the following with the correct form of the indicated adjective.

1. Les romans sont _intéressants_
   intéressant
2. Les pièces sont _merveilleuses_
   merveilleux
3. Les châteaux sont _médiévaux_.
   médiéval
4. Les livres sont _nouveaux_
   nouveau
5. Il passe les examens _finals_.
   final
6. Les hommes sont _grands_.
   grand
7. Les chandails sont _bleus_.
   bleu
8. Les poissons sont _frais_. frais
9. Ce sont des accidents _fatals_.
   fatal
10. Les murs sont _épais_. épais
11. Ce sont des réseaux _social_. social
12. Les peintures sont _belles_. beau
13. Ces lois sont _légales_ légal
14. Les questions sont _intelligentes_
    intelligent
15. Les robes sont _bleues_ bleu
16. Les garçons sont _heureux_
    heureux
17. Ces tableaux sont _beaux_. beau

Agreement Problems of Certain Adjectives

1. Certain adjectives placed before a noun are invariable and are attached to the noun with a hyphen.

une **demi**-heure	*a half hour*
des **demi**-frères	*half brothers*
la **mi**-septembre	*(in) mid-September*
les yeux **mi**-clos	*half closed eyes*

But:

| une heure et **demie** | *one and one-half hours* |

2. The adjective **nu** is invariable when it precedes a noun without an article.

   nu-pieds   *barefoot*

   But:

   les pieds **nus**   *bare feet*

3. **Ci-joint** and **ci-inclus** are invariable when placed before the noun.

   Vous trouverez **ci-joint** les documents que vous m'avez demandés.
   You will find attached the documents you requested.

   But:

   Vous trouverez deux documents **ci-joints.**
   You will find two documents attached.

4. **Haut** and **bas** are invariable before an article and a noun.

   Haut les mains!   *Hands up!*

5. When the adjective precedes the noun **gens,** it is feminine. When it follows, it is masculine.

   les **bonnes** gens   *good people*
   les gens **âgés**   *old people*

6. The nouns **amour, délice** and **orgue** are masculine in the singular and feminine in the plural.

   un amour joyeux   *a joyous love*
   des amours joyeuses   *joyous loves*

   un délice superbe   *a superb delight*
   des délices superbes   *superb delights*

   le bel orgue   *the beautiful organ*
   les belles orgues   *the beautiful organs*

Adjectives of Color

1. Normally, the adjective of color agrees with the noun it modifies.

   une robe **blanche**   *a white dress*
   des yeux **bruns**   *brown eyes*

2. When the adjective of color is a compound adjective, it is invariable.

   des yeux **bleu clair**   *light blue eyes*
   des chaussures **noir et blanc**   *black and white shoes*
   une robe **vert foncé**   *a dark green dress*
   des robes **bleu ciel**   *sky blue dresses*

3. If the adjective can also be a noun used as an adjective, it is invariable.

   des robes **orange**   *orange dresses*
   des joues **ivoire**   *ivory cheeks*
   une robe **chocolat**   *a chocolate colored dress*

4. The adjective **marron** is invariable.

    une robe **marron**   *a brown dress*

5. The adjective **châtain** agrees with a masculine plural noun.

    des cheveux **châtains**   *chestnut brown hair*

12. Complete the following sentences with the correct form of the indicated adjective.

  1. Il est sorti _____-pieds. *nu*
  2. Il y a beaucoup de _____ gens ici. *vieux*
  3. Elle va partir à onze heures et _____. *demi*
  4. Ce sont mes _____-sœurs. *demi*
  5. Il est sorti la tête _____. *nu*
  6. Les yeux _____-clos, elle rêvait. *mi*
  7. Vous trouverez deux pièces _____. *ci-joint*
  8. Restez une _____-heure ici. *demi*
  9. _____ les mains! *haut*
  10. Ce sont des gens _____. *âgé*
  11. Donne-moi mes souliers _____. *marron*
  12. Elle a les yeux _____. *brun foncé*
  13. Ce sont des amours _____. *joyeux*
  14. Ce sont de _____ orgues. *beau*

Compound Adjectives

1. Except for adjectives of color, when each of the two parts of the compound adjective modifies the noun, both adjectives agree with the noun.

    une fille **sourde-muette**   *a deaf-mute girl*

2. When the first part of the compound adjective ends in **-o** or **-i,** this part of the adjective is invariable.

    une pièce **tragi-comique**   *a tragicomic play*
    des lois **anglo-saxonnes**   *Anglo-Saxon laws*

3. If the compound adjective is formed with an invariable word plus an adjective, only the adjective agrees with the noun.

    des pays **nord-africains**   *North African countries*
    l'**avant-dernière** fois   *the next-to-the-last time*
    des pays **sous-développés**   *underdeveloped countries*

4. If the first term of the compound adjective has an adverbial quality, it is invariable.

    des enfants **nouveau-nés**   *newborn children*

    But:

    les fenêtres **grandes ouvertes**   *wide-open windows*
    des fraises **fraîches cueillies**   *freshly picked strawberries*

13. Complete the following sentences with the correct form of the indicated compound adjective.

1. C'est une histoire _____. *tragi-comique*
2. C'est une fille _____. *sourd-muet*
3. Ce sont des lapins _____. *nouveau-né*
4. Les gens _____ parlent espagnol. *sud-américain*
5. Ce sont des pays _____. *sous-développé*
6. Gardez les fenêtres _____. *grand ouvert*

Position of Adjectives

Normally, most adjectives follow the noun in French, particularly:

1. those indicating color or shape

une robe bleue	*a blue dress*
une maison carrée	*a square house*

2. adjectives of nationality, origin, religion, profession, or classification, or those that refer to the arts

une fille française	*a French girl*
une peinture parisienne	*a Parisian painting*
une église catholique	*a Catholic church*
une ville municipale	*a municipal city*
une école secondaire	*a secondary school*
le parti libéral	*the Liberal party*
l'art classique	*classical art*
le style roman	*Romanesque style*

3. those formed from a past or present participle

la porte ouverte	*the open door*
une vie animée	*a lively life*
la semaine passée	*last week*

4. those modified by an adverb

une conversation complètement bête *a completely stupid conversation*

The following adjectives normally precede the noun.

autre	*other*	**vilain**	*ugly, naughty*
jeune	*young*	**bon**	*good*
même	*same*	**grand**	*big, great*
court*	*short*	**gros**	*fat*
haut	*high, tall*	**long**	*long*
joli	*pretty*	**gentil***	*nice*
mauvais	*bad*	**beau**	*beautiful, handsome*
méchant†	*bad, naughty*	**nouveau**	*new*
meilleur*	*better, best*	**vieux**	*old*
petit	*small*	**vrai***	*true*

───────────

*These adjectives can be placed before or after the noun.

†**Méchant** usually follows the noun, but it precedes sometimes.

For emphasis many of these adjectives can be placed after the noun.

une fille jeune   *a young girl (a girl still young)*

When these adjectives are modified by short adverbs, they can either precede or follow the noun.

un homme très beau
un très bel homme

When the adjective precedes the noun, the **s** or **x** is pronounced **z** before a word beginning with a vowel.

de nouveaux‿étudiants
ᶻ

les autres‿amis
ᶻ

Grand is linked to a word beginning with a vowel with a **t** sound.

un grand‿ami
ᵗ

Long is linked to a word beginning with a vowel with a **k** sound.

un long‿entretien
ᵏ

In the plural, **des** becomes **de** or **d'** before an adjective that precedes a noun.

un nouveau roman	*a new novel*
de nouveaux romans	*some new novels*

When an adjective is an integral part of the noun, the article is **des.**

des jeunes filles	*some young girls*
des petits pois	*some peas*
des jeunes gens	*young people*

When two adjectives are used together, they retain their usual position.

une jolie robe bleue   *a pretty blue dress*

When two adjectives have the same position, they can be joined by the conjunction **et.**

une femme intéressante et intelligente

If an adjective is an integral part of the noun, another adjective can precede without using the conjunction **et.**

un petit jeune homme
un parfait honnête homme

When an adjective that is pronounced differently in the feminine and in the masculine forms modifies one or more nouns of different genders, place the masculine nouns closest to the adjective.

des questions et des problèmes sociaux   *social questions and problems*

The following adjectives that usually follow the noun can be placed before the noun in order to make a more personal or subjective statement.

célèbre	*famous*
énorme	*huge, enormous*

excellent	*excellent*
fameux	*famous*
formidable	*wonderful*
magnifique	*magnificent*
terrible	*terrible*
triste	*sad*
un peintre célèbre	*a famous painter (accepted fact)*
un célèbre peintre	*a famous painter (my opinion)*

14. Describe the things in the room, using the indicated adjective, according to the model.

un chat   *jeune*
Il y a un jeune chat.

un tapis   *bleu*
Il y a un tapis bleu.

1. un tableau   *joli*
2. une chaise   *vieux*
3. une peinture   *intéressant*
4. un livre   *bon*
5. un divan-lit   *gros*
6. une lampe   *petit*
7. un fauteuil   *confortable*
8. une cheminée   *grand*
9. un tapis   *oriental*
10. une chaise   *rouge*

15. Rewrite the following sentences in the plural.

1. C'est un livre intéressant.
2. C'est un film formidable.
3. C'est une conférence importante.
4. C'est un bon ami.
5. C'est une autre histoire.
6. C'est une bonne école.
7. C'est un vieil ami.
8. C'est un bel écrivain.
9. C'est une vieille amie.
10. C'est une grande maison.
11. C'est un nouvel hôtel.
12. C'est une jeune fille.
13. C'est un petit pois.

16. Anne has just won the lottery and is going on a shopping spree. Tell what she buys. Follow the model.

une maison   *grand, blanc*
Elle achète une grande maison blanche.

1. un stéréo   *grand, japonais*
2. une robe   *long, bleu*
3. un chien   *gentil, petit, amusant*
4. des meubles   *beau, français*
5. des chaussures   *nouveau, italien*
6. des gants   *beau, noir*
7. un ordinateur   *nouveau, fantastique*
8. un diamant   *gros, brillant*
9. un chat   *petit, jeune*
10. des peintures   *joli, vieux*

17. Describe yourself, your friends and your relatives.

Je suis...
Je suis une fille sportive.

Ma tante est...
Ma tante est intelligente et intéressante.

1. Je suis...	6. Ma tante est...
2. Mon père est...	7. Mon oncle est...
3. Ma mère est...	8. Mon cousin (Ma cousine) est (Mes cousins sont)...
4. Ma sœur est (Mes sœurs sont)...	9. Mon ami(e) est...
5. Mon frère est (Mes frères sont)...	10. Mes ami(e)s sont...

Adjectives that Change Meaning According to Position

Some adjectives have a different meaning depending on whether they precede or follow the noun.

amer	une **amère** expérience	*a bitter (painful) experience*
	un goût **amer**	*a bitter taste*
ancien	un **ancien** professeur	*a former teacher*
	un professeur **ancien**	*an old (ancient) teacher*
bon	un homme **bon**	*a kind man*
	un **bon** homme	*a good man*
brave	un **brave** homme	*a good fellow, a kind man*
	un homme **brave**	*a courageous man*
certain	un **certain** risque	*a certain risk, some risk*
	un risque **certain**	*an unquestionable risk*
	une **certaine** élégance	*a particular elegance*
	une élégance **certaine**	*an indisputable elegance*
	un **certain** jour	*one day*
cher	un **cher** ami	*a dear friend*
	une robe **chère**	*an expensive dress*
dernier	la **dernière** semaine de l'année	*the last week of the year*
	la semaine **dernière**	*last week*
différent	**différentes** personnes	*various persons*
	des personnes **différentes**	*different persons*
divers	**diverses** circonstances	*several circumstances*
	des circonstances **diverses**	*various circumstances*
faux	une **fausse** note	*a note out of tune*
	une note **fausse**	*a wrong note*
grand	un **grand** écrivain	*a great writer*
	un écrivain **grand**	*a tall writer*
honnête	une **honnête** femme	*a virtuous woman*
	une femme **honnête**	*an honest woman*
jeune	un **jeune** homme	*a young man*
	un homme **jeune**	*a man still young*
maigre	une **maigre** existence	*a poor, meager existence*
	une femme **maigre**	*a thin (skinny) woman*
malhonnête	un **malhonnête** homme	*a dishonest man*
	un homme **malhonnête**	*a rude man*

même	la **même** chose	*the same thing*
	la chose **même**	*the thing itself*
	le jour **même**	*the very day*
	même le professeur	*even the teacher*
moyen	le **Moyen** Âge	*the Middle Ages*
	l'âge **moyen**	*middle age*
nouveau	une **nouvelle** robe	*a new (different) dress*
	une robe **nouvelle**	*a new (style) dress*
pauvre	un **pauvre** garçon	*a poor (unfortunate) boy*
	un garçon **pauvre**	*a poor (penniless) boy*
prochain	la **prochaine** fois	*the next time*
	la semaine **prochaine**	*next week*
propre	sa **propre** chambre	*his (her) own room*
	une chambre **propre**	*a clean room*
	les **propres** termes	*the very, actual words*
	les termes **propres**	*the right terms*
sale	un **sale** homme	*a bad man*
	un homme **sale**	*a dirty (physically) man*
seul	une **seule** personne	*only one person*
	une personne **seule**	*a single person*
triste	un **triste** livre	*a poor, worthless book*
	un livre **triste**	*a sad book*
vilain	un **vilain** personnage	*a disagreeable character*
	un personnage **vilain**	*an ugly character*
vrai	une **vraie** histoire	*quite a story*
	une histoire **vraie**	*a true story*

18. Follow the model.

pauvre   **Ce garçon n'a pas d'argent.**   **Ce garçon n'a pas d'amis.**
         C'est un garçon pauvre.   **C'est un pauvre garçon.**

1. *ancien*   Ce monument est vieux.
         Monsieur Dupont est mon professeur.
2. *brave*   Cet homme est courageux.
         Cet homme est bon.
3. *cher*   Ce chandail coûte beaucoup.
         C'est un ami fidèle.
4. *dernier*   La semaine passée il est allé au cinéma.
         C'est la semaine finale du trimestre.
5. *différent*   Diverses personnes sont venues.
         De nouvelles personnes sont venues.
6. *grand*   C'est un écrivain célèbre.
         C'est un écrivain de grande taille.
7. *pauvre*   Ce garçon est pitoyable.
         Ce garçon n'a pas d'argent.

8. *propre*   Cette chambre est nette.
             C'est ma chambre à moi.
9. *maigre*   Cette femme ne pèse pas beaucoup.
             Cette vie n'est pas agréable.

19. Rewrite each of the following sentences, inserting the correct form of the indicated adjective in the correct position.

   ancien **Ce monument qui est vieux est un _____ monument _____.**
              Ce monument qui est vieux est un monument ancien.

   1. *vrai*   C'est une histoire incroyable. C'est une _____ histoire _____.
                    Ce film raconte la vie de Van Gogh. C'est une _____ histoire _____.
   2. *certain*   Tu vas sûrement tout perdre. C'est un _____ risque _____.
                    Si tu joues à la Bourse, tu vas courir un _____ risque _____.
   3. *même*   Elle est arrivée le _____ jour _____ comme prévu.
                    Maintenant, _____ le professeur _____ va être d'accord avec vous.
                    Marcher et *aller à pied* sont presque la _____ chose _____.
   4. *nouveau*   Je viens d'acheter cette robe; c'est une _____ robe _____.
                    Au printemps, les maisons de haute couture vont présenter une collection de _____ robes _____.
   5. *seul*   Une _____ personne _____ ne peut pas tout faire.
                    Mon _____ souci _____ c'est ma famille.
   6. *vilain*   Ce garçon est désagréable. C'est un _____ garçon _____.
                    Ce garçon n'est pas beau. C'est un _____ garçon _____.
   7. *faux*   Le piano ne marche pas bien. J'entends une _____ note _____.
                    Il faut chanter la note *b*, pas la note *c*. C'est une _____ note _____.
   8. *sale*   C'est un _____ manteau _____.
                    Cet homme n'est pas gentil. C'est un _____ homme _____.
   9. *triste*   Cette histoire ne vaut rien. C'est une _____ histoire _____.
                    Cette histoire me fait pleurer. C'est une _____ histoire _____.
  10. *malhonnête* Un homme qui extorque de l'argent aux autres est un _____ homme _____.
                    Un homme qui dit des grossièretés est un _____ homme _____.
  11. *prochain*   Je vous verrai la _____ semaine _____.
                    La _____ fois _____, dites la vérité.
  12. *divers*   À la réunion, _____ personnes _____ discutent des _____ circonstances _____.
  13. *amer*   Ce thé a un _____ goût _____.
                    C'était une _____ expérience _____.

Formation of Adverbs

Most adverbs are formed by adding **-ment** to the feminine form of the adjective. Adverbs modify a verb, an adjective, or another adverb, and they are invariable.

Regular Forms

	Adjective		Adverb
Masculine	Feminine		
final	finale	**finalement**	*finally*
fort	forte	**fortement**	*strongly*

parfait	parfaite	**parfaitement**	*perfectly*
extrême	extrême	**extrêmement**	*extremely*
facile	facile	**facilement**	*easily*
rapide	rapide	**rapidement**	*rapidly*
naturel	naturelle	**naturellement**	*naturally*
complet	complète	**complètement**	*completely*
amer	amère	**amèrement**	*bitterly*
heureux	heureuse	**heureusement**	*happily*
sérieux	sérieuse	**sérieusement**	*seriously*
doux	douce	**doucement**	*sweetly*
attentif	attentive	**attentivement**	*attentively*
franc	franche	**franchement**	*frankly*
long	longue	**longuement**	*at length*

20. Follow the model.

Comment travaille-t-il? *facile*
Il travaille facilement.

1. Comment chante-t-elle? *doux*
2. Comment a-t-il prononcé? *parfait*
3. Comment étudie-t-elle? *serieux*
4. Comment danse-t-elle? *naturel*
5. Quand a-t-il compris? *final*
6. Comment est-il parti? *soudain*
7. Comment agit-il? *dangereux*
8. Comment parle-t-il? *rapide*
9. Comment répond-elle? *franc*
10. Comment écoute-t-il? *attentif*

Adverbs Formed from Adjectives Ending in a Vowel

If the masculine adjective ends in a vowel other than a mute **e,** the ending **-ment** is added to the masculine form of the adjective to form the adverb.

Masculine Adjective	*Adverb*	
hardi	**hardiment**	*boldly*
poli	**poliment**	*politely*
vrai	**vraiment**	*truly*
absolu	**absolument**	*absolutely*
résolu	**résolument**	*resolutely*

Exception:

gai	**gaîment** or **gaiement**	*gaily*

Some adjectives ending in **-u** in the masculine add a circumflex to the **u** when forming the adverb.

Masculine Adjective	*Adverb*	
assidu	**assidûment**	*attentively*
continu	**continûment**	*continually*
cru	**crûment**	*coarsely*

21. Follow the model.

Comment parle-t-il? *poli*
Il parle poliment.

1. Comment agit-il? *hardi*
2. Comment agit-elle? *résolu*
3. Comment chantent-elles? *gai*
4. Comment parle-t-il? *continu*
5. Comment parle-t-il? *cru*

Adverbs Ending in -*ément*

Some adjectives ending in a mute **e** change the **e** to **é** before adding **-ment** to form the adverb.

Adjective		Adverb	
Masculine	*Feminine*		
aveugle	aveugle	**aveuglément**	*blindly*
commode	commode	**commodément**	*conveniently*
commun	commune	**communément**	*commonly*
confus	confuse	**confusément**	*confusingly*
énorme	énorme	**énormément**	*enormously*
exquis	exquise	**exquisément**	*exquisitely*
importun	importune	**importunément**	*importunately, irritatingly*
obscur	obscure	**obscurément**	*obscurely*
opportun	opportune	**opportunément**	*opportunely*
précis	précise	**précisément**	*precisely*
profond	profonde	**profondément**	*profoundly*
uniforme	uniforme	**uniformément**	*uniformly*

22. Complete the following sentences with the adverb formed from the indicated adjective.

1. Pierre explique _____ la situation. *confus*
2. Le philosophe parle _____. *profond*
3. L'homme est _____ habillé. *exquis*
4. L'homme entre _____ dans l'affaire. *aveugle*
5. C'est _____ cela. *précis*
6. Elle a fait cela _____. *opportun*

Adverbs Ending in -*amment* and -*emment*

Adjectives ending in **-ant** and **-ent** in the masculine singular change **-ant** to **-amment** and **-ent** to **-emment** to form adverbs.

Masculine *Adjective*	*Adverb*	
abondant	**abondamment**	*abundantly*
brillant	**brillamment**	*brilliantly*
constant	**constamment**	*constantly*
courant	**couramment**	*fluently*
puissant	**puissamment**	*powerfully*
décent	**décemment**	*decently*
évident	**évidemment**	*evidently*
fréquent	**fréquemment**	*frequently*

patient	**patiemment**	*patiently*
prudent	**prudemment**	*wisely*

Exceptions:

Masculine Adjective	Adverb	
lent	**lentement**	*slowly*
présent	**présentement**	*presently*
véhément	**véhémentement**	*vehemently*

23. Complete the following sentences with the adverb formed from the indicated adjective.

1. Il parle _____ le français.   *courant*
2. Elle va _____ à ce restaurant.   *fréquent*
3. Le chimiste travaille _____.   *patient*
4. Le conférencier parle _____.   *brillant*
5. L'homme agit _____.   *décent*
6. _____, il est parti.   *évident*
7. La fille agit _____.   *prudent*
8. Le professeur écoute _____.   *patient*
9. Elle travaille _____.   *constant*
10. Le garçon marche _____.   *lent*
11. Le criminel agit _____.   *véhément*
12. Ce livre est _____ illustré.   *abondant*

Irregular Adverbs

Some adverbs have irregular stems.

Adjective		Adverb	
Masculine	Feminine		
bref	brève	**brièvement**	*briefly*
gentil	gentille	**gentiment**	*nicely*
impuni	impunie	**impunément**	*with impunity*

Some adverbs differ altogether from the corresponding adjective.

Adjective		Adverb	
Masculine	Feminine		
bon	bonne	**bien**	*well*
mauvais	mauvaise	**mal**	*badly*
meilleur	meilleure	**mieux**	*better*
moindre	moindre	**moins**	*less*
petit	petite	**peu**	*little*

Elle chante **bien**.	*She sings well.*
Il écrit **mal**.	*He writes badly.*
Il va **mieux**.	*He is better.*
Il travaille **peu**.	*He does little work.*

You can distinguish between **bon** / **mauvais** and **bien** / **mal** by remembering that the adjectives **bon** and **mauvais** modify nouns whereas the adverbs **bien** and **mal** modify verbs.

Elle est **bonne (mauvaise)** en mathématiques.
She is good (bad) in mathematics.

Elle parle **bien (mal)** le français.
She speaks French well (badly).

Some adverbs are identical to the masculine singular adjective.

Adjective and Adverb

bas   *low*
   Il parle **bas.**   *He speaks low.*
bon   *good*
   Ça sent **bon.**   *That smells good.*
chaud   *warm*
   Il fait **chaud.**   *It is warm (weather).*
cher   *expensive*
   Les robes coûtent **cher.**   *The dresses are expensive.*
clair   *clearly*
   Elle voit **clair.**   *She understands.*
court   *short*
   Il s'arrête **court.**   *He stops short.*
dur   *hard*
   Elle travaille **dur.**   *She works hard.*
faux   *false*
   Il chante **faux.**   *He sings out of tune.*
fort   *loudly, strongly*
   Il cric **fort.**   *He shouts loudly.*
haut   *loudly*
   Il parle **haut.**   *He speaks loudly.*
juste   *straight*
   Elle tire **juste.**   *She shoots straight.*
mauvais   *bad*
   Ça sent **mauvais.**   *That smells bad.*
net   *clean, short*
   Elle s'arrête **net.**   *She stops short.*

24. Complete the following sentences with the correct form of the adverb formed from the indicated adjective.

  1. Le conférencier parle _____.   *bref*
  2. Il a agi _____.   *gentil*
  3. Elle parle _____ le français.   *bon*
  4. L'élève écrit _____.   *mauvais*
  5. Cette fille parle _____.   *petit*
  6. Elle voit _____.   *clair*
  7. Le garçon parle _____.   *bas*
  8. Ces chandails coûtent _____.   *cher*
  9. Il travaille _____.   *dur*
 10. Elle chante _____.   *bon*
 11. Elle s'arrête _____.   *court*
 12. Il crie _____.   *fort*

Position of Adverbs

In simple tenses, adverbs follow the verb.

Il parle **rapidement**.	*He speaks rapidly.*
Elle chante **bien**.	*She sings well.*

In compound tenses, short, common adverbs and some adverbs of manner are placed between the auxiliary verb and the past participle. Some of these are: **assez, bien, beaucoup, bientôt, déjà, encore, enfin, jamais, mal, mieux, moins, souvent, toujours, trop** and **vite**.

Elle a **beaucoup** parlé.	*She spoke a lot.*
Nous avons **bien** dormi.	*We slept well.*
Elle est **vite** descendue.	*She came down quickly.*
Elle a **trop** bu.	*She drank too much.*

Adverbs of place and certain adverbs of time such as **hier, aujourd'hui, demain, avant-hier, après demain, autrefois, tard** and adverbs ending in **-ment** usually follow the past participle.

Elle veut voyager **partout**.	*She wants to travel everywhere.*
Elle est arrivée **hier**.	*She arrived yesterday.*
Il est parti **tard**.	*He left late.*
On l'a rencontré **là-bas**.	*He was met there.*
Elle a compris **facilement**.	*She understood easily.*

The adverb that modifies an infinitive can be placed before or after it.

Je voudrais **toujours** garder mon sang-froid.
Je voudrais garder **toujours** mon sang-froid.
I always want to keep my cool.

Some adverbs may appear at the beginning or end of the sentence. when they modify the entire sentence.

Finalement, elle est arrivée.	*Finally, she arrived.*
Elle est arrivée **finalement**.	*She arrived finally.*
Heureusement, il l'a bien fait.	*Happily, he did it well.*
Il l'a bien fait, **heureusement**.	*He did it well, happily.*

Many adverbs of time may also appear at the beginning of a sentence.

Enfin, il a fini.	*Finally, he finished.*
Aujourd'hui nous irons au cinéma.	*Today we will go to the movies.*
Demain nous partirons.	*Tomorrow we will leave.*

25. Complete the following sentences placing the adverbs in the correct position.

Vous avez parlé. *bien*
Vous avez bien parlé.

1. Il court. *rapidement*
2. La situation est impossible. *absolument*
3. Elle a voyagé. *beaucoup*
4. Il a étudié. *bien*
5. Nous avons mangé. *déjà*
6. Nous y sommes allés. *souvent*
7. Elle est arrivée. *hier*
8. Elle a travaillé. *patiemment*
9. Elle va travailler. *trop*
10. J'ai mangé. *assez*

26. Follow the model.

A-t-elle fini? *heureusement*
Heureusement, elle a fini.

1. Êtes-vous content?   *naturellement*
2. Va-t-il être à l'heure?   *certainement*
3. Est-il triste?   *évidemment*
4. Est-elle arrivée?   *finalement*
5. Est-elle arrivée à l'heure?   *heureusement*

Comparison of Adjectives and Adverbs

Regular Comparisons

The comparative is formed by placing **plus, moins** or **aussi** before and **que** after the adjective or adverb.

Comparison of superiority
plus... que   *more ... than*

Cette robe est **plus** belle **que** l'autre.
This dress is prettier than the other.
Il parle **plus** vite **que** moi.
He speaks more rapidly than I.

Comparison of equality

aussi... que   *as ... as*

Elle est **aussi** intelligente **que** moi.
She is as intelligent as I am.
Il parle **aussi** couramment **que** Pierre.
He speaks as fluently as Peter.

Comparison of inferiority

moins... que   *less ... than*

Ce tailleur est **moins** cher **que** l'autre.
This suit is less expensive than the other.
Ce garçon agit **moins** poliment **que** l'autre.
This boy acts less politely than the other.

Note that the disjunctive pronoun follows **que.**[1]

Je suis **plus** intelligent **que lui.**
I am more intelligent than he.

In negative sentences, **aussi** can become **si.**

Affirmative

Elle parle **aussi** vite **que** son frère.
She speaks as quickly as her brother.

Negative

Elle ne parle pas **si** vite **que** son frère.
She does not speak as quickly as her brother.

Plus and **moins** do not change in negative sentences.

Elle ne parle pas **plus** vite **que** son frère.
She does not speak more quickly than her brother.

---

[1] See Chapter 8 for a review of disjunctive pronouns.

Elle ne parle pas **moins** vite **que** son frère.
She does not speak less quickly than her brother.

Plus and **moins** used as adverbs of quantity require **de** before a numeral.

Je travaille **plus de** soixante heures par semaine.
I work more than sixty hours per week.
Il y a **moins de** vingt personnes inscrites au cours.
There are fewer than twenty people enrolled in the course.

But:

Il peut porter **plus que** deux kilos.
He can carry more than two kilos.

When there is a clause depending on the comparative, the expletive **ne** must be used before the subordinate verb. The **ne** does not make the verb negative.

Il est **plus** intelligent **que** vous **ne** le pensez.
He is more intelligent than you think.
Elle est **plus** intelligente **qu'**elle **n'**en a l'air.
She is more intelligent than she appears.

27. Follow the model.

Marie est grande. *less . . . than*
Marie est moins grande que sa sœur.

1. Anne est intelligente. *more . . . than*
2. Cet enfant est poli. *as . . . as*
3. Elle est patiente. *less . . . than*
4. Annette est sérieuse. *more . . . than*
5. Il est gentil. *as . . . as*
6. Hélène parle intelligemment. *more . . . than*
7. Cet homme conduit dangereusement. *as . . . as*
8. Vous chantez doucement. *less . . . than*
9. Judith attend patiemment. *more . . . than*
10. Vous agissez poliment. *as . . . as*

28. Follow the model.

Elle est petite. Hélène est plus petite.
Hélène est plus petite qu'elle.

1. Il est grand. Georges est plus grand.
2. Je suis intelligent. Pierre est plus intelligent.
3. Nous travaillons patiemment. Les autres travaillent plus patiemment.
4. Elle danse gaiement. Hélène danse aussi gaiement.
5. Ils écoutent attentivement. Pierre écoute aussi attentivement.
6. Elles sont intelligentes. Marc est moins intelligent.

29. Rewrite the following sentences in the negative.

1. Il parle plus vite que moi.
2. Il répond aussi intelligemment que Georges.
3. Il chante moins doucement que Pierre.
4. Elle est plus belle que Babeth.
5. Elle est aussi gentille que sa sœur.

30. Combine the two sentences according to the model.

> **Vous croyez qu'elle est douée. Elle est plus douée.**
> **Elle est plus douée que vous ne le croyez.**

> **Il a l'air intelligent. Il est plus intelligent.**
> **Il est plus intelligent qu'il n'en a l'air.**

1. Vous croyez qu'il est bête. Il est moins bête.
2. Vous trouvez qu'elle est intelligente. Elle est plus intelligente.
3. Vous pensez qu'il est drôle. Il est moins drôle.
4. Il a l'air méchant. Il est plus méchant.
5. Cette chanson a l'air compliquée. Elle est moins compliquée.

Comparative Followed by a Noun

Followed by a noun, **plus... que** becomes **plus de... que, aussi... que** becomes **autant de... que** and **moins... que** becomes **moins de... que**.

> J'ai **plus de** livres **que** lui.
> *I have more books than he does.*
> Elle a **autant d'**argent **que** moi.
> *She has as much money as I.*
> Elle a **moins de** livres **que** moi.
> *She has fewer books than I.*

31. Follow the model.

> **Pierre a des livres.** *more*
> **Pierre a plus de livres que moi.**

1. Anne a de l'argent. *as much*
2. Elle a des robes. *fewer*
3. Il a des autos. *more*
4. Elle a des gâteaux. *as many*
5. Vous avez des peintures. *more*
6. Vous avez des CD. *as many*
7. Il a mangé des tartes. *more ... than*
8. Elle a pris des livres. *fewer ... than*

Superlative of Adjectives and Adverbs

The superlative of an adjective is formed by adding the definite article **le, la** or **les** to the comparative form.

> Marc est l'étudiant **le plus intelligent** de la classe.
> *Mark is the most intelligent boy in the class.*
> Cette peinture est **la plus belle** de toutes.
> *This painting is the most beautiful of all.*
> Ces peintures sont **les moins intéressantes** du musée.
> *These paintings are the least interesting in the museum.*

If an adjective normally precedes the noun, the superlative will also precede the noun. If the adjective normally follows the noun, the superlative will normally follow.

> Pierre est **un gentil garçon.**
> *Peter is a nice boy.*

Pierre est **le plus gentil garçon** de la classe.
Peter is the nicest boy in the class.
Marie est **une fille intelligente.**
Mary is an intelligent girl.
Marie est **la fille la plus intelligente** de la classe.
Mary is the most intelligent girl in the class.

Note that the preposition **de** follows the superlative even when it means *in.*

When a verb follows the superlative, it is usually in the subjunctive.[2]

> **C'est le film le plus intéressant que j'aie vu.**
> **C'est la plus gentille fille que je connaisse.**

The superlative of adverbs is formed by adding **le** to the comparative.

> Ce garçon parle **le plus couramment.**
> *This boy speaks the most fluently.*
> Cette fille chante **le plus fort.**
> *This girl sings the loudest.*

32. Follow the models.

> **Ce garçon est beau?**
> **Oui, c'est le plus beau garçon du village.**

> **Cette fille est intelligente?**
> **Oui, c'est la fille la plus intelligente du village.**

1. Cette fille est intéressante?	6. Ce professeur est exigeant?
2. Cette rue est petite?	7. Cette église est vieille?
3. Ces enfants sont amusants?	8. Ces filles sont intelligentes?
4. Ce jardin est joli?	9. Ce musée est grand?
5. Ce garçon est honnête?	10. Cette peinture est belle?

33. Follow the models.

> **Pierre parle vite?**
> **Oui, il parle le plus vite de tous.**

> **Anne parle vite?**
> **Oui, elle parle le plus vite de toutes.**

1. Georges chante fort?	4. Le professeur parle profondément?
2. Marie travaille sérieusement?	5. Anne chante brillamment?
3. Hélène danse exquisément?	

Irregular Comparatives and Superlatives

The adjective **bon** and the adverb **bien** are irregular in comparisons of superiority.

---

[2] See Chapter 5 for subjunctive forms.

	Comparative	*Superlative*
bon(s), bonne(s)	**meilleur(s), meilleure(s)**	**le, la, les meilleur(e)(s)(es)**
	better	*the best*
bien	**mieux**	**le mieux**
	better	*the best*

Ce livre est **meilleur** que l'autre.
This book is better than the other.
Cette pomme est **meilleure** que l'autre.
This apple is better than the other.
Ces peintures sont **les meilleures** de toutes.
These paintings are the best of all.
Elle parle **mieux** que lui.
She speaks better than he.
Elle chante **le mieux** de toutes.
She sings the best of all.

Comparative and superlative forms of **bon** can be placed before or after the noun.

Il n'y a pas de **meilleures** méthodes.
Il est parmi les peintres **les meilleurs.**

Moins and **aussi** are used with **bon** and **bien**.

Ce livre est **moins (aussi) bon que** l'autre.
Elle parle **moins (aussi) bien que** lui.

Mauvais and **mal** have irregular as well as regular forms.

	Comparative	*Superlative*
mauvais(e)(es)	**plus mauvais(e)(es)**	**le, la, les plus mauvais(e)(es)**
	pire	**le, la, les pire(s)**
	worse	*the worst*
mal	**plus mal**	**le plus mal**
	pis	**le pis**
	worse	*the worst*

Cette note est **plus mauvaise que** l'autre.
Cette note est **pire que** l'autre.
This grade is worse than the other.
Cette note est **la plus mauvaise** de toutes.
Cette note est **la pire** de toutes.
This grade is the worst of all.
Il chante **plus mal que** Marie.
Il chante **pis que** Marie.
He sings worse than Mary.
Il chante **le plus mal** de tous.
He sings the worst of all.
Le pis de l'affaire c'est que vous avez échoué.
The worst of the matter is that you failed.

Note: **le pis** can only be used as a noun.

Plus mauvais and **le plus mauvais** are generally used in a concrete sense.

Cette automobile est **plus mauvaise que** l'autre.
This automobile is worse than the other.

Pire and **le pire** are generally used in a moral sense.

Il est **pire que** Pierre.
He is worse than Peter.

Petit has regular and irregular forms.

	Comparative	Superlative
petit(e)(s)(es)	**plus petit(e)(s)(es)**	**le, la, les plus petit(e)(s)(es)**
	moindre(s)	**le, la, les moindre(s)**
	smaller	*the smallest*

Plus petit and **le plus petit** are used with things you can measure.

Mon auto est **plus petite que** la sienne.
My car is smaller than his (hers).

Moindre and **le moindre** are used in an abstract sense.

Je n'ai pas **la moindre** idée.
I don't have the slightest (least) idea.

The comparative of **beaucoup** is **plus** or **davantage**.

Pierre a **beaucoup de** livres.
Peter has many books.
Georges a **plus de** livres.
George has more books.
Georges en a **plus**.
George has more.

Davantage is used to indicate a comparison of superiority and is generally placed at the end of the sentence.

Cette femme est très intelligente mais sa fille l'est **davantage**.
This woman is very intelligent but her daughter is even more so.

The comparative of **peu** is **moins**.

André travaille **peu**.
Andrew works little.
Pierre travaille **moins**.
Peter works less.

34. Complete the following with an appropriate comparison of superiority.

1. Ce livre est bon mais celui-là est _____.
2. Ce garçon chante bien mais Pierre chante _____.
3. Cette peinture est bonne mais celle-là est _____.
4. Il parle bien mais Pierre parle _____.
5. Ce tableau est mauvais mais celui-là est _____.
6. Il chante mal mais Pierre chante _____.

7. André a beaucoup de livres. Georges en a _____.
8. Marie dessine un peu. Lisette dessine _____.
9. Ces écoles sont bonnes, mais celles-ci sont _____ de toutes.
10. Pierre travaille mal, mais André travaille _____ de tous.
11. Cette maison est petite. C'est _____ de toutes.
12. Je ne sais pas la réponse. Je n'ai pas _____ idée.

35. Follow the models.

Ce livre-ci est bon.
Ce livre-ci est aussi bon que ce livre-là.
Ce livre-ci est moins bon que ce livre-là.
Ce livre-ci est meilleur que ce livre-là.
Ce livre-ci est le meilleur de tous.

1. Ce gâteau-ci est bon.
2. Ces fromages-ci sont bons.
3. Cette orange-ci est bonne.
4. Ces tomates-ci sont bonnes.
5. Ce beurre-ci est mauvais.
6. Cette tarte-ci est mauvaise.

Il chante bien.
Il chante aussi bien que vous.
Il chante moins bien que vous.
Il chante mieux que vous.
Il chante le mieux de tous.

7. Elle chante bien.
8. Il écrit bien.
9. Il travaille mal.

Adjectives without Comparative and Superlative Forms

Some adjectives introducing their complement by the preposition **à** have no comparative or superlative forms.

inférieur à	*inferior to*
supérieur à	*superior to*
antérieur à	*anterior to*
postérieur à	*posterior to*
intérieur à	*interior to*
extérieur à	*exterior to*

Les œufs bruns sont-ils **supérieurs** aux œufs blancs?
Are brown eggs superior to white eggs?

Some adjectives that already express comparisons of inferiority or superiority do not have special comparative forms.

aîné, -e	*older, oldest*
cadet, cadette	*younger, youngest*
premier, première	*first*
dernier, dernière	*last*
principal, -e	*principal*

C'est mon frère **cadet.**
He's my younger brother.

Useful Phrases with Comparatives and Superlatives

plus... plus	*the more ... the more*
moins... moins	*the less ... the less*
plus... moins	*the more ... the less*

Plus je lis ce livre, **plus** je l'aime.
The more I read this book, the more I like it.
Moins je lis, **moins** j'apprends.
The less I read, the less I learn.
Plus je fais le ménage, **moins** j'en ai envie.
The more I do housework, the less I want to.

de plus en plus	*more and more*
de moins en moins	*less and less*
de mieux en mieux	*better and better*

Ce travail devient **de plus en plus** difficile.
This work is becoming more and more difficult.
Le climat est **de moins en moins** agréable.
The climate is less and less agreeable.
Elle chante **de mieux en mieux.**
She sings better and better.

d'autant plus que	*all the more ... as, because*

Il est **d'autant plus** heureux ici **qu'**il a un jardin.
He is all the more happy here because he has a garden.

tant mieux	*so much the better*
tant pis	*so much the worse*
de mal en pis	*from bad to worse*

Les choses vont **de mal en pis.**
Things go from bad to worse.

36. Write the following sentences in French.

1. The child talks more and more each day.
2. The more he works, the more he understands.
3. So much the better!
4. The economy goes from bad to worse.
5. He is all the more happy because he lives in the country.
6. The sick person eats better and better.
7. Mary is my older sister.

Possessive Adjectives

In French **de** and the name of the person show possession.

le livre de Paul
Paul's book

la mère de Marie et de Georges
Mary and George's mother
les livres des garçons
the boys' books

Following are the forms for the possessive adjectives.

	Masculine singular	Masculine or feminine singular before a vowel	Feminine singular	Plural
my	**mon**	**mon**	**ma**	**mes**
your (fam.)	**ton**	**ton**	**ta**	**tes**
his, her, its	**son**	**son**	**sa**	**ses**
our	**notre**	**notre**	**notre**	**nos**
your	**votre**	**votre**	**votre**	**vos**
their	**leur**	**leur**	**leur**	**leurs**

The possessive adjective agrees in number and in gender with the noun modified, i.e., with the object possessed, not with the possessor.

mon frère	*my brother*
ma sœur	*my sister*
mes frères	*my brothers*
Elle a **son livre.**	*She has her book.*
Il a **son livre.**	*He has his book.*

Note that **mon, ton** and **son** are used before feminine nouns or adjectives beginning with a vowel or silent **h.**

mon amie Hélène	*my friend Helen*
mon histoire préférée	*my favorite story*

The possessive adjective must be repeated before each noun.

Je dois écrire à **ma sœur,** à **mes parents** et à **mon oncle.**

Note that French uses the singular possessive adjective when only one object is possessed by each person.

Ils attachent leur ceinture de sécurité. (Each person has only one seatbelt.)
They fasten their seatbelts.

Use of the Definite Article as a Possessive

Possessive adjectives are not used when referring to parts of the body or clothing, or with mental faculties, when the possessor is clearly indicated by the use of the indirect object pronoun before the verb.

Il a les mains dans les poches.
He has his hands in his pockets.
Elle lui a fait mal au bras.
She hurt his arm.
Lève la main.
Raise your hand.
Il a baissé la tête.
He lowered his head.

Il a perdu la mémoire.
He lost his memory.

When the possessor has not been mentioned, the possessive adjective can be used.

Ses yeux étaient d'un noir profond.
Elle avait **les yeux** d'un noir profond.

In the last sentence, the possessor **elle** is indicated and, therefore, the definite article is used; however, after **regarder, montrer** or **voir** and when you want to emphasize the part of the body, the possessive adjectives are used with parts of the body.

Montre-moi tes mains.
Show me your hands.
Donne-moi ta main gauche.
Give me your left hand.
Elle regarde ses cheveux.
She looks at his hair.

With *on, personne, tout le monde*

When the object possessed is in the same clause as **on, personne** and **tout le monde,** the third person singular possessive adjectives **son, sa, ses** are used.

On aime son père et sa mère.
Tout le monde veut faire de son mieux.

If, however, the object possessed is in a different clause from the one where **on** is used, the possessive adjectives **notre** and **votre** are used.

On n'est pas méchant par nature. Ce sont les circonstances qui nous forcent à l'être malgré notre désir.

With *chacun*

If **chacun** is a subject or object, **son, sa, ses** are used.

Chacun a son défaut.
Each one has his(her) own faults.

If a plural subject is modified by **chacun,** the possessive adjective agrees with the subject.

Nous avons apporté chacun nos provisions.
Ils feront chacun son (leur) devoir.
Ils sont partis chacun de son (leur) côté.

The third person can be singular or plural.

The idea of possession can also be expressed by using **être à** plus a disjunctive pronoun.

Ce livre est à moi.
C'est mon propre livre.
This is my own book.

It can also be expressed by a demonstrative pronoun plus **de** plus a noun.

mon auto et celle[3] de mon père
my car and my father's (car)

---

[3] See Chapter 8 for demonstrative pronouns.

To avoid ambiguity in translating *his* or *her*, a prepositional phrase **à lui** or **à elle** may be used.

Il parle à **son père à elle.** *(her father)*
Il parle à **son père à lui.** *(his father)*

37. Tell what the people are packing to go on vacation. Complete the following, choosing the correct form of the possessive adjective.

1. *mon, ma, mes* J'ai _____ robe, _____ blouses et _____ pantalon.
2. *ton, ta, tes* Voilà _____ appareil photographique, _____ cellule, et _____ filtres.
3. *son, sa, ses* Il a _____ chemise, _____ imperméable et _____ chaussures.
4. *notre, nos* Nous avons _____ sac de couchage et _____ provisions.
5. *votre, vos* Vous avez _____ gants et _____ chapeau.
6. *leur, leurs* Ils ont _____ cravates et _____ liste des adresses.

38. Follow the model.

C'est le livre de Paul.
C'est son livre.

1. C'est le cahier de Pierre.
2. C'est le livre de Marie.
3. C'est la photo de Georges.
4. Ce sont les amies de Marie.
5. C'est l'amie de Paul.
6. Ce sont les lettres du professeur.
7. C'est l'école des garçons.
8. C'est l'adresse de Babeth.
9. Ce sont les livres de l'écrivain.
10. C'est l'auto de Monsieur et de Madame Dupont.
11. Ce sont les amis des garçons.
12. Ce sont les livres des professeurs.

39. The following people are bringing friends and relatives to a party. Whom are the people bringing? Follow the model.

J'invite _____ cousin.
J'invite *mon* cousin.

1. Nous invitons _____ cousines.
2. Nicole invite _____ ami Pierre.
3. J'invite _____ oncle Antoine.
4. Monsieur et Madame Dupont invitent _____ voisins.
5. Tu invites _____ mère.
6. Paul invite _____ cousine Antoinette.
7. Nous invitons _____ père.
8. Vous invitez _____ mère.
9. J'invite _____ amies.
10. Tu invites _____ professeurs.
11. David et Pierre invitent _____ tante.
12. J'invite _____ sœur Babeth.
13. Le professeur invite _____ élèves.
14. Tu invites _____ amie Anne.
15. Vous invitez _____ parents.

40. Complete the following sentences with the appropriate possessive adjective or definite article.

1. (*My*) _____ auto est en panne.
2. (*Your, fam.*) _____ livre est intéressant.
3. J'écris à (*my*) _____ mère.
4. J'aime (*his*) _____ cravate.
5. Il parle à (*her*) _____ père.
6. Ils lisent (*their*) _____ journal.
7. Paul parle à (*his*) _____ amie.
8. Ils ont (*their*) _____ billets.
9. Elle veut (*her*) _____ argent.
10. Il écrit à (*his*) _____ *mère.*
11. Elle adore (*her*) _____ père.
12. Nous écoutons (*our*) _____ professeurs.
13. Vous avez (*your*) _____ livres.
14. Tu as (*your*) _____ robe.
15. (*Your, formal*) _____ père m'a téléphoné hier soir.
16. (*My*) _____ amies viennent me voir souvent.
17. Elle écrit à (*her*) _____ parents.
18. Elle aime (*his*) _____ livres.
19. Nous aimons (*our*) _____ appartement.
20. Il a (*his*) _____ mains sur la table.
21. Elle a levé (*her*) _____ main.
22. Elle brosse (*his*) _____ cheveux.
23. Montre-moi (*your, fam.*) _____ mains.
24. On lui a rendu _____ liberté.
25. Vous avez apporté chacun _____ provisions.
26. Personne n'a oublié _____ livre.

41. Form sentences using a possessive adjective according to the model.

la maison... de Pierre
C'est sa maison à lui.

1. le père... de Marie
2. la sœur... de Pierre
3. le livre... à moi
4. la propriété... de M. et de Mme Dupont
5. les stylos... de Gisèle
6. le chien... à toi
7. les enfants... à nous
8. la bicyclette... à vous

42. You are planning a trip. What do you pack in your suitcase? Follow the model, using possessive adjectives.

Je mets mes sous-vêtements, mon chapeau, mon maillot de bain, mes robes, etc.,
dans ma valise.

Demonstrative Adjectives

The demonstrative adjectives *this, that, these, those* are as follows:

Masculine singular		Feminine singular	Plural
Before a consonant	Before a vowel or mute **h**		
ce	cet	cette	ces

Ce garçon est beau.
Cet artiste est intelligent.
Cette fille est belle.
Ces livres sont intéressants.
Ces peintures sont belles.

To make a clear distinction between *this* and *that*, the suffix **-ci** (*this*) or **-là** (*that*) is added.

Je veux ce livre-ci.   *I want this book.*
Je ne veux pas ce livre-là.   *I don't want that book.*

43. Complete the following with the appropriate demonstrative adjective.

1. J'aime _____ roman.
2. Il a écrit _____ pièce.
3. _____ artiste travaille bien.
4. Je veux _____ livres d'art.
5. _____ animaux sont féroces.
6. Parlez à _____ enfant.
7. _____ église est vieille.
8. _____ robes sont belles.
9. Nous allons déjeuner dans _____ restaurant.
10. _____ route va à Nice.

44. Madame Dupont is buying fruit for a fruit salad for her lunch. She is very particular about what she buys. Follow the model.

des pommes
Je voudrais ces pommes-ci, pas ces pommes-là.

1. une orange
2. un abricot
3. des cerises
4. une pomme
5. un pamplemousse
6. des fraises

Indefinite Adjectives

Following are some of the most common indefinite adjectives.

1. **autre, autres**   *another, other, different*

   Je voudrais essayer **une autre** robe.
   I would like to try on another dress.
   Avez-vous **d'autres** livres?
   Do you have any other books?

Note that the plural of **un autre** or **une autre** is **d'autres**.

un autre film
another film
d'autres films
other films

In spoken language, **autre** is also used to reinforce a first or second person plural subject pronoun.

Nous autres, nous viendrons.
As for us, we'll come.

Autre is used without an article or demonstrative adjective in certain expressions.

Autres temps, autres mœurs.
Other days, other ways.
Ça, c'est autre chose.
That's another thing.

2. **aucun(e)... ne, nul(le)... ne, ne... aucun(e)**   *no*

> **Aucun** travail **n'**est trop difficile.
> **Nul** travail **n'**est trop difficile.
> *No work is too difficult.*
> Il **n'**y a **aucun** homme ici.
> *There is no man here.*
> Il **n'**y a **aucune** peinture.
> *There is no painting.*

Aucun... ne can mean *any, a single, one single.*

> **Cet article est meilleur qu'aucun livre.**
> *This article is better than any book.*
> **Aucun homme ne peut faire cela.**
> *Not a single man can do that.*

3. **certain(e), certain(e)s**   *certain, some*

Certain is placed before the noun. Sometimes **certain** can mean the same thing as **quelque** (*some*).

> Une **certaine** Madame Leroi vous attend.
> *A certain Mrs. Leroy is waiting for you.*
> **Certains** mots anglais se sont infiltrés dans la langue française.
> *Certain English words have infiltrated into the French language.*
> **Certaines** situations sont difficiles; d'autres ne le sont pas.
> *Certain situations are difficult; others are not.*

Certain can be placed after the noun. In this case it has the meaning of *sure* or *certain*.

> **Ce spectacle est un succès certain.**
> *This show is a certain (undisputable) success.*

4. **chaque**   *each, every*

> **Chaque** personne a son pays.
> *Each person has his (her) country.*
> Il dit cela **chaque** fois.
> *He says that every time.*

5. **divers(es), différent(e)s, maint(e)s**   *several, various*

> **Divers** professeurs ont proposé **différents** projets.
> *Various teachers proposed various projects.*
> **Maintes** fois elle a proposé une solution.
> *Many times she proposed a solution.*

Divers after a noun stresses a variety of items.

> Il a travaillé dans des occupations **diverses.**
> *He worked in various occupations.*

Différent can be placed after the noun and can be used in the singular.

> Il a proposé une solution **différente.**
> *He proposed a different solution.*

6. **maint** *many a, various, many*

> **Mainte** personne voudrait faire cela.
> *Many a person would like to do that.*

Maintes fois elle vous a dit de ne pas suivre cette route.
Many times she told you not to go on this path.

7. **même**   *same, itself, very, even*

After a noun, **même** means *itself*.

C'est homme est l'honnêteté **même**.
This man is honesty itself.

After a noun or a pronoun, **même** means *very, even, himself,* etc. When **même** follows a pronoun, it is connected to the pronoun with a hyphen.

Il a annoncé sa candidature ce jour **même**.
He announced his candidacy that very day.
Même son meilleur ami ne le croit pas.
Even his best friend does not believe him.
Ses parents **mêmes** ne le croient pas.
His parents themselves don't believe him.
Lui-même[4] ne savait quoi dire.
He himself did not know what to say.
Écrivez-la **vous-même**.
Write it yourself.

Before a noun and preceded by the article, it means *same*.

C'est **le même livre**.
It's the same book.
Nous lisons **les mêmes journaux**.
We read the same newspapers.

8. **n'importe**   *no matter*

N'importe combines with **quel, quelle, quels, quelles** to signify *no matter what (which)*.

Téléphonez-moi à **n'importe quelle** heure.
Telephone me at any hour.

9. **plusieurs**   *several*

Elle a **plusieurs** livres.
She has several books.
Il a **plusieurs** chemises.
He has several shirts.

Plusieurs is invariable.

10. **quelque**   *a little, some, few*

In the singular, **quelque** means *a little*.

Il me reste **quelque** temps.
I have a little time left.

Or it may mean *some, any kind of*.

Je voudrais trouver **quelque** poste.
I would like to find any (some) kind of job.

---

[4] See Chapter 8 for disjunctive pronouns.

In the plural, **quelque** means *a few, some* or *several*.

> Elle a acheté **quelques** livres.
> *She bought a few (some) books.*
> Il a **quelques** amis.
> *He has some (several) friends.*

Quelque can be an adverb and, therefore, invariable when it is used before a number and means **environ** *(about, approximately, around)*.

> J'ai fait **quelque** cent mètres avant d'arriver à une route pavée.
> *I walked about one hundred meters before arriving at a paved road.*

11. **quelque... que**   *whatever, however*
    quel, quelle, quels, quelles... que   *whatever*

Quelque and the interrogative adjective **quel** combine with the relative pronoun **que** to mean *whatever*. The verb that follows is always in the subjunctive. Before a noun **quelque** is an adjective and is variable.

> **Quelques** peurs **que** vous ayez, conquérez-les.
> *Whatever fears you have, conquer them.*

Before a descriptive adjective, **quelque** is an adverb and, therefore, invariable.

> **Quelque** difficiles **que** soient les problèmes, persévérez.
> *However difficult the problems are, persevere.*

Before an adverb, it is another adverb and, therefore, invariable.

> **Quelque** bêtement **que** vous agissiez, je vous aime toujours.
> *However stupidly you act, I always like you.*

Quel que is written as two words when it is followed by a verb (almost always the verb **être**). It agrees with the subject.

> **Quel que** soit[5] votre métier, travaillez bien.
> *Whatever your profession, work well.*
> **Quelle que** soit la difficulté, surpassez-la.
> *Whatever the difficulty, surpass it.*
> **Quels que** soient[5] les problèmes, ne vous inquiétez pas.
> *Whatever the problems, don't get upset.*

12. **quelconque**   *just any*

> Ce n'est pas une peinture **quelconque.** C'est une peinture de Picasso.
> *This is not just any painting. It's a painting by Picasso.*

13. **je ne sais quel(le)(s)(les)**   *I don't know*
    on ne sait quel(le)(s)(les)   *one doesn't know*
    Dieu sait quel(le)(s)(les)   *God only knows*
    etc.

These expressions are used to indicate an approximate resemblance. They are similar in meaning to **certain** in an undetermined sense.

> **Je ne sais quelle** personne a dit « Il n'y a pas de fumée sans feu. »
> *I don't know who said: "There is no smoke without fire."*

---

[5] See Chapter 5 for review of subjunctive forms.

Il le fera **Dieu sait quel jour.**
He'll do it some day or other. (God only knows when.)
Elle a **je ne sais quelles** idées.
She has some ideas or others.

14. **tel** (*masc. sing.*), **tels** (*masc. pl.*), **telle** (*fem. sing.*), **telles** (*fem. pl.*)   *such, such a, like, as*

Tel est mon avis.
Such is my opinion.
Je n'ai jamais vu **un tel** film.
I never saw such a film.
Tel père, **tel** fils.
Like father, like son.
Il faut parler français **tel que** les Français le parlent.
You must speak French as the French do.
Un homme **tel que** lui mérite des louanges.
A man such as he deserves praise.
telle ou **telle** personne
such and such a person
Elle est partie **telle une flèche.**
She shot off like an arrow.

Use **si** instead of **tel** in expressions containing an adjective.

Avez-vous jamais vu une **si** belle peinture?
Have you ever seen such a beautiful painting?
Avez-vous jamais lu des livres **si** amusants?
Have you ever read such amusing books?

15. **tout** (*masc. sing.*), **tous** (*masc. pl.*), **toute** (*fem. sing.*), **toutes** (*fem. pl.*)   *all, every, the whole*

In the singular, **tout** means *each* or *every* when it is used without an article.

Tout homme a son pays.
Every man has his country.
Toute femme mérite cela.
Every woman deserves that.

When followed by an article or a possessive adjective, it means *the whole, the entire.*

Tout le pays est fertile.
The whole country is fertile.
Toute la montagne est couverte de neige.
The whole mountain is covered with snow.
Je serai honnête **toute ma** vie.
I will be honest my whole life.

Tout le monde means *everyone.*

In certain expressions, **tout** means *only.*

Pour **toute** réponse, il souriait.
His only answer was to smile.

In the plural, **tout** means *all* or *every.*

Toutes les personnes ont besoin de repos.
All people need rest.

Toutes les chemises sont chères.
All the shirts are expensive.
Elle y va **tous les** jours.
She goes there every day.

Tout is invariable when using the name of an author to mean the ensemble of his or her works.

J'ai lu **tout Simone de Beauvoir.**

Tout is an adverb and is invariable when used to mean *entire* or *complete*.

ma vie **tout entière**
my entire life
Nous sommes **tout seuls.**
We are all alone.

Tout as a pronoun means *everything*.

Il a **tout** fait, **tout** vu.
He did and he saw everything.
Tout est beau.
Everything is beautiful.

Tout is also invariable before a feminine word beginning with a vowel or silent **h.**

Elle est **tout agréable, tout heureuse.**
She is altogether agreeable, altogether happy.

However, the adverb **tout** must agree in gender and number before a feminine adjective beginning with a consonant or aspirate **h.**

Elle est **toute surprise, toute honteuse.**
She is altogether surprised, altogether ashamed.

45. Complete the following sentences with the correct French expression for the English words in parentheses.

1. Je cherche _____ *(some kind of)* travail.
2. Elle a acheté _____ *(some)* robes.
3. Il y a _____ *(several)* livres sur la table.
4. J'ai _____ *(certain)* choses à faire.
5. J'ai discuté la situation avec _____ *(various)* personnes.
6. _____ *(Every)* homme veut sa liberté.
7. _____ *(Every)* fois qu'il ouvre la bouche, il m'ennuie.
8. _____ *(All)* les hommes sont mortels.
9. Avez-vous une _____ *(other)* idée?
10. Je n'ai _____ *(no)* idée.
11. _____ *(Even)* le professeur ne dira pas cela.
12. Il est parti ce jour _____ *(very)*.
13. Il dit toujours la _____ *(same)* chose.
14. Avez-vous jamais entendu _____ *(such a)* histoire?
15. _____ *(Like)* mère, _____ *(like)* fille.
16. _____ *(Such)* est mon but.
17. _____ *(Whatever)* soit votre opinion, ne dites rien.
18. Ce n'est pas une auto _____ *(just any)*. C'est une Cadillac.
19. _____ *(Another)* temps, _____ *(other)* endroits.
20. Elle est _____ *(altogether)* surprise _____ *(altogether)* heureuse.

21. _____ *(Whatever)* mesures que vous preniez, je vous appuie.
22. Écoutez un disque _____ *(any)*.
23. Avez-vous jamais lu de _____ *(such)* beaux poèmes?
24. Il a couru _____ *(some)* deux cents mètres.
25. Elle est la bonté _____ *(itself)*.
26. Avez-vous _____ *(other)* livres?
27. _____ *(No)* travail n'est trop difficile.
28. _____ est parfait. *(Everything)*
29. _____ fois elle a proposé la solution. *(Many)*

Review

46. Mary and John get along well since they are so much alike. Tell how Mary is like John. Follow the models.

Jean est toujours content.
Marie est toujours contente aussi.

Jean n'est jamais triste.
Marie n'est jamais triste non plus.

1. Jean est intelligent.
2. Jean est fort.
3. Jean est sûr de lui-meme.
4. Jean est honnête.
5. Jean est gentil.
6. Jean est bon.
7. Jean n'est pas sot.
8. Jean n'est pas gros.
9. Jean est discret.
10. Jean est fier.
11. Jean est sérieux.
12. Jean est roux.
13. Jean est créateur.
14. Jean est sportif.
15. Jean est franc.
16. Jean n'est pas malin.

47. Describe the house. Put the correct form of the adjective in parentheses in the correct place and use the conjunction **et** when necessary. Follow the models.

C'est une (petit, noir) _____ maison _____.
C'est une *petite maison noire*.

C'est une (intéressant) _____ maison _____.
C'est une *maison intéressante*.

1. C'est une (grand, blanc) _____ maison _____ aux (bleu foncé) _____ volets _____.
2. Derrière la maison il y a un (très joli) _____ jardin _____ avec des fleurs aux (vif) _____ couleurs _____.
3. Dans le salon il y a de (beau, vieux) _____ meubles _____, une (beau, noir et blanc) _____ chaise _____, une (vieux, marron) _____ lampe _____ avec un (vieux, marron) _____ abat-jour _____.
4. Sur une table il y a des (frais cueilli) _____ fleurs _____ et une (beau, petit) _____ photo _____.
5. Sur la photo, il y a une (petit, jeune, roux) _____ fille _____, aux (bleu clair) _____ yeux _____, et aux (ivoire) _____ joues _____ et un (beau, blond, sérieux) _____ homme _____ aux (châtain) _____ cheveux

_____. Ils ont l'air d'être des (royal) _____ gens _____. C'est ma (favori) _____ photo _____.

6. Sur une (autre) _____ table _____ il y a une (grand, merveilleux) _____ statue _____ d'une (gros, malin) _____ chatte _____ aux (long) _____ griffes _____.

7. Au mur il y a de (gros) _____ peintures _____ de nos (natal, nord-africain) _____ villages _____.

8. Il y a une (grand) _____ cuisine _____ avec un (vieux) _____ évier _____, une (vieux) _____ cuisinière _____ et un (vieux) _____ réfrigérateur _____. On sent l'(doux) _____ odeur _____ des épices malgré les (grand-ouvert) _____ fenêtres _____.

9. Dans la salle à manger, il y a une (grand, ancien) _____ table _____ de (français) _____ style _____.

10. Dans la chambre, il y a de (nouveau, élégant) _____ meubles _____, une (beau, nouveau) _____ armoire _____, un (bon) _____ lit _____ et une (grand, nouveau) _____ commode _____.

48. Follow the model.

C'est mon _____ professeur _____. *former*
C'est mon *ancien professeur*.

1. C'est une _____ chaise _____. *expensive*
2. C'est un _____ homme _____. *courageous*
3. C'est une _____ fille _____. *poor (penniless)*
4. C'est une _____ robe _____. *clean*
5. Il est parti le _____ jour _____. *very*
6. Ce sont de _____ bottes _____. *new (different)*

49. Describe things you own.

J'ai une petite auto rouge et japonaise.
J'ai une jolie robe bleu-clair.

Continue.

50. Answer the questions using one or two of the adjectives listed below or adjectives of your own choice. You can use the words more than once.

japonais	grand	bleu	fantastique
américain	petit	brun	sérieux
français	long	châtain	comique
italien	court	blond	tragique

Quelle sorte de chambre avez-vous?
J'ai une grande chambre verte.

1. Quelle sorte d'autos préférez-vous?
2. Quelle sorte de restaurants aimez-vous?
3. Quelle sorte de films préférez-vous?
4. Quelle sorte d'hôtels préférez-vous?
5. Quelle sorte de cuisine aimez-vous?
6. Quelle sorte de cheveux avez-vous?

51. Follow the model. Make necessary changes in the placement of adjectives.

> **Comment parle-t-il?**   *sérieux*
> **Il parle sérieusement.**

1. Comment parle-t-il?   *résolu*
2. Quand vient-il?   *fréquent*
3. Comment parle-t-il?   *courant*
4. Comment travaille-t-elle?   *continu*
5. Comment a-t-il dormi?   *bon*
6. Quand est-il-parti?   *tard*
7. Quand a-t-il fini?   *final*
8. A-t-il bien mangé?   *heureux*
9. Quand a-t-elle fini?   *hier*
10. Comment chante-t-elle?   *bien*
11. Comment parle-t-il?   *haut*
12. Comment voit-il?   *clair*
13. Comment crie-t-il?   *fort*

52. Show how the following people do things in a manner that reflects their personality. Follow the models.

> **Robert / calme   Il parle...**
> **Robert *est calme*.**
> **Il parle *calmement*.**

> **Marie et Solange / discret   Elles parlent...**
> **Marie et Solange *sont discrètes*.**
> **Elles parlent *discrètement*.**

1. Pierre / sérieux   Il travaille...
2. Anne / précis   Elle parle...
3. Yvette / attentif   Elle écoute...
4. Jean / franc   Il répond...
5. Jacques et Charles / intelligent   Ils répondent...
6. Marie et Jeanne / gentil   Elles agissent...
7. André et Marc / patient   Ils écoutent...
8. Diane / brillant   Elle résout le problème...
9. Paul et Philippe / véhément   Ils agissent...
10. David et Georges / loyal   Ils agissent...
11. Éric et Roger / lent   Ils marchent...
12. Nicole / naturel   Elle agit...

53. Compare the cities. You may substitute names of cities you know. Follow the models.

> **Les parcs de la ville A sont jolis.**
> **Les parcs de la ville A sont aussi jolis que les parcs de la ville B.**
> **Les parcs de la ville A sont moins jolis que les parcs de la ville C.**
> **Les parcs de la ville A ne sont pas si jolis que les parcs de la ville C.**
> **Les parcs de la ville A sont plus jolis que les parcs de la ville D.**
> **Les parcs de la ville C sont les plus jolis de tous.**

1. Les attractions de la ville A sont bonnes.
2. Les restaurants de la ville A sont bons.
3. Les magasins de la ville A sont chics.
4. La pollution de la ville A est mauvaise.
5. Les habitants de la ville A marchent vite.
6. Les habitants de la ville A vivent bien.

La ville A a des musées.
La ville A a plus de musées que la ville B.
La ville A a moins de musées que la ville C.
La ville A a autant de musées que la ville D.

7. La ville A a des théâtres.
8. La ville A a des cafés.

54. Describe the students in the classroom. Follow the model. Then make similar comparisons for students in your classroom.

Pierre est un petit garçon.
Pierre est le plus petit garçon de la classe.

1. Marie est une fille intelligente.
2. Hélène est une jolie fille.
3. André est un bel homme.
4. Henri est un garçon intéressant.

55. To whom do the following things belong? Complete the following sentences using the correct demonstrative and possessive adjectives. Follow the model.

_____ **bracelet est à Marie; c'est** _____ **bracelet.**
Ce **bracelet est à Marie; c'est** *son* **bracelet.**

1. _____ livre est à moi; c'est _____ livre.
2. _____ souliers sont à Paul; ce sont _____ souliers.
3. _____ raquette de tennis est à toi; c'est _____ raquette de tennis.
4. _____ auto est à Yvette; c'est _____ auto.
5. _____ bicyclette est à Charles; c'est _____ bicyclette.
6. _____ disques compacts sont à vous; ce sont _____ disques compacts.
7. _____ journaux sont à Solange et à moi; ce sont _____ journaux.
8. _____ skis sont à moi; ce sont _____ skis.
9. _____ appareil photographique est à toi; c'est _____ appareil photographique.
10. _____ micro-ordinateur est à Marc et à André; c'est _____ micro-ordinateur.
11. _____ dictionnaire est à vous; c'est _____ dictionnaire.
12. _____ voiture est à moi; c'est _____ voiture.
13. _____ billets sont à Nicole et à Anne; ce sont _____ billets.
14. _____ photos sont à toi; ce sont _____ photos.
15. _____ maison est à nous; c'est _____ maison.

56. Complete the following with the correct definite article or possessive adjective.

1. Il a _____ mains sur la table. *his*
2. Regardez _____ mains. *your (formal)*
3. On a _____ responsabilité. *one's*
4. Lève _____ main. *your*

57. You are in a department store. Tell what things you want to buy. Follow the model.

le livre
Je veux ce livre-ci, pas ce livre-là.

1. la robe
2. l'appareil photographique
3. le disque compact
4. les cravates

58. Change the sentences, using the indicated words. Make all necessary changes.

Pierre a des livres.   *plusieurs*
Pierre a plusieurs livres.

1. Marie a des journaux.   *quelque*
2. Hélène a beaucoup d'amis.   *plusieurs*
3. Il a du temps.   *quelque*
4. Des problèmes sont difficiles à résoudre.   *certain*
5. Nous avons parlé à différentes personnes.   *divers*
6. Tout homme veut réussir.   *chaque*
7. Avez-vous des CD?   *autre*
8. J'ai vu les maisons.   *tout*
9. Il n'y a pas de livre ici.   *aucun*
10. J'ai mangé les gâteaux.   *tout*
11. Son ennemi le croit.   *même*
12. Je n'ai jamais vu une pièce.   *tel*
13. C'est mon choix.   *tel*
14. L'homme veut être heureux.   *tout*
15. Des livres sont intéressants.   *autre*
16. Il a couru cent mètres.   *quelque*
17. Elle est grande.   *tout*
18. Prenez un livre.   *quelconque*

CHAPTER 3

Prepositions

Uses of Certain Prepositions

A preposition is an invariable word which introduces an element of a sentence that it unites or subordinates in a certain way to another element of the sentence. Prepositions can establish many kinds of connections or relationships between various parts of a sentence. They can indicate place, time, cause, goal, means, manner, possession, and so on.

> Il va **au** bureau.
> *He goes to the office.*
> Il habite ici **depuis** deux ans.
> *He has been living here for two years.*
> le livre **de** ma mère
> *my mother's book (the book of my mother)*
> une machine **à** coudre
> *a sewing machine (a machine for sewing)*
> Il parle **d'**une voix basse.
> *He speaks in a low voice.*
> Il le fait **avec** hésitation.
> *He does it with hesitation.*

A prepositional locution is a group of words that have the same role as a preposition.

Prepositions	*Prepositional locution*
Il est **devant** l'école.	Il est **en face de** l'école.
Il travaille **pour** gagner de l'argent.	Il travaille **afin de** gagner de l'argent.

Prepositions and prepositional locutions are generally followed by a noun or noun group, a pronoun or an infinitive.

> Elle le fait **pour ses enfants.**
> Elle le fait **pour eux.**
> Elle le fait **pour gagner de l'argent.**

The difficulty for English speakers is that often a preposition in English has several French counterparts, and the correct translation depends on the meaning in the sentence. For example, the preposition *with* in English can be translated in various ways in French, depending on the context.

> Il va au cinéma **avec** moi.
> *He is going to the movies with me.*
> Il écrit **avec** un crayon.
> *He writes with a pencil.*
> Il écrit **de** la main gauche.
> *He writes with his left hand.*
> Elle embrasse son père **avec** joie.
> *She embraces her father with joy.*
> Elle danse **de** joie.
> *She danses with joy.*
> Elle parle **d'**une voix forte.
> *She speaks with a strong voice.*
> Le ciel est couvert **de** nuages.
> *The sky is covered with clouds.*
> Il marche la tête haute. (no preposition)
> *He walks with his head held high.*
> L'alphabet commence **par** la lettre **a**.
> *The alphabet begins with the letter a.*

The correct uses of various prepositions are learned through practice. In most cases there are no rules. Each expression needs to be learned individually. The discussion here is not exhaustive. Please consult a good dictionary for further examples of the uses of various prepositions.

Prepositions to Indicate Location or Direction to or from a Place

See also *Prepositions with Geographical Names*, pages 73–76.

à, de, dans, en, chez

à, *to, in, at*

With names of places, **à** can indicate location or direction *in, at* or *to* some place:

> Jean est **à l'**école.
> *John is in (at) school.*
> J'allais souvent **à** Paris.
> *I went to Paris often.*
> Marie va **au** bureau tous les jours.
> *Mary goes to the office every day.*
> Il va **à l'**école à huit heures.
> *He goes to school at eight o'clock.*
> Il retourne **à la** maison à trois heures.
> *He returns home at three o'clock.*

de, *from, about*

De indicates the place of origin with the verbs **venir, sortir, arriver, s'éloigner, partir,** etc.

> Je reviens **du** bureau.
> *I am coming back from the office.*

Elle est arrivée **de** Rome.
She arrived from Rome.

For contractions of the definite article with the prepositions **à** and **de**, see *Contractions of the Definite Article*, pp. 14–15.

dans, en, *in, into*

Dans is always used with an article. **En** is rarely used with an article.

Dans la classe, on ne peut pas fumer.
Nous sommes **en** classe.
Nous allons **en** ville.

Dans is used to indicate place more precisely than **à** or **en** and often means **à l'intérieur de** (*inside*).

en ville	*in town, to town*
dans la ville	*in the town, inside the town*
en classe	*in class*
dans la classe de français	*in French class*
Est-ce qu'elle est **à** l'école?	*Is she in school?*
Oui, elle est **en** classe.	*Yes, she's in class.*
Oui, elle est **dans** la classe de chimie.	*Yes, she's in chemistry class.*
Il est **à** la maison?	*Is he at home?*
Oui, il est **dans** la cuisine.	*Yes, he's in the kitchen.*

Dans can indicate the place in which a thing can be found.

L'enfant met du chocolat **dans** la bouche.
Elle met l'argenterie **dans** les sacs et elle met les sacs **dans** le tiroir.
Il met ses clefs **dans** sa poche.

With the verb **prendre**, **dans** means *out of.*

Prenez deux dollars **dans** mon sac.
Take two dollars out of my bag.

Dans is used with streets and avenues, but **sur** is used with the names of rural routes and boulevards. The verb **habiter** can be followed directly by the street name without the article.

Il habite **dans l'avenue à côté.**
Elle habite **dans la rue à côté.**
Nous habitons **sur la route 11.**
L'école est **sur le boulevard Saint-Michel.**
Il **habite avenue** Foch. or
Il **habite dans l'avenue** Foch.

chez, *to, at the house of, at someone's place*

Chez is used with a person, a person's name, a pronoun, a person's profession or business, a group or society.

Nous irons **chez Marie** vendredi soir.
We will go to Mary's house (on) Friday night.
Il viendra **chez moi** samedi.
He will come to my home (on) Saturday.
J'achète du pain **chez le boulanger.**
I buy bread at the baker's.

Je vais **chez le médecin** demain.
I am going to the doctor's tomorrow.
Chez les Français, on mange bien.
In French homes, one eats well.

Chez can also mean "in a person's work," figuratively speaking.

Chez cet auteur il y a beaucoup d'ironie.
In this author's work, there is a lot of irony.

Chez is also used in the following expressions.

Faites comme **chez vous.**
Make yourself at home. (Do as you do at home.)
Chez vous tout va bien.
Everything is well with you.

1. Complete the following sentences with the preposition **à, de, dans, en, chez** or **sur** plus the definite article when necessary.

1. Pierre est _____ bureau. Il est _____ salle de conférence.
2. Elle est _____ université. Elle est _____ classe. Elle est _____ classe de mathématiques.
3. Il y a beaucoup de magasins _____ l'avenue des Champs-Élysées.
4. Venez _____ nous demain soir.
5. Il range les assiettes _____ le placard.
6. Le matin, nous allons _____ supermarché; l'après-midi nous allons _____ le médecin.
7. Prenez les stylos _____ le tiroir.
8. Il sort _____ bureau à six heures et il retourne _____ maison à sept heures.
9. Il y a beaucoup d'étudiants _____ le boulevard Saint-Michel.
10. Nous irons _____ ville demain pour faire des courses.

Prepositions with Geographical Names

à

With names of places **à** can mean *in, at,* or *to* a place.

The preposition **à** is used before the names of most cities.

Il va **à Paris.**	*He is going to Paris.*
Elle est **à Genève.**	*She is in Geneva.*

The names of some cities contain a definite article: **à la** is used before feminine names and **au** is used before masculine names.

Elle va **à la Havane.**	*She goes to Havana.*
Ils ont débarqué **au Havre.**	*They landed in Le Havre.*

The preposition **à** is also used with masculine names of some small islands. Before feminine names of a few small islands the definite article **la** is included before the name.

à Chypre
à Cuba
à Haïti
à Madagascar

à la Guadeloupe
à la Martinique
à la Réunion

See also **en** below.

One always says **en route pour** or **passer par** with the name of a place. One can use **pour** after the verb **partir**, but more often **à, en** and **vers** replace **pour**.

En route pour Marseille, elle s'est arrêtée à Lyon.
On the way to Marseille, she stopped in Lyon.
Elles **ont passé par** l'Allemagne et la France.
They passed through Germany and France.
Je **suis parti à (pour)** la Martinique.
I left for Martinique.

en

The preposition **en** is used with names of feminine countries or continents. Almost all names of countries ending in a mute **e** are feminine. (Exception: **le Mexique.**)

Je vais **en France.**	*I am going to France.*
Nous irons **en Afrique.**	*We are going to Africa.*
Nous sommes **en Europe.**	*We are in Europe.*

With names of American states and Canadian provinces, **en** is used if the French form of the noun ends in **e** or **ie**. It is also used with **Ontario** and **Saskatchewan.**

en Californie
en Pennsylvanie
en Floride
en Nouvelle-Écosse
en Colombie-Britannique
en Ontario
en Saskatchewan

But:

au Nouveau-Mexique
au Nouveau-Brunswick
à Terre-Neuve *Newfoundland*
au Québec
au Manitoba
à l'île-du-Prince-Édouard

En is used before the names of some small islands.

en Corse
en Islande
en Nouvelle-Guinée
en Sardaigne

See also **à** p.73

au

The preposition **au** is used with masculine countries and means *in* or *to*.

Elle va **au Mexique.**	*She is going to Mexico.*
Nous sommes **au Canada.**	*We are in Canada.*

Elle va **au Danemark.**	*She is going to Denmark.*
Il va **au Portugal.**	*He is going to Portugal.*

The preposition **aux** is used with **États-Unis** since the word is plural.

New York est **aux États-Unis.**
New York is in the United States.

dans

The preposition **dans** (*in, at,* or *to*) is used before names of continents qualified by another expression.

Nous irons **dans l'Amérique du Sud.**
We are going to South America.

In spoken language, **en** may be used with names of continents.

Nous allons **en Amérique du Sud.**
We are going to South America.

When the name of a city or country is accompanied by a complement or an adjective, **dans le (l', la, les)** is used instead of **en.**

J'aimerais vivre **dans la France du xxiᵉ siècle.**
Nous allons voyager **dans toute la France.**
Ils vont **dans l'Italie du Nord.**

Dans le (l') is used with masculine nouns of most French and Canadian provinces, and American states.

Dans l'État de, dans la province de, dans le territoire de are also used.

dans le Vermont
dans le Colorado
dans l'État de Vermont
dans le territoire du Yukon

But:

au Nouveau-Mexique
au Nouveau-Brunswick
à Terre-Neuve *Newfoundland*
au Québec
dans la province de Québec

de

De is used to mean *from* or *of* and is used many times <u>without</u> the definite article before the names of feminine countries, provinces and states and masculine countries beginning with a vowel.

Il est **de Paris.**	*He is from Paris.*
Elle revient **d'Angleterre.**	*She is coming back from England.*
Il étudie l'histoire **de France.**	*He studies the history of France.*
Je viens **de Californie.**	*I am coming from California.*

But:

Paris est la capitale **de la France.**
Paris is the capital of France.

De is used to mean *from* or *of* and is used <u>with</u> the definite article before the names of masculine countries, provinces or states except those beginning with a vowel.

> J'ai envoyé le paquet **du Canada.**
> Elle vient **des États-Unis.**
> Il vient **du Québec.**

2. Complete the following sentences with the correct preposition plus the definite article.

1. Nous allons _____ France.
2. Elle est allée _____ Haïti et _____ Martinique.
3. Je suis _____ Paris et elle vient _____ Lyon.
4. Nous irons _____ Afrique et _____ Afrique du Nord.
5. Il demeure _____ Paris.
6. Il a voyagé _____ Mexique et _____ Amérique du Sud.
7. En route _____ l'Espagne, ils ont passé _____ la France.
8. L'action a lieu _____ Angleterre et _____ Italie.
9. J'ai demeuré _____ Californie, _____ Vermont et _____ Nouveau-Mexique.
10. San Francisco se trouve _____ États-Unis.
11. Il revient _____ Mexique, mais elle revient _____ Espagne.
12. Elle habite _____ Canada _____ Terre-Neuve.
13. Il va _____ San Francisco _____ Californie.
14. Il part _____ Haïti, et elle part _____ Cuba.

3. Answer the following questions. Follow the model.

> **Où se trouve la tour Eiffel?**
> **La tour Eiffel se trouve à Paris, en France.**

1. Où se trouve la Maison Blanche?
2. Où se trouve le Taj Mahal?
3. Où se trouvent les Pyramides?
4. Où se trouve le Parthénon?
5. Où parle-t-on allemand?
6. Où parle-t-on chinois?
7. Où parle-t-on japonais?
8. Où parle-t-on anglais?

Prepositions with Modes of Transportation

The prepositions **à** and **en** and sometimes **par** are used with means of travel when you wish to describe by what means someone is traveling.

à	en	par
à bicyclette*	en auto	**par le** train
à cheval	en autobus	
à motocyclette	en avion	
à pied	en métro	
à vélo*	en bateau	
	en taxi	
	en voiture	

---

*You may also hear **en bicyclette** and **en vélo.**

Note that **à** and **en** are used without the definite article and **par** is used with the definite article.

To describe how someone enters or leaves a vehicle, use **monter dans** or **descendre de,** or **embarquer dans** or **débarquer de.**

monter **dans** un autobus	descendre **d'**un autobus
to get on a bus	*to get off a bus*
monter **dans** une voiture	descendre **d'**une voiture
to get into a car	*to get out of a car*
monter **dans** un train	descendre **d'**un train
to get on a train	*to get off a train*
embarquer **dans** un bateau	débarquer **d'**un bateau
to get on a boat	*to get off a boat*

When referring to mailing a letter or a package, you use the preposition **par** with the means of transportation.

envoyer le paquet **par avion** ou **par bateau**

4. Complete the following sentences with the correct preposition to indicate how the people travel and mail things.

   1. Le cowboy va _____ cheval.
   2. Elle va au bureau _____ voiture ou _____ métro.
   3. Il va de New York à Paris _____ avion.
   4. Le petit va à l'école _____ pied.
   5. Le conducteur voyage _____ train.
   6. Le marin voyage _____ bateau.
   7. Elle va en ville _____ autobus.
   8. Elles vont au théâtre _____ taxi.
   9. Préfères-tu voyager _____ bicyclette ou _____ vélo?
   10. J'enverrai la lettre _____ avion et non _____ bateau.

5. Answer the following personalized questions. Use the prepositions **à, en** or **par** plus a method of transportation.

   1. Comment vas-tu à l'école? aux cours?
   2. Comment vas-tu à la banque?
   3. Comment envoies-tu ce colis?
   4. Comment vas-tu au théâtre?
   5. Comment vas-tu au restaurant?

Prepositions with Expressions of Time

à, at

Il reviendra **à** cinq heures précises.
He'll return at exactly five o'clock.

dans, en, **in**

Dans (*in*) can indicate the time after which a certain thing can be done. It can mean **après** (*after*) or **à la fin de** (*at the end of*).

Je le ferai **dans** une heure.
I'll do it in one hour. (after an hour has passed).
(It is now two o'clock. I'll do it at three o'clock.)
L'avion arrive **dans** trois heures.
The plane arrives in three hours.
(It is now eight o'clock. The plane arrives at eleven o'clock.)
Il reviendra **dans** quatre heures.
He'll return in four hours.
Elle aura fini **dans** un mois.
She will have finished in a month.

En (*in*) indicates the time necessary for the accomplishment of an action, the time in which something will be completed or accomplished (duration of an action).

Je le ferai **en** deux heures.
I will do it in two hours' time.
(It will take me two hours to do it.)
Le bateau traverse l'Atlantique **en** cinq jours.
The boat crosses the Atlantic in five days.

avant, **before** and *après,* **after**

Avant is used to mean *before* (*in time*) and **après** is used to mean *after* (*in time*).

Elle est arrivée **avant** les autres.
She arrived before the others.
Il est arrivé **après** Pierre.
He arrived after Peter.

Remember that the prepositions **devant** (*before* or *in front of*) and **derrière** (*after* or *behind*) are used with places.

Il est **devant** la maison.
He is in front of the house.
La table est **derrière** le divan.
The table is behind the couch.

6. Complete the following with the prepositions **à, dans, en, avant** or **après**.

1. Voyons! Il est une heure maintenant. Je l'aurai fini _____ trois heures. Donc, je l'aurai fini _____ quatre heures.
2. Ce projet ne prendra pas beaucoup de temps. Je pourrai le terminer _____ une demi-heure.
3. L'avion décolle _____ six heures précises.
4. Marie est arrivée à trois heures. Hélène est arrivée à trois heures et quart. Marie est arrivée _____ Hélène et Hélène est arrivée _____ Marie.

7. Complete the following sentences with the preposition **dans** or **en.** Follow the models.

Nous recevrons des invités _____ deux jours.
Nous recevrons des invités *dans* deux jours.

Elle finit l'exercice _____ dix minutes.
Elle finit l'exercice *en* dix minutes.

1. Le danseur a changé de costume _____ quinze minutes.
2. Je suis occupé maintenant, mais je peux vous aider _____ une demi-heure.
3. Nos invités arriveront _____ une heure.
4. _____ cent ans le monde sera différent.
5. Le dîner sera prêt _____ deux heures.
6. Tu auras ma décision _____ dix jours ouvrables.
7. Il a couru dix kilomètres _____ trente minutes.
8. Le chien a très vite mangé son dîner. Il l'a mangé _____ trois minutes.

Prepositions Used to Join Two Nouns

To Indicate Function or to Join a Noun that Modifies Another Noun

The prepositions **à** and **de** can introduce a noun that modifies or qualifies another noun and indicates the function of the preceding noun. In French a noun with a complement is often the same as an English expression composed of two nouns written either as two words or as a single compound word. The first noun in English is the complement in French. Study the following:

à	de
un verre à eau	**un verre d'eau**
a water glass (a glass for water)	*a glass of water*
une tasse à café	**une tasse de café**
a coffee cup (a cup for coffee)	*a cup of coffee*
une lime à ongles	**mon professeur de maths**
a nail file	*my math teacher*
une brosse à dents	**une agence de voyages**
a toothbrush	*a travel agency*
une cuiller à soupe	**une robe de chambre**
a soupspoon	*a bathrobe*
une cuiller à thé	**une salle de bains**
a teaspoon	*a bathroom*

To Mean *with*

Used with the article, **à** can mean *with*. **À** replaces **avec** when you wish to indicate that the second noun is a distinct part of the first one.

de la soupe aux légumes
vegetable soup (soup with vegetables)
du café au lait
coffee with milk
la fille aux yeux bleus
the girl with blue eyes
la maison au toit rouge
the house with the red roof
la glace à la vanille
vanilla ice cream (ice cream made with vanilla)
l'homme à la barbe blanche
the man with the white beard

une tarte aux pommes
an apple pie (a pie made with apples)
une peinture à l'huile
an oil painting (a painting made with oil)

To Introduce the Material from Which an Object is Made

De and **en** are used to introduce the material from which an object is made.

une robe **de** soie
des bas **de** nylon
un portefeuille **en** cuir
un bracelet **en** or

Usage determines whether you should use **de** or **en**. Often, either preposition is possible. **De** is usually used to indicate the type of object one is talking about and **en** emphasizes the material from which the object is made.

un sac **de** cuir
a leather bag

un sac **en** cuir
a bag made of leather

Prepositions of Cause

De can also indicate a relationship of cause between the verb and the noun complement. It is translated by *with, of, for* or *from*.

Il danse **de** joie.
He dances for joy.
Je meurs **de** faim.
I'm dying of hunger.
Elle écrit **de** la main gauche.
She writes with her left hand.
La rue est couverte **de** neige.
The street is covered with snow.

Prepositions After Indefinite Pronouns

When **quelque chose, rien, quelqu'un** and **personne** are modified by an adjective, the adjective is introduced by **de.**

Il mange quelque chose de bon.
He eats something good.
C'est quelqu'un de très adroit.
He's someone very skillful.
Il n'y a eu personne de blessé dans la tempête.
No one was hurt in the storm.
Il ne dit rien d'intelligent.
He says nothing intelligent.

8. Complete the following sentences with the correct preposition **à, de** or **en.** Combine with the definite article when necessary.

    1. Il faut mettre du thé dans les tasses _____ thé.
    2. Je voudrais boire un verre _____ lait.

3. Elle a pleuré _____ joie quand elle a appris qu'il n'y avait personne _____ blessé dans l'accident.
4. Je mets ma robe _____ chambre dans la salle _____ bains.
5. Il mange de la soupe _____ tomates, une tarte _____ pommes et de la glace _____ chocolat.
6. Je fais ma toilette. Je me brosse les dents avec une brosse _____ dents. Je fais le soin des mains avec une lime _____ ongles.
7. Voilà mon professeur _____ histoire.
8. Je n'ai pas mangé depuis hier. Je meurs _____ faim.
9. L'homme _____ barbe noire parle à la fille _____ cheveux noirs.
10. Je vais acheter une bague _____ argent, un sac _____ cuir, et une robe _____ laine.
11. Il écrit _____ la main droite.
12. Ce professeur est quelqu'un _____ très intelligent.

Prepositions in Adverbial Clauses of Manner

In many adverbial phrases where *in, by* or *on* are used in English, **à** is used in French.

Il parle **à voix basse.**
He speaks in a low voice.
Il parle **à haute voix.**
He speaks aloud (with a loud voice, loudly).
Mettez les vêtements **au soleil** pour les faire sécher.
Put the clothes in the sun to make them dry.
Ce chandail est fait **à la main.**
This sweater is made by hand.
Il a les papiers **à la main.**
He has the papers in hand.
Le train est arrivé **à l'heure.**
The train arrived on time.
Ce bâtiment a été construit **au temps de** Louis XIV.
This building was constructed in the time of Louis XIV.
Les soldats marchent **à grands pas.**
The soldiers march in giant steps.

In an adverbial clause of manner, **de** introduces the noun modified by the indefinite article.

Il parle **d'une voix faible.**
He speaks with a weak voice.
Il me regarde **d'un air furieux.**
He looks at me with a furious expression (furiously).
Elle le fait **d'une manière adroite.**
She does it skillfully.

When the noun is not modified by an indefinite article, **avec** is used.

Il me parle **avec faiblesse.**
He speaks to me weakly.
Il me regarde **avec fureur.**
He looks at me furiously.
Il le fait **avec adresse.**
He does it skillfully.

9. Complete the following sentences with the prepositions **à, de** or **avec.**

1. Elle l'a regardé _____ curiosité.
2. Elle l'a regardé _____ un air curieux.
3. Je ne peux pas vous entendre. Parlez _____ haute voix.
4. Il me répond _____ un ton faible.
5. Il me répond _____ faiblesse.
6. Il a le document _____ la main.

Prepositions to Introduce an Infinitive Depending on a Noun or Adjective

To Indicate Function, Result or Tendency

The preposition **à** can introduce an infinitive that indicates the function of the preceding noun or the use to which an object is destined. Often **à** has the meaning of *for*. The infinitive complement is often the equivalent of an expression with "-ing" in English.

du papier à écrire
writing paper (paper for writing)
une machine à écrire / à laver / à coudre
a typewriter (a machine for writing) / a washing machine (a machine for washing) / a sewing machine (a machine for sewing)
une salle à manger
a dining room (a room for dining)
une chambre à coucher
a bedroom (a room for sleeping)
un fer à repasser
an iron
de l'eau à boire
drinking water (water for drinking)
une maison à vendre / à louer
a house for sale / for rent

À can introduce an infinitive phrase that describes a preceding noun in terms of a possible result.

C'est un bruit à réveiller tout le monde.
It's a noise that could wake everyone up.
C'est une tâche à rendre fou.
This is a task that can drive you crazy.
Ce sont des cris à rendre sourd.
These are shouts that can make you deaf.
Ce sont des larmes à faire pitié.
These are tears that can make you feel pity.
C'est un exercice à recopier.
This is an exercise to be recopied.

À can also introduce an infinitive phrase that intensifies the meaning of an adjective.

une histoire triste à en pleurer
a story sad enough to make you cry
un animal laid à faire peur
an animal ugly enough to make you afraid

After an adjective, **à** introduces an infinitive that indicates the action to which the adjective applies.

> **C'est facile à faire.**
> *It's easy to do.*
> **C'est difficile à comprendre.**
> *It's difficult to understand.*
> **C'est bon à manger.**
> *It's good to eat.*

After Expressions of Duration, Length of Time and Position of the Body

À introduces an infinitive after certain expressions indicating duration, length of time and position of the body. À plus the infinitive is used to describe what the subject does during this time or in this position.

> **Il passe son temps à travailler.** (duration)
> *He spends his time working.*
> **Elle reste assise à lire.** (position)
> *She remains seated while reading.*
> **Il met longtemps à apprendre cela.** (time)
> *He takes a long time to learn that.*
> **Elle est debout à travailler.**
> *She works standing up.*

Generally, infinitives following an adjective or noun are preceded by **de.**

Je suis heureux d'être ici.	*I am happy to be here.*
Je suis étonné d'apprendre cette nouvelle.	*I am surprised to hear this news.*
J'ai peur de sortir la nuit.	*I am afraid to go out at night.*
J'ai envie de partir.	*I want to leave.*
Il avait raison de faire cela.	*He was right to do that.*
J'ai l'occasion de faire cela.	*I have the chance to do that.*

After the impersonal **il** + **être** + adjective, **de** precedes the infinitive.

Il est bon de se reposer.	*It is good to rest.*
Il est nécessaire d'étudier.	*It is necessary to study.*

When an infinitive depends on another verb, it is often introduced by **à** or **de.** For a detailed analysis, see *The Use of the Prepositions **à** and **de** before an Infinitive*, pp. 227–229.

10. Complete the following sentences with the correct preposition **à** or **de.**

1. Ce sont des devoirs _____ refaire.
2. Mets les vêtements sales dans la machine _____ laver.
3. Il est dangereux _____ ne pas faire attention.
4. Cet appartement _____ louer a une grande salle _____ manger.
5. Il a tort _____ dire cela.
6. Cet exercice est difficile _____ faire.
7. Il a honte _____ avoir volé la bicyclette.
8. C'est une histoire amusante _____ en rire aux éclats.
9. C'est un problème _____ rendre fou.
10. J'ai l'intention _____ partir demain.

Following is a list of some common prepositions.

à	*to, at, in, on*
après	*after, next to*
avant	*before (time)*
avec	*with*
chez	*at (to)_____ 's house*
contre	*against*
dans	*in, inside, into*
de	*of, from, with, etc.*
depuis	*since, from*
derrière	*behind, after*
devant	*before, in front of*
durant	*during*
en	*in, to*
entre	*between, among*
envers	*toward (moral tendency)*
hors (de)	*outside (of)*
jusque	*until, up to*
malgré	*in spite of*
par	*by, through*
parmi	*among*
pendant	*during*
pour	*for, in order to (+ infinitive)*
près	*near*
sans	*without*
sauf	*except*
selon	*according to*
sous	*under*
suivant	*following*
sur	*on, upon*
vers	*toward (direction)*

Following is a list of principal prepositional locutions.

à cause de	*because of*
à côté de	*beside*
afin de	*in order to*
à force de	*by means of*
à la mode de	*in the manner of*
à l'exception de	*except*
à l'exclusion de	*to the exclusion of*
à moins de	*unless*
à raison de	*at the rate of*
à travers	*through*
au dedans	*inside, within*
au dehors de	*outside of*
au-delà de	*above, beyond, past*
au-dessous de	*below*
au-dessus de	*above*
au lieu de	*instead of*
au milieu de	*in the middle of*
auprès de	*near*

autour de	*around*
aux environs de	*in the vicinity of*
d'après	*according to*
de façon à	*so as to*
de manière à	*so as to*
de peur de	*for fear of*
en bas de	*at the bottom of*
en dedans de	*inside, on the inside of, within*
en dehors de	*outside of*
en dépit de	*in spite of*
en face de	*in front of, facing*
en haut de	*at the top of*
en raison de	*because of*
grâce à	*thanks to*
hors de	*outside of*
jusqu'à	*until, up to*
jusque dans	*up into*
loin de	*far from*
par dedans	*inside, through the inside*
par dehors	*by the outside*
par delà	*beyond*
par-dessous	*under*
par-dessus	*over, above, on top of*
par devant	*before, in front*
par rapport à	*with regard to, in relation to*
près de	*near*
proche de	*near*

For other uses of prepositions, see the following:

For the use of **après** with the past infinitive, see page 222.
For the use of **en** with the present participle, see pages 140–141 and 221.
For the use of **par** with an infinitive, see page 141.
For the use of **par** with the passive voice, see page 230.
For the use of prepositions with the year, months and seasons, see pages 94–95.
For the use of **de** with measurements and age, see page 93.
For the use of the prepositions **à** and **de** before infinitives see pages 227–228.
For the use of **à** and **de** to show possession, see pages 54–55.
For the use of **de** to introduce a complement of a superlative, see page 50.

Review

11. Translate the following.

1. a cup of tea
2. a teacup
3. a glass of water
4. a water glass
5. a soupspoon
6. a cherry pie
7. chocolate ice cream
8. a bicycle for sale
9. the man with brown eyes
10. tomato soup

11. a travel agency
12. a geography teacher

13. a dress made of silk
14. a silk dress

12. Complete the following with the correct preposition or preposition plus definite article to show how and where people are traveling or where people live.

1. Il va _____ New York _____ Californie _____ avion.
2. Elle va _____ Paris _____ Lyon _____ train.
3. Il voyage _____ Japon _____ bateau.
4. Il va _____ école _____ pied.
5. Envoyez cette lettre _____ avion et non _____ bateau.
6. Il va _____ médecin _____ taxi.
7. Il habite l'avenue Foch _____ Paris, _____ France.
8. Elle habite _____ le boulevard Métropolitain _____ Montréal, _____ Québec, _____ Canada.
9. Elle revient _____ bureau _____ métro.
10. Il va _____ Italie du Sud _____ Italie du Nord _____ autobus.
11. Elle va _____ boulanger _____ vélo.
12. Il va faire du ski _____ Colorado _____ États-Unis.
13. Il va prendre du soleil _____ Haïti ou _____ Martinique.
14. Il va _____ Buenos Aires _____ Argentine _____ l'Amérique du Sud.

13. Complete the following with the correct preposition or preposition plus the definite article.

D'habitude, Monsieur Leclerc va _____ usine _____ mardi _____ vendredi. Il y va _____
      (1)   (2)   (3)   (4)
auto. Il revient _____ bureau _____ six heures du soir d'habitude.
     (5)   (6)

Mais aujourd'hui, c'est lundi et il ne travaille pas. Ses enfants sont _____ école. Ils sont
                                         (7)
_____ classe, spécifiquement dans la classe _____ français. Sa femme est _____ bureau où elle
 (8)   (9)   (10)
travaille comme programmeuse dans l'industrie de l'informatique. Lui, il est _____ la maison
                                               (11)
maintenant. Il est _____ la cuisine où il reste debout _____ travailler.
          (12)   (13)

Et comme il travaille! Le matin, il passe son temps _____ faire le ménage. Il met les
                                  (14)
vêtements sales dans la machine _____ laver; il range les verres _____ eau et les tasses
                        (15)   (16)
_____ café, les cuillers _____ soupe, etc. _____ les placards. Il époussette les meubles et il
 (17)   (18)   (19)
passe l'aspirateur.

À midi il prend son déjeuner. Il mange de la soupe _____ légumes, un sandwich _____
                              (20)   (21)
jambon, et comme dessert une glace _____ fraises. Comme boisson il boit du café _____ lait.
                   (22)   (23)

Maintenant il est _____ la cuisinière électrique en train de préparer le dîner. Il porte un
          (24)
tablier _____ plastique. Le dîner qu'il prépare va être bon _____ manger. Il fait la cuisine
     (25)   (26)
_____ une manière professionnelle, _____ l'adresse d'un grand chef. Pendant qu'il prépare le
 (27)   (28)

dîner, il chante _____ haute voix. Il veut finir la préparation du dîner _____ l'arrivée des autres.
(29)   (30)

Il peut compléter cette tâche _____ deux heures. Il n'a pas le temps de se reposer maintenant. Il
(31)

lira le journal _____ deux heures. Il aura fini ses tâches _____ deux heures. Il est quatre heures
(32)   (33)

maintenant; donc, il pourra lire _____ six heures.
(34)

_____ les Leclerc, tout est bien organisé grâce aux efforts de M. Leclerc. Lui, c'est
(35)

quelqu'un _____ extraordinaire.
(36)

CHAPTER 4

Numbers, Dates, Time

Numbers

Cardinal Numbers

The cardinal numbers in French are:

0 zéro	22 vingt-deux	72 soixante-douze
1 un	23 vingt-trois	73 soixante-treize
2 deux	24 vingt-quatre	74 soixante-quatorze
3 trois	25 vingt-cinq	75 soixante-quinze
4 quatre	26 vingt-six	76 soixante-seize
5 cinq	27 vingt-sept	77 soixante-dix-sept
6 six	28 vingt-huit	78 soixante-dix-huit
7 sept	29 vingt-neuf	79 soixante-dix-neuf
8 huit	30 trente	80 quatre-vingts
9 neuf	31 trente et un	81 quatre-vingt-un
10 dix	32 trente-deux	82 quatre-vingt-deux
11 onze	40 quarante	90 quatre-vingt-dix
12 douze	41 quarante et un	91 quatre-vingt-onze
13 treize	42 quarante-deux	92 quatre-vingt-douze
14 quatorze	50 cinquante	99 quatre-vingt-dix-neuf
15 quinze	51 cinquante et un	100 cent
16 seize	52 cinquante-deux	101 cent un
17 dix-sept	60 soixante	102 cent deux
18 dix-huit	61 soixante et un	120 cent vingt
19 dix-neuf	62 soixante-deux	199 cent quatre-vingt-dix-neuf
20 vingt	70 soixante-dix	200 deux cents
21 vingt et un	71 soixante et onze	201 deux cent un

202 deux cent deux	1 000 mille	1 972 mil (mille) neuf cent
300 trois cents	1 001 mille un	soixante-douze
400 quatre cents	1 100 mille cent	dix-neuf cent
500 cinq cents	onze cents	soixante-douze
600 six cents	1 200 mille deux cent	2 000 deux mille
700 sept cents	douze cents	1 000 000 un million
800 huit cents	1 900 mille neuf cents	2 000 000 deux millions
900 neuf cents	dix-neuf cents	1 000 000 000 un milliard
		1 000 000 000 000 un billion

Note that in numbers **21, 31, 41, 51, 61, 71,** the conjunction **et** is used. There is no hyphen.

vingt et un
quarante et un

Et is not used in **81, 91, 101.** Note the hyphens in **81** and **91.**

quatre-vingt-un
quatre-vingt-onze
cent un

When **vingt** and **cent** are multiplied, they become plural.

quatre vingts
deux cents

When **vingt** and **cent** are followed by another number, they are singular.

vingt-neuf
quatre-vingt-huit
cent quatre
deux cent douze

Mille is never plural.

cinq mille
deux mille cinquante

Million is preceded by the indefinite article.

un million de touristes

Note that **un million, un milliard** and **un billion** are like nouns of quantity and take **de (d')** before a following noun.

un million de femmes
un milliard d'insectes
un billion d'habitants

In France and Quebec a comma is used in place of the decimal point used with numbers in the United States and English Canada. Instead of a comma used with numbers in the United States and English Canada, a period or a space is used in France and a space is used in Quebec. In France it is becoming more common to use a space instead of a period, although a period is more frequently used with thousands, millions or billions.

France	Quebec	United States and English Canada
1.121.000 or 1 121 000	1 121 000	1,121,000
3,50	3,50	3.50
1.360,50 or 1 360,50	1 360,50	1,360.50

Following are some expressions with cardinal numbers.

tous les trois ans	*every three years*
une année sur trois	
toutes les cinq minutes	*every five minutes*
dans huit jours	*in a week*
tous les quinze jours	*every two weeks*
tous les deux kilomètres	*every two kilometers*
une femme sur dix	*one woman in ten*
quatre-vingts pour cent de	*eighty percent of*
un à un	*one by one*

1. Write the following numbers and expressions in French.

1. 10	14. 100
2. 19	15. 200
3. 20	16. 565
4. 21	17. 798
5. 27	18. 1 124
6. 31	19. 1 145 792
7. 61	20. 2 954
8. 70	21. two by two
9. 72	22. every two weeks
10. 80	23. one person in ten
11. 84	24. every two years
12. 90	25. every ten minutes
13. 99	

Ordinal Numbers

Most ordinal numbers are formed by adding the suffix **-ième** to the cardinal number. If the cardinal number ends in a mute **e,** the **e** is dropped before adding the suffix.

deux	**deuxième**
scpt	**septième**
quatorze	**quatorzième**
seize	**seizième**
cinquante et un	**cinquante et unième**
cent	**centième**
deux cent trois	**deux cent troisième**
mille	**millième**

Exceptions:

un, une	*first*	**premier, première**
cinq	*fifth*	**cinquième** (**u** is added)
neuf	*ninth*	**neuvième** (**f** becomes **v**)

Second, seconde can replace **deuxième. Deuxième** is usually used when there are more than two elements.

La première fois j'ai refusé; la **deuxième** fois j'ai accepté.
La première fois j'ai refusé; la **seconde** fois j'ai accepté.
la **deuxième** classe ou la **seconde** classe (avion, bateau, train)

But:

voyager en **seconde,** une **seconde** fois

In titles of rulers, the cardinal numbers are used except for **premier, première** (*first*).

François premier
Louis quatorze

In certain fixed expressions, **tiers** and **tierce** are used instead of **troisième.**

le **tiers** état
the third estate
une **tierce** personne
a third party
le **tiers**-monde
the third world

When cardinal and ordinal numbers are used together, the cardinal number precedes the ordinal.

les deux premières semaines
the first two weeks

2. Complete the following sentences with the correct ordinal number.

1. Janvier est le (1) _____ mois de l'année.
2. Septembre est le (9) _____ mois de l'année.
3. Mai est le (5) _____ mois de l'année.
4. La (1) _____ fois j'ai dit oui.
5. Mardi est le (2) _____ jour de la semaine.
6. C'est la (101) _____ fois que j'ai entendu cette chanson.
7. C'est la (2) _____ fois qu'il a fait cela.
8. Il faut demander l'avis d'une (3) _____ personne.

3. Write the following in French.

1. Napoleon I
2. Louis XV
3. the first two years
4. the last two days

Collective Numbers

To express an approximate quantity, the suffix **-aine** is added to the cardinal number. If the cardinal number ends in a mute **e,** the **e** is dropped before adding **-aine.** The **x** of **dix** becomes **z.**

Environ	10	**une dizaine**
(*Around*)	12	**une douzaine**
	15	**une quinzaine**
	20	**une vingtaine**
	40	**une quarantaine**
	50	**une cinquantaine**
	60	**une soixantaine**
	100	**une centaine**

Exceptions:

Environ		
	1 000	**un millier**
	1 000 000	**un million**
	1 000 000 000	**un milliard**
	1 000 000 000 000	**un billion**

When used before a noun, the preposition **de** is used.

Il y avait **une vingtaine de** personnes dans la salle.
Je voudrais **une douzaine de** poires.

Note that all collective numbers are feminine except for **un millier, un million, un milliard, un billion.**

Approximate quantity can also be expressed by using **à peu près, environ, quelque** and **dans les.**

Il y a **à peu près trente** élèves dans cette classe.
There are approximately thirty pupils in this class.
Il a **environ trente** ans.
He is around thirty years old.
Elle gagne **dans les trente mille** dollars par an.
She earns around thirty thousand dollars a year.

4. Follow the model.

Je voudrais des pommes. *12*
Je voudrais une douzaine de pommes.

1. Je voudrais des pêches. *10*
2. Je voudrais des poires. *20*
3. Je voudrais des pommes. *30*
4. Il y a des gens dans cette salle. *1 000 000*
5. Elle gagne 30 000$ par an. *dans les*

Fractions

Normally, the cardinal number and the ordinal number are used together to form fractions.

2/5 **deux cinquièmes**
3/8 **trois huitièmes**

Certain fractions have special forms.

1/2	**un demi (une demie), la moitié**	6 1/2	**six et demi**
1/3	**un tiers**	5 1/3	**cinq et un tiers**
2/3	**deux tiers**		
1/4	**un quart**	9 1/4	**neuf et un quart**
3/4	**trois quarts**		

J'ai bu **la moitié de la bouteille.**
I drank half the bottle.
Je voudrais **une demi-bouteille** de vin.
I want a half-bottle of wine.

When a number with **demi** modifies a noun, **et demi** or **et demie** will follow the noun.

> **Il est quatre heures et demie.**
> *It is half past four.*
> **J'ai vingt ans et demi.**
> *I am twenty and a half years old.*

5. Write the following numbers in French.

1. 1/2
2. a half bottle
3. 21 1/2
4. 1/3
5. 3/4
6. 7/16
7. 10 1/4

Arithmetical Operations

The verb **faire** (*to do, to make*) is used in arithmetical operations. The plural **font** is used for addition, subtraction, and multiplication. The singular **fait** is used for division.

> **Addition** (*Addition*)
> **3 et 3 font 6.**
> **Soustraction** (*Subtraction*)
> **5 moins 1 font 4.**
> **Multiplication** (*Multiplication*)
> **5 fois 10 font 50.**
> **Division** (*Division*)
> **10 divisé par 2 fait 5.**

Dimensions

Length, width, height and depth are expressed in the following ways.

> **Ce mur est long (haut) de cinq mètres (5 m).**
> **Ce mur a cinq mètres (5 m) de long (de longueur) / de haut (de hauteur).**
> *This wall is five meters (5 m) long/high.*

> **Cette table est large d'un mètre cinquante (de 1 m 50).**
> **Cette table a un mètre cinquante (1 m 50) de large (de largeur).**
> *This table is one and one-half meters (1 1/2 m) wide.*

> **La piscine est profonde de trois mètres (3 m).**
> **La piscine a trois mètres (3 m) de profondeur.**
> *The swimming pool is three meters (3 m) deep.*

Following is an example of how to measure something.

> **Cette boîte a trente centimètres (30 cm) de long (de longueur) sur vingt-quatre centimètres (24 cm) de large (de largeur) sur vingt-six centimètres (26 cm) de haut (de hauteur).**
> *This box is thirty centimeters (30 cm) long by twenty-four centimeters (24 cm) wide by twenty-six centimeters (26 cm) high.*

6. Write the following in French.

1. $10 + 5 = 15$
2. $18 - 6 = 12$

3. $8 \times 12 = 96$
4. $50 \div 5 = 10$
5. This box is 15 cm long by 10 cm wide by 8 cm high.

7. Give the dimensions in French for your room, your computer, the windows in your room, your French classroom, one of your notebooks.

Dates

Days

lundi	*Monday*	**vendredi**	*Friday*
mardi	*Tuesday*	**samedi**	*Saturday*
mercredi	*Wednesday*	**dimanche**	*Sunday*
jeudi	*Thursday*		

Months

janvier	*January*
février	*February*
mars	*March*
avril	*April*
mai	*May*
juin	*June*
juillet	*July*
août	*August*
septembre	*September*
octobre	*October*
novembre	*November*
décembre	*December*

Note that the days of the week and the months of the year are not capitalized.

Dates are written as follows:

Quel jour est-ce aujourd'hui?
Quel jour sommes-nous aujourd'hui?
What day is it today?
C'est aujourd'hui le samedi dix mai.
Today is Saturday, May 10.
C'est aujourd'hui le lundi quatorze juillet deux mille huit.
Today is Monday, July 14, 2008.
le 10 mai 1998
May 10, 1998
le vendredi 9 mai 2008
Friday, May 9, 2008

Note the following:

au mois de juin	*in the month of June*
en juin	*in June*
le premier juin	*June 1, the first of June*
le deux juin	*June 2*

Seasons

le printemps	*spring*
l'été	*summer*
l'automne	*fall*
l'hiver	*winter*

The seasons are all masculine. Note the prepositions that are used with the seasons:

au printemps	*in spring*
en été	*in summer*
en automne	*in fall*
en hiver	*in winter*

8. Write the following in French.

1. Monday, June 25
2. Tuesday, December 4
3. in the month of January
4. in June
5. April 1
6. What day is it today?
7. Today is Friday, December 22, 2018.
8. in spring
9. in summer
10. in winter

Time

The expression for *What time is it?* is **Quelle heure est-il?** Time in French is expressed as follows:

1:00 A.M.	**une heure**	1 h	01:00
1:00 P.M.	**treize heures**	13 h	13:00
2:00 A.M.	**deux heures**	2 h	02:00
2:00 P.M.	**quatorze heures**	14 h	14:00
12:00 midnight	**minuit**	24 h (0 h)	24:00 (00:00)
12:00 noon	**midi**	12 h	12:00
12:30 A.M.	**minuit et demi**	0 h 30	00:30
12:30 P.M.	**midi et demi**	12 h 30	12:30
5:15 A.M.	**cinq heures et quart** **cinq heures quinze**	5 h 15	05:15
5:15 P.M.	**dix-sept heures et quart** **dix-sept heures quinze**	17 h 15	17:15
6:30 A.M.	**six heures et demie** **six heures trente**	6 h 30	06:30
6:30 P.M.	**dix-huit heures et demie** **dix-huit heures trente**	18 h 30	18:30
6:40 A.M.	**sept heures moins vingt**	6 h 40	06:40
6:40 P.M.	**dix-huit heures quarante**	18 h 40	18:40
7:45 A.M.	**sept heures quarante-cinq**	7 h 45	07:45
7:45 P.M.	**dix-neuf heures quarante-cinq**	19 h 45	19:45

There are two ways of expressing the half hour or 15 minutes before or after the hour.

Il est deux heures et quart.
Il est deux heures quinze.
It is 2:15.

Il est huit heures et demie.
Il est huit heures trente.
It is 8:30.

Il est neuf heures moins le quart.
Il est huit heures quarante-cinq.
It is 8:45.

When it is more than 30 minutes past the hour, the number of minutes is subtracted from the next hour.

Il est minuit moins vingt.
It is 11:40.
Il est six heures moins vingt-cinq.
It is 5:35.

The word **demi** agrees with the noun when it follows.

midi et demi
minuit et demi
une heure et demie
deux heures et demie

When **demi** precedes the noun, it is hyphenated and does not agree.

une demi-heure

Official time in France is based on the 24-hour system. Minutes are always added to the hour.

0 h	**zéro heure (minuit)**
08 h 40	**huit heures quarante (du matin)**
13 h	**treize heures (une heure de l'après-midi)**
20 h 50	**vingt heures cinquante (huit heures cinquante du soir)**

Le train part à 15 h 20 (15:20).
The train leaves at 3:20 P.M.

To express A.M. or P.M., the expressions **du matin, du soir, de l'après-midi** are added to the time not expressed in the 24-hour system.

six heures du matin	*six o'clock in the morning*
deux heures de l'après-midi	*two o'clock in the afternoon*
huit heures du soir	*eight o'clock in the evening*

9. Write the following times in French.

1. It is 1:00 A.M.
2. It is 3:45 P.M.
3. It is 8:30 A.M.
4. It is noon.
5. It is midnight.
6. It is 9:15 P.M.
7. It is 12:30 P.M.
8. It is 12:30 A.M.
9. It is 10:25 P.M.
10. It is 9:40 A.M.

10. Write the above exercise in the 24-hour system.

Review

11. Complete the following with the correct dates and seasons to show when the following holidays are celebrated. Follow the model.
la fête nationale du Québec
On célèbre la fête nationale du Québec le 24 juin en été.
Juin est le sixième mois de l'année.

1. L'Hallowe'en (la veille de la Toussaint)
2. Noël

3. la fête nationale en France
4. la fête du travail en France
5. le jour de l'An
6. la fête de la Saint-Patrice

12. Write the following arithmetical problems in French.

1. $78 + 20 = 98$
2. $1/3 + 2/3 = 1$
3. $1\,000 + 1\,500 = 2\,500$
4. $3/4 - 1/2 = 1/4$
5. $1\,000 \times 1\,000 = 1\,000\,000$
6. $80\% \times 100 = 80$
7. $1\,200 \div 100 = 12$
8. $1\,000\,000\,000 \div 1\,000\,000 = 1\,000$
9. $2 \times 25 = 50$
10. $1955 - 1850 = 105$

13. Anne has a busy day. Tell what she does and at what time. Change the time in her schedule to conversational time, according to the model.

14 h   rencontrer une amie
Elle rencontre une amie à deux heures de l'après-midi.

1. 6 h 45   se lever
2. 7 h   prendre le petit déjeuner
3. 7 h 30   partir pour l'université
4. 8 h   avoir son cours de français
5. 8 h 50   prendre un café
6. 9 h 15   avoir son cours d'histoire
7. 12 h 15   prendre le déjeuner à la cafétéria
8. 13 h   travailler dans la bibliothèque
9. 16 h 45   rentrer chez elle
10. 18 h 30   prendre le dîner
11. 20 h 10   aller au cinéma
12. 24 h   se coucher

14. Answer the following personalized questions.

1. Quelle est ta date de naissance?
2. Où vas-tu le lundi?
3. Où es-tu allé(e) lundi dernier?
4. D'habitude, où vas-tu le samedi?
5. Où vas-tu samedi prochain?
6. À quelle heure te lèves-tu?
7. À quelle heure te couches-tu?
8. À peu près combien d'habitants est-ce qu'il y a dans ta ville?

CHAPTER 5

Verbs

French verbs at first appear to be difficult to the native English-speaker, but they are really not as difficult as they appear. Fortunately, each verb is not unique; it does not function as an entity unto itself. Many verbs that are formed in the same way can be grouped together in classes or conjugations. This greatly facilitates learning verb forms. As you will observe in subsequent parts of this chapter, even many so-called irregular verbs have characteristics in common and thus can be grouped together.

Moods and Tenses

In French there are six moods of the verb: **l'indicatif** (indicative), **le subjonctif** (subjunctive), **le conditionnel** (conditional), **l'impératif** (imperative), **l'infinitif** (infinitive) and **le participe** (participle). A mood relates to an aspect of the verb but does not tell you about the time. It tells you how the speaker views a statement. The timing of the verb is indicated by the tenses present, past and future. These tenses are divided into simple tenses and compound tenses. A simple tense has one single word. A compound tense is made up of an auxiliary (helping) verb and a past participle.

The indicative mood is used to indicate facts, events, etc. Most of the tenses you use in conversation are in the indicative mood.
The subjunctive mood is used to express feeling or emotion, to express opinions, doubts and subjective conditions.
The conditional mood expresses verbs tied to a condition.
The imperative mood expresses commands, orders, or wishes. It is not divided into tenses.
The infinitive has a fixed ending.
The participle can be used as a verb or an adjective.

L'INDICATIF
INDICATIVE

Simple Tenses	Compound Tenses
présent	**passé composé**
present	*conversational past*
imparfait	**plus-que-parfait**
imperfect	*pluperfect (past perfect)*
futur	**futur antérieur**
future	*future perfect (future anterior)*
passé simple	**passé antérieur**
literary past (simple past)	*past perfect (past anterior)*

LE SUBJONCTIF
SUBJUNCTIVE

Simple Tense	*Compound Tense*
présent	passé
present subjunctive	*past subjunctive*

LE CONDITIONNEL
CONDITIONAL

Simple Tense	*Compound Tense*
présent	passé
present	*past*

L'IMPÉRATIF
IMPERATIVE

L'INFINITIF
INFINITIVE

Simple Tense	*Compound Tense*
présent	passé
present infinitive	*past infinitive*

LE PARTICIPE
PARTICIPLE

participe présent	participe passé
present participle	*past participle*

Subject Personal Pronouns

In French, unlike in some other languages, the personal subject pronoun or a noun must be used with the verb. There are three ways to express the pronoun *you*. To address a friend, relative or close associate, the pronoun **tu** is used. This is called the familiar singular form. To address someone whom you do not know well or someone older than yourself, the pronoun **vous** is used. This is called the formal singular form. To address two or more people, either friends or mere acquaintances, **vous** is also used. **Vous** is the plural for both the familiar **tu** singular form and the formal **vous** singular form.

The third person singular pronoun **on** is an indefinite pronoun meaning *one, they, we* or *people*.

The subject pronouns are:

	Singular		*Plural*	
1st person	**je**	*I*	**nous**	*we*
2nd person	**tu**	*you*	**vous**	*you*
3rd person	**il** (masculine)	*he*	**ils**	*they*
	elle (feminine)	*she*	**elles**	*they*
	on (impersonal)	*one, people, they*		

The Present Tense

First Conjugation Verbs

Regular first conjugation verbs are commonly referred to as **-er** verbs since their infinitives end in **-er**. Many of the most frequently used verbs belong to the first conjugation.

In order to form the present tense of **-er** verbs, the infinitive ending **-er** is dropped. To the root are added the personal endings **-e, -es, -e, -ons, -ez, -ent.**

parler

je parl**e**	nous parl**ons**
tu parl**es**	vous parl**ez**
il, elle, on parl**e**	ils, elles parl**ent**

travailler

je travaill**e**	nous travaill**ons**
tu travaill**es**	vous travaill**ez**
il, elle, on travaill**e**	ils, elles travaill**ent**

Il parle français.
Tu chantes bien.
Je porte un parapluie.
Elles traversent la rue.
Nous travaillons bien.
Vous regardez la télévision.

Below is a partial list of **-er** verbs.

briller	*to shine*	**louer**	*to rent*
cacher	*to hide*	**marcher**	*to walk*
casser	*to break*	**monter**	*to climb, to go up*
chanter	*to sing*	**montrer**	*to show*
chercher	*to look for*	**parler**	*to speak*
commander	*to order*	**passer**	*to spend (time)*
compter	*to count*	**porter**	*to carry, to wear*
danser	*to dance*	**préparer**	*to prepare*
décider	*to decide*	**présenter**	*to present*
déjeuner	*to have lunch*	**quitter**	*to leave*
demander	*to ask*	**raconter**	*to tell (a story)*
dessiner	*to draw*	**refuser**	*to refuse*
dîner	*to dine*	**regarder**	*to look at*
donner	*to give*	**rencontrer**	*to meet*
fermer	*to close*	**rester**	*to stay*
fouiller	*to rummage through*	**retourner**	*to return*
fréquenter	*to frequent*	**sauter**	*to jump*
gagner	*to win, to earn*	**télécharger**	*to download*
garder	*to keep*	**tomber**	*to fall*
goûter	*to taste*	**travailler**	*to work*
jouer	*to play*	**traverser**	*to cross*
laisser	*to leave*	**tromper**	*to deceive*
laver	*to wash*	**visiter**	*to visit*

1. Complete the verbs in the following sentences with the appropriate ending.

1. Le soleil brill _____.
2. L'enfant cass _____ le jouet.
3. On cherch _____ le cadeau.
4. Je gagn _____ le prix.
5. Je donn _____ le livre à Pierre.
6. Tu ferm _____ la porte.

7. Tu fréquent _____ ce restaurant.
8. Ils chant _____ une chanson.
9. Les adolescents pass _____ beaucoup de temps sur l'Internet.
10. Nous march _____ dans le parc.
11. Nous mont _____ dans la tour.
12. Vous port _____ un bel habit.
13. Vous prépar _____ le dîner.
14. Vous rest _____ ici.

2. Complete the following sentences with the correct form of the indicated verb.

1. L'homme _____ un appartement. *louer*
2. Nous _____ français. *parler*
3. Elles _____ les peintures. *regarder*
4. Vous _____ à la maison. *rester*
5. Je _____ dans un bureau. *travailler*
6. Les enfants _____ dans l'escalier. *tomber*
7. Tu _____ la rue. *traverser*
8. La fille _____ une histoire. *raconter*
9. Ils _____ leurs amis au café. *rencontrer*
10. Nous _____ beaucoup de questions. *poser*
11. Vous _____ un poste dans le centre-ville. *chercher*
12. Je _____ cette vue. *dessiner*
13. Tu _____ des chansons sur ton smartphone. *télécharger*
14. Nous _____ de la soupe, du poulet et une salade. *commander*
15. Elles _____ souvent au restaurant. *dîner*

3. Choose the correct form of one of the verbs listed below to logically complete the following sentences.

fouiller / cacher / garder / fermer / fréquenter / déjeuner

1. Je _____ le cadeau de Noël.
2. Tu _____ ce quartier.
3. Nous _____ à midi.
4. Ils _____ le souvenir.
5. Vous _____ la porte.
6. Elle _____ dans le tiroir.

4. Complete the following paragraph with the correct forms of the indicated verb.

Pendant la semaine, nous _____ (travailler) beaucoup. Nous _____ (préparer) nos leçons dans la maison d'étudiants ou dans la bibliothèque. Nous _____ (passer) des heures dans la bibliothèque. Nous _____ (travailler) trois soirs par semaine dans un restaurant, mais nous ne _____ (gagner) pas beaucoup d'argent. Le samedi après-midi, nous _____ (jouer) au football ou nous _____ (parler) à nos amis au téléphone et le soir nous _____ (danser) à la discothèque.

5. Form sentences by combining the elements of column A with the appropriate element of column B. Be sure to put the verb in the correct form.

A	B
1. Elle / danser	la fenêtre
2. Nous / louer	une histoire
3. Ils / jouer	le vin
4. Tu / goûter	un appartement
5. Je / raconter	dans le parc
6. Vous / fermer	à la discothèque

6. Answer the following personalized questions.

1. Quand prépares-tu tes leçons? Où?
2. Passes-tu beaucoup de temps à étudier?
3. Travailles-tu? Où? Quand? Gagnes-tu beaucoup d'argent?
4. Passes-tu beaucoup de temps avec tes ami(e)s? Où?
5. Parles-tu français et anglais?
6. Où déjeunes-tu? À quelle heure?
7. Où dînes-tu? À quelle heure?

Verbs Beginning with a Vowel

Many verbs beginning with a vowel or silent **h** are **-er** verbs. They are conjugated like **-er** verbs, but a few special problems must be noted. The pronoun **je** becomes **j'**. This is called elision. In spoken French, in the **nous, vous, ils** and **elles** forms, a **z** sound is heard between the pronoun and a following verb. This is called liaison. The **n** of **on** is pronounced before words beginning with a vowel. Study the following:

aimer

j'aime	nous‿aimons
tu aimes	vous‿aimez
il, elle aime	ils‿aiment
on‿aime	elles‿aiment

Below is a partial list of some common **-er** verbs beginning with a vowel or silent **h**.

abandonner	*to abandon*	**embrasser**	*to kiss, to embrace*
accrocher	*to hang*	**emporter**	*to carry away*
admirer	*to admire*	**enseigner**	*to teach*
aider	*to help*	**entourer**	*to surround*
aimer	*to like, to love*	**entrer**	*to enter*
allumer	*to light*	**épouser**	*to marry*
amuser	*to amuse*	**étudier**	*to study*
apporter	*to bring*	**expliquer**	*to explain*
arriver	*to arrive*	**exprimer**	*to express*
attacher	*to attach*	**habiter**	*to live (in)*
attirer	*to attract*	**imaginer**	*to imagine*
attraper	*to catch*	**inspirer**	*to inspire*
avaler	*to swallow*	**inviter**	*to invite*
avouer	*to admit*	**irriter**	*to irritate*
échapper	*to escape*	**opposer**	*to oppose*
échouer	*to fail*	**oser**	*to dare*
écouter	*to listen to*	**oublier**	*to forget*
écraser	*to crush*	**utiliser**	*to use*

J'avale la pilule.
Nous‿arrivons à l'heure.
Vous‿osez le faire.
Elles‿admirent les statues.
Il échoue à l'examen.
Tu attrapes le ballon.

7. Rewrite the following sentences, putting the verbs in the singular.

1. Nous allumons la lampe.
2. Nous oublions son nom.
3. Nous attirons une foule.
4. Nous arrivons en retard.
5. Nous apportons le déjeuner.

8. Rewrite the following sentences, inserting the correct form of the indicated verb. Make all necessary changes.

1. Je _____ la peinture moderne.   *aimer*
2. Nous _____ à l'heure.   *arriver*
3. Tu _____ le livre.   *oublier*
4. Je _____ mes amis.   *aider*
5. Vous _____ le français.   *enseigner*
6. Ils _____ l'histoire.   *étudier*
7. Elles _____ à Paris.   *habiter*
8. Je _____ des CD.   *écouter*
9. Le garçon _____ le bifteck.   *apporter*
10. Nous _____ nos défauts.   *avouer*

9. Complete the following story with the correct form of the indicated verbs.

Je m'appelle Élisabeth Pierron. J'_____ (habiter) dans un appartement à Paris. Je suis étudiante à HECJF (Hautes Études Commerciales Jeunes Filles). J'_____ (étudier) beaucoup; donc, je n'_____ (échouer) pas aux examens. Le samedi soir j' _____ (inviter) mes amies à une surboum. Nous _____ (écouter) des CD. Nous _____ (aimer) les chansons de Céline Dion.

10. Answer the following personalized questions.

1. Qui admires-tu?
2. Écoutes-tu la radio? Quelle station?
3. Comment emportes-tu tes livres?
4. Où étudies-tu?
5. Où habites-tu?
6. Quels CD écoutes-tu? Quel chanteur aimes-tu?

Verbs with Spelling Changes

Verbs ending in -*cer* and -*ger*

Verbs ending in **-cer** add a cedilla to the **c** before the letters **a** or **o** in order to retain the soft **c** sound.

avancer	*to advance*	**nous avançons**
commencer	*to begin*	**nous commençons**
lancer	*to throw*	**nous lançons**

Verbs ending in **-ger** add an **e** after the **g** before the letters **a** and **o** in order to maintain the soft **g** sound.

changer	*to change*	**nous changeons**
manger	*to eat*	**nous mangeons**
nager	*to swim*	**nous nageons**

11. Complete the following sentences with the correct form of the indicated verb.

1. Nous _____ la leçon. *commencer*
2. Nous _____ le travail. *recommencer*
3. Nous _____. *avancer*
4. Nous _____ beaucoup. *manger*
5. Nous _____ de place. *changer*
6. Nous _____ dans la rivière. *nager*

12. Complete the following sentences with the correct form of the indicated verb, according to the model.

Elle _____ le travail, mais nous ne le _____ pas. *commencer*
Elle *commence* le travail, mais nous ne le *commençons* pas.

1. Nous _____ le cours de français mais elles ne le _____ pas. *commencer*
2. Tu _____ seul, mais nous _____ en groupe. *voyager*
3. Elles _____ du pain, mais nous n'en _____ pas. *manger*
4. Je _____ la leçon, mais vous ne la _____ pas. *commencer*
5. Je _____ bien, mais vous ne _____ pas bien. *nager*
6. Il _____ la balle, mais elles ne la _____ pas. *lancer*

13. Answer the following personalized questions.

1. Qu'est-ce que tu manges au petit déjeuner? au déjeuner? au dîner?
2. Quand tu sors avec tes ami(e)s, qu'est-ce que vous mangez au café?
3. Toi et tes ami(e)s, est-ce que vous nagez?
4. À quelle heure commence ton cours de français?

Verbs with -é- in the infinitive

Verbs which have **-é-** in the next to the last syllable of the infinitive change **-é-** to **-è-** in all forms except the **nous** and **vous** forms.

compléter

je complète
tu complètes
il, elle, on complète
nous complétons
vous complétez
ils, elles complètent

Some of the most common of these verbs are:

céder	*to yield, to cede*	**posséder**	*to possess*
célébrer	*to celebrate*	**précéder**	*to precede*
compléter	*to complete*	**préférer**	*to prefer*
considérer	*to consider*	**protéger**	*to protect*
espérer	*to hope*	**répéter**	*to repeat*
interpréter	*to interpret*		

14. Rewrite the following sentences, putting the verbs in the singular.

1. Vous cédez votre place.
2. Nous considérons ce poste.
3. Nous célébrons la fête.
4. Vous répétez les exercices.
5. Vous préférez partir de bonne heure.

15. Rewrite the following sentences, putting the verbs in the plural.

1. J'espère le voir.
2. Je cède à ses demandes.

3. Tu préfères venir à huit heures.
4. Tu interprètes le poème.

16. Complete the following sentences with the correct form of the indicated verb.

1. Vous _____ le poème. *interpréter*
2. Elles _____ le travail. *compléter*
3. Nous _____ nos amis. *protéger*
4. Je _____ aller au cinéma. *préférer*
5. Ces hommes _____ cette profession. *considérer*
6. Tu _____ à ses demandes. *céder*

17. Answer the following personalized questions.

1. Quelles fêtes célèbres-tu? Quelles fêtes célèbrent tes ami(e)s?
2. Possèdes-tu beaucoup de livres?
3. Quels films préfères-tu?
4. Qu'est-ce que tu espères devenir?
5. Considères-tu les deux côtés d'une question?

Verbs with -*e*- in the infinitive

In some verbs which contain -e- in the next to the last syllable of the infinitive, the -e- changes to -è- in all forms except the **nous** and **vous** forms. Study the following.

lever

je lève

tu lèves

il, elle, on lève

nous levons

vous levez

ils, elles lèvent

Some of the most common of these verbs are:

acheter	*to buy*
mener	*to lead*
amener	*to bring, to lead toward*
emmener	*to take away, to lead away*
promener	*to take a walk*
lever	*to raise*
élever	*to raise*
enlever	*to remove, to take off*
geler	*to freeze*
peser	*to weigh*

In other verbs with -**e**- in the infinitive, the final consonant is doubled in all but the **nous** and **vous** forms.

jeter

je jette

tu jettes

il, elle, on jette

nous jetons

vous jetez

ils, elles jettent

Two verbs belonging to this group are:

appeler	*to call*
jeter	*to throw (away)*

18. Rewrite the following sentences, putting the verbs in the singular.

1. Nous levons le rideau.
2. Vous pesez cinquante kilos.
3. Nous gelons en hiver.
4. Vous menez une vie tranquille.
5. Nous appelons un taxi.
6. Vous jetez la balle.

19. Rewrite the following sentences, putting the verbs in the plural.

1. J'achète des livres.
2. Tu lèves le rideau.
3. J'enlève les ordures.
4. Tu emmènes le chien dans de longues promenades.
5. J'appelle Pierre.
6. Tu jettes le livre.

20. Complete the following sentences with the correct form of the indicated verb.

1. Elle _____ une vie tranquille.　*mener*
2. Les ouvriers _____ le papier dans la corbeille.　*jeter*
3. Vous _____ le journal.　*jeter*
4. Elles _____ un taxi.　*appeler*
5. Nous _____ la tache.　*enlever*
6. Ces paquets _____ deux kilos.　*peser*
7. Tu _____ le garçon.　*appeler*
8. Vous _____ vos enfants à l'exposition.　*mener*
9. J'_____ une voiture.　*acheter*
10. Nous _____ les copains.　*appeler*

21. Answer the following personalized questions.

1. Combien pèses-tu?
2. Qu'est-ce que tu achètes au supermarché?
3. Mènes-tu une vie intéressante?
4. Où jettes-tu les ordures?

Verbs with -*yer* in the infinitive

Verbs whose infinitive ends in **-oyer, -uyer** and **-ayer** change **-y-** to **-i-** in all but the **nous** and **vous** forms.

nettoyer

je nettoie	nous nettoyons
tu nettoies	vous nettoyez
il, elle, on nettoie	ils, elles nettoient

Verbs in **-ayer** can keep the **y** in all forms of the conjugation.

Some common **-yer** verbs are:

balayer	*to sweep*
employer	*to use*
ennuyer	*to bore*
envoyer	*to send*

essayer	*to try*
essuyer	*to wipe*
nettoyer	*to clean*
payer	*to pay (for)*

22. Complete the following sentences with the correct form of the indicated verb.

1. La femme de ménage _____ la salle. *nettoyer*
2. Tu _____ la lettre par avion. *envoyer*
3. Je _____ la facture. *payer*
4. Ils _____ les fenêtres. *essuyer*
5. Ces livres m'_____. *ennuyer*
6. Nous _____ une bonne. *employer*
7. Vous _____ l'addition. *payer*

23. Rewrite the following, putting the verbs in the singular.

1. Nous payons ces dettes.
2. Vous employez une femme de ménage.
3. Vous essayez de réussir.
4. Nous envoyons des messages (des textos).
5. Ils nettoient les meubles.
6. Elles essaient de le faire.

24. Answer the following personalized questions.

1. Emploies-tu un stylo ou un crayon pour écrire?
2. Nettoies-tu ta chambre? Balaies-tu le plancher?
3. Envoies-tu des messages (des textos) à tes ami(e)s?
4. Essaies-tu de parler français?

Second Conjugation Verbs

Verbs whose infinitive ends in **-ir** are second conjugation verbs. The endings **-is, -is, -it, -issons, -issez, -issent** are added to the stem.

finir	choisir
je fin**is**	je chois**is**
tu fin**is**	tu chois**is**
il, elle, on fin**it**	il, elle, on chois**it**
nous fin**issons**	nous chois**issons**
vous fin**issez**	vous chois**issez**
ils, elles fin**issent**	ils, elles chois**issent**

Je finis ma leçon.
Tu obéis aux lois.
Elle punit l'enfant.
Nous choisissons une peinture.
Vous remplissez la tasse.
Ils réussissent à l'examen.

Below is a list of the most common **-ir** verbs.

| accomplir | *to accomplish* | applaudir | *to applaud* |
| agrandir | *to enlarge* | bâtir | *to build* |

choisir	*to choose*	**punir**	*to punish*
embellir	*to embellish*	**réfléchir**	*to think, to reflect*
envahir	*to invade*	**remplir**	*to fill*
finir	*to finish*	**réunir**	*to reunite*
grandir	*to become bigger*	**réussir**	*to succeed*
obéir	*to obey*	**saisir**	*to seize*

25. Complete the following sentences with the correct verb ending.

1. Il chois _____ du poulet rôti.
2. L'artiste embell _____ la salle.
3. Je réuss _____ à l'examen.
4. Je sais _____ l'occasion.
5. Tu rempl _____ le verre.
6. Tu fin _____ ta leçon.
7. Les juges pun _____ les criminels.
8. Ils obé _____ aux lois.
9. Nous applaud _____ beaucoup.
10. Nous bât _____ une maison.
11. Vous envah _____ la province.
12. Vous grand _____ beaucoup.

26. Complete the following sentences with the correct form of the indicated verb.

1. Je _____ la tasse de café.   *remplir*
2. Nous _____ les deux amis.   *réunir*
3. Ils _____ au professeur.   *obéir*
4. L'ami _____ un cadeau.   *choisir*
5. Tu _____ aux injustices.   *réfléchir*
6. Vous _____ la maison.   *agrandir*
7. Les soldats _____ le territoire.   *envahir*
8. On _____ les coupables.   *punir*
9. Nous _____ nos devoirs.   *finir*
10. Vous _____ tout ce que vous entreprenez.   *réussir*

27. Choose the correct form of one of the verbs listed below to logically complete the following sentences.

applaudir / réussir / remplir / accomplir / saisir / punir

1. Tu _____ l'occasion.
2. Il _____ le verre.
3. Vous _____ le chat méchant.
4. Elles _____ à la fin du concert.
5. Nous _____ la tâche.
6. Je _____ à l'examen.

28. Form sentences by combining the elements of column A with the appropriate element of column B. Be sure to put the verb in the correct form.

A	B
1. Nous / bâtir	à l'examen
2. Les enfants / grandir	le travail
3. Il / réussir	aux lois
4. Vous / choisir	une maison à la campagne
5. Je / finir	chaque année
6. Tu / obéir	votre programme d'études

29. Answer the following personalized questions.

    1. Accomplis-tu tout ce que tu veux?
    2. Quand applaudis-tu?
    3. Finis-tu tes devoirs avant de sortir avec tes ami(e)s?
    4. À quoi réfléchis-tu?
    5. Obéis-tu aux lois?

Third Conjugation Verbs

Verbs whose infinitive ends in **-re** are third conjugation verbs. The endings **-s, -s, -, -ons, -ez, -ent** are added to the stem.

répondre	**entendre**
je répond**s**	j'entend**s**
tu répond**s**	tu entend**s**
il, elle, on répond	il, elle, on entend
nous répond**ons**	nous entend**ons**
vous répond**ez**	vous entend**ez**
ils, elles répond**ent**	ils, elles entend**ent**

Below is a list of some common **-re** verbs.

attendre	*to wait for*	**perdre**	*to lose*
défendre	*to defend*	**rendre**	*to give back*
descendre	*to go down, to descend*	**répandre**	*to spread*
entendre	*to hear*	**répondre**	*to answer*
fendre	*to split*	**tendre**	*to pull, to set (a trap)*
fondre	*to melt*	**vendre**	*to sell*
pendre	*to hang*		

Je réponds à la question.
Tu attends tes amis.
Il descend l'escalier.
Nous vendons la maison.
Vous entendez du bruit.
Elles perdent l'espoir.

30. Complete the following sentences with the correct form of the indicated verb.

    1. L'avocat _____ son client.   *défendre*
    2. La glace _____.   *fondre*
    3. Je _____ aux questions.   *répondre*
    4. Je _____ l'escalier.   *descendre*
    5. Tu _____ la peinture.   *pendre*
    6. Tu _____ du bruit.   *entendre*
    7. Les charpentiers _____ du bois.   *fendre*
    8. Elles _____ la nouvelle.   *répandre*
    9. Nous _____ l'auto.   *vendre*
    10. Nous _____ les devoirs au professeur.   *rendre*
    11. Vous _____ la clef.   *perdre*
    12. Vous _____ la corde.   *tendre*

31. Rewrite the following sentences, putting the verbs in the plural.

    1. Elle vend l'auto.
    3. J'entends le professeur.
    2. Tu descends sur la place.
    4. Il fend du bois.

32. Rewrite the following sentences, putting the verbs in the singular.

    1. Ils entendent du bruit.
    2. Vous attendez le train.
    3. Elles perdent le match.
    4. Nous défendons cet homme.

33. Form sentences by combining the elements of column A with the appropriate element of column B. Be sure to put the verb in the correct form.

A	B
1. Vous / tendre	la maison
2. Je / entendre	l'espoir
3. Elles / descendre	à la question
4. Nous / perdre	les devoirs au professeur
5. Il / rendre	la rue
6. Je / attendre	un piège pour la souris
7. Tu / vendre	la chanson
8. Ils / répondre	un copain devant le cinéma

34. Answer the following personalized questions.

    1. Défends-tu tes ami(e)s?
    2. Qu'est-ce que tu perds souvent?
    3. Rends-tu tes devoirs à l'heure qu'il faut?
    4. Réponds-tu aux questions en classe?
    5. Vends-tu quelque chose? Quoi?

Irregular Verbs

Verbs like *ouvrir*

Some verbs, although the infinitive ends in **-ir**, are conjugated like regular **-er** verbs. Some of the most common are **ouvrir** (*to open*), **couvrir** (*to cover*), **recouvrir** (*to cover again, cover completely*), **découvrir** (*to discover*), **offrir** (*to offer*), **souffrir (de)** (*to suffer*), **cueillir** (*to pick, to gather*), **accueillir** (*to welcome*), and **recueillir** (*to collect, to pick, to gather*).

ouvrir	cueillir
j'ouvre	je cueille
tu ouvres	tu cueilles
il, elle, on ouvre	il, elle, on cueille
nous ouvrons	nous cueillons
vous ouvrez	vous cueillez
ils, elles ouvrent	ils, elles cueillent

35. Complete the following sentences with the correct form of the indicated verb.

    1. Les paysannes _____ les fleurs. *cueillir*
    2. J'_____ la porte. *ouvrir*
    3. Elle _____ les invités. *accueillir*

4. Vous _____ un cadeau.   *offrir*
5. Tu _____ beaucoup.   *souffrir*
6. Nous _____ la fenêtre.   *ouvrir*
7. L'enfant _____ un nouveau jouet.   *découvrir*
8. La neige _____ la terre.   *recouvrir*
9. Nous _____ la boîte.   *recouvrir*
10. Elles _____ d'une maladie étrange.   *souffrir*

36. Answer the following personalized questions.

1. Souffres-tu d'un rhume de temps en temps?
2. Qu'est-ce que tu découvres en faisant des voyages?
3. Accueilles-tu tes invité(e)s à bras ouverts?
4. Qu'est-ce que tu offres comme cadeaux d'anniversaire à tes ami(e)s?
5. Ouvres-tu la fenêtre quand il fait chaud?

Verbs like *courir, rire, rompre, conclure*

Some verbs whose infinitives end in **-ir** or **-re** are conjugated like regular **-re** verbs except in the **il, elle, on** form where a **t** is added to the stem. Some of the most common are **courir** (*to run*), **parcourir** (*to pass through, to pass over, to tour*), **secourir** (*to help, to assist*), **rire** (*to laugh*), **sourire** (*to smile*), **conclure** (*to conclude*), **rompre** (*to break*) and its derivatives **corrompre** (*to corrupt, to spoil*) and **interrompre** (*to interrupt*).

courir	**rire**
je cours	je ris
tu cours	tu ris
il, elle, on cour**t**	il, elle, on ri**t**
nous courons	nous rions
vous courez	vous riez
ils, elles courent	ils, elles rient

rompre	**conclure**
je romps	je conclus
tu romps	tu conclus
il, elle, on romp**t**	il, elle, on conclu**t**
nous rompons	nous concluons
vous rompez	vous concluez
ils, elles rompent	ils, elles concluent

37. Rewrite the following sentences, putting the verbs in the singular.

1. Ils rient aux éclats.
2. Elles courent vite.
3. Ils concluent l'accord.
4. Elles sourient beaucoup.
5. Ils rompent les liens.
6. Elles interrompent le professeur.

38. Complete the following sentences with the correct form of the indicated verb.

1. L'enfant _____ vers son père.   *courir*
2. Elles _____ à haute voix.   *rire*
3. La chaleur _____ la viande.   *corrompre*
4. Vous _____ vos amis.   *secourir*
5. Tu _____ le discours.   *conclure*
6. Tu _____ les liens.   *rompre*

7. Je _____ aux éclats.   *rire*
8. Nous _____ le monde.   *parcourir*
9. Il _____ beaucoup.   *rire*
10. Nous _____ beaucoup.   *sourire*
11. Nous _____ l'entretien.   *interrompre*
12. Tu _____ très vite.   *courir*
13. Les hommes d'affaires _____ l'accord.   *conclure*
14. Ils _____ leur travail.   *interrompre*
15. Vous _____ au spectacle.   *rire*

39. Complete.

1. Je ris quand...   4. J'interromps quand...
2. Je cours quand...   5. Je romps...
3. Je souris quand...

Battre and mettre

The verbs **battre** (*to beat, to hit, to win*) and its derivatives **se battre** (*to fight*) and **combattre** (*to combat*), and **mettre** (*to put, to place, to wear* or *to put on* — clothes, *to turn on* — radio or T.V., *to set* — table) and its derivatives **admettre** (*to admit*), **permettre** (*to permit*), **promettre** (*to promise*), **remettre** (*to put back*), **soumettre** (*to overcome, to submit, to subjugate, to subject*), **se mettre à** (*to begin*) and **transmettre** (*to transmit*) are conjugated like regular **-re** verbs except that the double **t** becomes a single **t** in the singular forms.

battre	**mettre**
je bats	je mets
tu bats	tu mets
il, elle, on bat	il, elle, on met
nous battons	nous mettons
vous battez	vous mettez
ils, elles battent	ils, elles mettent

40. Rewrite the following sentences, putting the verbs in the singular.

1. Nous mettons les vêtements dans l'armoire.
2. Vous battez le tapis.
3. Ils remettent le travail à demain.
4. Elles promettent d'aller avec moi.

41. Rewrite the following sentences, putting the verbs in the plural.

1. Il admet le crime.   3. Tu mets la nappe sur la table.
2. L'armée soumet les rebelles.   4. Je bats le linge pour le nettoyer.

42. Complete the following sentences with the correct form of the indicated verb.

1. Elles _____ le record.   *battre*
2. Tu _____ la question aux autres.   *soumettre*
3. Elle _____ d'y aller.   *promettre*
4. Nous _____ les livres sur l'étagère.   *remettre*
5. Vous _____ dans l'armée.   *combattre*
6. Je _____ le tapis.   *battre*

7. Tu _____ les livres sur la table. *mettre*
8. Les soldats _____ les rebelles. *soumettre*
9. Vous _____ que vous avez tort. *admettre*
10. Il lui _____ d'y aller. *permettre*
11. Nous _____ le message. *transmettre*
12. Je lui _____ de venir. *promettre*

43. Answer the following personalized questions.

1. Promets-tu de dire toujours la vérité?
2. Remets-tu tes vêtements dans l'armoire?
3. L'admets-tu quand tu as tort?
4. Qu'est-ce que tu remets à demain?

Verbs like *partir*

Verbs like **partir** (*to leave*), **dormir** (*to sleep*), **s'endormir** (*to fall asleep*), **mentir** (*to tell a lie*), **servir** (*to serve*), **sentir** (*to feel, to smell*) and **sortir** (*to leave, to go out*) are conjugated like regular **-re** verbs in the plural. The regular **-re** endings are added to the stem of the first and second person singular forms after the final consonant has been dropped. A **t** is added to the third person singular form after the final consonant has been dropped. In the plural, note the consonant sounds **t** in **partir**, **mentir**, **sentir** and **sortir**; **m** in **dormir** and **v** in **servir**.

partir	**dormir**	**servir**
je **pars**	je **dors**	je **sers**
tu **pars**	tu **dors**	tu **sers**
il, elle, on **part**	il, elle, on **dort**	il, elle, on **sert**
nous partons	nous dormons	nous servons
vous partez	vous dormez	vous servez
ils, elles partent	ils, elles dorment	ils, elles servent

44. Complete the following sentences with the correct form of the indicated verb.

1. Il _____ tout le temps. *mentir*
2. Elle _____ de la salle. *sortir*
3. Je _____ le dîner. *servir*
4. Je _____ pour l'aéroport. *partir*
5. Tu _____ huit heures. *dormir*
6. Tu _____ les fleurs. *sentir*
7. Ils _____ de bonne heure. *partir*
8. Elles _____ souvent le samedi soir. *sortir*
9. Nous _____ du thé. *servir*
10. Nous ne _____ jamais. *mentir*
11. Vous _____ ce soir. *sortir*
12. Vous _____ bien. *dormir*

45. Rewrite the following sentences, putting the verbs in the singular.

1. Nous partons à huit heures.
2. Vous dormez bien.
3. Vous servez des apéritifs.
4. Elles servent un bon repas.
5. Ils sentent l'odeur fraîche.
6. Elles dorment huit heures.

46. Rewrite the following sentences, putting the verbs in the plural.

1. Je sors de la classe.
2. Il ment au professeur.
3. Elle dort sur le divan.
4. Tu pars de bonne heure.

47. Complete the following.

1. Je dors _____ heures la nuit.
2. Je sors avec mes ami(e)s _____.
3. Je sers _____ quand j'ai des invité(e)s.

Vaincre

Vaincre (*to conquer*) and **convaincre** (*to convince*) are conjugated like regular **-re** verbs except that the **c** changes to **qu** in the plural.

vaincre

je vaincs	nous vain**qu**ons
tu vaincs	vous vain**qu**ez
il, elle, on vainc	ils, elles vain**qu**ent

48. Rewrite the following sentences, putting the verbs in the plural.

1. Je vaincs le rival.
2. Tu vaincs la difficulté.
3. Il convainc le sceptique.
4. Elle convainc l'homme de sa culpabilité.

49. Rewrite the following sentences, using the cues provided.

Ils vainquent l'ennemi.
Je _____.
Vous _____.
Elles _____.
Nous _____.
Tu _____.

Verbs like *connaître*

Connaître (*to know someone or to be acquainted with someone, some place or thing*) and similar verbs such as **apparaître** (*to appear, to seem*), **disparaître** (*to disappear*), **paraître** (*to seem, to appear*), **reconnaître** (*to recognize*) and **naître** (*to be born*) are conjugated alike. Note the circumflex over the **i** in the third person singular.

connaître

je connais
tu connais
il, elle, on connaît
nous connaissons
vous connaissez
ils, elles connaissent

Haïr (*to hate*) is conjugated like **connaître** in the singular, except that there is no circumflex on the **i** in the third person singular. Note the dieresis on the **i** in the plural.

haïr

je hais
tu hais
il, elle, on hait

nous haïssons
vous haïssez
ils, elles haïssent

50. Complete the following sentences with the correct form of the indicated verb.

1. Elles _____ les Dupont.   *connaître*
2. Ils _____ cet homme.   *reconnaître*
3. Une étoile _____ à l'horizon.   *apparaître*
4. Un enfant _____ chaque minute.   *naître*
5. Elle _____ dans le brouillard.   *disparaître*
6. Il _____ l'injustice.   *haïr*
7. Il _____ facile de le faire.   *paraître*
8. Nous _____ nos amis.   *reconnaître*
9. Nous _____ cette ville.   *connaître*
10. Vous _____ la pauvreté.   *haïr*
11. Vous _____ cette chanson.   *reconnaître*
12. Je _____ cette femme.   *connaître*
13. Je _____ dans la neige.   *disparaître*
14. Tu _____ les menteurs.   *haïr*
15. Tu _____ ces romans.   *connaître*

51. Rewrite the following sentences, putting the verbs in the singular.

1. Les invités paraissent à la porte.
2. Nous connaissons les Leclerc.
3. Vous reconnaissez le criminel.
4. Ils haïssent la bureaucratie.
5. Ils disparaissent souvent.

52. Rewrite the following sentences, putting the verbs in the plural.

1. Je reconnais cet enfant.
2. Tu connais le poète.
3. Elle hait l'injustice.
4. Cet homme paraît malade.
5. Le chien disparaît derrière l'arbre.

53. Complete the following sentences.

1. Je connais...
2. Je reconnais...
3. Je hais...

Plaire and *se taire*

Plaire (à) (*to be pleasing*), **déplaire (à)** (*to displease*) and **se taire** (*to be quiet*) are conjugated like **connaître** except that there is only one **s** in the plural forms. There is no circumflex on the **i** in the third person singular of **se taire**.

plaire	se taire
je plais	je me tais
tu plais	tu te tais
il, elle, on plaît	il, elle, on se tait
nous plaisons	nous nous taisons
vous plaisez	vous vous taisez
ils, elles plaisent	ils, elles se taisent

See Reflexive Verbs, pages 132–134.

54. Rewrite the following sentences, putting the verbs in the singular.

1. Ils plaisent à tout le monde.
2. Elles se taisent pendant le concert.
3. Nous plaisons à Marie.
4. Vous vous taisez pendant la conférence.

55. Rewrite the following sentences, putting the verbs in the plural.

1. Il plaît à cette femme.
2. Elle se tait pendant le spectacle.
3. Tu plais à tout le monde.
4. Je me tais maintenant.
5. Ce livre déplaît à Pierre.

56. Complete the following.

1. … me plaît.
2. … me plaisent.
3. Je me tais quand…

Verbs with Infinitives Ending in *-ire*

Lire, dire, conduire, traduire

Many verbs whose infinitives end in **-ire** have a base ending in a **z** sound in the plural. Belonging to this group are **lire** (*to read*), **élire** (*to elect*), **dire** (*to speak, to tell, to say*), **interdire** (*to forbid*), **suffire** (*to be sufficient*), **conduire** (*to conduct, to drive*), **produire** (*to produce*), **traduire** (*to translate*), **construire** (*to build*), **reconstruire** (*to rebuild, to reconstruct*), **détruire** (*to destroy*), **cuire** (*to cook*) and **nuire** (*to do harm*). These verbs add the endings **-s, -s, -t, -sons, -sez, -sent** to the stem. The second person plural of **dire (vous dites)** is an exception.

lire	dire	conduire
je lis	je dis	je conduis
tu lis	tu dis	tu conduis
il, elle, on lit	il, elle, on dit	il, elle, on conduit
nous lis**ons**	nous dis**ons**	nous conduis**ons**
vous lis**ez**	vous di**tes**	vous conduis**ez**
ils, elles lis**ent**	ils, elles dis**ent**	ils, elles conduis**ent**

57. Rewrite the following sentences, putting the verbs in the singular.

1. Les troupes détruisent la ville.
2. Ils élisent un président.
3. Vous dites la vérité.
4. Vous traduisez la phrase.
5. Nous lisons un roman.
6. Nous conduisons une Citroën.

58. Rewrite the following sentences, putting the verbs in the plural.

1. Elle lit *Le Monde* tous les jours.
2. Il conduit une Renault.
3. Je dis la vérité.
4. Je détruis le livre.
5. Tu produis un nouveau jouet.
6. Tu dis bonjour.

59. Complete the following sentences with the correct form of the indicated verb.

1. Elle _____ un poème. *lire*
2. Vous _____ au revoir. *dire*
3. Ça _____. *suffire*
4. Je _____ bien. *conduire*
5. Les ouvriers _____ le pont. *reconstruire*
6. L'armée _____ la ville. *détruire*
7. Nous _____ les phrases. *traduire*
8. Ce panneau nous _____ de marcher sur le gazon. *interdire*
9. Tu _____ un hôtel. *reconstruire*
10. On _____ une maison. *construire*

60. Answer the following personalized questions.

1. Lis-tu souvent?
2. Quel journal lis-tu?
3. Dis-tu toujours la vérité?
4. Conduis-tu une auto? Quelle marque d'auto conduis-tu?

Écrire, vivre, suivre

Écrire (*to write*), **décrire** (*to describe*), **vivre** (*to live*), **survivre (à)** (*to survive*), **suivre** (*to follow, to take a course or class*), **poursuivre** (*to pursue, to follow up*) and **s'ensuivre** (*to come after, to follow*) are conjugated alike. Note the **v** in the plural forms.

écrire	vivre	suivre
j'écris	je vis	je suis
tu écris	tu vis	tu suis
il, elle, on écrit	il, elle, on vit	il, elle, on suit
nous écrivons	nous vivons	nous suivons
vous écrivez	vous vivez	vous suivez
ils, elles écrivent	ils, elles vivent	ils, elles suivent

61. Complete the following sentences with the correct form of the indicated verb.

1. Elles _____ ce sentier. *suivre*
2. Les romanciers _____ des romans. *écrire*
3. Nous _____ la fête. *décrire*
4. Nous _____ un cours de français. *suivre*
5. Vous _____ une lettre. *écrire*
6. Vous _____ bien ici. *vivre*
7. Elle _____ un cours de chimie. *suivre*
8. Il _____ souvent à ses parents. *écrire*
9. Je _____ la scène. *décrire*
10. Je _____ cet homme. *poursuivre*
11. Tu _____ cette route. *suivre*
12. Tu _____ au xxe siècle. *vivre*

62. Rewrite the following sentences, putting the verbs in the plural.

1. Je vis bien ici.
2. Tu suis ce cours.
3. Elle écrit un poème.
4. Il décrit le match.

63. Rewrite the following sentences, putting the verbs in the singular.

1. Elles survivent à l'accident.
2. Ils écrivent les devoirs.
3. Nous vivons bien.
4. Vous suivez un cours de français.

64. Answer the following personalized questions.

1. À qui écris-tu des cartes d'anniversaire?
2. Écris-tu des cartes postales quand tu es en vacances?
3. Vis-tu une vie intéressante?
4. Quels cours suis-tu?

Croire, voir **and** *mourir*

Like **-yer** verbs, **croire** (*to believe*) and **voir** (*to see*), **prévoir** (*to foresee*) and **revoir** (*to see again*) have an internal vowel change. The **i** changes to **y** in the **nous** and **vous** forms. The other forms are conjugated like regular **-re** verbs except in the third person singular, where a **t** is added to the stem.

croire	voir
je crois	je vois
tu crois	tu vois
il, elle, on croit	il, elle, on voit
nous croyons	nous voyons
vous croyez	vous voyez
ils, elles croient	ils, elles voient

Fuir (*to flee*) and **s'enfuir** (*to flee, run away*) have the same vowel change in the first and second person plural.

fuir

je fuis
tu fuis
il, elle, on fuit
nous fuyons
vous fuyez
ils, elles fuient

Mourir (*to die*) has an internal vowel change from **ou** to **eu** in the singular and the third person plural.

mourir

je meurs
tu meurs
il, elle, on meurt
nous mourons
vous mourez
ils, elles meurent

65. Complete the following sentences with the correct form of the indicated verb.

1. Nous _____ l'histoire. *croire*
2. Nous _____ clair. *voir*
3. Nous _____ de la salle. *s'enfuir*
4. Vous _____ qu'elle a raison. *croire*
5. Vous _____ votre ami. *croire*
6. Vous _____ la nouvelle dans le journal. *voir*

66. Change the sentence, using the cues given.

Nous mourons de faim.
Vous _____.
Il _____.

Je _____.
Tu _____.
Elles _____.

67. Rewrite the following sentences, putting the verbs in the singular.

1. Elles le voient.
2. Nous croyons en Dieu.
3. Vous fuyez sa présence.
4. Ils croient cette histoire.
5. Ils meurent de fatigue.
6. Nous mourons de peur.

68. Rewrite the following sentences, changing the first verb to the plural.

1. Je vois qu'il a tort.
2. Elle croit que vous êtes fatigué.
3. Il s'enfuit de la salle précipitamment.
4. Tu meurs de faim.
5. Tu crois l'histoire.

69. Answer the following personalized questions.

1. Crois-tu à la chance?
2. À quoi crois-tu?
3. Qu'est-ce que tu prévois?
4. De quoi meurs-tu?

Verbs like *craindre, peindre, joindre*

Craindre (*to fear*), **plaindre** (*to pity, to feel sorry for*), **se plaindre** (*to complain*), **atteindre** (*to reach*), **éteindre** (*to put out, to extinguish*), **peindre** (*to paint*), **joindre** (*to join, to unite*) and **rejoindre** (*to rejoin, to reunite*) are conjugated similarly. They have an internal change from **n** to **gn** in the plural.

craindre	peindre	joindre
je crains	je peins	je joins
tu crains	tu peins	tu joins
il, elle, on craint	il, elle, on peint	il, elle, on joint
nous craignons	nous peignons	nous joignons
vous craignez	vous peignez	vous joignez
ils, elles craignent	ils, elles peignent	ils, elles joignent

70. Complete the following sentences with the correct form of the indicated verb.

1. Elles _____ la pluie. *craindre*
2. Ils _____ l'utile à l'agréable. *joindre*
3. Nous _____ la lumière. *éteindre*
4. Nous _____ le sommet. *atteindre*
5. Vous me _____ trop. *plaindre*
6. Vous _____ un portrait. *peindre*
7. Elle _____ d'être en retard. *craindre*
8. Il _____ un paysage. *peindre*
9. Je vous _____. *plaindre*
10. Je _____ mes amis au café. *rejoindre*
11. Tu _____ l'examen. *craindre*
12. Tu _____ les murs de la maison. *peindre*

71. Rewrite the following sentences, putting the verbs in the plural.

1. Je crains cet homme.
2. Tu rejoins Pierre à l'heure.
3. Il peint un paysage.
4. Elle se plaint de tout.
5. Elle joint les deux bouts.

72. Rewrite the following sentences, putting the verbs in the singular.

1. Elles craignent de répondre. 4. Ils vous plaignent.
2. Nous peignons le mur. 5. Nous joignons les deux bouts.
3. Vous éteignez la lumière.

73. Follow the model.

Je crains le professeur, mais vous ne le _____ pas.
Je crains le professeur, mais vous ne le *craignez pas.*

1. Je rejoins les copains, mais vous ne les _____ pas.
2. Il craint l'examen, mais nous ne le _____ pas.
3. Tu peins le mur, mais ils ne le _____ pas.
4. Vous éteignez la lumière, mais je ne l'_____ pas.
5. Nous plaignons les misérables, mais tu ne les _____ pas.
6. Elles atteignent ce but, mais il ne l'_____ pas.

74. Complete the following.

1. Je crains _____, mais je ne crains pas _____.
2. Je peins _____.
3. Je rejoins _____ à _____ heures.
4. Je me plains de _____.

Verbs like *prendre*

   Prendre (*to take, to take* or *to eat* — food, a meal, *to drink* — beverage, *to buy* — a ticket), **apprendre** (*to learn*), **comprendre** (*to understand*), **reprendre** (*to take back*) and **surprendre** (*to surprise*) are conjugated like regular **-re** verbs in the singular. In the plural, the final **-d** is dropped from the stem and the regular endings are added. The consonant **n** is doubled in the third person plural.

prendre
je prends
tu prends
il, elle, on prend
nous pre**nons**
vous pre**nez**
ils, elles pre**nnent**

75. Rewrite the following sentences, putting the verbs in the plural.

1. Je prends le déjeuner à midi. 4. Tu surprends l'enfant.
2. J'apprends les verbes. 5. Il comprend le français.
3. Tu reprends le CD. 6. Cette nouvelle nous surprend.

76. Complete the following sentences with the correct form of the indicated verb.

1. Je _____ la leçon. *comprendre*
2. Elle _____ son ami. *surprendre*
3. Nous _____ nos places. *prendre*
4. Elles _____ les difficultés. *comprendre*
5. Tu _____ le poème. *apprendre*

6. Vous _____ l'autobus.   *prendre*
7. Il _____ ses possessions.   *reprendre*

77. Answer the following personalized questions.

1. Quelles langues apprends-tu?
2. Comprends-tu tes ami(e)s?
3. Quand surprends-tu tes ami(e)s?
4. À quelle heure prends-tu le dîner?

Venir and *tenir*

Venir (*to come*) and its derivatives **revenir** (*to come back*), **convenir** (*to be convenient*), **devenir** (*to become*), **redevenir** (*to become again*), **parvenir** (*to reach, to attain*) and **se souvenir (de)** (*to remember*); **tenir** (*to have, to hold*) and its derivatives **appartenir** (*to belong to*), **contenir** (*to hold, to contain*), **maintenir** (*to maintain*), **obtenir** (*to obtain*) and **retenir** (*to retain*) are conjugated alike.

Note the vowel change from **-e-** to **-ie-** in the singular forms and the third person plural. Note the double consonant **nn** in the third person plural.

Tenir à plus an infinitive means *to be anxious to*. **Tenir à** plus a noun means *to like very much, to be attached to*.

venir	tenir
je v**ien**s	je t**ien**s
tu v**ien**s	tu t**ien**s
il, elle, on v**ien**t	il, elle, on t**ien**t
nous venons	nous tenons
vous venez	vous tenez
ils, elles v**ienn**ent	ils, elles t**ienn**ent

78. Complete the following sentences with the correct form of the indicated verb.

1. Ils _____ maintenant.   *venir*
2. Elles _____ une chambre à l'hotel.   *retenir*
3. Cette robe vous _____ bien.   *convenir*
4. Ce gant vous _____.   *appartenir*
5. Je _____ tout de suite.   *revenir*
6. Je _____ fatigué.   *devenir*
7. Tu _____ le prix.   *obtenir*
8. Tu _____ à tes fins.   *parvenir*
9. Nous _____ de ce voyage.   *revenir*
10. Nous _____ à vous voir.   *tenir*
11. Vous _____ votre opinion.   *maintenir*
12. Vous _____ de bons résultats.   *obtenir*

79. Rewrite the following sentences, putting the verbs in the singular.

1. Ils viennent tout de suite.
2. Vous devenez riches.
3. Nous maintenons notre position.
4. Les boîtes contiennent des papiers.
5. Nous parvenons à un âge avancé.

80. Rewrite the following sentences, putting the verbs in the plural.

1. Il tient à vous voir.
2. Elle vient tout de suite.
3. Ce livre vous appartient.
4. Tu obtiens le prix.
5. Je viens maintenant.

81. Answer the following personalized questions.

1. Avec l'âge, deviens-tu plus patient(e)? plus libéral(e)? plus optimiste?
2. Quand reviens-tu des vacances, en général?

3. De quelle ville viens-tu?
4. Tes ami(e)s viennent-ils (elles) souvent chez toi?

Acquérir and *conquérir*

Acquérir (*to acquire, to buy, to gain*) and **conquérir** (*to conquer, to win*) have an internal vowel change from **é** to **ie** in all but the **nous** and **vous** forms. Study the following.

acquérir

j' acquiers
tu acquiers
il, elle, on acquiert
nous acquérons
vous acquérez
ils, elles acquièrent

82. Rewrite the following sentences, putting the verbs in the singular.

1. Nous acquérons de l'expérience.
2. Nous conquérons son affection.
3. Vous acquérez une maison.
4. Vous conquérez l'ennemi.

83. Complete the following sentences with the correct form of the indicated verb.

1. J'_____ une auto. *acquérir*
2. Elles _____ son estime. *conquérir*
3. Tu _____ une maison. *acquérir*
4. Vous _____ beaucoup de livres. *acquérir*
5. Il _____ l'ennemi. *conquérir*
6. Nous _____ son affection. *conquérir*

Pouvoir, vouloir, pleuvoir

Pouvoir (*to be able to*), **vouloir** (*to want, to wish*) and **pleuvoir** (*to rain*) are conjugated similarly. Note the change from **ou** to **eu** in the stem of **vouloir** and **pouvoir** in all but the first and second person plural forms. **Pleuvoir** has only a third person singular form since it is an impersonal verb and only the pronoun **il** is used.

pouvoir	**vouloir**	**pleuvoir**
je **peux**	je **veux**	
tu **peux**	tu **veux**	
il, elle, on **peut**	il, elle, on **veut**	il **pleut**
nous **pouvons**	nous **voulons**	
vous **pouvez**	vous **voulez**	
ils, elles **peuvent**	ils, elles **veulent**	

84. Complete the following sentences with the correct form of the indicated verb.

1. Les garçons _____ aller à la piscine. *pouvoir*
2. Je _____ de l'argent. *vouloir*
3. Tu _____ partir. *pouvoir*
4. Elle _____ m'accompagner. *vouloir*
5. Nous _____ attendre. *vouloir*
6. Vous _____ voir le film. *pouvoir*

85. Rewrite the following sentences, putting the verbs in the singular.

1. Nous pouvons partir maintenant.
2. Nous voulons revenir demain.
3. Vous pouvez sortir maintenant.
4. Vous voulez rester ici.
5. Ils peuvent venir ce soir.
6. Elles veulent savoir la réponse.

86. Rewrite the following sentences in the plural.

1. Je peux attendre une minute.
2. Je veux sortir maintenant.
3. Il veut jouer au football samedi.
4. Elle peut rester ici si elle le veut.

87. Follow the model.

Je / aller au musée
Je peux aller au musée et je veux aller au musée maintenant.

1. Je / partir
2. Vous / jouer au football
3. Nous / sortir ce soir
4. Il / voir ce film
5. Tu / aller au cinéma
6. Elles / réussir

88. Complete the following.

1. Avec 1 000 $, je veux…
2. Avec 1 000 $, je peux…

Boire, devoir, recevoir

Boire (*to drink*), **devoir** (*to owe, to have to*), **recevoir** (*to receive*), **apercevoir** (*to perceive*) and **décevoir** (*to disappoint, to deceive*) are conjugated similarly. Note the cedilla on the **c** in the singular and third person plural forms of **recevoir** and its derivatives. Note the internal vowel change in the first and second person plural forms. Note also the **v** in all plural forms.

boire	devoir	recevoir
je **bois**	je **dois**	je **reçois**
tu **bois**	tu **dois**	tu **reçois**
il, elle, on **boit**	il, elle, on **doit**	il, elle, on **reçoit**
nous **buvons**	nous **devons**	nous **recevons**
vous **buvez**	vous **devez**	vous **recevez**
ils, elles **boivent**	ils, elles **doivent**	ils, elles **reçoivent**

89. Complete the following sentences with the correct form of the indicated verb.

1. Les enfants _____ beaucoup de lait.   *boire*
2. Elles _____ beaucoup de courriels.   *recevoir*
3. Ils _____ de l'argent à Pierre.   *devoir*
4. Marie _____ un coup de téléphone.   *recevoir*
5. Elle _____ partir de bonne heure.   *devoir*
6. Il vous _____.   *décevoir*
7. Je _____ du café.   *boire*
8. Je _____ des paquets.   *recevoir*
9. Tu _____ une tache sur la robe.   *apercevoir*
10. Tu _____ une lettre.   *recevoir*
11. Nous _____ du vin.   *boire*
12. Nous _____ beaucoup de lettres.   *recevoir*
13. Vous _____ vos amis.   *décevoir*
14. Vous _____ de l'eau.   *boire*

90. Follow the model.

> Je _____ partir, mais vous ne _____ pas partir.   *devoir*
> Je *dois* partir, mais vous ne *devez* pas partir.

1. Je _____ de l'eau, mais vous n'en _____ pas.   *boire*
2. Tu _____ un cadeau, mais nous n'en _____ pas.   *recevoir*
3. Je _____ de l'argent, mais vous n'en _____ pas.   *devoir*
4. Vous _____ du vin, mais ils n'en _____ pas.   *boire*
5. Nous _____ cent francs, mais elles ne _____ rien.   *devoir*

91. Rewrite the following sentences, putting the verbs in the plural.

1. Je dois de l'argent.
2. Je reçois une carte postale.
3. Tu bois du vin.
4. Tu reçois la lettre.
5. Il déçoit le professeur.
6. Elle reçoit de l'argent.

92. Answer the following personalized questions.

1. Si tu es malade, qu'est-ce que tu dois faire?
2. Qu'est-ce que tu bois au petit déjeuner? au déjeuner? au dîner?
3. Reçois-tu des cadeaux d'anniversaire? Qu'est-ce que tu reçois?
4. Quand reçois-tu des cadeaux?

Avoir

The verb **avoir** (*to have*) is completely irregular. Study the following.

<table>
<tr><td>j'**ai**</td><td>nous **avons**</td></tr>
<tr><td>tu **as**</td><td>vous **avez**</td></tr>
<tr><td>il, elle, on **a**</td><td>ils, elles **ont**</td></tr>
</table>

93. Complete the following sentences with the correct form of the verb **avoir.**

1. Il _____ sommeil.
2. Elle _____ faim.
3. Tu _____ beaucoup d'amis.
4. Tu _____ tort.
5. J'_____ froid.
6. J'_____ chaud.
7. Nous _____ une Renault.
8. Nous _____ de la chance.
9. Vous _____ honte.
10. Vous _____ peur.
11. Ils _____ soif.
12. Elles _____ raison.

94. Some friends are getting ready to go on a trip and are checking to be sure no one has forgotten anything. Follow the model.

> **Il a ses valises. Et vous?**
> **Nous avons nos valises aussi.**

1. Il a les billets. Et les amies?
2. Nous avons de l'argent. Et toi?
3. Tu as ton passeport. Et nous?
4. Ils ont les billets. Et les autres?
5. J'ai des cartes de crédit. Et Pierre?
6. Ils ont leurs visas. Et vous, Marie et Anne?

95. Mary and her friends are getting ready to go on a picnic. Who is bringing the provisions? Follow the model.

Qui a les pommes?   *Tu*
Tu as les pommes.

1. Qui a les sandwichs?   *Je*
2. Qui a le couvert?   *Vous*
3. Qui a le dessert?   *Nous*
4. Qui a le panier?   *Anne*
5. Qui a les boissons?   *Michel et André*
6. Qui a les serviettes?   *Pierre*
7. Qui a le tire-bouchon?   *Tu*

96. Answer the following personalized questions.

1. As-tu beaucoup d'ami(e)s?
2. Quand tu as tort, est-ce que tu l'admets?
3. As-tu des cartes de crédit?
4. As-tu beaucoup d'ami(e)s sur Facebook?

Être

The verb **être** (*to be*) is completely irregular. Study the following.

je **suis**   nous **sommes**
tu **es**   vous **êtes**
il, elle, on **est**   ils, elles **sont**

97. Complete the following sentences with the correct form of the verb **être**.

1. Il _____ français.
2. Elle _____ petite.
3. Tu _____ fatigué.
4. Tu _____ gentil.
5. Je _____ en retard.
6. Je _____ à l'heure.
7. Ils _____ malades.
8. Elles _____ heureuses.
9. Nous _____ contents.
10. Nous _____ fatiguées.
11. Vous _____ américain.
12. Vous _____ françaises.

98. Rewrite the following sentences, changing the singular pronouns and verbs to the plural and the plural pronouns and verbs to the singular. Make all necessary changes.

1. Nous sommes françaises.
2. Il est heureux.
3. Elles sont malades.
4. Vous êtes loyaux.
5. Je suis fort.
6. Tu es grand.

99. What are the nationalities of the following people? Follow the model.

Elle / le Canada
Elle est du Canada. Elle est canadienne.

1. Je / la France
2. Il / l'Italie
3. Tu / les États-Unis
4. Nous / l'Allemagne
5. Elles / la Russie
6. Vous / la Chine

100. What are the following people's professions? Follow the model.

Je / médecin
Je suis médecin.

1. Elle / journaliste
2. Il / avocat
3. Elles / dentistes

    4. Nous / ingénieurs
    5. Tu / chirurgien
    6. Je / professeur

101. Answer the following personalized questions.

    1. D'où es-tu? D'où sont tes parents?
    2. Es-tu petit(e) ou grand(e)?
    3. Es-tu pessimiste ou optimiste?
    4. Es-tu heureux (heureuse)?

Aller

The verb **aller** (*to go*) is completely irregular. Study the following.

je **vais**	nous **allons**
tu **vas**	vous **allez**
il, elle, on **va**	ils, elles **vont**

102. Complete the following sentences with the correct form of the verb **aller.**

    1. Il _____ à Paris en voiture.   7. Ils _____ à la chasse.
    2. Elle _____ à la boutique.   8. Elles _____ au musée.
    3. Tu _____ à l'école.   9. Nous _____ à Paris.
    4. Tu _____ en ville.   10. Nous _____ au théâtre.
    5. Je _____ à pied.   11. Vous y _____ par le train.
    6. Je _____ au cinéma.   12. Vous _____ à la plage.

103. Say how the people are feeling. Follow the model.

Je / bien
Je vais bien.

    1. Nous / très bien   4. Tu / assez bien
    2. Vous / bien   5. Elle / mieux
    3. Ils / très mal   6. Je / mal

104. Say where the following people are going, based on what they want to do. Choose from the list below. Follow the model.

au restaurant / au cinéma / à la discothèque / à la boulangerie / à la piscine / à la bibliothèque / au théâtre

Il veut voir une pièce de théâtre.
Il va au théâtre.

    1. Elle veut danser.
    2. Tu veux lire.
    3. Nous voulons regarder un film.
    4. Je veux nager.
    5. Vous voulez manger.
    6. Anne et Michèle veulent acheter du pain.

105. Answer the following personalized questions.

    1. Où vas-tu le samedi?
    2. Comment vas-tu à l'école?
    3. Toi et tes ami(e)s, quand allez-vous au cinéma?
    4. Comment vas-tu aujourd'hui?

Faire

The verb **faire** (*to do, to make*) is completely irregular. Study the following.

je **fais**	nous **faisons**
tu **fais**	vous **faites**
il, elle, on **fait**	ils, elles **font**

106. Complete the following sentences with the correct form of the verb **faire.**

1. Il _____ froid.
2. Elle _____ la salade.
3. Je _____ la leçon.
4. Je _____ un gâteau.
5. Tu _____ du golf.
6. Tu _____ ton droit.
7. Elles _____ du bien.
8. Ils _____ du ski.
9. Nous _____ du bruit.
10. Nous _____ du piano.
11. Vous _____ du sport.
12. Vous _____ votre possible.

107. Change the sentence, using the cue provided.

Je fais fortune.
Tu _____.
Nous _____.
Ils _____.
Elle _____.
Vous _____.

108. What do the people do in the following places? Complete the sentences choosing from the list below. Put the verb **faire** in the correct form.

faire la vaisselle	faire des réparations à l'auto
faire le ménage	faire du ski
faire attention	faire une promenade

1. Elle _____ dans le garage.
2. Nous _____ dans la cuisine.
3. Tu _____ dans le salon.
4. Les enfants _____ dans le parc.
5. Vous _____ en classe.
6. Je _____ dans les Alpes.

109. Answer the following personalized questions.

1. Quand fais-tu attention?
2. Fais-tu le ménage? Qu'est-ce que tu fais?
3. Où fais-tu des promenades?
4. Quel sport fais-tu?

Savoir

The verb **savoir** (*to know a fact, to know how to*) is completely irregular. Study the following.

je **sais**	nous **savons**
tu **sais**	vous **savez**
il, elle, on **sait**	ils, elles **savent**

110. Complete the following sentences with the correct form of the verb **savoir.**

1. Il _____ la vérité.
2. Elle _____ la réponse.
3. Je _____ parler français.
4. Je _____ la date de sa naissance.
5. Tu _____ son nom.
6. Tu _____ qu'il arrive.
7. Elles _____ jouer du piano.
8. Ils _____ son adresse.
9. Nous _____ où elle va.
10. Nous _____ conduire une voiture.
11. Vous _____ quand l'avion va partir.
12. Vous _____ qu'elles sont contentes.

111. Rewrite the following sentences, putting **savoir** in the plural.

1. Je sais qu'elle est malade.
2. Tu sais où elle habite.
3. Il sait faire du ski.
4. Elle sait faire la cuisine.

112. Tell what the people know how to do based on the information given. Choose from the list below. Follow the model.

bien écrire réparer les autos
parler espagnol faire la cuisine
jouer du piano bien conduire
guérir les maladies

Il est journaliste.
Il sait bien écrire.

1. Nous sommes médecins.
2. Elle est mécanicienne.
3. Je suis musicien.
4. Vous êtes un grand chef.
5. Ils habitent en Espagne.
6. Tu es chauffeur de taxi.

113. Write what you know how to do. Use **je sais** + an infinitive.

Je sais jouer du piano.

Valoir **and** *falloir*

The verbs **valoir** (*to be worth*) and **falloir** (*to be necessary*) are irregular. Study the following.

valoir	falloir
je **vaux**	
tu **vaux**	
il, elle, on **vaut**	il **faut**
nous **valons**	
vous **valez**	
ils, elles **valent**	

Il vaut mieux plus an infinitive means *it is better to.*

114. Complete the following sentences with the correct form of the indicated verb.

    1. Il _____ la peine de le faire.   *valoir*
    2. Il _____ partir de bonne heure.   *falloir*
    3. Ces robes _____ le prix.   *valoir*
    4. Vous _____ bien votre frère.   *valoir*

115. Rewrite the following, substituting the words provided.

    Il faut rentrer de bonne heure.
    _____ arriver _____.
    Il vaut mieux _____.
    _____ venir _____.

116. Complete the following sentences.

    1. Pour réussir, il faut...
    2. Pour obtenir de bonnes notes, il faut...
    3. Pour être heureux, il faut...
    4. Pour avoir beaucoup d'ami(e)s, il faut...
    5. Pour gagner de l'argent, il faut...

Special Uses of the Present Tense

The present tense in French is used the same as in English to express an action which is going on in the present. Note, however, that special auxiliary or helping verbs such as *am, are, is* in English are not used in French. The present tense is also used, as in English, to express habitual actions taking place in the present or a permanent situation.

    Elle dort maintenant.
    She is sleeping now.
    Tous les matins, ils vont à l'école.
    Every morning they go to school.
    La neige est blanche.
    Snow is white.

To insist on the duration of an action, use **être en train de** plus an infinitive.

    Il est en train de s'habiller.
    He's getting dressed.

The present tense can be used to express the immediate future.

    J'arrive dans cinq minutes.
    I'll come in five minutes.

Depuis, il y a... que, voilà... que, and *ça fait... que* plus the present tense

A special use of the present tense is with the time expressions **depuis, il y a... que, voilà... que,** and **ça fait... que** to express an action which began in the past but continues into the present.

Depuis quand attend-elle?	*How long has she been waiting?*
Elle attend depuis une semaine. **Il y a une semaine qu'elle attend.** **Voilà une semaine qu'elle attend.** **Ça fait une semaine qu'elle attend.**	*She has been waiting for a week.*

Depuis can mean *for* or *since*. Study the following.

Depuis quand habite-t-elle ici?	*Since when has she been living here?*
Elle habite ici depuis novembre.	*She has been living here since November.*
Depuis combien de temps habitez-vous ici?	*For how long have you been living here?*
Nous habitons ici depuis trois ans.	*We have been living here for three years.*

You will note that in English the past tense (present perfect) is used. Since the action continues into the present, the present tense must be used in French.

Note that **une heure** may mean *one o'clock*. To say *since one o'clock* use **depuis.** To say *for an hour,* use **il y a... que, voilà... que** or **ça fait... que.**

J'attends depuis deux heures.	*I have been waiting since two o'clock.*
Il y a deux heures que j'attends.	*I have been waiting for two hours.*

Venir de **plus the infinitive**

The present tense of **venir de** plus the infinitive is used to describe something that has just happened recently. It means *to have just done something*.

Elle **vient d'**arriver.	*She has just arrived.*
Elle **vient de** voir ce film.	*She has just seen this film.*

117. Complete the following sentences with the appropriate form of the indicated verb.

1. Nous _____ Pierre depuis cinq ans.   *connaître*
2. Elle _____ ici depuis deux ans.   *être*
3. Il y a un an que je _____ ici.   *demeurer*
4. Ça fait deux mois que nous _____ le français.   *apprendre*
5. Il y a longtemps que vous _____ ce poème.   *écrire*

118. Change the sentence according to the model.

Je travaille depuis une heure.
Il y a une heure que je travaille.
Ça fait une heure que je travaille.
Voilà une heure que je travaille.

1. Je lis ce poème depuis une heure.
2. J'attends l'autobus depuis cinq minutes.
3. Elle cherche ce livre depuis deux semaines.
4. Ils dorment depuis longtemps.

119. Answer the following questions, using the cue provided.

1. Depuis quand travaillez-vous?   *depuis une heure*
2. Depuis quand habite-t-il ici?   *Il y a deux ans*
3. Depuis quand attends-tu le train?   *Ça fait 15 minutes*
4. Depuis quand conduisez-vous une auto?   *depuis l'âge de 18 ans*
5. Depuis quand attendez-vous un taxi?   *Voilà dix minutes*
6. Depuis quand étudie-t-il le français?   *Il y a longtemps*
7. Depuis quand lisent-ils?   *depuis une heure*
8. Depuis quand jouez-vous de la guitare?   *Il y a un mois*
9. Vient-elle d'arriver?   *Oui,... il y a deux minutes*
10. Venez-vous de finir le travail?   *Oui,... il y a une heure*

120. Answer the following personalized questions.

1. Depuis combien de temps étudies-tu le français?
2. Depuis combien de temps habites-tu ici?
3. Depuis quand ta famille habite-t-elle à _____?
4. Depuis quand es-tu à l'université?

121. You have just returned from the grocery store. What have you just purchased? Use **je viens de (d')** + infinitive in your answers.

Je viens d'acheter des pommes, etc.

Review

122. Complete the following sentences with the appropriate form of the present tense of the indicated verb.

1. Je _____ voyager en avion. *préférer*
2. Tu _____ une carte à tes parents. *envoyer*
3. Nous _____ le travail. *commencer*
4. Elle _____ le garçon. *appeler*
5. Vous _____ une nouvelle robe. *choisir*
6. Tu _____ un cadeau à Pierre. *offrir*
7. Elle _____ aux éclats. *rire*
8. Ils _____ leurs passions. *vaincre*
9. Nous _____ cette histoire. *croire*
10. Il _____ de faim. *mourir*
11. Elle _____ cet homme. *connaître*
12. Cela me _____ . *plaire*
13. Je _____ le couvert. *mettre*
14. Vous _____ beaucoup de voyages. *faire*
15. Elle _____ huit heures. *dormir*
16. Nous _____ la phrase. *traduire*
17. Elle _____ ce boulevard. *suivre*
18. Vous _____ sa réponse. *craindre*
19. Elle _____ un portrait. *peindre*
20. Nous _____ la leçon. *comprendre*
21. Ils _____ tout de suite. *revenir*
22. Elles _____ le faire. *pouvoir*
23. Vous _____ partir. *vouloir*
24. Marie _____ une lettre. *recevoir*
25. Vous _____ travailler. *devoir*
26. Nous _____ du vin. *boire*
27. Elle _____ qu'il _____. *savoir, venir*
28. Nous _____ beaucoup d'amis. *avoir*
29. Vous _____ contents. *être*
30. Je _____ à l'école. *aller*
31. Il _____ arriver de bonne heure. *falloir*

123. Form sentences using the subjects and verbs given and choosing a logical completion from the list below. Follow the model.

les liens
les fenêtres quand il fait chaud
au restaurant
dans une usine
cet homme de partir
un bon film au cinéma
beaucoup de journaux
mon ami devant le cinéma
aux examens
du sel dans le ragoût
leur maison

cette chanson
sa leçon
ici souvent
une vie tranquille
dans le lac
la police quand nous voyons un crime
toujours les réponses
le faire
beaucoup de lettres
tout le temps

Je / travailler
Je travaille dans une usine.

1. Vous / manger
2. Les garçons / nager
3. Nous / appeler
4. Je / réussir
5. Les hommes / rompre
6. Ils / vendre
7. Nous / ouvrir
8. Les chefs / mettre
9. Je / attendre
10. Les bébés / dormir
11. Marie / mener
12. Georges / convaincre
13. Nous / connaître
14. Vous / lire
15. Angèle / apprendre
16. Les Pierron / venir
17. Les enfants / voir
18. Je / pouvoir
19. David / recevoir
20. Nous / savoir

124. Answer the following personalized questions. Use the present tense in your answers.

Qu'est-ce que tu fais au supermarché?
J'achète des provisions au supermarché.

1. Qu'est-ce que tu fais au grand magasin?
2. Qu'est-ce que tu fais au cinéma?
3. Qu'est-ce que tu fais au café?
4. Qu'est-ce que tu fais au restaurant?
5. Qu'est-ce que tu fais au magasin de vêtements?
6. Qu'est-ce que tu fais à l'université?
7. Qu'est-ce que tu fais dans la cuisine?
8. Qu'est-ce que tu fais au parc?
9. Qu'est-ce que tu fais à la bibliothèque?
10. Qu'est-ce que tu fais en classe?
11. Qu'est-ce que tu fais dans le jardin?
12. Qu'est-ce que tu fais au concert?
13. D'habitude, qu'est-ce que tu fais le matin? l'après-midi? le soir?
14. D'habitude, qu'est-ce que tu fais le samedi? le dimanche? le lundi?
15. Qu'est-ce que tu fais en vacances?

Reflexive / Pronominal Verbs

Reflexive verbs or pronominal verbs always have an object pronoun that refers to the same person or thing as the subject. The action of a reflexive verb is both executed and received by the subject. Since the subject also receives the action, an additional pronoun is needed. This is called the reflexive pronoun. Study the following.

se réveiller	s'habiller
je **me** réveille	je **m'**habille
tu **te** réveilles	tu **t'**habilles
il, elle, on **se** réveille	il, elle, on **s'**habille
nous **nous** réveillons	nous **nous** habillons
vous **vous** réveillez	vous **vous** habillez
ils, elles **se** réveillent	ils, elles **s'**habillent

Note that **me** becomes **m'**, **te** becomes **t'** and **se** becomes **s'** before a vowel or a mute **h**.

Je **m'**habille.
Tu **t'**arrêtes.
Il **s'**amuse bien.

Reflexive verbs may be used with a strictly reflexive meaning as well as in other ways where the English equivalent does not use a reflexive verb.

Je me lave.	*I wash myself.*
Je me trompe.	*I am mistaken.*

Many reflexive verbs are conjugated like regular **-er** verbs or **-er** verbs with spelling changes. Following is a partial list.

-er *verbs*

s'amuser	to amuse oneself	se moquer de	to make fun of
s'arrêter	to stop	s'occuper de	to be busy with,
se blesser	to hurt oneself		to take care of
se brosser	to brush oneself	se passer	to happen
se coucher	to go to bed	se passer de	to do without
se débrouiller	to get along, to manage,	se peigner	to comb (one's hair)
	to handle a situation	se porter	to feel
se demander	to wonder	se presser	to hurry
se dépêcher	to hurry	se raser	to shave
se déshabiller	to get undressed	se rencontrer	to meet each other
se fâcher	to become angry	se reposer	to rest
s'habiller	to get dressed	se retrouver	to meet each other
s'intéresser à	to be interested in	se réveiller	to wake up
se laver	to wash	se tromper	to be mistaken
se maquiller	to put on makeup	se trouver	to be located, to be found
se marier	to get married		

Spelling change verbs

s'acheter	to buy for oneself	s'ennuyer	to become bored
s'appeler	to be named	se lever	to get up
se rappeler	to remember	se promener	to take a walk

Below is a list of irregular reflexive verbs with references to similarly conjugated non-reflexive verbs.

s'en aller	to go away	aller (p. 126)
s'endormir	to fall asleep	partir (p. 113)
s'entendre (avec)	to get along (with)	-re verbs (p. 109)
se plaindre	to complain	craindre (p. 119)

se sentir	*to feel*	partir (p. 113)
se souvenir de	*to remember*	venir (p. 121)
se taire	*to be quiet*	plaire (p. 115)

125. Complete the following with an appropriate reflexive pronoun.

1. Elle _____ endort à onze heures du soir.
2. Je _____ peigne dans la salle de bains.
3. Ils _____ trompent souvent.
4. Tu _____ habilles bien.
5. Nous _____ couchons de bonne heure.
6. Vous _____ dépêchez pour ne pas manquer le commencement du spectacle.
7. Je _____ arrête devant le cinéma.
8. Tu _____ débrouilles bien.
9. Il _____ rase chaque matin.
10. Nous _____ levons de bonne heure.

126. Complete the following sentences with the correct form of the indicated verb.

1. Il _____ à sept heures.　*se réveiller*
2. Je _____ pour arriver à l'heure.　*se dépêcher*
3. Tu _____ dans la salle de bains.　*se laver*
4. Nous _____ au café.　*se retrouver*
5. Vous _____ bien.　*se débrouiller*
6. Les hommes _____ le matin.　*se raser*
7. Elles _____ en blanc.　*s'habiller*
8. Je _____ Marie.　*s'appeler*
9. Tu _____ bien.　*s'amuser*
10. Elle _____ avec Jean.　*se marier*
11. Nous _____ dans le jardin.　*se promener*
12. Vous _____ de moi.　*se moquer*

127. Pierre describes his family's daily activities in the morning. Follow the model.

se réveiller à sept heures
Je me réveille à sept heures.
Ma sœur se réveille à sept heures aussi.
Mes parents se réveillent à sept heures aussi.
Oui, nous nous réveillons tous à sept heures.

1. se lever tout de suite
2. se laver dans la salle de bains
3. se brosser les dents
4. se peigner
5. s'habiller

128. Answer the following questions, choosing from the cues provided. Follow the model.

à dix heures
parce qu'il est fatigué
sur le divan
bien
Oui,... souvent
Marie
dans la salle de bains

de mes vacances
si nous recevrons une bonne note
dans une rue déserte
parce que la conférence commence
parce que le film n'est pas intéressant
à côté du bureau de poste

Où est-ce qu'il se peigne?
Il se peigne dans la salle de bains.

1. Comment vous appelez-vous?
2. Où se passe l'action?
3. Où se trouve la pharmacie?
4. Qu'est-ce que vous vous demandez?
5. Pourquoi vous ennuyez-vous?
6. Pourquoi s'en va-t-il?
7. À quelle heure se couchent-elles?
8. Se fâchent-ils?
9. Comment vous portez-vous?
10. De quoi vous souvenez-vous?
11. Pourquoi se tait-il?
12. Où est-ce que l'enfant s'endort?

129. Answer the following personalized questions.

1. À quelle heure est-ce que tu te lèves?
2. Est-ce que tu te laves dans la salle de bains?
3. Est-ce que tu te brosses les dents?
4. Est-ce que tu t'habilles tout de suite?
5. À quelle heure est-ce que tu te couches?
6. Quand est-ce que tu t'amuses?
7. Quand est-ce que tu te reposes?

S'asseoir

A common, completely irregular reflexive verb is **s'asseoir** (*to sit down*). Study the following forms.

s'asseoir	
je **m'assieds**	nous **nous** asseyons
tu **t'assieds**	vous **vous** asseyez
il, elle, on **s'assied**	ils, elles **s'asseyent**

130. Complete the following sentences with the correct form of the verb **s'asseoir.**

1. Il _____ à table.
2. Elle _____ devant le bureau.
3. Je _____ à ma place.
4. Je _____ en face du professeur.
5. Tu _____ au premier rang.
6. Tu _____ sur le balcon.
7. Ils _____ dans les fauteuils.
8. Elles _____ au théâtre.
9. Nous _____ parce que nous sommes fatigués.
10. Nous _____ à table.
11. Vous _____ devant le feu.
12. Vous _____ sur la chaise.

131. Rewrite the following sentences in the plural.

1. Il s'assied devant vous.
2. Je m'assieds devant le feu.
3. Tu t'assieds dans le fauteuil.
4. Elle s'assied au premier rang.

132. Rewrite the following sentences in the singular.

1. Nous nous asseyons.
2. Vous vous asseyez à table.

    3. Ils s'asseyent devant le bureau.
    4. Elles s'asseyent sur le balcon.

Reflexive Verbs with Parts of the Body

You will note that when a part of the body is used with reflexive verbs, the definite article rather than the possessive adjective is used.

    Je me lave | **la** | figure.   *I wash* | *my* | *face.*

    Je me lave | **les** | mains.   *I wash* | *my* | *hands.*

You will also note that when the noun is ordinarily plural in English, it is singular in French.

    Elles se lavent | **la figure.** | *They wash* | *their faces.* |

133. Complete the following sentences with the appropriate definite article.

    1. La fille se lave _____ figure.   3. Ils se brossent _____ dents.
    2. Elles se lavent _____ mains.   4. Ils se lavent _____ figure.

134. Say what you do in the morning. Use the following verbs: **se réveiller, se lever, se laver, se brosser, se couper.**

Reflexive versus Non-reflexive Verbs

Many verbs function both reflexively and non-reflexively. If the action reverts to the subject, the verb is reflexive. If, however, the action is performed on another person or object, the verb is not reflexive.

Reflexive:	Je me lave.	*I wash myself.*
Non-reflexive:	Je lave la voiture.	*I wash the car.*
Reflexive:	Je me lève.	*I get up.*
Non-reflexive:	Je lève la main.	*I raise my hand.*

The reflexive verb is also used to indicate reciprocal action.

Reflexive:	Nous nous aimons.	*We like each other.*
Non-reflexive:	Nous aimons nos amies.	*We like our friends.*
Reflexive:	Ils s'écrivent.	*They write to each other.*
Non-reflexive:	Il écrit à Marie.	*He writes to Mary.*

135. Complete the following sentences with the appropriate reflexive pronoun, when it is necessary.

    1. Je _____ lave dans la salle de bains.   5. Nous _____ couchons tôt.
    2. Je _____ lave la voiture.   6. Nous _____ couchons les enfants.
    3. Elle _____ lève la main.   7. Tu _____ habilles le bébé.
    4. Elle _____ lève de bonne heure.   8. Tu _____ habilles en noir.

136. Follow the model.

    Nous aimons nos amis et nos amis nous aiment.
    Nous nous aimons.

1. Nous écrivons à nos parents et ils nous écrivent.
2. Ils aiment leurs amis et leurs amis les aiment.
3. Ils regardent leurs copains et leurs copains les regardent.
4. Nous cherchons nos amis et nos amis nous cherchent.

Reflexive Verbs in the Infinitive

The reflexive pronoun always immediately precedes the reflexive verb in the infinitive. Note that the pronoun agrees with the subject.

Je vais **me promener.**	*I am going to take a walk.*
Tu vas **te peigner.**	*You are going to comb your hair.*
Il va **se raser.**	*He is going to shave.*
Nous allons **nous dépêcher.**	*We are going to hurry.*
Vous allez **vous amuser.**	*You are going to amuse yourself.*
Elles vont **s'asseoir.**	*They are going to sit down.*

See pages 242–244 for reflexive verbs in the negative.

137. Complete the following sentences with the correct form of the indicated reflexive verb.

1. Je vais _____. *s'asseoir*
2. Tu vas _____. *se raser*
3. Nous allons _____. *se peigner*
4. Ils vont _____. *se réveiller*
5. Elle va _____. *s'habiller*
6. Vous allez _____. *s'endormir*

138. Describe what the people do on a daily basis and what changes on Saturday. Follow the model.

Je me lève à sept heures (onze heures).
Samedi, je vais me lever à onze heures.

1. Mme Dupont se lève à six heures et demie. (neuf heures)
2. Vous vous couchez tôt. (tard)
3. Nous nous habillons avant le petit déjeuner. (après le petit déjeuner)
4. Pierre et Marie se parlent dix minutes au téléphone. (une heure)
5. Je me lave la figure. (les cheveux)
6. Tu te réveilles à sept heures. (dix heures)

Imperatives

Affirmative Imperatives

The imperative or command is the same form as the second person singular and the first and second person plural forms of the verb without the pronoun. For **-er** verbs, the **s** is dropped from the second person singular to form the imperative.

parler		finir		attendre	
Parle!	*Speak!*	Finis!	*Finish!*	Attends!	*Wait!*
Parlons!	*Let's speak!*	Finissons!	*Let's finish!*	Attendons!	*Let's wait!*
Parlez!	*Speak!*	Finissez!	*Finish!*	Attendez!	*Wait!*

The imperative forms of **aller** are **va, allons, allez. Va** becomes **vas** and the familiar imperative of **-er** verbs adds **s** before the pronouns **y** and **en.**

Vas-y!   Go there!   **Parles-en!**   Speak of, about it!

The imperatives of **être, avoir** and **savoir** are irregular.

être	avoir	savoir
Sois!	Aie!	Sache!
Soyons!	Ayons!	Sachons!
Soyez!	Ayez!	Sachez!

The imperative forms for these verbs are the subjunctive forms. See *The Subjunctive Mood,* pages 195–196.

139. Write the imperative forms for each of the following.

1. parler français
2. écouter le professeur
3. choisir un livre
4. réfléchir à ces idées
5. attendre le train
6. vendre l'auto
7. prendre le déjeuner
8. ouvrir la porte
9. boire du lait
10. écrire la lettre
11. partir maintenant
12. venir tout de suite
13. être honnête
14. avoir du courage
15. savoir le poème par cœur

140. Give your friend or friends advice. Follow the models.

à un(e) ami(e), puis à deux ami(e)s **faire attention en classe.**
Fais attention en classe. Faites attention en classe.

à un(e) ami(e), puis à deux ami(e)s:

1. faire les devoirs
2. étudier chaque jour
3. prendre de bonnes notes en classe
4. venir en classe à l'heure
5. lire les livres
6. écouter le professeur
7. être attentif (attentive)
8. savoir les leçons
9. avoir de la patience

141. Say that you agree with your friend's suggestions for weekend plans. Follow the model.

On regarde la télévision?
D'accord, regardons la télévision.

1. On fait des projets pour le week-end?
2. On va au cinéma?
3. On fait une promenade dans le parc?
4. On part à dix heures?
5. On prend un verre au café?
6. On écoute la musique?
7. On mange au restaurant?

142. Follow the model.

Tu es à l'heure.
Sois toujours à l'heure!

1. Tu es honnête.
2. Nous sommes en avance.
3. Vous êtes heureux.
4. Tu as de la patience.

5. Nous avons du courage.
6. Vous avez de la pitié.
7. Tu sais la vérité.

8. Nous savons la réponse.
9. Vous savez le poème par cœur.

The Affirmative Imperative of Reflexive Verbs

In the affirmative imperative, the reflexive pronoun follows the verb and is joined to it by a hyphen. Note that **te** changes to **toi** in the affirmative imperative.

Lève-toi!	*Get up!*
Levons-nous!	*Let's get up!*
Levez-vous!	*Get up!*

143. Follow the model.

se coucher / vous
Couchez-vous!

1. se lever / tu
2. s'amuser / vous

3. s'habiller vite / tu
4. se dépêcher / nous

The Negative Imperative

The imperative is made negative by placing **ne** or **n'** before the imperative form of the verb and **pas** after it.

Affirmative	*Negative*
Travaille!	**Ne** travaille **pas!**
Écoute!	**N'**écoute **pas!**

144. Rewrite the following imperatives in the negative.

1. Parlez!
2. Travaille!
3. Soyez en retard!
4. Restons ici!

5. Aie du courage!
6. Écoutez la conversation!
7. Arrivons à l'heure!

145. Tell the child not to do the following. Follow the model.

toucher / le four
Ne touche pas le four.

1. toucher / la peinture
2. manger / la corde
3. être / méchant

4. aller / trop près de la piscine
5. boire / café

The Negative Imperative of Reflexive Verbs

In the negative imperative of reflexive verbs, the reflexive pronoun precedes the verb.

Affirmative	*Negative*
Réveille-toi!	Ne te réveille pas!
Réveillons-nous!	Ne nous réveillons pas!
Réveillez-vous!	Ne vous réveillez pas!

Note that the reflexive pronoun **te** does not change in the negative imperative.

146. You have given the following affirmative commands, but then change your mind. Change the affirmative commands to negative ones.

1. Couche-toi!
2. Habille-toi!
3. Dépêchez-vous!

4. Promenez-vous dans le parc!
5. Réveillons-nous!

The Present Participle

Formation

The present participle is formed by dropping the ending **-ons** from the first person plural of the present tense and adding **-ant**.

nous parlons	**parlant**
nous finissons	**finissant**
nous répondons	**répondant**
nous dormons	**dormant**
nous craignons	**craignant**

Only **avoir, être** and **savoir** are irregular.

avoir	**ayant**
être	**étant**
savoir	**sachant**

Use

When the present participle is used as an adjective, it agrees with the noun it modifies.

une fille **souriante**	*a smiling girl*
Il parle d'une voix **menaçante.**	*He speaks with a menacing voice.*

The present participle is invariable when it is used to express an action that takes place at the same time as the action of the principal verb.

Je vois mon père **faisant** la cuisine.
I see my father cooking.

The present participle can be replaced by **qui** plus a verb.

Je vois mon père **faisant (qui fait)** la cuisine.
I see my father cooking (who is cooking).

The present participle can also express cause.

Étant professeur, il veut enseigner.
Since he is a teacher, he wants to teach.

The present participle is often used after the preposition **en. En** means *by, while, upon, although.*

On apprend le français **en étudiant.**
One learns French by studying.

En me promenant, j'ai rencontré mon ami.
While taking a walk, I met my friend.
En arrivant, j'ai vu Marie.
Upon arriving, I saw Mary.
Tout **en** vous **aimant,** je reconnais vos défauts.
Although I like you, I recognize your faults.

By doing something is expressed in French by **en** plus the present participle except after the verbs **commencer** and **finir. Par** with the infinitive is used with these verbs. **À** plus the infinitive is used after **s'amuser.**

Il a fini **par travailler.**   *He finally started working.*
Elle a commencé **par faire** l'appel. *She began by calling the roll.*
Les enfants s'amusent **à jouer** dans le parc. *The children are having fun (amusing themselves by) playing in the park.*

With prepositions other than **en,** the infinitive is used rather than the present participle. (See *Uses of the Infinitive,* pp. 221–222.)

Il part **sans** rien **dire.**   *He left without saying anything.*
Faites le ménage **avant d'aller** au cinéma. *Do the housework before going to the movies.*

147. Say that the following people do two things at the same time. Follow the model.

Il écoute la musique quand il travaille.
Il écoute la musique en travaillant.

1. J'écoute la radio quand je fais mes devoirs.
2. Pierre regarde la télévision quand il mange.
3. Anne écoute la musique quand elle s'habille.
4. Nous écoutons les nouvelles à la radio quand nous conduisons.
5. Vous lisez quand vous attendez l'autobus.
6. Le chef chante quand il prépare le repas.

148. Say that something else happens while the following people do things.

Quand il sort, il tombe.
En sortant, il tombe.

1. Quand il se promène, il rencontre son ami Paul.
2. Pendant qu'elle descend la rue, elle tombe.
3. Pendant qu'elle raconte une histoire amusante, elle rit.
4. Quand il regarde la télévision, il s'endort.
5. Pendant que les spectateurs se lèvent, ils crient bravo.

149. Change the sentences to show how people can accomplish things.

On travaille et on apprend.
C'est en travaillant qu'on apprend.

1. On étudie et on reçoit de bonnes notes.
2. On joue du piano tous les jours et on apprend à bien jouer.
3. On a de l'ambition et on devient chef d'entreprise.
4. On court tous les jours et on reste en forme.

5. On est généreux et on a de bons amis.
6. On sait les verbes et on réussit à l'examen de français.
7. On mange moins et on maigrit.
8. On travaille et on gagne de l'argent.

150. Say what the people are doing. Follow the model.

> **Que fait-il?** *étudier / manger*
> **Il étudie en mangeant.**

1. Que fait-il?   *se brûler la main / faire la cuisine*
2. Que fait-elle?   *s'ennuyer / faire ce travail*
3. Que faites-vous?   *s'amuser / nager*
4. Que font-elles?   *entrer / courir*
5. Que fait-il?   *parler / dormir*
6. Que fait-elle?   *finir / dormir*
7. Que fait-il?   *commencer / remercier les invités*

151. Follow the model.

> **Il est professeur et il veut enseigner.**
> **Étant professeur, il veut enseigner.**

1. Il est chirurgien et il veut travailler à l'hôpital.
2. Elle a de l'argent et elle peut voyager partout.
3. Nous voulons réussir et nous travaillons.
4. Il dit au revoir et il part.
5. Je sais la leçon et maintenant je peux jouer avec mes amis.

152. Complete the following sentences. Use present participles in your answers.

> **J'apprends le français en...**
> **J'apprends le français en étudiant tous les jours.**

1. J'apprends le français en...
2. Je réussis aux examens en...
3. J'étudie en...
4. J'écoute les nouvelles à la radio en...

The Imperfect Tense

Regular Forms

The imperfect tense is formed by dropping the **-ons** ending from the first person plural of the present tense and adding the endings **-ais, -ais, -ait, -ions, -iez, -aient.**

parler (base: **parlons**)	finir (base: **finissons**)
je parl**ais**	je finiss**ais**
tu parl**ais**	tu finiss**ais**
il, elle, on parl**ait**	il, elle, on finiss**ait**
nous parl**ions**	nous finiss**ions**
vous parl**iez**	vous finiss**iez**
ils, elles parl**aient**	ils, elles finiss**aient**

Note that despite spelling changes, the singular forms and the third person plural are pronounced the same.

Verbs with Spelling Changes

Note the spelling changes before **a** in verbs ending in **-cer** and **-ger.**

commencer	**manger**
je commen**ç**ais	je mang**e**ais
tu commen**ç**ais	tu mang**e**ais
il, elle, on commen**ç**ait	il, elle, on mang**e**ait
ils, elles commen**ç**aient	ils, elles mang**e**aient

But:

nous commencions	nous mangions
vous commenciez	vous mangiez

Note that verbs with stems ending in **-i** have a double **i** in the **nous** and **vous** forms of the imperfect.

present	*imperfect*
nous étudions	nous étud**ii**ons
vous riez	vous r**ii**ez

Être

The imperfect tense of the verb **être** has an irregular stem to which the regular endings are added.

j'**étais**
tu **étais**
il, elle, on **était**
nous **étions**
vous **étiez**
ils, elles **étaient**

153. Rewrite the following sentences in the imperfect tense.

1. Nous travaillons beaucoup.
2. Nous prenons le petit déjeuner à huit heures.
3. Nous pouvons le faire.
4. Nous attendons longtemps.
5. Nous écrivons beaucoup de lettres.
6. Nous lisons des romans policiers.
7. Nous voyons clair.
8. Nous rions souvent.
9. Nous craignons de partir.
10. Nous venons souvent.
11. Nous nous débrouillons.
12. Nous nous couchons de bonne heure.

154. Complete the following sentences with the correct form of the imperfect tense of the indicated verb.

1. Je _____ de place. *changer*
2. Je _____ des livres d'occasion. *vendre*
3. Tu _____ à haute voix. *parler*
4. Tu _____ la musique classique. *préférer*
5. Elle _____ une femme de ménage. *employer*
6. Il _____ ce cours. *suivre*
7. Elles _____ le petit déjeuner à sept heures. *prendre*
8. Ils _____ réussir. *vouloir*
9. Nous _____ la vérité. *dire*
10. Nous _____ du vin. *boire*
11. Vous _____ vos devoirs. *faire*

12. Vous _____ des histoires.   *lire*
13. Ils _____ souvent au restaurant.   *manger*
14. Nous _____ tous les jours.   *étudier*
15. Elles _____ de bonne heure.   *se lever*

155. Rewrite the following sentences in the imperfect tense.

1. Je suis content.
2. Tu es heureux.
3. Elle est fatiguée.
4. Nous sommes malades.
5. Vous êtes triste.
6. Ils sont enfants.

156. Rewrite the following sentences in the imperfect tense.

1. Ils peuvent chanter.
2. Nous apprenons le français.
3. Je sors souvent.
4. Tu as beaucoup de temps.
5. Elle vient nous voir.
6. Vous buvez du lait.
7. Il ment souvent.
8. Elle croit ses amis.
9. Nous sommes heureuses.
10. Elle se dépêche.
11. Vous vous habillez bien.
12. Ils se promènent dans le parc.

157. Rewrite the following paragraph, putting the verbs in the imperfect tense.

J'ai 40 ans. Tous les jours je me lève à six heures et demie. Je me lave et puis je me brosse les dents. Je m'habille avec soin. Je prends le train pour aller en ville. Je travaille dur pendant la journée. Je rentre tard le soir. Je mange le dîner. Je joue avec les enfants et ensuite, je me couche tôt. Ah! Métro, boulot, dodo!

158. Complete the following with the correct form of the imperfect tense of the appropriate verb. Choose from the list below.

s'amuser, apporter, danser, avoir, aller, boire, préparer, gagner, être, inviter, jouer, sortir, écouter, manger

Quand j'_____ jeune, j'_____ beaucoup d'amis. Je _____ souvent avec eux. Nous _____ _____ beaucoup. Nous _____ souvent au cinéma, nous _____ souvent aux cartes. C'était Robert qui _____ toujours. Tous les vendredis soirs, l'un d'entre nous _____ les autres à une fête. Les uns _____ des CD. Les autres _____ des choses à manger. Nous _____, nous _____, nous _____ les CD, nous _____.

Uses of the Imperfect Tense

Continuing or Habitual Action

The imperfect tense is used less in English than in French. It is used to describe activities in the past. The imperfect tense is used to indicate actions begun in the past but not necessarily completed. It is used to express those past actions which are habitual or customary. Some common adverbs and adverbial expressions which would indicate continuance and thus frequently use the imperfect are:

toujours	*always*
fréquemment	*frequently*
d'habitude	*usually*
habituellement	*usually*
souvent	*often*

bien des fois	*often, many times*
autrefois	*formerly, in the past*
quelquefois	*sometimes*
parfois	*sometimes*
rarement	*rarely*
de temps en temps	*sometimes, from time to time*
tout le temps	*all the time*
tous les jours (lundis)	*every day (Monday)*
en ce temps-là	*at that time*
chaque année (jour, mois, matin, soir)	*every year (day, month, morning, evening)*
le lundi (le mardi, etc.)	*on Mondays (on Tuesdays, etc.)*

Study the following examples.

Elles **mangeaient toujours** dans ce restaurant.	*They always used to eat at this restaurant.*
Il **venait** me voir **fréquemment**.	*He came to see me frequently.*
Chaque été, j'**allais** à la plage.	*Every summer I went to the beach.*
Je **jouais** au football **souvent**.	*I played football often.*
Nous **allions bien des fois** à Paris.	*We went to Paris many times.*
Il **travaillait tous les jours**.	*He worked every day.*
En ce temps-là, je **chantais** bien.	*At that time, I sang well.*
Il ne **pleuvait jamais** là où nous **habitions**.	*It never rained (would never rain) where we used to live.*

The imperfect tense is used to describe what people were doing rather than report what people did.

Ils chantaient pendant que les filles bavardaient.
They were singing while the girls were talking.

159. Say that the following people used to do the same things they do now. Rewrite the following sentences in the imperfect tense.

1. Chaque année, elle va en vacances.
2. Nous lisons souvent.
3. Nous rentrons toujours à la même heure.
4. Elle fait des courses tous les jours.
5. Chaque matin, elles achètent des baguettes.
6. D'habitude, je mange des croissants au petit déjeuner.
7. Bien des fois, vous savez vous débrouiller.
8. Tu voyages fréquemment.
9. Elle va en Europe chaque été.
10. Il craint le tonnerre.
11. Il fait du ski quelquefois.
12. De temps en temps, vous dites des bêtises.

160. Say that you used to do the following. Follow the model.

Joues-tu au football?   *quand j'étais jeune*
Pas maintenant, mais quand j'étais jeune, je jouais au football.

1. Lis-tu souvent?   *en ce temps-là*
2. Riez-vous?   *quand j'étais jeune*
3. Chantes-tu bien?   *autrefois*
4. Vous couchez-vous de bonne heure?   *quand j'étais jeune*

161. Say what you used to do when you were younger.

1. Quand j'étais jeune,...
2. Chaque été,...
3. Tous les matins,...
4. Tous les soirs,...
5. Tous les samedis,...

With Verbs Denoting Mental Activity or Conditions

Since most mental processes involve duration or continuance, verbs which deal with mental activities or conditions are often expressed in the imperfect when used in the past. The most common of these verbs are:

aimer	*to like*
avoir	*to have*
croire	*to believe*
désirer	*to desire, to want*
espérer	*to hope*
être	*to be*
penser	*to think*
pouvoir	*to be able to*
préférer	*to prefer*
regretter	*to be sorry*
savoir	*to know*
vouloir	*to want*

162. Rewrite the following sentences in the past.

1. Je ne veux pas partir.
2. Vous regrettez les jours passés.
3. Nous pouvons venir tous les samedis.
4. Il ne sait pas les réponses.
5. Elles croient que vous avez raison.
6. Nous espérons recevoir de bonnes notes.
7. À quoi penses-tu?
8. Nous sommes désolés de ne pas pouvoir venir.
9. Elle préfère voyager en auto.
10. Je le désire beaucoup.

163. Complete the following, giving at least two personalized answers for each item.

1. Je voulais toujours...
2. Je ne voulais jamais...
3. Je préférais...
4. Je pouvais...
5. Je ne pouvais jamais...
6. Je regrettais...
7. J'aimais...

Descriptions in the Past

The imperfect tense is used to describe conditions or circumstances that accompanied a past action or to designate a condition in the past that no longer exists.

Il faisait beau.
The weather was nice.
Il avait de la chance.
He was lucky.

Il portait une chemise blanche.
He wore a white shirt.
Le Louvre était le palais des rois de France.
The Louvre was the palace of the kings of France.
Louis XIV était roi de France.
Louis XIV was king of France.

164. Rewrite the following sentences in the past. Describe the setting and the people at the skating rink.

1. Il est huit heures du soir.
2. Il fait froid.
3. Les étoiles brillent dans le ciel.
4. Il y a beaucoup de monde sur la patinoire.
5. Il y a un homme qui a à peu près soixante ans.
6. Une fille fait du patinage avec son ami.
7. Elle est blonde et lui, il est brun.
8. Ils portent de beaux patins.
9. Ils sont heureux.

165. Complete the following paragraph with the correct form of the imperfect of the indicated verbs.

Chaque été, nous _____ (passer) des vacances idéales au bord d'un lac. Nous _____ (avoir) de la chance parce qu'il _____ (faire) un temps merveilleux tous les jours. Nous _____ (porter) un maillot de bain toute la journée. Le jour, il _____ (faire) chaud mais le soir _____ (être) plus frais. La lune et les étoiles _____ (briller) dans le ciel. Nous _____ (être) très heureux en ce temps-là. Nous ne _____ (vouloir) pas rentrer chez nous.

Si and the Imperfect Tense

Si and the **on** or **nous** form of the verb in the imperfect tense can be used as a kind of imperative to express a wish or suggestion.

Si on jouait au tennis?	*How about playing tennis?*
Si nous jouions au tennis?	*Suppose we play tennis?*
Il a une nouvelle voiture.	*He has a new car.*
Si j'avais une nouvelle voiture aussi!	*If only I had a new car, too!*

166. Susan complains that she and her husband never do or buy things. Her husband proposes to do the following.

Nous ne jouons jamais au golf!
Si on jouait au golf?
Si nous jouions au golf?

1. Nous ne jouons jamais aux cartes.
2. Nous ne faisons jamais de ski.
3. Nous n'allons jamais au cinéma.
4. Nous ne dînons jamais au restaurant.
5. Nous n'achetons jamais une nouvelle voiture.

Depuis, il y avait… que, voilà… que, ça faisait… que and the Imperfect Tense

Depuis, il y avait… que, voilà… que and **ça faisait… que** are used with the imperfect tense to mean *had been.*

Depuis quand attendait-il?	*How long had he been waiting?*

Il attendait depuis dix minutes.	
Voilà dix minutes qu'il attendait.	*He had been waiting for ten minutes.*
Il y avait dix minutes qu'il attendait.	
Ça faisait dix minutes qu'il attendait.	

Venir de in the Imperfect Tense

Venir de in the imperfect tense is the past tense of *to have just done something*.

Il **venait d'**arriver.	*He had just arrived.*

167. Complete the following sentences with the appropriate form of the imperfect tense of the indicated verb.

1. Depuis quand _____ vous? *travailler*
2. Elle _____ ce livre depuis deux ans. *écrire*
3. Voilà longtemps que mon grand-père _____ aller au cinéma. *vouloir*
4. Il y avait deux mois que Jean _____ Marie. *connaître*
5. Voilà deux ans que j' _____ la médecine. *étudier*
6. Depuis quand _____ -ils ce bâtiment? *construire*
7. Nous _____ la vérité depuis longtemps. *savoir*
8. Vous _____ ici depuis trois mois. *habiter*
9. Vous _____ partir. *venir de*
10. Elle _____ téléphoner. *venir de*

The Conversational Past Tense (Passé Composé) of Verbs Conjugated with Avoir

The *Passé Composé* of *-er* Verbs

The *passé composé* or conversational past tense is used when talking about something that happened and was completed at a definite time in the past. The *passé composé* of most verbs is formed by adding the present tense of the auxiliary verb **avoir** to the past participle. The past participle of **-er** verbs is formed by adding **-é** to the infinitive stem.

Infinitive: parler
Past participle: **parlé**

j'ai parlé
tu as parlé
il, elle, on a parlé
nous avons parlé
vous avez parlé
ils, elles ont parlé

Short adverbs precede the past participle.

Elle a **bien** chanté. *She sang well.*

But:

Elle a chanté **lentement**. *She sang slowly.*

See Chapter 7 for negative forms.

168. Rewrite the following sentences in the *passé composé*.

1. J'oublie ma valise.
2. Elle prépare un bon repas.
3. Nous ramassons les papiers.
4. Vous sautez de joie.
5. Elles goûtent le vin.
6. Tu portes une nouvelle robe.
7. Le petit frappe à la porte.
8. Ils appellent leurs amis.
9. Je paie l'addition.
10. Je mange vite.
11. Elle garde toujours le secret.
12. Elle achète déjà des cadeaux pour Noël.
13. Je travaille vite.
14. Le conférencier quitte la salle.
15. Il jette les ordures.
16. Tu cherches partout.
17. Je chasse le gibier.
18. Nous dînons au restaurant.
19. Vous fermez la porte.
20. Elles louent l'appartement.

169. Tell what you did. Write sentences, using the cues provided. Put the verbs in the *passé composé*.

écouter... samedi
J'ai écouté des CD samedi.

1. manger... samedi dernier
2. acheter... récemment
3. travailler... hier
4. étudier... hier soir
5. regarder... à la télé récemment
6. danser... avec mes ami(e)s

The *Passé Composé* of *-ir* Verbs

The past participle of **-ir** verbs is formed by adding **-i** to the infinitive stem. Some verbs whose infinitive ends in **-ir** have regular past participles even though they are irregular in the present tense.

finir	**fini**
choisir	**choisi**
dormir	**dormi**
mentir	**menti**
servir	**servi**
accueillir	**accueilli**
cueillir	**cueilli**

170. Rewrite the following sentences in the *passé composé*.

1. Ils applaudissent le concert.
2. Je choisis un beau tapis.
3. Elle remplit la tasse de café.
4. Nous réfléchissons aux problèmes.
5. La police saisit le criminel.
6. Vous dormez bien.
7. Tu obéis aux lois.
8. Vous accomplissez déjà la tâche.
9. Les écoliers finissent leurs devoirs.
10. Les ouvriers bâtissent une maison.

171. Complete the following paragraph with the correct form of the *passé composé* of the indicated verbs.

Samedi dernier, parce que nous _____ (finir) nos devoirs avant midi, nous _____ (saisir) l'occasion pour aller au théâtre. Nous _____ (choisir) des places au balcon. Le spectacle était merveilleux. Tout le monde _____ (applaudir) à la fin de la pièce.

The *Passé Composé* of *-re* Verbs

The past participle of **-re** verbs is formed by adding **-u** to the infinitive stem. Some **-re** verbs that are irregular in the present tense have regular past participles.

vendre	**vendu**
répondre	**répondu**
battre	**battu**
rompre	**rompu**
vaincre	**vaincu**

172. Rewrite the following sentences in the *passé composé*.

1. Le bûcheron fend du bois.
2. Nous entendons du bruit.
3. Ils rompent les liens.
4. Vous vainquez le problème.
5. Il bat le tapis.
6. Elle répond vite.
7. La marchande vend des légumes.
8. La glace fond.
9. Tu attends tes amis.
10. L'avocat défend son client.

173. Answer the following personalized questions.

1. Quand as-tu attendu trop longtemps?
2. As-tu répondu aux questions en classe?
3. Qu'est-ce que tu as vendu?
4. As-tu défendu un(e) ami(e)?
5. Qu'est-ce que tu as perdu cette année?

Irregular Past Participles

Past participle ending in *-é*

être	**été**

Past participle ending in *-i*, *-is*, *-it*

-i

rire	**ri**
sourire	**souri**
suffire	**suffi**
suivre	**suivi**

-is

acquérir	**acquis**
conquérir	**conquis**
mettre	**mis**
prendre	**pris**
apprendre	**appris**
comprendre	**compris**
surprendre	**surpris**
reprendre	**repris**

-it

dire	**dit**
écrire	**écrit**
décrire	**décrit**
conduire	**conduit**
construire	**construit**

cuire	**cuit**
détruire	**détruit**
produire	**produit**
reconstruire	**reconstruit**
traduire	**traduit**

Past participle ending in -*ait*

faire	**fait**

174. Complete the following sentences with the correct form of the past participle of the indicated verb.

1. Elle a _____ à l'heure.   *être*
2. Il a _____ un bon voyage.   *faire*
3. Vous avez _____ en disant cela.   *sourire*
4. Ces réponses ont _____.   *suffire*
5. Nous avons _____ un cours de français.   *suivre*
6. Ils ont _____ une collection de peintures.   *acquérir*
7. J'ai _____ les livres sur l'étagère.   *mettre*
8. Tu as _____ le dîner à sept heures.   *prendre*
9. Nous avons _____ la leçon.   *comprendre*
10. La police a _____ le voleur.   *surprendre*
11. Il a _____ une Renault.   *conduire*
12. L'architecte a _____ une belle maison.   *construire*
13. Ils ont _____ des œufs.   *cuire*
14. Les bombes ont _____ la ville.   *détruire*
15. Le traducteur a _____ le roman.   *traduire*
16. Elles vous ont _____ cela.   *dire*
17. Vous avez _____ beaucoup de cartes postales.   *écrire*
18. Il a _____ la scène.   *décrire*

175. Rewrite the following sentences in the *passé composé*.

1. Elle suit un cours d'histoire.
2. L'élève apprend l'alphabet.
3. Vous écrivez vos devoirs.
4. Nous faisons des progrès.
5. Je dis la vérité.
6. Ils surprennent leurs amis.
7. Tu ris aux éclats.
8. Elle suit ce boulevard.
9. Ils construisent un pont.
10. Elle met le couvert.

176. Mary's friends are giving her a surprise birthday party. Form sentences from the following in the *passé composé*.

1. André et Sylvie / écrire / les invitations
2. Anne et Suzette / mettre / la table
3. Pierre / produire / les décorations
4. Solange et Jean / acquérir / les provisions
5. Le jour de la fête tout le monde / surprendre / Marie
6. Tout le monde / dire / « Bon anniversaire »

Past participles ending in -*u*

Verbs with infinitives in **-aître, tenir** and its derivatives and **courir** and its derivatives add **-u** to the infinitive stem to form the past participle.

connaître	**connu**
reconnaître	**reconnu**
paraître	**paru**
apparaître	**apparu**

disparaître	**disparu**
tenir	**tenu**
convenir	**convenu**
courir	**couru**
secourir	**secouru**

Paraître and **apparaître** can also be conjugated with **être** in the *passé composé*.

Most verbs with infinitives in **-aire** and **-oir** and some other verbs are completely irregular since their past participles are not formed on the infinitive stem.

plaire	**plu**
déplaire	**déplu**
se taire	**tu**
devoir	**dû**
décevoir	**déçu**
apercevoir	**aperçu**
concevoir	**conçu**
recevoir	**reçu**
avoir	**eu**
boire	**bu**
croire	**cru**
pouvoir	**pu**
savoir	**su**
voir	**vu**
falloir	**fallu**
pleuvoir	**plu**
valoir	**valu**
vouloir	**voulu**
lire	**lu**
élire	**élu**
vivre	**vécu**
survivre	**survécu**

Note the circumflex on the **u** of **dû.** Note the cedilla on the **ç** of past participles ending in **çu.**
See Chapter 9 for special meanings of **pouvoir, savoir** and **vouloir** in the *passé composé*.

177. Complete the following sentences with the correct form of the past participle of the indicated verb.

1. Le soleil a _____ derrière les nuages. *disparaître*
2. J'ai _____ cet homme. *reconnaître*
3. Elles ont _____ deux places. *retenir*
4. Vous avez _____ vers votre ami. *courir*
5. Ce film m'a _____. *déplaire*
6. Vous avez _____ travailler dur. *devoir*
7. Elle a _____ un cadeau. *recevoir*
8. Nous avons _____ du café. *boire*
9. Elle a _____ la réponse. *avoir*
10. Tu as _____ cette histoire. *croire*
11. Elle a _____ la vérité. *savoir*
12. Nous avons _____ le faire. *pouvoir*
13. Vous avez _____ ce film. *voir*

14. Elle a _____ aller à la pêche. *vouloir*
15. Cette robe a _____ le prix. *valoir*
16. Vous avez _____ ce roman. *lire*
17. Elle a _____ au xixe siècle. *vivre*

178. Rewrite the following sentences in the *passé composé*.

1. Je connais les Leblanc.
2. Cette décision déplaît à ces gens.
3. Elle croit le professeur.
4. Il survit à ses parents.
5. Tu vois tes amis.
6. Elles reçoivent le prix.
7. Elle retient une chambre à l'hôtel.
8. Nous courons vite.
9. Ils maintiennent un air calme.
10. Vous apercevez quelque chose d'étrange.
11. Tu dois répondre.
12. Cet homme paraît étrange.
13. Elle lit les romans de Proust.
14. Cette conférence plaît à tout le monde.
15. Il a de l'argent.
16. Vous tenez votre promesse.
17. Ils élisent un président.
18. Nous reconnaissons cette peinture.
19. Nous buvons du lait.
20. Il veut faire ce devoir.

179. Answer the following personalized questions.

1. Qu'est-ce que tu as bu pour le petit déjeuner?
2. As-tu su répondre aux questions du professeur hier?
3. Quel film as-tu vu récemment? Le film t'a plu?
4. As-tu eu l'occasion de voir tes ami(e)s samedi dernier?
5. Quel livre as-tu lu récemment?
6. Qu'est-ce que tu as voulu oublier?
7. As-tu couru aujourd'hui?
8. Qui as-tu élu comme président(e) de ta classe?

Past participles ending in -*ert*

Some verbs whose infinitives end in **-rir** have past participles ending in **-ert.**

ouvrir	**ouvert**
couvrir	**couvert**
découvrir	**découvert**
offrir	**offert**
souffrir	**souffert**

180. Rewrite the following sentences in the *passé composé*.

1. Il ouvre la fenêtre.
2. Le biologiste découvre un microbe.
3. Vous souffrez d'un rhume.
4. Nous ouvrons les cadeaux.
5. La mère couvre l'enfant.
6. Il offre un cadeau à son ami.
7. Tu couvres le mur de peintures.
8. Je souffre de maux de tête.

181. Answer the following personalized questions.

1. Qu'est-ce que tu as offert à ton père / à ta mère / à ton ami(e) pour son anniversaire?
2. As-tu souffert d'une maladie? Laquelle?
3. De quoi as-tu couvert ton lit?
4. As-tu découvert quelque chose récemmment? Quoi?

Past participle of verbs ending in *-indre*

The past participles of verbs ending in **-indre** are irregular.

craindre	**craint**
plaindre	**plaint**
atteindre	**atteint**
éteindre	**éteint**
peindre	**peint**
joindre	**joint**
rejoindre	**rejoint**

182. Rewrite the following sentences in the *passé composé*.

1. Il atteint son but.
2. Elle craint cet homme.
3. Nous rejoignons nos amis.
4. Vous éteignez la lumière.
5. L'artiste peint un portrait.
6. Nous plaignons cet homme.
7. Vous craignez les rues désertes.
8. Nous rejoignons nos amis par téléphone.

183. Answer the following personalized questions.

1. As-tu atteint tes buts? Lesquels?
2. À quelle heure est-ce que tu as éteint les lumières hier soir?
3. Quand as-tu rejoint tes amis par téléphone?
4. As-tu peint un portrait? De qui?

Agreement of the Past Participle with Verbs Conjugated with *avoir*

The past participle of verbs using **avoir** in the *passé composé* agrees in number and in gender with a preceding direct object.

> Voilà **la lettre** que j'ai **écrite.**
> Voilà **les photos** que j'ai **prises.**
> Voilà **l'homme** que j'ai **craint.**
> Voilà **les disques** que j'ai **achetés.**

Most past participles sound alike in the masculine and feminine except for those ending in a consonant.

> les hommes que j'ai **vus**
> la femme que j'ai **vue**
>
> *But:*
>
> la lettre que j'ai **écrite**
> le poème que j'ai **écrit**

Compare the masculine and feminine of the following past participles.

Masculine	*Feminine*
pris	**prise**
mis	**mise**
dit	**dite**
offert	**offerte**
écrit	**écrite**
craint	**crainte**

Note that there is no oral or written change for the masculine singular and plural when the past participle ends in **s**.

> le livre que j'ai **pris**
> les livres que j'ai **pris**

The past participle of verbs conjugated with **avoir** is invariable

1. when it is used with an impersonal verb:

> la pluie qu'**il y a eu**

2. when the past participle is followed by a complementary infinitive and it is the infinitive that relates to the preceding direct object:

> les tâches qu'elle a **dû compléter**

See also pages 223–226.

The past participle of certain intransitively used verbs accompanied by a unit of price, weight, distance, length, time, etc., is invariable.

> **les deux heures** que j'ai **couru** (intransitive)

> *But:*

> **les dangers** que j'ai **courus** (transitive)

> **les cent kilos** que j'ai **pesé**

> *But:*

> **les paquets** que j'ai **pesés**

184. Complete the following sentences with the correct form of the past participle of the indicated verb.

1. Voilà la place que j'ai _____. *prendre*
2. Voilà le billet que j'ai _____. *prendre*
3. Voilà la ville qu'il a _____. *peindre*
4. Voilà le tableau qu'il a _____. *peindre*
5. Voilà les dames que j'ai _____. *craindre*
6. Voilà les hommes que j'ai _____. *craindre*
7. Voilà les peines que j'ai _____. *endurer*
8. Voilà les maux que j'ai _____. *endurer*
9. Voilà la photo que j'ai _____. *voir*
10. Voilà le film que j'ai _____. *voir*

185. Rewrite the following sentences according to the model.

J'ai écrit la lettre.
Quelle lettre avez-vous écrite?

1. J'ai appris la leçon.
2. J'ai compris le livre.
3. J'ai mis les CD.
4. J'ai couvert les murs.
5. J'ai dit la phrase.
6. J'ai conduit l'auto.
7. J'ai pris les blouses.
8. J'ai ouvert les fenêtres.
9. J'ai lu le poème.
10. J'ai craint le criminel.
11. J'ai vu les pièces.
12. J'ai cru l'histoire.

186. Add the correct ending to the past participle if necessary.

1. Les pommes que j'ai pesé_____ sont dans le panier.
2. les deux cents dollars que ces robes m'ont coûté_____
3. les deux cents kilos que j'ai pesé_____
4. les livres qu'elle n'a pas pu_____ terminer
5. les vingt ans que j'ai fait_____ ce travail
6. les larmes que cette situation m'a coûté_____

187. Respond to the commands by saying that you have already done the following.

Écris tes devoirs!
Je les ai déjà écrits.

1. Mange ton petit déjeuner!
2. Fais tes devoirs!
3. Écris ta composition!
4. Apprends les conjugaisons!
5. Achète les livres!

Review

188. You are the anchor for a television newscast. Give the news. Put the verbs in the *passé composé*.

Les Bleus / gagner / la coupe du monde
Les Bleus ont gagné la coupe du monde.

1. Le président / faire / le tour de l'Afrique
2. Les habitants / élire / un nouveau président
3. La femme du président / visiter / les écoles
4. Le président / accueillir / les représentants des autres pays
5. Le président / répondre / aux questions des journalistes
6. Deux savants américains / découvrir / une nouvelle étoile
7. Les athlètes américains / recevoir / trois médailles d'or aux Jeux olympiques
8. Tout le monde / rire / au spectacle hier soir
9. La police / surprendre / un voleur à la banque

The Passé Composé *of Verbs Conjugated with* Être

The following verbs use **être** as the helping verb in the *passé composé*. Study the following past participles.

| aller | **allé** | *to go* |
| venir | **venu** | *to come* |

entrer	**entré**	*to enter*
sortir	**sorti**	*to leave, to go out*
arriver	**arrivé**	*to arrive*
partir	**parti**	*to leave*
monter	**monté**	*to go up, to get on (transport)*
descendre	**descendu**	*to go down, to get off (transport)*
naître	**né**	*to be born*
mourir	**mort**	*to die*
revenir	**revenu**	*to come back*
retourner	**retourné**	*to go back*
tomber	**tombé**	*to fall*
rester	**resté**	*to stay*
rentrer	**rentré**	*to return*
devenir	**devenu**	*to become*

It is helpful to think of the first 12 of these verbs as opposite pairs.

With verbs conjugated with **être,** the past participle agrees in number and in gender with the subject.

aller

je suis **allé(e)**	nous sommes **allé(e)s**
tu es **allé(e)**	vous êtes **allé(e)(s)(es)**
il, on est **allé**	ils sont **allés**
elle est **allée**	elles sont **allées**

189. Complete the following sentences with the correct form of the *passé composé* of the indicated verb.

1. Elle _____ au théâtre.   *aller*
2. Il _____ dans la salle.   *entrer*
3. Elles _____ à l'heure.   *arriver*
4. Ils _____ dans le taxi.   *monter*
5. Elle _____ à huit heures du soir.   *naître*
6. Il _____ chez lui.   *retourner*
7. Elles _____ sur le trottoir.   *tomber*
8. Ils _____ chez eux.   *rester*
9. Elle _____ à minuit.   *rentrer*
10. Il _____ ce soir.   *sortir*
11. Elles _____ de bonne heure.   *partir*
12. Ils _____ nous voir.   *venir*
13. Elle _____ du train.   *descendre*
14. Il _____ tard hier.   *revenir*
15. Elles _____ riches.   *devenir*
16. Ils _____ dans l'accident.   *mourir*

190. Rewrite the following sentences in the *passé composé.*

1. Elle monte dans le wagon.
2. Nous (f.) arrivons de bonne heure.
3. Monsieur, vous rentrez tard.
4. Pierre et Georges, vous devenez ennuyeux.
5. Marie et Lucille, vous revenez trop tard.
6. Nous (m.) restons chez nous.
7. Vous (f. sing). mourez de faim.
8. Nous (f.) partons de bonne heure.
9. Je (f.) rentre chez moi.
10. Tu (m.) descends dans la rue.
11. Vous (f. pl.) entrez dans l'atelier.
12. Les bonnes viennent à l'heure.
13. Les enfants tombent dans l'escalier.
14. Je (m.) vais au bureau.
15. Tu (f.) vas au restaurant.
16. Il part à l'heure.

191. Mary and John went to France on their vacation. Say what they did.

> **aller en France**
> **Ils sont allés en France.**

1. partir pour Paris le 24 juin à huit heures du soir
2. arriver à l'aéroport Charles de Gaulle à neuf heures du matin
3. rester deux semaines à l'hôtel
4. sortir tous les soirs pour dîner et pour aller aux spectacles
5. monter dans le train pour aller en Provence
6. descendre quatre heures plus tard à Aix-en-Provence
7. retourner à Paris une semaine plus tard
8. revenir aux États-Unis

192. Answer the following personalized questions.

1. Quand es-tu né(e)?
2. Es-tu sorti(e) samedi dernier? À quelle heure es-tu parti(e)? Où es-tu allé(e)?
3. Quand es-tu revenu(e) chez toi?
4. Comment es-tu venu(e) en classe aujourd'hui?
5. Connais-tu quelqu'un qui est devenu célèbre?
6. Ta famille et toi, où êtes-vous allé(e)s l'été dernier?

Monter, descendre, sortir, entrer, rentrer with *être* and *avoir* in the *Passé Composé*

When **monter, descendre, entrer, rentrer,** and **sortir** have direct objects, they use **avoir** rather than **être** as the auxiliary verb in the *passé composé*.

Elle est montée.	*She went up.*
Elle a monté l'escalier.	*She went up the stairs.*
Elle est descendue.	*She came down.*
Elle a descendu les valises.	*She brought the suitcases down.*
Elle est entrée dans la salle.	*She entered the room.*
Elle a entré les données dans son ordinateur.	*She entered the data into her computer.*
Elle est rentrée très tard hier soir.	*She returned very late last night.*
Elle a rentré le journal du matin.	*She brought in the morning newspaper.*
Elle est sortie.	*She went out.*
Elle a sorti de l'argent.	*She got out some money.*

Passer with *être* and *avoir* in the *Passé Composé*

When **passer** means *to pass by, to come by, to stop by, to be over,* etc., it is conjugated with **être**. When it means *to spend time* or *to take an exam,* etc., it is conjugated with **avoir**.

Il est passé me voir samedi soir.	*He stopped by to see me Saturday evening.*
Sa vie est passée.	*Her life is over.*
Elle a passé une année en France.	*She spent a year in France.*
Elle a passé son examen de français en juin.	*She took her French exam in June.*

193. Rewrite the following sentences in the *passé composé*.

1. Elle monte vite.
2. Elle monte l'escalier.
3. Nous (f.) descendons du train.
4. Nous descendons la valise.
5. Elles sortent samedi.
6. Elles sortent l'argenterie du tiroir.
7. Il monte dans sa chambre.
8. Ils descendent les valises.
9. Nous sortons de l'argent.
10. Elles descendent de l'autobus.
11. Nous passons nos vacances au bord de la mer.
12. Nous passons près d'ici samedi.
13. Il entre dans la salle de classe.
14. Il entre les notes dans son cahier.
15. Elle rentre très tard.
16. Elle rentre le courrier.

The *Passé Composé* of Reflexive Verbs

All reflexive verbs are conjugated with **être** in the *passé composé*.

se lever

je me suis levé(e)	nous nous sommes levé(e)s
tu t'es levé(e)	vous vous êtcs lcvé(c)(s)(es)
il, on s'est levé	ils se sont levés
elle s'est levée	elles se sont levées

The past participle of **s'asseoir** is **assis**.

Agreement of the Past Participle with Reflexive Pronouns

The past participle of a reflexive verb agrees in number and in gender with the reflexive pronoun when it is used as a direct object.

> **Elle s'est lavée.**   *She washed herself.*

Se is the direct object and therefore the past participle agrees.

When the direct object is not the reflexive pronoun, there is no agreement.

> **Elle s'est lavé les mains.**   *She washed her hands.*

Les mains is the direct object and therefore there is no agreement. But if **les mains** is replaced by the object pronoun **les,** the participle will agree with the preceding direct object **les.**

> Elle se **les** est **lavées.**   *She washed them.*

When a reciprocal reflexive verb is in the *passé composé*, there is no agreement if the corresponding non-reflexive verb takes an indirect object.

> Elles **se** sont écrit.   *They wrote to each other.*

In the above sentence, **se** is the indirect object and therefore there is no agreement.

> Ils **se** sont **vus.**   *They saw each other.*

Se is the direct object and therefore there is agreement.

194. Complete the following sentences with the correct form of the *passé composé* of the indicated verb.

1. Elle _____ hier.   *se dépêcher*
2. Il _____ ce matin.   *se raser*
3. Elles _____ hier.   *s'ennuyer*
4. Ils _____ du voyage.   *se souvenir*
5. Je (m.) _____ immédiatement.   *s'asseoir*
6. Je (f.) _____ hier soir.   *se tromper*

7. Tu (m.) _____ à sept heures.   *se réveiller*
8. Tu (f.) _____ les mains.   *se laver*
9. Vous (m. pl.) _____ dans le parc.   *s'amuser*
10. Vous (f. pl.) _____ en bleu.   *s'habiller*
11. Nous (m. pl.) _____ hier soir.   *se reposer*
12. Nous (f. pl.) _____ tout de suite.   *s'endormir*

195.   Rewrite the following sentences in the *passé composé*.

1. Il se débrouille bien.
2. Elle se lève de bonne heure.
3. Nous (f.) nous amusons bien.
4. Hélène et Marie, vous vous trompez.
5. Elles se retrouvent devant le musée.
6. Elle se lave les mains.
7. Ils se brossent les dents.
8. Je (f.) m'assieds devant le feu.
9. Elles se couchent dans le lit.
10. Tu (m.) te réveilles à huit heures.
11. Vous (f. sing.) vous peignez.
12. Je (m.) me trompe.
13. Nous (m.) nous dépêchons.
14. Pierre et Jean, vous vous rasez.
15. Elles se téléphonent.

196.   Write about John and Mary's wedding day. Put the verbs in the *passé composé*.

1. Jean et Marie / se lever / à huit heures
2. Marie / se maquiller avec soin
3. Elle / s'habiller / en blanc
4. Jean / se raser / avec soin
5. Les demoiselles d'honneur / s'habiller / en rose
6. Les placeurs / se dépêcher / pour arriver à l'église à l'heure
7. Les invités / se rencontrer / à l'église
8. Marie et Jean / se marier / à onze heures
9. Tout le monde / se réunir / pour la réception
10. Les invités / se parler / et / ils / s'amuser à la réception

Uses of the Passé Composé

Present Perfect

The passé *composé* is the present perfect tense. The action or condition expressed by the present perfect is either completed in the very recent past or completed in the distant past but still has meaning for the present. The time of the completion is indefinite.

Elles ont été malades.	*They have been sick.*
Ils sont allés à Paris trois fois.	*They went to Paris three times.*
Ils sont revenus de Montréal.	*They came back from Montreal.*

Past Action

The *passé composé* is used to relate what happened at a definite time in the past or what happened next. It is used to indicate an action or a condition that was completed or ended in the past. Some common time expressions that are used with the *passé composé* are:

hier	*yesterday*
avant-hier	*the day before yesterday*
hier soir	*last night*
l'autre jour	*the other day*
un samedi (un dimanche, etc.)	*one Saturday (one Sunday, etc.)*

CHAPTER 5 *Verbs*

161

une fois, deux fois	once, twice
plusieurs fois	several times
quelquefois	sometimes
la semaine dernière (passée)	last week
l'année passée (dernière)	last year

197. Complete the following sentences with the appropriate form of the *passé composé* of the indicated verb.

1. Hier, nous _____ au cinéma. *aller*
2. On _____ la cathédrale au douzième siècle. *bâtir*
3. Elle _____ son ami l'autre jour. *voir*
4. Ils _____ me voir hier soir. *venir*
5. Vous _____ en Europe l'année dernière. *voyager*
6. Elle _____ de bonne heure hier soir. *se coucher*
7. Nous _____ la maison la semaine dernière. *louer*
8. Christophe Colomb _____ les Antilles. *découvrir*
9. Elle _____ cela avant-hier. *dire*
10. Il _____ ce matin. *se raser*

198. When was the last time you did the following?

aller au théâtre
Je suis allé(e) au théâtre hier soir (l'an passé, l'année passée, etc.).

1. manger au restaurant
2. aller au cinéma
3. jouer au tennis
4. faire la cuisine
5. se coucher très tard
6. se réveiller très tard
7. recevoir un cadeau
8. voir ton grand-père

Differences between the *Passé Composé* and the Imperfect Tense

Specific action versus habitual or continuing action

You have already learned the basic uses of the imperfect tense and the *passé composé*. The imperfect tense is used to describe continuing action, habitual action or past action of long duration. The *passé composé* is used to express an action which definitely began and was completed in the past. Even though the action may have taken place in the past for an extended period of time, the *passé composé* is used if the action has been terminated.

Il **a joué** au football **hier.**
Il **jouait** au football **tous les samedis.**

Elle **a parlé une fois** au professeur.
Elle **parlait souvent** au professeur.

199. Rewrite the following, changing **l'autre jour** to **bien des fois.** Make all necessary changes.

1. Elle est venue me voir l'autre jour.
2. Tu l'as vu l'autre jour.
3. Pierre a dit cela l'autre jour.
4. Nous avons reçu des lettres l'autre jour.
5. Vous l'avez appelé l'autre jour.

200. Rewrite the following, changing **tous les ans** to **l'année passée.**

1. Elle venait me voir tous les ans.
2. J'allais à Paris tous les ans.
3. Je voyais Marie tous les ans.
4. Nous voyagions en Europe tous les ans.
5. Elle jouait ce rôle tous les ans.

201. Rewrite the following in either the *passé composé* or the imperfect tense according to the indicated time expression.

     1. Ils ont regardé la télévision hier soir.
         _____ chaque soir.
     2. En ce temps-là, il jouait au tennis.
         L'autre jour _____.
     3. Elle répétait cette phrase bien des fois.
         _____ une fois.
     4. Pierre est venu ici hier.
         _____ tous les dimanches.
     5. Nous allions à ce restaurant tous les samedis.
         _____ samedi dernier.
     6. Hier soir, nous avons discuté politique.
         Souvent _____.
     7. Ta mère était toujours malade.
         _____ pendant deux ans.
     8. Pendant son dernier voyage, elle a payé par cartes de crédit.
         Pendant tous ses voyages, _____.
     9. Nous y sommes allés l'année dernière.
         _____ de temps en temps.
   10. D'habitude, il dormait jusqu'à sept heures.
         Ce matin, _____.

202. Answer the following according to the model. Use the *passé composé* or the imperfect tense.

     Lire le journal?   *Oui, hier*
     Oui, j'ai lu le journal *hier*.

     1. Recevoir la carte?   *Oui, hier*
     2. Habiter à New York?   *Oui, l'année dernière*
     3. Aller au concert?   *Oui, tous les dimanches*
     4. Travailler beaucoup?   *Oui, en ce temps-là*
     5. Dormir beaucoup?   *Oui, hier soir*
     6. Conduire cette auto?   *Oui, toujours*
     7. Nager beaucoup?   *Oui, l'été dernier*
     8. Aller à la plage?   *Oui, la semaine dernière*

203. Write what you did last night, last week and last year, every Saturday, usually, one Saturday.

     1. Hier soir...   4. Tous les samedis...
     2. La semaine dernière...   5. Habituellement...
     3. L'année dernière...   6. Un samedi...

With *souvent, parfois, quelquefois*

Depending on the speaker's point of view, either the *passé composé* or the imperfect can be used with expressions such as **souvent, parfois** or **quelquefois.**

The *passé composé* is used for a series of specific completed actions.

     Je **suis allé souvent** à la campagne.   *I went to the country often (on several occasions).*

The imperfect is used for habitual occurrences.

     J'allais souvent à la campagne.   *I used to go to the country often (on a regular basis).*

204. Say that you did the following things on a regular basis. Then say that you did them often or on several occasions.

> **aller au cinéma**
> **J'allais souvent au cinéma.**
> **Je suis allé(e) souvent au cinéma.**

1. aller au théâtre
2. jouer au tennis
3. lire des romans
4. manger au restaurant
5. faire des excursions à bicyclette

Specific action versus ongoing action

The imperfect tense is used to describe what was taking place and continuing to take place in the past when something else happened. The latter action is expressed in the *passé composé*. If the actions occurred simultaneously, the two actions are in the same tense.

> **Quand je suis arrivé, ils dansaient.**
> *When I arrived, they were dancing.*
> **Elle mangeait quand le téléphone a sonné.**
> *She was eating when the telephone rang.*
> **Pendant que nous dormions, il a neigé.**
> *While we were sleeping, it snowed.*
>
> **Paul est venu et Marie est partie.**
> *Paul came and Mary left.*
> **Les enfants jouaient pendant que leurs parents les regardaient.**
> *The children were playing while their parents were watching them.*

Sometimes the tense will change, depending upon whether the speaker wishes to portray the event as a background condition or something that happened.

> **Un homme a vendu la peinture et l'autre l'a achetée.**
> *One man sold the painting and the other bought it.*
> (Here the speaker is merely reporting what took place.)
>
> **Un homme vendait la peinture et l'autre l'achetait.**
> *One man was selling the painting and the other was buying it.*
> (Here the speaker wishes to describe the background, what was taking place.)
>
> **J'ai eu peur quand le voleur est entré dans la maison.**
> *I became afraid when the thief entered the house.*
> (change in state of mind)
>
> **J'avais peur quand le voleur est entré dans la maison.**
> *I was afraid when the thief entered the house.*
> (description of state of mind)

205. Complete the following sentences with the appropriate form of either the *passé composé* or the imperfect tense of the indicated verbs to show what the people were doing when something else happened.

1. Je _____ quand elle _____ à la porte. *lire, frapper*
2. Elle _____ une promenade quand elle _____ un billet de cent euros sur le trottoir. *faire, découvrir*
3. Elles _____ quand tu _____. *manger, téléphoner*

4. Nous _____ sa connaissance quand nous _____ en Europe.   *faire, être*
5. Marie _____ avec sa mère quand je _____.   *parler, entrer*
6. Je vous _____ quand vous _____ du théâtre.   *voir, sortir*
7. Pendant qu'il _____ son déjeuner, il _____ la mauvaise nouvelle à la radio.   *prendre, entendre*
8. Je _____ quand le téléphone _____.   *dormir, sonner*
9. Elles _____ des élections quand il _____ les résultats.   *discuter, annoncer*
10. Pendant que nous _____ en vacances, des cambrioleurs _____ dans notre maison.   *être, entrer*

206. Complete the following sentences as if you were telling someone what happened.

1. Un homme _____ et un autre _____ du vin.   *manger, boire*
2. La police _____ et le voleur _____.   *entrer, partir*
3. Pierre _____ les valises et Marie _____ les billets.   *faire, prendre*
4. Le bébé _____ et le chien _____.   *pleurer, aboyer*
5. Ma mère _____ le repas pendant que je _____ le couvert.   *préparer, mettre*

207. Rewrite the sentences of the previous exercise as if you were describing to someone what was happening.

208. What were you doing when something else happened?

Le téléphone a sonné.
Je dormais quand le téléphone a sonné.

1. Il a commencé à pleuvoir.
2. Quelqu'un a frappé à la porte.
3. Tu es tombé(e).
4. Tu as entendu le tonnerre.
5. Les lumières se sont éteintes.

Events versus background

The imperfect tense is used to describe the background conditions to an event in the *passé composé*. In other words, the imperfect tense relates the conditions, state of mind or actions that were going on and the *passé composé* relates what happened or what happened next.

Event	*Background or Conditions*
J'ai fait une promenade hier.	**Il faisait beau.**
	J'étais de bonne humeur.
J'ai mangé très vite	**parce que j'avais très faim.**

209. Tell why the following people did certain things. Follow the model.

Roland / aller à la plage / faire beau
Roland est allé à la plage parce qu'il faisait beau.

1. Pierre / aller chez le médecin / être malade
2. Monsieur et Madame Dupont / aller en vacances / avoir besoin de repos
3. Nicole / manger / avoir faim
4. Nous / se dépêcher / être en retard
5. Vous / mettre un imperméable / pleuvoir
6. Tu / nager / vouloir être en forme

210. Rewrite the following story in the past.

> C'est le sept juillet. Il est quatre heures de l'après-midi. Il fait très chaud. Je fais des courses. Pendant que je me promène le long du boulevard, je rencontre mon amie. Nous décidons d'aller chez le bijoutier. Pendant que nous regardons les bracelets et les colliers, un homme entre dans le magasin. Il a à peu près 25 ans. Il a les cheveux noirs. Il porte un pantalon noir, une chemise verte et un masque au visage. Il tire un révolver et il demande de l'argent au caissier. Le caissier a peur et il lui donne de l'argent. Mais heureusement, un autre employé voit le vol et appelle la police. La police arrive et arrête le voleur.

Verbs with different meanings in the imperfect and *passé composé*

Some verbs have different meanings in the imperfect and the *passé composé*.

avoir

Il avait soif.	*He was thirsty.*
Il a eu soif.	*He became thirsty.*

connaître

Elle connaissait ma cousine.	*She knew my cousin.*
Elle a connu ma cousine.	*She met my cousin.*

pouvoir

Je pouvais sortir.	*I could leave* (it was easy for me).
J'ai pu sortir.	*I could leave* (and I did).

savoir

Je savais la réponse.	*I knew the answer.*
J'ai su la réponse.	*I found out the answer.*

vouloir

Elle voulait rester deux semaines.	*She wanted to stay for two weeks.*
Elle a voulu rester deux semaines.	*She tried to stay for two weeks.*
Elle ne voulait pas rester deux semaines.	*She didn't want to stay for two weeks.*
Elle n'a pas voulu rester deux semaines.	*She refused to stay for two weeks.*

211. Write the following sentences in French. Use the verbs **avoir, connaître, pouvoir, savoir** or **vouloir**.

1. Did you know the name of the teacher?
   No, but I found out his name last night.
2. Have you met my husband?
   I already knew him.
3. Did she want to spend the evening at the movies?
   Yes, but she couldn't do it.
4. Did you want to leave at five o'clock?
   No, I didn't want to leave at five o'clock.
5. Did you try to leave at five o'clock?
   No, I refused to leave at five o'clock.
6. I was able to play, but I refused to play that.
7. Were you hungry at three o'clock?
   No, but I became hungry at five o'clock.

Review

212. Rewrite the following sentences in the *passé composé*.

1. Tu parles beaucoup.
2. Elles dorment bien.
3. Ils répondent à la question.
4. Elles suivent les instructions.
5. Elle descend l'escalier.
6. Nous (f.) nous levons de bonne heure.
7. Nous (m.) allons au musée.
8. Elle monte dans le wagon.
9. Nous prenons les billets.
10. Il fait la leçon.
11. Elles montent les bagages.
12. Je reconnais cet homme.
13. Il revient tout de suite.
14. Elles écrivent les devoirs.
15. Elles se promènent dans le parc.
16. Cette peinture me plaît.
17. Vous recevez la lettre.
18. Tu lis le roman.
19. Ils vivent bien ici.
20. Vous peignez ce paysage.
21. Elle ouvre la fenêtre.
22. Voilà les photos que je vous offre.
23. Voilà les pièces que je lis.
24. Elles se débrouillent bien.

213. Answer the questions according to the model.

Te rases-tu aujourd'hui?
Non, mais je me suis rasé hier.

1. Apprends-tu cette leçon aujourd'hui?
2. Veut-il aller au cinéma aujourd'hui?
3. La comprenez-vous aujourd'hui?
4. Vous souvenez-vous de la réponse aujourd'hui?
5. Vaut-il le prix aujourd'hui?
6. Rit-elle aujourd'hui?
7. Souffrez-vous d'un rhume aujourd'hui?
8. Disons-nous la vérité aujourd'hui?
9. Revient-elle à huit heures aujourd'hui?
10. Mettez-vous un imperméable aujourd'hui?
11. Reste-t-il jusqu'à dix heures aujourd'hui?
12. Vois-tu Pierre aujourd'hui?

214. When was the last time you did the following? Use an expression of time such as **samedi, samedi dernier, l'année dernière, la semaine passée,** etc. in your answers. Follow the model.

aller au théâtre
Je suis allé au théâtre l'année dernière.

1. aller au cinéma
2. téléphoner à tes parents
3. danser à la discothèque
4. jouer d'un instrument de musique
5. faire un voyage
6. prendre des vacances

215. Describe a trip you have taken, using the indicated verbs.

faire un voyage
J'ai fait un voyage en Europe.

1. aller
2. partir
3. arriver
4. rester
5. prendre des repas
6. visiter
7. voir
8. acheter
9. revenir

216. Complete the following sentences with the correct form of the *passé composé* or imperfect tense of the indicated verb.

1. Chaque jour, Pierre _____ à la Faculté de Médecine où il _____ aux cours d'anatomie et où il _____ ses amis.   *aller, assister, voir*
2. Samedi dernier, nous _____ de bonne heure. Nous _____ et ensuite, nous _____ le reste de la journée à nous amuser.   *se lever, travailler, passer*
3. D'habitude, Monsieur Leroi _____ au bureau en métro. Il _____ huit heures par jour et ensuite, il _____ à la maison pour revoir sa famille.   *aller, travailler, rentrer*
4. Hier soir, ils _____ aux cartes, ils _____ la télévision, ils _____ des CD et ensuite, ils _____.   *jouer, regarder, écouter, se coucher*
5. Bien des fois, nous _____ notre temps pour aller à l'école et nous _____ en route.   *prendre, s'amuser*
6. L'année passée, nous _____ un voyage en Europe où nous _____ des monuments historiques et où nous _____.   *faire, voir, s'amuser*

217. Rewrite the following paragraph, putting the verbs in the imperfect or *passé composé*.

Il est sept heures du matin. Je vais dans les montagnes parce que je veux faire du ski. Il fait froid et il fait du vent mais le soleil brille. Je porte un beau costume de ski. J'arrive au chalet. J'achète mon billet pour les remonte-pentes et je fais la queue pour monter la montagne. Je remarque qu'il y a beaucoup de monde sur les pistes de ski. Je monte. Je descends. Je suis très content(e). Je sais bien faire du ski. Mais malheureusement, à la quatrième descente, je tombe. Je me casse la jambe. On m'emmène à l'hôpital où on met ma jambe dans du plâtre. La journée qui commence bien finit mal.

218. Complete the following sentences to say what happened when you were doing the following.

Je lisais un roman quand...
Je lisais un roman quand le téléphone a sonné.

1. Je dormais quand...
2. Je faisais mes devoirs quand...
3. Je parlais au téléphone quand...
4. J'allais à la bibliothèque quand...
5. Je regardais la télévision quand...

219. Rewrite the following paragraph in the past. Put the verbs in the imperfect or the *passé composé*.

Anne a de la chance. Elle passe l'été chez une famille française qui habite dans la banlieue de Paris. Elle fait ses valises une semaine à l'avance. Le jour de son départ, elle se réveille tôt parce qu'elle ne peut pas dormir. Pour le petit déjeuner, elle prend seulement des rôties et elle boit un peu de café. Pour le déjeuner elle mange seulement un sandwich. L'après-midi, elle prend l'avion pour Paris. Le voyage semble être long. La famille avec qui elle va vivre la rencontre à l'aéroport. Elle passe un été formidable avec cette famille française. Elle s'entend bien avec la fille de la famille. Toutes les deux font beaucoup de choses ensemble. Elles font des promenades dans le jardin du Luxembourg; elles voient les monuments historiques; elles montent la tour Eiffel; elles regardent les peintures au Louvre et au musée d'Orsay; elles prennent des repas formidables dans de bons restaurants; elles font les courses. Anne s'achète un beau chandail et une robe. La robe qu'elle achète est très chic. Tous les samedis les deux filles sortent avec un groupe d'amis et ils s'amusent à la discothèque. C'est un été formidable.

220. Tell about your day last Saturday. Choose from the verbs in the list below and put them in the *passé composé* or the imperfect.

se réveiller	rencontrer des amis
se lever	se promener
avoir soif, faim	aller au cinéma
prendré... pour le petit déjeuner	manger au restaurant
boire	danser toute la nuit
s'habiller	être fatigué(e)
se raser / se maquiller	se coucher

Je me suis réveillé(e) à... heures.

Continue.

The Literary Past Tense (Passé Simple)

The *passé simple* or literary past tense is a past tense that designates a completed action in the past with no relation to the present tense. The *passé simple* is used in literary contexts whereas the *passé composé* is used in conversation and in informal writing.

The *Passé Simple* of *-er* Verbs

The *passé simple* of regular **-er** verbs is formed by dropping the **-er** ending from the infinitive and adding the endings **-ai, -as, -a, -âmes, -âtes, -èrent.** Note that some **-er** verbs that are irregular in the present tense are regular in the *passé simple*.

parler	aller
je parl**ai**	j'all**ai**
tu parl**as**	tu all**as**
il, elle, on parl**a**	il, elle, on all**a**
nous parl**âmes**	nous all**âmes**
vous parl**âtes**	vous all**âtes**
ils, elles parl**èrent**	ils, elles all**èrent**

Remember that **-cer** verbs add a cedilla to the **c** before the vowel **a** and that **-ger** verbs add **e** before the vowel **a.**

commencer	**il commença**
manger	**il mangea**

221. Rewrite the following sentences in the *passé simple*.

1. On a publié le livre en 1973.
2. On a brûlé Jeanne d'Arc en 1431 à Rouen.
3. Tu as acheté ce CD.
4. Tu as appelé ton père.
5. J'ai emmené mes amis avec moi.
6. J'ai envoyé le télégramme.
7. Nous sommes allés à Paris.
8. Nous avons trouvé ce livre.
9. Vous avez célébré la fête.
10. Vous êtes arrivées à l'heure.
11. Les Américains ont débarqué en Normandie en 1944.
12. Ils ont commencé la construction de la cathédrale en 1150.

222. Rewrite the following sentences in the *passé composé*.

1. Il chercha son père.
2. Nous donnâmes de l'argent à nos amis.
3. Elles méditèrent sur l'avenir.
4. Je frappai à la porte.
5. Vous devinâtes les résultats.
6. Tu montas vite.
7. Nous comptâmes notre argent.
8. Ils marchèrent dans les rues désertes.
9. Je retournai chez moi.
10. Elle alla à l'église.

The *Passé Simple* of *-ir* and *-re* Verbs

To form the *passé simple* of **-ir** and **-re** verbs, the endings **-is, -is, -it, -îmes, -îtes, -irent** are added to the infinitive stem.

finir	attendre
je fin**is**	j'attend**is**
tu fin**is**	tu attend**is**
il, elle, on fin**it**	il, elle, on attend**it**
nous fin**îmes**	nous attend**îmes**
vous fin**îtes**	vous attend**îtes**
ils, elles fin**irent**	ils, elles attend**irent**

Note that the singular forms of the present tense and the *passé simple* are identical for regular **-ir** verbs.

223. Complete the following sentences with the correct form of the *passé simple* of the indicated verb.

1. Christophe Colomb _____ le Nouveau Monde.   *découvrir*
2. Elle _____ sa mère.   *attendre*
3. Tu _____ la salle.   *embellir*
4. Tu _____ tes amis.   *défendre*
5. J'_____ les acteurs.   *applaudir*
6. Je _____ tout de suite.   *partir*
7. Nous _____ le fil.   *perdre*
8. Nous _____ la lecture.   *finir*
9. Vous _____ à l'examen.   *réussir*
10. Vous _____ des fleurs.   *vendre*
11. Ils _____ des chemises.   *choisir*
12. Elles _____ aux questions.   *répondre*

224. Rewrite the following sentences in the *passé composé*.

1. Ils découvrirent la vérité.
2. Nous réfléchîmes aux problèmes.
3. Il agrandit le palais.
4. Vous répandîtes la nouvelle.
5. Je vendis des timbres.
6. Tu rendis tes devoirs.
7. Elles finirent leurs devoirs.
8. Vous descendîtes le boulevard.

Irregular Verbs Building the *Passé Simple* upon the Past Participle

For most irregular verbs, the stem for the *passé simple* is the past participle. The endings **-s, -s, -t, -^mes, -^tes, -rent** are added to this stem.

Verbs with past participles ending in -*i*

The *passé simple* of many irregular verbs whose infinitive ends in **-ir** or **-re** is formed by adding the endings **-s, -s, -t, -^mes, -^tes, -rent** to the past participle. Note that they are like **finir** in the *passé simple*.

Infinitive	Past participle	Passé simple
dormir	dormi	**je dormis, nous dormîmes**
mentir	menti	**je mentis, nous mentîmes**
partir	parti	**je partis, nous partîmes**
sentir	senti	**je sentis, nous sentîmes**
servir	servi	**je servis, nous servîmes**
sortir	sorti	**je sortis, nous sortîmes**
rire	ri	**je ris, nous rîmes**
sourire	souri	**je souris, nous sourîmes**
suffire	suffi	**je suffis, nous suffîmes**
suivre	suivi	**je suivis, nous suivîmes**

Verbs with past participles ending in -*i* plus a consonant

The final consonant of the past participle of these verbs is replaced by the endings **-s, -s, -t, -^mes, -^tes, -rent**.

Infinitive	Past participle	Passé simple
acquérir	acquis	**j'acquis, nous acquîmes**
dire	dit	**je dis, nous dîmes**
mettre	mis	**je mis, nous mîmes**
prendre (and its derivatives)	pris	**je pris, nous prîmes**

225. Rewrite the following sentences in the *passé simple*.

1. Elle a suivi la route.
2. Tu es parti.
3. Je suis sortie.
4. Nous avons menti.
5. Vous avez dormi huit heures.
6. Ils ont ri aux éclats.
7. Elle a acquis les peintures.
8. J'ai mis le couvert.
9. Tu as dit la vérité.
10. Nous avons pris le déjeuner.
11. Vous avez appris la vérité.
12. Ils ont compris la situation.

226. Rewrite the following sentences in the *passé composé*.

1. Nous sortîmes ce soir-là.
2. Elle suivit la route pour Dijon.
3. Elles prirent les livres.
4. Vous mîtes votre manteau.
5. Tu servis un bon repas.
6. Je souris en entrant.

Verbs with past participles ending in -*u*

<table>
<tr><td colspan="2" align="center">**pouvoir**</td></tr>
<tr><td align="right">je **pus**</td><td align="right">nous **pûmes**</td></tr>
<tr><td align="right">tu **pus**</td><td align="right">vous **pûtes**</td></tr>
<tr><td align="right">il, elle, on **put**</td><td align="right">ils, elles **purent**</td></tr>
</table>

<table>
<tr><td colspan="2" align="center">**avoir**</td></tr>
<tr><td align="right">j'**eus**</td><td align="right">nous **eûmes**</td></tr>
<tr><td align="right">tu **eus**</td><td align="right">vous **eûtes**</td></tr>
<tr><td align="right">il, elle, on **eut**</td><td align="right">ils, elles **eurent**</td></tr>
</table>

Pouvoir and avoir can be used as a pattern for the following verbs.

Infinitive	Past participle	Passé simple
avoir	eu	j'eus, nous eûmes
boire	bu	je bus, nous bûmes
connaître	connu	je connus, nous connûmes
courir	couru	je courus, nous courûmes
croire	cru	je crus, nous crûmes
devoir	dû	je dus, nous dûmes
lire	lu	je lus, nous lûmes
paraître	paru	je parus, nous parûmes
plaire	plu	je plus, nous plûmes
pouvoir	pu	je pus, nous pûmes
recevoir	reçu	je reçus, nous reçûmes
savoir	su	je sus, nous sûmes
se taire	tu	je me tus, nous nous tûmes
valoir	valu	je valus, nous valûmes
vivre	vécu	je vécus, nous vécûmes
vouloir	voulu	je voulus, nous voulûmes

227. Rewrite the following sentences in the *passé simple*.

1. Elle a bu trop de vin.
2. Il a vite couru.
3. Tu as voulu venir.
4. Tu as pu le faire.
5. J'ai cru l'histoire.
6. J'ai reconnu cet homme.
7. Nous avons lu *les Misérables*.
8. Nous avons reçu la lettre.
9. Vous avez dû travailler.
10. Vous avez eu des difficultés.
11. Ce livre a paru chez un grand éditeur.
12. Ils ont vécu à Londres.

228. Complete the following sentences with the correct form of the *passé simple* of the indicated verb.

1. Nous _____ trop de café.   *boire*
2. Elles nous _____.   *reconnaître*
3. Tu _____ la carte.   *recevoir*
4. Je _____ à New York.   *vivre*
5. Vous _____ l'histoire.   *lire*
6. Ils _____ venir.   *pouvoir*
7. Elle _____ à tout le monde.   *plaire*
8. Nous _____ le professeur.   *croire*

Irregular Verbs not Building the *Passé Simple* upon the Past Participle

Some verbs add the endings -s, -s, -t, -^mes, -^tes, -rent to an irregular stem. Note that all contain the vowel i except **mourir, être, venir** and **tenir**.

Infinitive	Past participle	Passé simple
battre	battu	je battis, nous battîmes
rompre	rompu	je rompis, nous rompîmes
offrir	offert	j'offris, nous offrîmes
ouvrir	ouvert	j'ouvris, nous ouvrîmes
couvrir	couvert	je couvris, nous couvrîmes
souffrir	souffert	je souffris, nous souffrîmes
vaincre	vaincu	je vainquis, nous vainquîmes

écrire	écrit	**j'écrivis, nous écrivîmes**
conduire	conduit	**je conduisis, nous conduisîmes**
traduire	traduit	**je traduisis, nous traduisîmes**
naître	né	**je naquis, nous naquîmes**
voir	vu	**je vis, nous vîmes**
craindre	craint	**je craignis, nous craignîmes**
joindre	joint	**je joignis, nous joignîmes**
peindre	peint	**je peignis, nous peignîmes**
faire	fait	**je fis, nous fîmes**
mourir	mort	**je mourus, nous mourûmes**
être	été	**je fus, nous fûmes**
tenir	tenu	**je tins, nous tînmes**
venir	venu	**je vins, nous vînmes**

229. Complete the following sentences with the correct form of the *passé simple* of the indicated verb.

1. Elle _____ les liens. *rompre*
2. Nous _____ le tapis. *battre*
3. Vous _____ du vin. *offrir*
4. Il _____ à la gare. *conduire*
5. Ils _____ le roman. *traduire*
6. Tu _____ tes amis. *convaincre*
7. Nous _____ une lettre. *écrire*
8. Victor Hugo _____ en 1802. *naître*
9. Vous _____ vos copains. *voir*
10. L'artiste _____ le portrait. *peindre*
11. Vous _____ l'examen final. *craindre*
12. Nous _____ nos amis. *rejoindre*
13. Il _____ de son mieux. *faire*
14. Nous _____ du tennis. *faire*
15. Je _____ content. *être*
16. Ils _____ malades. *être*
17. Albert Camus _____ dans un accident. *mourir*
18. Il _____ de Paris. *venir*
19. Nous _____ une chambre à l'hôtel. *retenir*
20. Elles _____ ce soir. *revenir*

230. Rewrite the following sentences in the *passé composé*.

1. Il traduisit le livre.
2. Ils écrivirent des romans.
3. Il fut roi de France.
4. Je vins te voir.
5. Elles rejoignirent leurs amis.
6. Ils vinrent de Paris.
7. Nous ouvrîmes la porte.
8. Vous souffrîtes beaucoup.
9. Elle naquit à Paris.
10. Nous vîmes le film.

Review

231. What did the following people do? Rewrite the following sentences in the *passé composé*.

1. Samuel de Champlain fonda Québec en 1608.
2. Pierre et Marie Curie découvrirent le radium.
3. Edgar Degas peignit des portraits et des scènes de danse.
4. Napoléon vainquit l'ennemi dans beaucoup de batailles.

5. Albert Camus mourut dans un accident de voiture.
6. Le peuple de Paris détruisit la Bastille.
7. Charles de Gaulle fut président de la Cinquième République.
8. Le Corbusier fit bâtir beaucoup de bâtiments célèbres.
9. Jean Anouilh écrivit *Antigone*.
10. Louis XIV devint roi de France en 1643.

232. Tell the story of Evangeline, putting the verbs in the *passé simple*.

Longfellow / écrire / l'histoire d'Évangéline.
Longfellow écrivit l'histoire d'Évangéline.

1. Les Acadiens / être / agriculteurs
2. Un fermier, Bénédict Bellefontaine, / avoir / une fille
3. La fille / s'appeler / Évangéline
4. Évangéline / tomber amoureuse / de Gabriel Lajeunesse
5. Mais elle / ne pas épouser / Gabriel
6. Les Anglais / chasser / les Acadiens de leur pays
7. Ils / brûler / leurs maisons
8. Ils / déporter / les Acadiens
9. Évangéline / essayer / de retrouver Gabriel
10. Un jour/ en Pennsylvanie, elle / aller/ dans un hôpital pour soigner les malades
11. Là, / elle / retrouver / Gabriel, vieux et malade
12. Gabriel / mourir / et il / partir / de la vie d'Évangéline pour toujours

The Future

Aller with an Infinitive

The immediate future can be expressed by using the verb **aller** with an infinitive. This is the equivalent of the English *to be going to*.

Je vais travailler ici.
I am going to work here.
Nous allons nous reposer.
We are going to rest.
Ils vont venir à sept heures.
They are going to come at seven o'clock.

233. Complete the following sentences with the appropriate form of the verb **aller**.

1. Je _____ partir demain.
2. Nous _____ faire du ski.
3. Qui _____ mettre le couvert?
4. Vous _____ nager dans la mer.
5. Elles _____ faire le repas.
6. Tu _____ voyager en avion.

234. Rewrite the following sentences in the future, using **aller** with the infinitive.

1. Nous faisons les valises.
2. Je regarde la télévision.
3. Elle parle au professeur.
4. Vous sortez de bonne heure.
5. Ils habitent à New York.
6. Tu viens tout de suite.
7. Nous buvons du café.
8. Vous lisez le journal.
9. Il sait les résultats.
10. Vous finissez le travail.

235. Say what you and your friends are going to do. Complete the following. Use **aller** + an infinitive.

    1. Demain, je...
    2. Dans trois heures, je...
    3. Cet après-midi, mon ami(e) et moi, nous...
    4. Ce soir, mes ami(e)s...

Regular Forms of the Future Tense

The future tense of most verbs is formed by adding **-ai, -as, -a, -ons, -ez, -ont** to the infinitive. The final **-e** of **-re** verbs is dropped before adding the future endings. The future tense is used as in English to express an event or describe a condition that will take place in the future.

parler	**finir**	**attendre**
je parler**ai**	je finir**ai**	j'attendr**ai**
tu parler**as**	tu finir**as**	tu attendr**as**
il, elle, on parler**a**	il, elle, on finir**a**	il, elle, on attendr**a**
nous parler**ons**	nous finir**ons**	nous attendr**ons**
vous parler**ez**	vous finir**ez**	vous attendr**ez**
ils, elles parler**ont**	ils, elles finir**ont**	ils, elles attendr**ont**

Note that the second and third person singular forms sound alike; the first person singular and the second person plural sound alike; and the first and third person plurals sound alike. The forms are all spelled differently, however.

For **-er** verbs, if the infinitive stem ends in two pronounced consonants, the **e** is pronounced.

    je parl_e_rai

If the stem ends in one pronounced consonant, the **e** is not pronounced.

    je dîn_e_rai

236. Complete the following sentences with the correct form of the future tense of the indicated verb.

    1. Il _____ du problème avec nous. *discuter*
    2. Elle _____ à l'heure. *finir*
    3. Tu _____ les livres. *vendre*
    4. Tu _____ de cela plus tard. *parler*
    5. Je _____ du bifteck ce soir. *manger*
    6. Je _____ la tasse de café. *remplir*
    7. Vous _____ aux lois. *obéir*
    8. Vous _____ à la question demain. *répondre*
    9. Nous _____ tous par hélicoptère dans cinquante ans. *voyager*
    10. Nous _____ les instructions. *suivre*
    11. Ils _____ de bonne heure. *se réveiller*
    12. Elles _____ leurs devoirs demain. *rendre*

237. Say what the people are going to do. Rewrite the following sentences in the future tense.

    1. Nous allons regarder la télévision.
    2. Vous allez étudier davantage.
    3. Je vais écrire des cartes postales.
    4. Il va plaire à cette fille.
    5. Elles vont dormir huit heures.
    6. L'artiste va peindre un portrait.
    7. Tu vas conduire prudemment.
    8. Elle va dire la vérité.
    9. Elles vont rejoindre leurs amis.
    10. Vous allez suivre les instructions.
    11. Je vais prendre le déjeuner à midi.
    12. Elle va se coucher à dix heures.

Verbs Using the Third Person Singular Form of the Present Tense as the Future Stem

Some verbs use the third person singular form of the present tense rather than the infinitive as the future stem.

Verbs ending in *-yer*

Infinitive	Base	Future
employer	il emploie	j'emploierai, nous emploierons
ennuyer	il ennuie	j'ennuierai, nous ennuierons
essayer	il essaie	j'essaierai, nous essaierons
essuyer	il essuie	j'essuierai, nous essuierons
nettoyer	il nettoie	je nettoierai, nous nettoierons
payer	il paie	je paierai, nous paierons

Verbs with *-e-* in the infinitive

Infinitive	Base	Future
acheter	il achète	j'achèterai, nous achèterons
lever	il lève	je lèverai, nous lèverons
mener	il mène	je mènerai, nous mènerons
peser	il pèse	je pèserai, nous pèserons
appeler	il appelle	j'appellerai, nous appellerons
jeter	il jette	je jetterai, nous jetterons

238. Rewrite the following sentences in the future tense.

1. Elle nettoie sa chambre.
2. Il paie ses dettes.
3. Elle essaie de partir.
4. Il ennuie ses amis.
5. On achète des bonbons.
6. Elle mène une vie tranquille.
7. Elle lève le rideau.
8. Il appelle ses amis.
9. Elle jette la lettre dans la corbeille.

239. Complete the following sentences with the correct form of the future tense of the indicated verb.

1. Nous _____ la salle. *nettoyer*
2. Vous _____ vos amis au téléphone. *appeler*
3. Ils _____ les enfants au cinéma. *emmener*
4. Je _____ les fruits. *peser*
5. Tu _____ la tache. *enlever*
6. Elle _____ cette viande. *jeter*
7. Il _____ du pain. *acheter*
8. Nous _____ de faire ce travail. *essayer*

240. Write what chores the family members will do.

Maman / acheter / les provisions au supermarché
Maman achètera les provisions au supermarché.

1. Maman / payer / les factures
2. Papa / jeter / les ordures
3. Les enfants / nettoyer / leur chambre
4. Anne / acheter / du pain à l'épicerie
5. Maman / enlever / la tache sur le divan
6. Elle / employer / un nouveau produit pour l'enlever

7. Papa / emmener / le chien chez le vétérinaire
8. Ma sœur / appeler / une amie pour l'inviter à dîner
9. Nous / essayer / de finir nos tâches avant six heures.

Verbs with Irregular Future Stems

Some verbs have completely irregular future stems to which the regular future endings are added.

Infinitive	*Future*
cueillir	**je cueillerai, nous cueillerons**
s'asseoir	**je m'assiérai, nous nous assiérons**
aller	**j'irai, nous irons**
avoir	**j'aurai, nous aurons**
être	**je serai, nous serons**
faire	**je ferai, nous ferons**
savoir	**je saurai, nous saurons**
falloir	**il faudra**
valoir	**je vaudrai, nous vaudrons**
vouloir	**je voudrai, nous voudrons**
apercevoir	**j'apercevrai, nous apercevrons**
décevoir	**je décevrai, nous décevrons**
devoir	**je devrai, nous devrons**
pleuvoir	**il pleuvra**
recevoir	**je recevrai, nous recevrons**
courir	**je courrai, nous courrons**
secourir	**je secourrai, nous secourrons**
mourir	**je mourrai, nous mourrons**
pouvoir	**je pourrai, nous pourrons**
voir	**je verrai, nous verrons**
envoyer	**j'enverrai, nous enverrons**
tenir (and its derivatives)	**je tiendrai, nous tiendrons**
venir (and its derivatives)	**je viendrai, nous viendrons**

241. Complete the following sentences with the correct form of the future tense of the indicated verb.

1. Elles _____ des fleurs.   *cueillir*
2. Ils _____ à table.   *s'asseoir*
3. Nous _____ à Paris.   *aller*
4. Il _____ besoin d'une voiture.   *avoir*
5. Vous _____ à l'heure.   *être*
6. Nous le _____ exprès.   *faire*
7. Vous _____ le poème par cœur   *savoir*
8. Il _____ le faire.   *falloir*
9. Il _____ mieux vous coucher maintenant.   *valoir*
10. Nous _____ lire ce livre.   *vouloir*
11. Nous _____ quelque chose d'étrange ici.   *apercevoir*
12. Il _____ ses amis.   *décevoir*
13. Tu _____ partir.   *devoir*
14. Il _____ à verse.   *pleuvoir*
15. Elle _____ une lettre demain.   *recevoir*
16. Tu _____ à la maison.   *courir*
17. Elles _____ les pauvres.   *secourir*
18. Il _____ à l'hôpital.   *mourir*

19. Elle _____ jouer ce rôle. *pouvoir*
20. Ils _____ leurs amis ce soir. *voir*
21. Tu _____ la lettre par avion. *envoyer*
22. Elles _____ avec nous. *venir*
23. Il _____ sa place. *retenir*
24. Nous _____ demain. *revenir*

242. Follow the model.

A-t-elle reçu une invitation?
Non, mais la prochaine fois, elle recevra une invitation.

1. Ont-ils pu finir à l'heure?	13. Avez-vous fait de votre mieux?
2. Avez-vous fait le voyage en avion?	14. As-tu cueilli des fleurs?
3. Ont-ils su la vérité?	15. Ont-ils été à l'heure?
4. Êtes-vous allé voir ce film?	16. As-tu voulu sortir?
5. A-t-il eu confiance en son ami?	17. A-t-il fallu le faire?
6. As-tu envoyé la lettre par avion?	18. As-tu dû le faire?
7. A-t-elle vu Pierre?	19. Avez-vous aperçu l'incendie?
8. Avez-vous retenu une chambre?	20. Vous êtes-vous assis au premier rang?
9. Est-elle venue avec André?	21. A-t-il plu?
10. A-t-il reçu une bonne note?	22. Est-il mort hier?
11. Avez-vous secouru les pauvres?	23. Avez-vous couru?
12. A-t-il valu la peine d'y aller?	

243. Your family is taking a trip to France. Say what you and your family will do there. Form sentences from the following and use the future tense in your sentences. Follow the model.

Ma famille / faire / un voyage en France
Ma famille fera un voyage en France.

1. Ma famille / partir / le 22 juin
2. Elle / prendre / le vol 476 sur Air France
3. Nous / être / en France pendant un mois
4. D'abord / nous / aller / à Paris
5. Ma sœur / faire / des courses sur le boulevard Haussmann
6. Mon petit frère / courir / dans le jardin du Luxembourg
7. Mes parents / regarder / les peintures au Louvre et au musée d'Orsay.
8. Nous / aller/ au théâtre plusieurs fois
9. Je / faire / une excursion aux châteaux de la Loire
10. Nous / pouvoir / aller en Normandie pour visiter le Mont Saint-Michel
11. Il / valoir / la peine d'y aller
12. Nous / avoir / aussi l'occasion d'aller en Provence
13. Je / envoyer / beaucoup de cartes postales à mes ami(e)s
14. Malheureusement, nous / devoir / rentrer avant la fin du mois de juillet

Special Uses of the Future Tense

After certain conjunctions

The future tense is used after the following conjunctions when the verb of the main clause is in the future tense. The future time is implied in the dependent clause. Note that the present tense is often used in English.

quand
lorsque } *when*
au moment où

dès que
aussitôt que }   *as soon as*

pendant que
tandis que }   *while (at the same time as)*

Quand
Lorsque
Au moment où }   **Pierre arrivera, je le verrai.**

When Peter arrives, I will see him.

Je le verrai { quand / lorsqu' / au moment où } **il arrivera.**

I will see him when he arrives.

**Dès que
Aussitôt que** } **vous viendrez, nous dînerons.**

As soon as you come, we will eat dinner.

Nous dînerons { **dès que / aussitôt que** } **vous viendrez.**

We will eat as soon as you come.

**Pendant que
Tandis que** } **le garçon jouera de la guitare, les filles chanteront.**

While the boy plays the guitar, the girls will sing.

Le garçon jouera de la guitare { **pendant que / tandis que** } **les filles chanteront.**

The boy will play the guitar while the girls sing.

The verb will also be in the future tense after these conjunctions with an imperative that refers to an action that will take place in the future.

Dites-moi quand il arrivera.
Tell me when he will arrive.
Parlez à Jean dès qu'il arrivera.
Speak to John as soon as he arrives.

If the action is habitual, the present tense is used after these conjunctions.

Tous les jours je le vois quand il part pour l'école.
Every day I see him when he leaves for school.

244. Complete the following sentences with the correct form of the future tense of the indicated verb.

    1. Quand il _____, nous _____. *arriver, manger*
    2. Lorsque je _____ Paul, je lui _____ le livre. *voir, donner*
    3. Dès qu'il _____ le travail, je le _____. *finir, payer*
    4. Aussitôt que nous _____, nous _____. *terminer, sortir*
    5. Tandis que l'enfant _____, je _____ le journal. *dormir, lire*
    6. Pendant que les garçons _____ la cuisine, les filles _____ le couvert. *faire, mettre*
    7. Téléphonez-moi quand vous _____ venir. *pouvoir*
    8. Payez quand vous _____. *vouloir*
    9. Écrivez-moi une carte quand vous _____ en Europe. *voyager*
    10. Nous _____ au moment où nos amis _____. *partir, arriver*

245. Say what the following people will be able to do and when. Use the cues provided.

    Il veut avoir de l'argent pour pouvoir faire un voyage en France.   ***Quand***
    Quand il aura de l'argent, il pourra faire un voyage en France.

    1. Il veut être astronaute pour aller à la lune.   *Quand*
    2. Marie veut obtenir son doctorat pour enseigner à l'université.   *Dès que*
    3. Nous voulons réussir à nos examens pour travailler.   *Aussitôt que*
    4. Elle veut être présidente pour changer le système.   *Dès que*
    5. Elle veut devenir médecin pour découvrir un nouveau médicament contre le cancer.   *Quand*
    6. Il veut avoir de l'argent pour aller en Europe.   *Dès que*
    7. Elle veut le voir pour lui dire « Bon anniversaire. »   *Lorsque*

After *penser que, savoir que, espérer que, ne pas savoir si* and in indirect discourse

    The present or future tense can be used after **penser que, savoir que, espérer que, ne pas savoir si** and in indirect discourse when the main clause is in the present.

    Je pense qu'il viendra.
    Je pense qu'il vient.

    Je sais qu'il viendra.
    Je sais qu'il vient.

    J'espère qu'il viendra.
    J'espère qu'il vient.

    Je ne sais pas s'il viendra.
    Je ne sais pas s'il vient.

    The future tense is also used in indirect discourse to express a future action when the main clause is in the present tense.

    Il dit qu'il viendra.
    He says he will come.
    Il me demande si nous irons au théâtre.
    He asks me whether we will go to the theater.

246. Rewrite the following sentences, putting the second verb in the future tense.

    1. Je pense qu'elle étudie.   4. Je crois qu'ils viennent.
    2. Je sais qu'il vient.   5. Je ne sais pas s'il veut y aller.
    3. J'espère que nous arrivons à l'heure.   6. Je ne sais pas si elle peut venir.

247. Follow the model.

> **Elle dit qu'elle va venir.**
> **Elle dit qu'elle viendra.**

    1. Il dit qu'il va sortir.
    2. Elle dit qu'elle va pouvoir le faire.
    3. Elles disent qu'elles vont travailler.
    4. Ils disent qu'ils vont savoir le poème par cœur.

248. Complete the sentences, using verbs in the future tense.

    1. Mon ami(e) dit que (qu')...   3. Mes ami(e)s disent que...
    2. Je dis que...

To express probability

    In familiar conversational French, the future is sometimes used to express supposition or probability, particularly with **avoir** or **être.** Since these forms are used in conversation, the meaning is often conveyed by intonation. The future of probability is never used out of context.

> J'entends la radio. Il **sera** à la maison.
> *I hear the radio. He must be at home.*
> Il court vite. Il **aura** froid.
> *He is running fast. He must be cold.*
> Elle ne mange pas. Elle **sera** malade.
> *She does not eat. She must be sick.*

249. Complete the following sentences with the correct form of the future tense of the indicated verb.

    1. Il _____ à la maison. Je vois de la lumière.   *être*
    2. Il n'est pas au bureau aujourd'hui. Il _____ malade.   *être*
    3. Il _____ faim. Il en a l'air.   *avoir*
    4. Ils courent. Ils _____ peur.   *avoir*

250. Rewrite the following sentences, using the future of probability.

    1. Elle n'est pas dans sa chambre. Elle est (probablement) avec Pierre.
    2. Regardez ce qu'ils achètent. Ils ont (probablement) de l'argent à jeter.
    3. Comme elle court! Elle a (probablement) peur.
    4. Elles viennent me voir. Elles ont (probablement) besoin de moi.
    5. Elle ne mange pas. Elle est (probablement) malade.

251. Translate the following sentences, using the future tense.

    1. He must be afraid.   3. He must be sick.
    2. He is probably home.   4. She must be cold.

Review

252. Complete the following sentences with the correct form of the future tense of the indicated verb.

    1. Elles _____ devant le cinéma.   *attendre*
    2. Il _____ trois heures.   *être*
    3. Quand il _____, nous _____ le travail.   *venir, faire*

4. Aussitôt qu'elles _____, nous _____ au cinéma.   *venir, aller*
5. Elle _____ la chambre bientôt. *nettoyer*
6. Vous _____ une vie tranquille ici.   *mener*
7. Tu _____ à cette question.   *réfléchir*
8. Elle _____ vous aider.   *savoir*
9. Ils _____ leurs amis samedi prochain.   *voir*
10. Nous _____ le faire.   *pouvoir*
11. Elle _____ besoin de ce livre.   *avoir*
12. Il _____ le faire.   *falloir*
13. Nous _____ à table.   *s'asseoir*
14. Ils _____ de faim.   *mourir*
15. Vous _____ voir ce film.   *vouloir*

253. Form sentences in the future to show the predictions about the students in the yearbook.

Marie / être pilote / aller partout dans le monde.
Marie sera pilote. Elle ira partout dans le monde.

1. Pierre / gagner à la loterie / acheter une villa
2. Anne / devenir millionnaire / faire le tour du monde
3. Nicole / être chirurgienne / savoir guérir les gens malades
4. Martine et Sylvie / découvrir un remède contre le cancer / obtenir le prix Nobel
5. Monique / se marier / avoir trois enfants
6. Georges et Nicole / être astronautes / pouvoir voyager en fusée
7. Tu / courir dans le marathon / recevoir une médaille d'or
8. Nous / pouvoir voyager partout / voir beaucoup de sites historiques
9. Vous / être écrivain / écrire un roman
10. Paul / aller habiter à la campagne / mener une vie tranquille

254. Tell what you are going to do next Saturday. Choose from the verbs in the list below and put them in the future.

se réveiller	rencontrer des ami(e)s
se lever	se promener
prendre... pour le petit déjeuner	aller au cinéma
lire le journal	manger au restaurant
s'habiller	danser toute la nuit
se raser / se maquiller	être fatigué(e)
avoir du temps pour voir mes ami(e)s	se coucher

255. Complete the following with as many personalized answers as you can. Use the future tense.

L'année prochaine,...
L'année prochaine, je suivrai un cours d'histoire.
Dans 100 ans,...
Dans 100 ans, le monde sera différent.

1. Demain, je (j')...
2. L'année prochaine,...
3. Dans dix ans,...
4. Dans 20 ans,...
5. Dans 50 ans,...
6. Quand il fera beau,...
7. Quand il pleuvra,...
8. Lorsque j'aurai beaucoup d'argent,...
9. Mes ami(e)s disent que...
10. Je sais que...

The Conditional

Formation of the Present Conditional

The present conditional is formed by adding the endings **-ais, -ais, -ait, -ions, -iez, -aient** to the future stem of the verb. Note that the endings are the same as those for the imperfect tense.

parler	finir	attendre
je parler**ais**	je finir**ais**	j'attendr**ais**
tu parler**ais**	tu finir**ais**	tu attendr**ais**
il, elle, on parler**ait**	il, elle, on finir**ait**	il, elle, on attendr**ait**
nous parler**ions**	nous finir**ions**	nous attendr**ions**
vous parler**iez**	vous finir**iez**	vous attendr**iez**
ils, elles parler**aient**	ils, elles finir**aient**	ils, elles attendr**aient**

Verbs that have irregular stems in the future tense have the same irregular stem in the conditional.

Infinitive	*Conditional*
employer	**j'emploierais, nous emploierions**
acheter	**j'achèterais, nous achèterions**
appeler	**j'appellerais, nous appellerions**
cueillir	**je cueillerais, nous cueillerions**
s'asseoir	**je m'assiérais, nous nous assiérions**
aller	**j'irais, nous irions**
avoir	**j'aurais, nous aurions**
être	**je serais, nous serions**
faire	**je ferais, nous ferions**
savoir	**je saurais, nous saurions**
falloir	**il faudrait**
valoir	**je vaudrais, nous voudrions**
vouloir	**je voudrais, nous voudrions**
apercevoir	**j'apercevrais, nous apercevrions**
décevoir	**je décevrais, nous décevrions**
devoir	**je devrais, nous devrions**
pleuvoir	**il pleuvrait**
recevoir	**je recevrais, nous recevrions**
courir	**je courrais, nous courrions**
secourir	**je secourrais, nous secourrions**
mourir	**je mourrais, nous mourrions**
pouvoir	**je pourrais, nous pourrions**
voir	**je verrais, nous verrions**
envoyer	**j'enverrais, nous enverrions**
tenir (and its derivatives)	**je tiendrais, nous tiendrions**
venir (and its derivatives)	**je viendrais, nous viendrions**

256. Rewrite the following sentences in the conditional.

1. Je dînerai en ville.
2. Tu resteras à la maison.
3. Elle prendra l'avion.
4. Nous paierons nos dettes.
5. Vous viendrez à trois heures.
6. Il sera de retour à huit heures.
7. Elle aura faim.
8. Nous le ferons.
9. Elle enverra la lettre par avion.
10. Il mourra de remords.
11. Elles verront leurs amis.
12. Vous pourrez voir ce film.
13. Ils secourront les pauvres.
14. Nous nous assiérons devant le feu.

257. Complete the following sentences with the correct form of the conditional of the indicated verb.

1. Elles _____ dans la mer, mais l'eau est trop froide. *nager*
2. J'_____ un sonnet, mais je ne suis pas poète. *écrire*
3. Il me _____, mais il n'a pas d'argent. *payer*
4. Pourquoi n'_____-vous pas en avion? *aller*
5. Elles _____ tout de suite, mais il n'y a pas de vol avant mardi. *venir*
6. Nous _____ à New York, mais nous avions autre chose à faire. *être*
7. Il le _____ tout de suite. *faire*
8. Il _____ la lettre par avion. *envoyer*
9. Nous _____ tous les détails. *savoir*
10. Vous _____ de bonne heure. *se coucher*
11. Je _____ à table. *s'asseoir*
12. Tu _____ tes amis. *recevoir*
13. Vous _____ le faire. *pouvoir*
14. Nous _____ travailler. *devoir*
15. Ils _____ les billets s'ils avaient le temps. *acheter*
16. J'_____ un stylo si j'en avais un. *employer*
17. Il _____ les pierres de Carnac en Bretagne. *voir*
18. Je _____ vous voir. *vouloir*
19. Nous _____ soif. *avoir*
20. Il _____ de faim. *mourir*

Uses of the Conditional

To express the idea *would*

The conditional describes an action that would happen in certain circumstances. It is translated by *would* in English.

> **Dans ce cas-là, je viendrais.**
> *In that case, I would come.*
> **À votre place, nous lui en parlerions.**
> *In your situation, we would speak to him about it.*

Do not confuse the meaning of the conditional with the verb **devoir**. In the present conditional **devoir** expresses necessity or obligation.

> Je **devrais** travailler.   *I should (ought to) study.*
> Je **travaillerais.**   *I would study.*

258. Follow the model.

> **Qu'est-ce que je devrais faire—accepter ou refuser?** *À votre place*
> **À votre place, j'accepterais.**

1. Qu'est-ce que je devrais faire—étudier ou sortir? *À votre place*
2. Qu'est-ce que je devrais faire—venir ou rester à la maison? *À votre place*
3. Qu'est-ce que je devrais faire—aller à Paris ou aller à Marseille? *Dans ce cas-là*
4. Qu'est-ce que je devrais faire—écrire ou téléphoner? *Dans ce cas-là*

259. Say that the following are not true. Use the conditional.

> **Anne a oublié mon nom.**
> **Ah! non, elle n'oublierait jamais ton (votre) nom.**

1. Les enfants ont fait des bêtises.
2. Pierre a menti.
3. J'ai échoué à mon examen de français.
4. Anne est rentrée tard hier soir.
5. Nous avons oublié de payer les factures.

After certain conjunctions

The conditional is used after **quand, lorsque, dès que, aussitôt que** and **tant que** when the main verb is in the conditional.

> **Il mangerait quand il arriverait.**
> *He would eat when he arrived.*
> **Il ferait le travail dès qu'il reviendrait.**
> *He would do the work as soon as he returned.*

It is also used after **au cas où.** The main verb can be in any tense.

> **J'attendrai encore une heure au cas où elle viendrait.**
> *I will wait another hour in case she comes.*

260. Complete the following sentences with the correct form of the conditional of the indicated verb.

1. Il _____ dès qu'il _____.　*finir, revenir*
2. Il _____ quand il _____ le temps.　*lire, avoir*
3. Elle _____ aussitôt que vous _____.　*comprendre, expliquer*
4. Elle _____ le faire lorsque vous lui _____ les instructions.　*pouvoir, donner*
5. Je ne sortirai pas au cas où il _____.　*rentrer*
6. Nous rentrons à la maison au cas où nos invités _____.　*revenir*

261. Complete the following sentences.

1. Je mangerais dès que...
2. J'écrirais quand...
3. Je resterai ici au cas où...

To soften a request, command or desire

The conditional is used to soften a request, command or desire.

> **Je voudrais vous dire quelque chose.**
> *I would like to tell you something.*
> **J'aimerais aller à Paris.**
> *I would like to go to Paris.*
> **Pourriez-vous m'aider?**
> *Could you help me?*
> **Voudriez-vous aller au cinéma?**
> *Would you like to go to the movies?*

262. Soften the following requests. Follow the models.

Attendez-moi.
Pourriez-vous m'attendre?

1. Venez tout de suite.
2. Conduisez-moi à l'aéroport.
3. Donnez-moi ce livre.
4. Aidez-moi.

Allons au cinéma!
Voudriez-vous aller au cinéma?

5. Dînons en ville!
6. Assistons à la conférence!
7. Allons voir ce film!
8. Prenons le train!

du café
Je voudrais du café.

9. du vin rouge
10. deux billets aller et retour

11. ce livre
12. ces chaussures

To express possibility or unsure action

The conditional is used to express a possible action or condition in the present. It is often used with exclamations or questions.

Quelle heure **serait**-il? Il **serait** trois heures.
What time could it be? It could be three o'clock already.

It is also used to describe an action that is unsure or not known to be true. It is often used by journalists and reporters.

Il **serait** à New York aujourd'hui.
He is rumored to be in New York today.
Il **aurait** une peinture de Braque.
He allegedly has a Braque painting.
Quel accident! Il y **aurait** trois morts.
What an accident! It is said there are three deaths.

263. Rewrite the following sentences, using the conditional of possibility.

1. (Peut-être) est-il huit heures? Ils sont arrivés.
2. Elle a (peut-être) bien 50 ans!
3. Comme il court! (Peut-être) sait-il les résultats.
4. (On dit qu') il fait sa médecine à Paris maintenant.

264. Translate the following sentences into French, using the conditional.

1. He is rumored to live in Paris.
2. She allegedly has a Picasso painting.

3. The president is rumored to be in New York.
4. It could be two o'clock already.

In indirect discourse

The conditional is used to express a future action in indirect discourse when the main verb is in the past tense. The present conditional can be equivalent to a simple future in the past.

Il m'a dit qu'il viendrait.
He told me he would come.
Il m'a demandé si je voyagerais en France.
He asked me if I would travel in France.
Je croyais qu'elle voudrait venir.
I thought she would want to come.

Remember that the future tense is used when the verb in the main clause is in the present tense.

Il dit qu'il viendra.
He says he will come.

265. Rewrite the following sentences, putting the verb in the main clause in the past tense. Make all necessary changes.

1. Il me dit qu'il sortira ce soir.
2. Elle m'assure qu'elle sera heureuse.
3. Il me demande si je mènerai une vie tranquille.
4. Elle dit qu'elle m'écrira.

266. Complete the following sentences with the correct form of the future or conditional of the indicated verb.

1. Elle dit qu'elle _____ la lettre. *écrire*
2. Il m'a demandé si je _____. *venir*
3. Il décide qu'il _____ le voyage en avion. *faire*
4. Elles ont dit qu'elles _____ peur. *avoir*
5. Nous avons dit que nous _____ le couvert. *mettre*
6. Elle dit qu'elle _____ le faire. *pouvoir*
7. Elle m'a assuré qu'elle _____ heureuse. *être*
8. Je dis que je ne _____ pas ici. *être*

Review

267. What would the following people do with a lot of money? Complete the following with the correct form of the conditional.

Avec beaucoup d'argent,

1. il _____ ses dettes. *payer*
2. nous _____ au Japon. *aller*
3. tu _____ le meilleur champagne. *boire*
4. il _____ le dépenser sagement. *falloir*
5. je _____ quand même. *mourir*
6. elle _____ le tour du monde. *faire*
7. vous _____ beaucoup de liberté. *avoir*
8. elles _____ quoi faire. *savoir*
9. nous _____ tous les pays du monde. *voir*
10. tu _____ des cadeaux à tous tes amis. *envoyer*
11. elle _____ acheter une nouvelle maison. *pouvoir*
12. il _____ plus ou moins heureux. *être*
13. ils _____ chez nous en avion. *venir*
14. vous _____ une nouvelle voiture. *acheter*

268. Complete the following with as many personalized answers as you can.

1. Dans ce cas-là, je...
2. À votre place, je...
3. Je mangerais quand...
4. Je sortirais quand...

5. J'aimerais...
6. Je voudrais...
7. Il / Elle m'a dit que (qu')...

Compound Tenses

The compound tenses are formed by using the appropriate tense of the auxiliary verb **avoir** or **être** and the past participle. Review the formation of the past participles on pages 148–157 and the passé composé on pages 148–159.

Pluperfect Tense (*Plus-que-parfait*)

The pluperfect tense (*plus-que-parfait*) is formed by using the imperfect tense of the verb **avoir** or **être** with the past participle.

parler	entrer	se lever
j'avais parlé	j'étais entré(e)	je m'étais levé(e)
tu avais parlé	tu étais entré(e)	tu t'étais levé(e)
il, elle, on avait parlé	il, on était entré	il, on s'était levé
nous avions parlé	elle était entrée	elle s'était levée
vous aviez parlé	nous étions entré(e)s	nous nous étions levé(e)s
ils, elles avaient parlé	vous étiez entré(e)(s)(es)	vous vous étiez levé(e)(s)(es)
	ils étaient entrés	ils s'étaient levés
	elles étaient entrées	elles s'étaient levées

The pluperfect tense is used the same in French as in English to express a past action completed prior to another past action that is either mentioned or understood from the context.

Elle avait parlé et ensuite nous sommes partis.
She had spoken and then we left.
Ils avaient déjà terminé quand je suis parti.
They had already finished when I left.
Elles étaient déjà descendues quand je suis entré.
They had already come down when I came in.
Elle m'a demandé si j'avais vu le film.
She asked me if I had seen the film.

It can also be used to express a habitual action when used after a conjunction of time.

Quand j'avais fini mes devoirs, j'allais souvent jouer avec mes amis.
When I had finished my homework, I often went to play with my friends.

269. Say that Madeleine asked what the people had done. Complete the following sentences with the appropriate form of the pluperfect tense of the indicated verb.

Madeleine a demandé si

1. nous (f.) _____ déjà _____. *arriver*
2. elle _____ ce roman. *lire*
3. tu _____ la valise. *faire*
4. le petit _____ le CD. *casser*
5. nous (m.) _____ déjà _____. *descendre*
6. ils _____. *manger*
7. j' (f.) _____ déjà _____. *partir*
8. vous (m. pl.) _____ du voyage. *revenir*
9. elle _____ de bonne heure. *se coucher*
10. nous (f.) _____ tard. *se lever*

270. Rewrite the following sentences according to the model to show what had already happened when something else took place.

Je suis partie et ensuite il est entré.
J'étais déjà partie quand il est entré.

1. Je suis revenu et ensuite elle est entrée.
2. Elles ont déjeuné et ensuite je suis arrivé.
3. J'ai fini mes devoirs et ensuite le téléphone a sonné.
4. Elle a écrit la lettre et ensuite son ami a frappé à la porte.
5. Les voleurs sont partis et ensuite la femme a crié.
6. Nous nous sommes couchés et ensuite il est revenu.

271. Follow the model.

Mangeaient-ils quand vous êtes arrivé?
Non, ils avaient déjà mangé quand je suis arrivé.

1. Regardais-tu la télévision quand on a annoncé le dîner?
2. Les étudiants faisaient-ils leurs devoirs quand le professeur est entré?
3. Sortiez-vous quand elles sont arrivées?
4. Rentraient-elles quand il a commencé à pleuvoir?
5. Lisait-elle le journal quand il est arrivé?
6. Ton père se rasait-il quand tu es parti?
7. Nous moquions-nous du politicien quand il est arrivé sur la scène?

272. Say what you did yesterday and why. Follow the model.

se lever de bonne heure ou se lever tard / se coucher de bonne heure ou se coucher tard
Je me suis levé(e) de bonne heure parce que je m'étais couché(e) de bonne heure.
ou
Je me suis levé(e) tard parce que je m'étais couché(e) tard.

1. prendre le petit déjeuner ou ne pas prendre le petit déjeuner / se lever de bonne heure ou se lever tard
2. avoir faim ou ne pas avoir faim / prendre le déjeuner ou ne pas prendre le déjeuner
3. réussir à l'examen de français ou échouer à l'examen de français / étudier ou ne pas étudier
4. arriver à l'heure ou arriver en retard / partir tôt ou partir tard
5. aller au cinéma ou ne pas aller au cinéma / finir mes devoirs à cinq heures ou finir mes devoirs à onze heures

Future Perfect Tense (*Futur Antérieur*)

The future perfect tense (*futur antérieur*) is formed by using the future tense of the auxiliary verb **avoir** or **être** with the past participle.

finir	**venir**	**se réveiller**
j'aurai fini	je serai venu(e)	je me serai réveillé(e)
tu auras fini	tu seras venu(e)	tu te seras réveillé(e)
il, elle, on aura fini	il, on sera venu	il, on se sera réveillé
nous aurons fini	elle sera venue	elle se sera réveillée
vous aurez fini	nous serons venu(e)s	nous nous serons réveillé(e)s
ils, elles auront fini	vous serez venu(e)(s)(es)	vous vous serez réveillé(e)(s)(es)
	ils seront venus	ils se seront réveillés
	elles seront venues	elles se seront réveillées

The future perfect tense is used to express a future action that will be completed prior to another future action.

Elles auront mangé avant mon arrivée.
They will have eaten before my arrival.
Il sera déjà parti quand vous arriverez.
He will have already left when you arrive.
Nous nous serons couchés quand vous reviendrez.
We will have already gone to bed when you return.
Demain à cette heure, nous serons arrivés en France.
Tomorrow at this time, we will have arrived in France.

The future perfect tense is used especially after the conjunctions **quand, après que, aussitôt que, dès que** and **tant que** with the future or future perfect in the main clause.

> **Après qu'elle sera partie, nous nous coucherons.**
> *After she has left, we'll go to bed.*

Like the future tense, the future perfect tense is often used to express probability. It is often used in this way with all verbs. See page 180.

> Il n'est pas ici. Il **sera parti.**
> *He is not here. He must have left.*
> Qu'est-ce que j'ai fait de mon journal? Je l'**aurai jeté!**
> *What did I do with my newspaper? I must have thrown it away!*

273. Complete the following sentences with the appropriate form of the future perfect of the indicated verb.

1. Nous _____ déjà _____ avec le directeur. *parler*
2. Vous _____ avant minuit. *rentrer*
3. Elles _____ le travail avant notre arrivée. *faire*
4. Tu _____ cela avant lundi. *apprendre*
5. Elle _____ ces disques avant la soirée. *acheter*
6. Elle _____ de Paris avant samedi. *rentrer*
7. Je _____ déjà _____ quand vous reviendrez. *partir*
8. Nous _____ cette exposition avant votre départ. *voir*
9. Vous _____ votre composition avant la fin de juin. *écrire*
10. Vous _____ quand ils reviendront. *se coucher*
11. Téléphonez-moi dès que vous _____ l'histoire. *lire*
12. Je vous le dirai aussitôt que j'_____ la voiture. *acheter*

274. Say what the people have to do first before they can do something else. Follow the model.

Je ne peux pas sortir. Il faut d'abord que je finisse le travail.
Je sortirai quand j'aurai fini le travail.

1. Je ne peux pas partir. Il faut d'abord qu'ils rentrent.
2. Ils ne peuvent pas aller mieux. Il faut d'abord qu'ils prennent le médicament.
3. Vous ne pouvez pas vous coucher. Il faut d'abord que vous éteigniez les lumières.
4. Tu ne peux pas avoir un diplôme. Il faut d'abord que tu étudies pendant quatre ans.
5. Nous ne pouvons pas résoudre le problème. Il faut d'abord que le professeur explique une chose.
6. Elle ne peut pas manger. Il faut d'abord qu'elle aille au supermarché.

275. Say that it will be too late in each case. Use the future and future perfect.

Il / venir / nous / partir
Il viendra quand nous serons parti(e)s.

1. Il / arriver / je / sortir
2. Elle / venir nous voir / nous / se coucher
3. Nous / arriver / le restaurant / être fermé
4. Il / apporter les hors d'œuvres / elles / finir le dîner
5. Il / répondre à la question / je / rendre mes devoirs

Past Conditional (*Passé du Conditionnel*)

The past conditional (*passé du conditionnel*) is formed by using the conditional tense of the auxiliary verb **avoir** or **être** and the past participle.

attendre	partir	se laver
j'aurais attendu	je serais parti(e)	je me serais lavé(e)
tu aurais attendu	tu serais parti(e)	tu te serais lavé(e)
il, elle, on aurait attendu	il, on serait parti	il, on se serait lavé
nous aurions attendu	elle serait partie	elle se serait lavée
vous auriez attendu	nous serions parti(e)s	nous nous serions lavé(e)s
ils, elles auraient attendu	vous seriez parti(e)(s)(es)	vous vous seriez lavé(e)(s)(es)
	ils seraient partis	ils se seraient lavés
	elles seraient parties	elles se seraient lavées

The past conditional is used to describe what would have taken place if something else had not interfered.

> **Dans ce cas-là, j'aurais refusé.**
> *In that case, I would have refused.*
> **Ils auraient fait le voyage, mais ils n'avaient pas assez d'argent.**
> *They would have taken the trip, but they didn't have enough money.*
> **Elle serait venue, mais elle n'avait pas d'auto.**
> *She would have come, but she didn't have a car.*
> **Il se serait rasé, mais il n'avait pas de rasoir.**
> *He would have shaved, but he didn't have a razor.*

Like the conditional, the past conditional is used to express a possible action in the past.

> **J'ai trouvé sa lettre. Serait-il venu en mon absence?**
> *I found his letter. Could it be that he came in my absence?*

It is also used to describe an action that is unsure. Like the present conditional, it is used by journalists and reporters.

> **Dix avions auraient été abattus hier.**
> *It is reported that ten planes were brought down yesterday.*

See page 185.

276. Complete the following sentences with the correct form of the past conditional of the indicated verb.

1. Ils _____, mais il a commencé à pleuvoir. *finir*
2. Nous _____ mais nous n'avions pas faim. *manger*
3. Nous _____ hier, mais il n'y avait pas de vol. *rentrer*
4. Elle _____ le petit, mais elle ne pouvait pas. *accompagner*
5. Tu _____ tes amis, mais ils ne sont pas venus. *voir*
6. Vous _____ de l'eau, mais vous n'avez pas eu soif. *boire*
7. Elle _____ le médicament, mais elle n'était pas malade. *prendre*
8. Dans ce cas-là, elle _____ venir. *pouvoir*
9. Dans ce cas-là, je _____. *se coucher*
10. Tu _____ en noir. *s'habiller*

277. Follow the model to show what the people would have done had they had certain things.

> **Elle / venir / auto**
> **Elle serait venue, mais elle n'avait pas d'auto.**

1. Il / se raser / rasoir
2. Elles / manger au restaurant / argent
3. Vous / faire un voyage / temps
4. Nous / écrire la lettre / papier
5. Je / partir / parapluie
6. Tu / ouvrir le paquet / couteau

278. Read what Pierre did. Then say what the following people would have done in his place. Follow the model.

Pierre a joué au tennis. Nous / nager dans la piscine
À sa place, nous aurions nagé dans la piscine.

1. Pierre a pris le bateau pour aller de New York en France. Je / avion
2. Pierre a mangé de la viande au restaurant. Nous / du poisson
3. Pierre s'est couché à trois heures du matin. Marie / avant minuit
4. Pierre a dépensé trop d'argent. Anne et Georges / faire des économies
5. Pierre est malade, mais il est allé au cinéma. Tu / rester chez toi

The Past Anterior (*Passé Antérieur*) and the *Passé Surcomposé*

The *passé antérieur* is formed by using the *passé simple* of the auxiliary verb **avoir** or **être** and the past participle.

finir	venir
j'eus fini	je fus venu(e)
tu eus fini	tu fus venu(e)
il, elle, on eut fini	il, on fut venu
nous eûmes fini	elle fut venue
vous eûtes fini	nous fûmes venu(e)s
ils, elles eurent fini	vous fûtes venu(e)(s)(es)
	ils furent venus
	elles furent venues

The *passé surcomposé* is a double compound tense formed by using the *passé composé* of the auxiliary verb **avoir** and the past participle. It is rarely used with verbs conjugated with **être** except when these verbs imply result, not action.

finir	arriver
j'ai eu fini	j'ai été arrivé(e)
tu as eu fini	tu as été arrivé(e)
il, elle, on a eu fini	il, on a été arrivé
nous avons eu fini	elle a été arrivée
vous avez eu fini	nous avons été arrivé(e)s
ils, elles ont eu fini	vous avez été arrivé(e)(s)(es)
	ils ont été arrivés
	elles ont été arrivées

Like the *plus-que-parfait*, the *passé antérieur* expresses a past action that occurred before another past action. It is usually used in subordinate clauses after **quand, lorsque, après que, aussitôt que, dès que** or **à peine** which indicate a past action immediately preceding another.

Quand il eut fini, il partit.
When he had finished, he left.
Lorsqu'elle fut arrivée, nous partîmes.
When she had arrived, we left.

Note that the subject and verb are inverted after **à peine**.

À peine eut-elle fini qu'elle partit.
She had hardly finished when she left.

The *passé antérieur* is only used in written language. In spoken language, it is replaced by the *passé surcomposé*.

Quand il a eu fini, il est parti.
When he had finished, he left.

279. Rewrite the following sentences in spoken language.

1. Quand il eut mangé, il partit.
2. Lorsqu'elles furent réunies, elles élurent un président.
3. Lorsque le professeur eut fini le discours, il descendit de l'estrade.
4. À peine eut-il fini que nous arrivâmes.
5. Après qu'ils furent guéris, ils retournèrent au travail.
6. Quand il fut arrivé, la conférence commença.

280. Rewrite the following sentences in written language.

1. Dès qu'elle a eu appris la nouvelle, elle a décidé de partir.
2. À peine a-t-elle eu reçu l'invitation qu'elle y a répondu.
3. À peine a-t-elle été entrée qu'elle a compris la situation.
4. Aussitôt qu'ils ont été partis, ils ont soupiré.

Review

281. Say what you and your family (*a*) had already done; (*b*) will have already done; (*c*) would have already done before the arrival of guests.

Nous / laver les légumes.
Nous avions lavé les légumes.
Nous aurons lavé les légumes.
Nous aurions lavé les légumes.

1. Papa / aller au supermarché
2. Pierre / nettoyer le salon
3. Marie / préparer / les hors d'œuvres
4. Marie et Pierre / mettre les couverts
5. Maman / faire les apéritifs
6. Je / mettre / la viande dans le four
7. Nous / se laver
8. Nous / s'habiller

282. Complete the following with personalized answers. Use the correct form of the *passé composé*, the pluperfect, the future or future perfect, the imperfect, conditional or past conditional.

1. Je ne suis pas allé(e) au cinéma parce que...
2. Je sortirai dès que...
3. À votre place, je (j')...
4. À l'âge de 30 ans, je (j')...
5. Je serais allé(e) au cinéma, mais...
6. Dès que j'aurai fini mes études, je (j')...
7. J'étais déjà parti(e) quand...

Si *Clauses*

Si (*if*) clauses are used to express conditions contrary to fact. For such clauses, there is a definite sequence of tenses to be followed.

Si *clause*	Result clause
Present indicative or *passé composé*	Future or imperative
Imperfect	Conditional
Pluperfect	Past Conditional

Study the following examples.

Si vous n'avez pas <u>compris</u>, <u>dites</u>-le-moi.
If you didn't understand, tell me.
Si vous n'avez pas <u>compris</u>, vous me le <u>direz</u>.
If you didn't understand, you will tell me.
Si j'<u>ai</u> assez d'argent, je <u>ferai</u> le voyage.
If I have enough money, I will take the trip.
Si j'<u>avais</u> assez d'argent, je <u>ferais</u> le voyage.
If I had enough money, I would take the trip.
Si j'<u>avais</u> eu assez d'argent, j'<u>aurais</u> fait le voyage.
If I had had enough money, I would have taken the trip.

Si vous <u>veniez</u>, nous <u>resterons</u>.
If you come, we will stay.
Si vous <u>veniez</u>, nous <u>resterions</u>.
If you came, we would stay.
Si vous <u>étiez venu</u>, nous <u>serions restés</u>.
If you had come, we would have stayed.

In sentences expressing general rules or conditions, the present tense can be used in both clauses.

Si j'ai faim, je mange.
If I am hungry, I eat.
Si on étudie, on reçoit de bonnes notes.
If one studies, one gets good grades.

Si becomes **s'** before the pronouns **il** and **ils,** but not before the pronouns **elle** and **elles.** The **si** clause can come first or second.

S'il a le temps, il viendra nous voir.
Elles viendront nous voir, <u>si elles</u> ont le temps.

283. Complete the following sentences with the appropriate form of the indicated verb.

1. Elles y iront si elles _____ le temps.   *avoir*
2. Si vous _____ à l'heure, je vous attendrai.   *être*
3. Je _____ s'il ne pleut pas.   *partir*
4. S'il fait beau, nous _____ une promenade.   *faire*
5. S'ils _____ assez de temps, ils viendraient.   *avoir*
6. Il paierait ses dettes s'il _____ de l'argent.   *avoir*
7. Si j'avais le temps, je le _____.   *faire*
8. Nous _____ chez nous s'il pleuvait.   *rester*
9. S'il _____ des billets, il serait allé au théâtre.   *prendre*
10. J'aurais été content si vous _____.   *venir*
11. S'il avait fait froid, il _____ son manteau.   *mettre*
12. Vous _____ à l'heure si vous étiez parti de bonne heure.   *arriver*

284. Answer the following questions: **Que feront les gens s'ils ont de l'argent? Que feraient les gens s'ils avaient de l'argent? Qu'est-ce que les gens auraient fait s'ils avaient eu de l'argent?** Follow the model.

Pierre / faire le tour du monde
Si Pierre a de l'argent, il fera le tour du monde.
Si Pierre avait de l'argent, il ferait le tour du monde.
Si Pierre avait eu de l'argent, il aurait fait le tour du monde.

1. Anne / acheter une Mercedes
2. Nous / aller en Europe
3. Tu / s'habiller bien
4. Marie et Nicole / venir nous voir plus souvent
5. Georges / ne pas travailler
6. Je / faire un long voyage
7. Les Dupont / vivre bien
8. Vous / avoir une grande maison

285. Combine an element from the first column with an element from the second column. Then form sentences with three **si** clauses as in the model.

1. S'il (pleuvoir), ils
2. Si elle (se casser) la jambe, elle
3. S'il (accepter) ce poste, il
4. Si nous (rentrer) trop tard, nos parents
5. Si tu (aller) en Égypte, tu
6. S'il (faire) beau, les enfants
7. Si vous (arriver) à l'aéroport à temps, vous
8. Si les étudiants (étudier), ils
9. Si je (avoir) sommeil, je
10. Si nous (être) en retard, nous

voir les Pyramides
dormir
mettre un imperméable
jouer dans le parc
aller à la salle d'urgence à l'hôpital
gagner beaucoup d'argent
se dépêcher
pouvoir prendre l'avion de 10 heures
réussir à l'examen
se fâcher

1. S'il pleut, ils mettront un imperméable.
S'il pleuvait, ils mettraient un imperméable.
S'il avait plu, ils auraient mis un imperméable.

Continue.

286. Answer the following questions with as many choices as you can think of.

Si tu vas en France, que feras-tu?
Si tu allais en France, que ferais-tu?

Si je vais en France, je monterai la tour Eiffel.
Si j'allais en France, je monterais la tour Eiffel.

Continue.

287. What would you do if . . .? Choose from the list below or add your own answers.

voyager partout dans le monde
travailler
se promener dans le parc
étudier

aller au cinéma
rester chez moi
manger un sandwich
appeler le médecin

Que ferais-tu

1. si tu voulais voir un film?
2. si tu avais besoin d'argent?
3. si tu voulais recevoir de bonnes notes?
4. si tu te sentais mal?
5. si tu gagnais à la loterie?
6. si tu avais faim?
7. s'il pleuvait?
8. s'il faisait du soleil?

288. Answer the following personalized questions.

1. Qu'est-ce que tu aurais fait si tu n'avais pas fait tes devoirs?
2. Où est-ce que tu serais allé(e) l'été dernier si tu avais eu assez d'argent?

3. Si tu avais vécu au dix-neuvième siècle, qui aurais-tu voulu être?
4. Qu'est-ce que tu aurais fait vendredi dernier si tu avais eu le temps?
5. Qu'est-ce que tu aurais fait si tu avais eu l'occasion d'aller en France l'année dernière?

The Subjunctive Mood

The indicative mood is used to report an action which is taking, has taken or will take place. The action is not dependent upon an opinion or condition. When the statement implies a truth, fact or probability, the indicative mood is used.

> **Marie mange beaucoup.**
> *Mary eats a lot.*
> **Je sais qu'il est parti.**
> *I know he left.*
> **Il est probable qu'il ira à New York.**
> *It is probable that he will go to New York.*
> **Il est vrai que la terre est ronde.**
> *It is true that the earth is round.*

The subjunctive is used to express an action which is dependent upon a subjective idea, opinion or condition. The idea in the dependent clause is either contrary to fact, or possible but not probable.

> **Le père veut que son fils devienne médecin.**
> *The father wants his son to become a doctor.*
> **Il faut qu'elle se réveille tôt.**
> *It is necessary for her to wake up early.*
> **Je doute qu'il vienne.**
> *I doubt that he is coming.*

In the first example, even though the father wants his son to become a doctor, it is not certain that the boy will carry out the father's desire. Therefore, the action is expressed in the subjunctive. In English an infinitive, rather than the subjunctive, is used.

> *The father wants his son to become a doctor.*

In French, however, a clause must be used.

(See *Uses of the Subjunctive*, beginning on page 200.)

Present Subjunctive

Regular Forms

The present subjunctive is formed by dropping the **-ent** ending from the third person plural of the present indicative and adding the endings **-e, -es, -e, -ions, -iez, -ent.**

	parler	**finir**	**attendre**
Base:	**ils parlent**	**ils finissent**	**ils attendent**
je	parle	finisse	j'attende
tu	parles	finisses	attendes
il, elle, on	parle	finisse	attende
nous	parlions	finissions	attendions
vous	parliez	finissiez	attendiez
ils, elles	parlent	finissent	attendent

Note that for **-er** verbs, there is no difference between the subjunctive and the present indicative in the **je, tu, il, elle, on, ils, elles** forms. The same is true for the third person plural of all regular subjunctive forms. Note that unlike the present indicative of regular **-ir** and **-re** verbs, there is no audible difference between the third person plural and the singular forms.

Present indicative	Subjunctive
il finit	**il finisse**
ils finissent	**ils finissent**
il attend	**il attende**
ils attendent	**ils attendent**

Note that verbs ending in **-ier**, such as **étudier** and **oublier**, and the verbs **rire** and **sourire** have a double **i** in the **nous** and **vous** forms since the base ends in **-i**.

Base	Subjunctive
ils étudient	**nous étudiions**
	vous étudiiez

Other verbs that are regular in the subjunctive are:

	Verb	Base
Verbs like	ouvrir	**ils ouvrent**
Verbs like	courir	**ils courent**
	rire	**ils rient**
	conclure	**ils concluent**
	rompre	**ils rompent**
	battre	**ils battent**
	mettre	**ils mettent**
	partir	**ils partent**
Verbs like	connaître	**ils connaissent**
	plaire	**ils plaisent**
	se taire	**ils se taisent**
	lire	**ils lisent**
	dire	**ils disent**
	conduire	**ils conduisent**
	traduire	**ils traduisent**
	dormir	**ils dorment**
	servir	**ils servent**
	suivre	**ils suivent**
	vivre	**ils vivent**
	vaincre	**ils vainquent**
	craindre	**ils craignent**
	joindre	**ils joignent**
	peindre	**ils peignent**
	s'asseoir	**ils s'asseyent**

289. Complete the following sentences with the correct form of the present subjunctive of each indicated verb.

    1. Il faut qu'elles _____.
       (parler, entrer, finir, réussir, attendre, répondre)
    2. Il ne veut pas qu'elle _____.
       (partir, sortir, mentir, se repentir, dormir)

3. Il veut que je _____.
   (rompre les liens, vaincre mes passions, craindre cet homme, peindre ce portrait)
4. Il est nécessaire que tu _____.
   (écrire la lettre, suivre la route, vivre ici, décrire la vue, servir le déjeuner)
5. Elle désire que nous _____.
   (parler, lire, dormir, disparaître, s'asseoir)
6. Il veut que vous _____.
   (sourire, étudier, rire, oublier ceci)

Spelling Changes in the Present Subjunctive

Verbs ending in **-yer**, such as **employer, envoyer, nettoyer, essayer, payer,** etc., and **croire** and **voir** change the **i** of the third person plural base to **y** in the **nous** and **vous** forms. The vowel changes are the same as those for the present indicative.

	envoyer	**croire**
Base:	**ils envoient**	**ils croient**
	j'envoie	je croie
	tu envoies	tu croies
	il, elle, on envoie	il, elle, on croie
	ils, elles envoient	ils, elles croient
	nous envoyions	nous croyions
	vous envoyiez	vous croyiez

Verbs with Internal Vowel Changes in the Present Subjunctive

Verbs with -é- in the infinitive

Verbs with **-é-** in the infinitive, such as **céder, compléter, considérer, espérer, préférer, répéter,** etc., change the **è** of the third person plural stem to **-é-** in the **nous** and **vous** forms.

	céder		
Base:	**ils cèdent**		
	je cède		
	tu cèdes	*But:*	**nous cédions**
	il, elle, on cède		**vous cédiez**
	ils, elles cèdent		

Verbs with -e- in the infinitive

Verbs with **-e-** in the infinitive, such as **acheter, appeler, jeter, lever, mener,** etc., change the base in the **nous** and **vous** forms. Verbs which in the present indicative change **-e-** to **-è-** in the singular and the third person plural forms retain the **e** in the **nous** and **vous** forms.

acheter

Base:	**ils achètent**
But:	**nous achetions**
	vous achetiez

Verbs which double the consonant in the third person plural have only one consonant in the **nous** and **vous** forms.

jeter

Base:	**ils jettent**
But:	**nous jetions**
	vous jetiez

In other words, the spelling changes are the same as those for the present indicative.

290. Complete the following sentences with the correct form of the present subjunctive of the indicated verb.

1. Il est essentiel qu'ils _____ le paquet. *envoyer*
2. Il est nécessaire que nous _____ la salle. *nettoyer*
3. Je veux qu'elles _____ l'histoire. *croire*
4. Elle veut que vous _____ ce film. *voir*
5. Il faut qu'ils _____ ce problème. *considérer*
6. Il faut que nous _____ nos places. *céder*
7. Il est important qu'ils _____ ce livre. *acheter*
8. Il est important que nous _____ le rideau. *lever*
9. Il faut qu'ils _____ leurs amis. *appeler*
10. Il est nécessaire que vous _____ ce papier. *jeter*

Prendre, tenir, venir

Prendre, tenir and **venir** also undergo an internal vowel change in the present subjunctive.

prendre

Base:	**ils prennent**
But:	**nous prenions**
	vous preniez

tenir

Base:	**ils tiennent**
But:	**nous tenions**
	vous teniez

venir

Base:	**ils viennent**
But:	**nous venions**
	vous veniez

One way to remember the subjunctive forms for spelling-change verbs and verbs with internal vowel changes is the following:

1. Add the endings to the third person present indicative base for the singular and third person plural forms.
2. Drop the ending **-ant** from the present participle before adding the endings to the **nous** and **vous** forms.

Example: **prendre**

Singular and third person plural

Base form	*Subjunctive*
ils prenn / ent	**je prenne**
	tu prennes
	il / elle / on prenne
	ils / elles prennent

Nous and **vous**

Base form	*Subjunctive*
pren / ant	**nous prenions**
	vous preniez

Verbs with Variable Bases in the Present Subjunctive

The following verbs have variable bases in the present subjunctive.

mourir

Base:	**ils meurent**
But:	**nous mourions**
	vous mouriez

recevoir (décevoir, concevoir), devoir

recevoir			**devoir**	
Base:	**ils reçoivent**		*Base:*	**ils doivent**
But:	**nous recevions**		*But:*	**nous devions**
	vous receviez			**vous deviez**

boire

Base:	**ils boivent**
But:	**nous buvions**
	vous buviez

Note that the base changes are the same for these verbs in the present indicative and the present subjunctive.

Present indicative	*Subjunctive*
nous mourons	**nous mourions**
nous recevons	**nous recevions**
nous buvons	**nous buvions**

291. Complete the following sentences with the correct form of the present subjunctive of the indicated verb.

1. Il faut qu'ils _____ leur temps. *prendre*
2. Il est important que vous _____ l'autobus. *prendre*
3. Il est possible qu'elle _____ à l'heure. *venir*
4. Il est important que vous _____ les places maintenant. *retenir*
5. Il est possible que le malade _____. *mourir*
6. Il est possible que vous _____ de fatigue. *mourir*
7. Il faut qu'ils _____ de l'argent. *recevoir*
8. Il est possible que nous _____ de l'argent. *recevoir*
9. Il faut que tu _____ le médicament. *boire*
10. Il vaut mieux que nous _____ du lait. *boire*

Verbs with Irregular Bases in the Present Subjunctive

The following verbs have irregular bases in the present subjunctive.

avoir	**être**
j'aie	je sois
tu aies	tu sois
il, elle, on ait	il, elle, on soit
ils, elles aient	ils, elles soient
nous ayons	nous soyons
vous ayez	vous soyez

pouvoir	faire
je puisse	je fasse
tu puisses	tu fasses
il, elle, on puisse	il, elle, on fasse
ils, elles puissent	ils, elles fassent
nous puissions	nous fassions
vous puissiez	vous fassiez

savoir	vouloir
je sache	je veuille
tu saches	tu veuilles
il, elle, on sache	il, elle, on veuille
ils, elles sachent	ils, elles veuillent
nous sachions	nous voulions
vous sachiez	vous vouliez

aller	valoir
j'aille	je vaille
tu ailles	tu vailles
il, elle, on aille	il, elle on vaille
ils, elles aillent	ils, elles vaillent
nous allions	nous valions
vous alliez	vous valiez

falloir	pleuvoir
il faille	il pleuve

292. Change the following sentences, substituting the words given.

1. Il est nécessaire que nous soyons à l'heure.   (vous, ils, elle, tu, je)
2. Il faut que tu aies de la patience.   (je, il, elles, nous, vous)
3. Il est bon que je puisse venir.   (nous, vous, ils, tu, elle)
4. Il est important que tu fasses le travail.   (je, il, elles, nous, vous)
5. Il faut que tu saches la vérité.   (vous, nous, ils, elle, je)
6. Il est possible qu'il veuille partir.   (nous, vous, tu, elles, je)
7. Il faut que j'aille au supermarché.   (tu, ils, elle, nous, vous)
8. Il est important que ça vaille le prix.   (elle, elles, il, ils)

Uses of the Subjunctive

Subjunctive in noun clauses

The subjunctive is required in clauses following verbs which denote desire, doubt, denial, necessity, fear, etc. The subjunctive verb usually appears in a clause introduced by **que.**

Some common expressions requiring the subjunctive are:

1. wish, preference or desire

vouloir	*to want*
bien vouloir	*to agree, to be willing*
désirer	*to wish, to desire*
préférer	*to prefer*

| aimer mieux | *to prefer* |
| souhaiter | *to wish* |

Je veux qu'il parte.
I want him to leave.

Note that **espérer** (*to hope*) is followed by the indicative.

J'espère qu'il viendra.
I hope he will come.

2. doubt

| douter | *to doubt* |

Je doute qu'il vienne.
I doubt he is coming (will come).

3. denial

| nier | *to deny* |

Elle nie qu'elle vous connaisse.
She denies that she knows you.

4. emotions and feelings

être content	*to be happy*
être heureux	*to be happy*
être triste	*to be sad*
être fâché	*to be angry*
être fier	*to be proud*
être désolé	*to be sorry*
être surpris	*to be surprised*
avoir peur	*to be afraid*
avoir crainte	*to be afraid*
craindre	*to fear*
regretter	*to be sorry*
être furieux	*to be mad, furious*
se fâcher	*to be angry*
se réjouir	*to rejoice, to be happy*

Je suis heureux que vous puissiez venir.
I am happy that you can come.
Elle est triste que nous partions.
She is sad that we are leaving.
Elle craint que nous n'attendions pas.
She is afraid that we will not wait.

5. an order, command or requirement (See page 212.)

commander	*to ask, to order*
exiger	*to demand*
ordonner	*to command, to order*

Il exige que nous soyons à l'heure.
He demands that we be on time.

6. permission or refusal of permission (See page 212.)

permettre	*to permit*
consentir	*to consent*
défendre	*to forbid*
empêcher	*to prevent*

Il permet que nous fassions cela.
He permits us to do that.
Il défend que nous fumions en classe.
He forbids us to smoke in class.

293. Complete the following sentences with the correct form of the present subjunctive of each indicated verb.

1. Je veux qu'ils _____.
   (parler, manger, écrire, dormir, venir, sortir, conduire)
2. Elle préfère que nous _____.
   (payer, céder, appeler le garçon, venir, boire, aller, être ici)
3. Pourquoi commandes-tu que je _____?
   (travailler, lire, venir, finir, sortir)
4. Elle craint que vous ne _____.
   (venir, comprendre, manger, attendre)

294. Say what the following people's wishes or feelings are. Follow the model.

Il veut que: Vous travaillez.
Il veut que vous travailliez.

A. Le professeur veut que:

1. Tu lis le livre.
2. Vous étudiez la leçon.
3. Nous complétons nos devoirs.
4. Elles savent les réponses.
5. Je fais attention en classe.
6. Il est à l'heure.

B. Je doute que:

1. Le politicien dit la vérité.
2. Tu pars à l'heure.
3. Il pleut demain.
4. Vous achetez cette maison.
5. Ils meurent de faim.
6. Nous prenons nos vacances sur la lune.

C. Pierre est heureux que:

1. Ses amis peuvent aller en Europe en été.
2. Babeth vient le voir.
3. Jeanne et Anne reçoivent de bonnes notes.
4. Claire peint un beau portrait.
5. Nous considérons son offre.
6. Vous recevez le prix.

D. Le médecin ordonne que:

1. Vous prenez les pilules quatre fois par jour.
2. Tu as de la patience.
3. La patiente se repose.
4. Nous buvons huit verres d'eau par jour.
5. Je suis un régime.
6. Vous êtes calme.

E. Anne regrette que:

1. Vous ne voulez pas venir à la surprise-partie.
2. Tu ne veux pas le faire.
3. Son amie n'obtient pas la médaille d'or.
4. Nous ne pouvons pas aller au cinéma avec elle.
5. Sa sœur n'est pas à la maison.

295. Complete the following sentences with the appropriate form of the indicated verb.

1. Je préfère que tu _____ l'auto. *conduire*
2. Elle craint que vous _____ en retard. *arriver*
3. Mes parents défendent que je _____. *fumer*
4. Il nie qu'il la _____. *connaître*
5. Je suis triste que vous _____ malade. *être*
6. Il ordonne que je _____ le travail. *faire*
7. Il permet que nous y _____. *aller*
8. Elle doute que vous le _____. *savoir*
9. Nous sommes contents qu'elles _____ venir. *vouloir*
10. Il veut que nous _____ son œuvre. *traduire*
11. Ils commandent que je _____ de bonne heure. *rentrer*
12. Nous sommes désolés qu'il ne _____ pas ce soir. *venir*
13. Il désire que je _____ la leçon. *comprendre*
14. Nous voulons que tout _____ bien. *aller*
15. Je préfère que vous ne _____ pas ce soir. *sortir*

296. React to the following. Use the appropriate expression of emotions and feelings. Use one of the following expressions in your answers.

être heureux	être content
avoir peur	regretter
être furieux	avoir peur
craindre	être désolé
être fâché	être surpris

Je suis heureux.
Je suis content(e) que tu sois (vous soyez) heureux.

1. Je suis malade.
2. Je ne fais pas mes devoirs.
3. Nous recevons de bonnes notes.
4. Ils vont en Europe cet été.
5. Elle ne fait pas attention en classe.
6. Il prend des risques.

Subjunctive with impersonal expressions that express opinion or emotions

The subjunctive is also required after many impersonal expressions that denote an element of subjectivity.

il est temps que	*it is time that*
il vaut (vaudrait) mieux que	*it is better that*
il est préférable que	*it is better that*
il faut (faudrait) que	*it is necessary that*
il est nécessaire que	*it is necessary that*
il est essentiel que	*it is essential that*
il importe que	*it is important that*
il est important que	*it is important that*
il suffit que	*it is enough that, it suffices that*
il est indispensable que	*it is indispensable that*
il convient que	*it is fitting that, it is proper that*
il est convenable que	*it is fitting that, it is proper that*
il est possible que	*it is possible that*
il se peut que	*it is possible that*
il est impossible que	*it is impossible that*
il est utile que	*it is useful that*
il est inutile que	*it is useless that*
il est douteux que	*it is doubtful that*
il est peu probable que	*it is unlikely that*
il n'est pas certain que	*it is uncertain that*
il est heureux que	*it is fortunate that*
il est bon que	*it is good that*
c'est (il est) dommage que	*it is a pity that*
il semble que	*it seems that*
il est honteux que	*it is shameful that*
il est triste que	*it is sad that*
il est surprenant que	*it is surprising that*
il est étonnant que	*it is surprising that*
il est urgent que	*it is urgent that*

Il est temps que vous veniez.
It is time for you to come.
Il faut que vous étudiiez.
It is necessary for you to study.
Il est douteux qu'il réussisse.
It is doubtful that he will succeed.
C'est dommage qu'elle ne vienne pas.
It's a pity that she is not coming.

If the opinion is a general one, then the impersonal expression is followed by the infinitive.

Il vaut mieux ne pas sortir par un temps pareil.
One shouldn't go out in such weather.
Il faut étudier pour réussir.
It is necessary to study to succeed.

The indicative is used with the following expressions.

il est certain que	*it is certain that*
il est sûr que	*it is sure that*
il est probable que	*it is probable that*
il est évident que	*it is evident that*
il est exact que	*it is correct that*
il est clair que	*it is clear that*
il est vrai que	*it is true that*
il est vraisemblable que	*it is conceivable that*
il paraît que	*it seems that*

Although **il semble que** is followed by the subjunctive, **il me semble que** is followed by the indicative.

Il semble qu'il maigrisse.
It seems he is getting thin.
Il me semble que je fais votre connaissance pour la première fois.
It seems to me that I am meeting you for the first time.

297. Complete the following sentences with the correct form of the present subjunctive of each indicated verb.

1. Il est possible qu'il le _____.
   (préparer, lire, recevoir, faire, savoir, perdre)
2. Il est nécessaire que nous le _____.
   (finir, manger, comprendre, suivre, faire, répéter, retenir)
3. Il est douteux que vous _____.
   (comprendre, venir, finir, sortir, savoir la réponse)
4. Il n'est pas certain qu'il _____.
   (réussir, comprendre, arriver, finir, répondre)

298. Introduce each of the following by the indicated expression.

1. Nous recevons ces lettres.   *Il est essentiel*
2. Je te le dis.   *Il suffit*
3. Tu es ici.   *Il vaut mieux*
4. Vous voulez venir.   *Il est bon*
5. Elle écrit ses devoirs.   *Il est important*
6. Ils vont au marché.   *Il faut*
7. Vous venez.   *Il est temps*
8. Vous êtes malade.   *C'est dommage*
9. Elles partent tout de suite.   *Il vaut mieux*
10. Tu réussis à l'examen.   *Il est heureux*
11. Paul peut venir.   *Il est douteux*
12. Tu mens.   *Il est honteux*
13. Ils savent la vérité.   *Il est bon*
14. On le craint.   *Il est possible*
15. Ils viendront demain.   *Il convient*

299. Respond to the following, using one of the impersonal expressions in the first column and one of the verbal endings in the second column. More than one of the impersonal expressions can be used with an ending.

Il faut que	étudier davantage
Il est important que	boire de l'eau
Il est nécessaire que	se dépêcher
Il vaudrait mieux que	faire ses devoirs
Il est urgent que	aller chez le médecin
	manger

J'ai faim.
Il faut que (Il est important que) tu manges.

1. Je suis malade.
2. J'ai échoué à l'examen.
3. Nous sommes en retard.

4. Elle veut sortir ce soir.
5. Ils ont soif.

Subjunctive with expressions of doubt

The indicative is used with expressions that denote certainty in the affirmative.

il est sûr que	*it is sure that*
il est certain que	*it is certain that*
il est probable que	*it is probable that*

The subjunctive is used in the negative and interrogative forms of the above expressions, since uncertainty is implied.

Indicative	*Subjunctive*
Il est sûr qu'il viendra.	**Il n'est pas sûr qu'il vienne.**
	Est-il sûr qu'il vienne?
Il est certain qu'elle comprend.	**Il n'est pas certain qu'elle comprenne.**
	Est-il certain qu'elle comprenne?
Il est probable qu'il le fera.	**Il n'est pas probable qu'il le fasse.**
	Est-il probable qu'il le fasse?

The indicative is used with affirmative forms of **croire** and **penser** since there is no uncertainty.

Je pense qu'il vient.
Je crois qu'elle comprend.

The subjunctive is used with the negative and interrogative forms of **croire** and **penser** when they express doubt or uncertainty.

Je ne crois pas qu'il vienne.
I don't believe he is coming. (But I don't know for sure.)
Croyez-vous qu'il vienne?
Do you think he is coming? (The answer is unknown for sure.)

You will note that many expressions that take the indicative are followed by a future tense.

Indicative	*Subjunctive*
Il est certain qu'il viendra.	**Il n'est pas certain qu'il vienne.**
Je crois qu'elles seront ici.	**Je ne crois pas qu'elles soient ici.**

Note that the conditional can also be used if the clause expresses a supposition or eventuality.

Je ne crois pas qu'il pourrait le faire.
I don't think he could do it.

300. Complete the following sentences with the correct form of the indicated verb.

1. Il cst sûr qu'il _____ ici demain. *être*
2. Il n'est pas sûr qu'elle le _____. *faire*
3. Est-il sûr qu'ils _____? *venir*
4. Il est certain qu'elles _____ demain. *venir*
5. Il n'est pas certain que nous _____ les résultats aujourd'hui. *savoir*
6. Est-il certain que vous y _____? *aller*
7. Il est probable qu'elle le _____. *faire*
8. Il n'est pas probable qu'il _____ les billets. *obtenir*
9. Est-il probable que nous _____ le travail? *finir*
10. Je pense qu'elle _____ raison. *avoir*
11. Je ne pense pas qu'elle _____ la réponse. *savoir*
12. Pensez-vous qu'il le _____ ? *croire*
13. Je crois qu'elle _____ venir. *vouloir*
14. Je ne crois pas qu'elles _____ le faire. *vouloir*
15. Croyez-vous que nous _____ le faire? *pouvoir*

301. Answer the following questions, according to the indicated cue.

1. Crois-tu que Jean le sache? *Non*
2. Êtes-vous certain que Pierre le sache? *Non*
3. Est-il probable qu'il conduise une auto? *Non*
4. Est-il sûr qu'ils viennent? *Non*
5. Croyez-vous qu'elles arrivent demain? *Non*
6. Est-il sûr qu'elle parte tout de suite? *Non*
7. Est-il probable qu'il vienne? *Non*
8. Êtes-vous certain que Jean vienne? *Non*

302. Give your opinion about the following. Introduce your comments with the following expressions:

Il est sûr que   Il n'est pas sûr que
Il est probable que   Il n'est pas probable que
Il est certain que   Il n'est pas certain que
Je pense que   Je ne pense pas que
Je crois que   Je ne crois pas que

Je serai élu président.
Il est sûr que tu seras (vous serez) élu président.
Il n'est pas probable que tu sois (vous soyez) élu président.

1. Les astronautes iront sur la lune.
2. Vous atteindrez l'âge de 50 ans.
3. Je recevrai de bonnes notes.
4. Tes professeurs sont trop exigeants.
5. Tu auras dix enfants.
6. Tes amis feront le tour du monde.
7. Tes amis seront toujours fidèles.
8. Nous prendrons nos vacances sur Mars.
9. Tu deviendras professeur.
10. Nous mourrons.

Subjunctive with subordinate conjunctions

The following conjunctions require the subjunctive.

1. Of time

avant que	*before*
en attendant que	*until*
jusqu'à ce que	*until*
aussi (de si) loin que	*far from as far back as*

On lui dira au revoir avant qu'il (ne) parte. (The (**ne**) is not negative. See p. 208.)
We will tell him good-bye before he leaves.

2. Of cause or negation

non que	*not that*
non pas que	*not that*
sans que	*without*

Elle est partie sans que je la voie.
She left without my seeing her.

3. Of purpose

afin que	*in order that*
pour que	*in order that*
de manière que	*so that*
de façon que	*so that*
de sorte que	*so that*
de crainte que	*for fear that*
de peur que	*for fear that*

Elle ne vous parle pas de peur que vous la réprimandiez.
She does not speak to you for fear that you will scold her.

In certain cases, **de manière que, de façon que** and **de sorte que** are followed by the indicative, particularly when the result is an accomplished and presumably irreversible deed or fact.

Les étudiants se taisaient de sorte que personne ne pouvait entendre le moindre bruit.
The students were so quiet you couldn't hear the slightest noise.

4. Of concession

bien que	*although*
quoique	*although*
encore que	*although*
malgré que	*in spite of*

Bien qu'il soit chez lui, il ne répond pas au téléphone.
Although he is at home, he does not answer the telephone.

5. Of condition

à condition que	*on condition that*
en cas que	*in case*
pourvu que	*provided that*
supposé que	*supposing that*
à moins que	*unless*
soit que... soit que	*whether ... or*

Ils iront à la plage à moins qu'il (ne) pleuve.
They will go to the beach unless it rains.

Ne is usually used after **à moins que, avant que, de peur que, de crainte que, de manière que, de sorte que** when the verb in the dependent clause is affirmative. When the verb is negative, **ne... pas** is used.

Nous nous réveillons tôt de peur qu'elle ne parte sans nous.
We are getting up early for fear that she will leave without us.
Nous nous réveillons tôt de peur qu'elle ne nous attende pas.
We are getting up early for fear that she will not wait for us.

The following conjunctions do not take the subjunctive.

aussitôt que	*as soon as*
dès que	*as soon as*
après que	*after*
pendant que	*while*
parce que	*because*

Review the use of conjunctions with the future and conditional tenses on pages 177–178 and 184.

303. Complete the following sentences with the correct form of each indicated expression.

1. À moins que tu ne _____, le professeur se fâchera.
   (savoir la leçon, faire tes devoirs, lire le roman, écrire la composition)
2. Quoiqu'il _____, je m'en irai.
   (neiger, faire froid, pleuvoir)
3. Il se couchera aussitôt qu'il _____.
   (être fatigué, arriver, rentrer, revenir)

304. Complete the following sentences with the correct form of the subjunctive of the indicated verb.

1. Je le verrai avant qu'il ne _____. *partir*
2. Je lui répondrai avant qu'elle ne _____. *sortir*
3. Je lirai en attendant qu'elle _____. *venir*
4. Il m'aidera jusqu'à ce que je _____ une meilleure note. *recevoir*
5. Je les attendrai jusqu'à ce qu'ils _____. *revenir*
6. Elle part sans qu'on lui _____ au revoir. *dire*
7. Je parlerai lentement pour que vous _____. *comprendre*
8. Je partirai tôt afin que je _____ arriver à l'heure. *pouvoir*
9. Il fera cela de sorte que nous _____ contents. *être*
10. De peur qu'il ne _____, je prendrai un parapluie. *pleuvoir*
11. Je resterai ici de crainte que mes amis n' _____. *arriver*
12. Quoiqu'il _____ riche, je ne l'aime pas. *être*
13. Bien qu'elles _____, elles ne réussissent pas. *étudier*
14. Nous sortirons ce soir à moins qu'il ne _____. *neiger*
15. Je vous attendrai pourvu que vous n' _____ pas trop en retard. *arriver*
16. À moins qu'il ne _____ beau, je ne sortirai pas. *faire*
17. À moins que tu ne _____ la leçon, il se fâchera. *savoir*

305. Complete the following sentences with the correct form of the indicated verb.

1. Aussitôt qu'il _____, nous partirons. *arriver*
2. Je me dépêche de peur qu'elle ne m' _____ pas. *attendre*
3. Dès qu'elle _____, nous mangerons. *venir*
4. Je vous l'expliquerai afin que vous le _____ mieux. *comprendre*
5. Ils chantaient pendant que je _____ de la guitare. *jouer*
6. Elle me verra avant que je ne _____. *partir*

Subjunctive as an imperative

The subjunctive may be used as an imperative when not talking to the person to whom the command is directed.

Qu'il parte tout de suite!
Let him leave immediately!
Qu'elle ne revienne jamais!
May she never return!

Vive le roi!
Long live the king!
Ainsi soit-il!
So be it!

Subjunctive after an affirmation

The subjunctive is used in the following expressions of affirmation.

que je sache	*that I know*
pas que je sache	*not that I know*
autant que je sache	*as much as I know*

Personne n'est à la porte, que je sache.
No one is at the door so far as I know.

306. Change the sentence according to the model.

Il part maintenant.
Qu'il parte maintenant!

1. Elle vient tout de suite.
2. Il conduit sagement.
3. Il répond au professeur.
4. Ils obéissent à leurs parents.
5. Elle apprend la leçon.
6. Elles disent la vérité.
7. Il sait la réponse.
8. Elles finissent leurs devoirs.

Subjunctive in relative clauses

Indefinite antecedent

The subjunctive is used in relative clauses when the antecedent (the word the clause modifies) is indefinite. In other words, it is used after a noun or pronoun representing someone or something that is not yet identified or found. If the antecedent is definite, the indicative is used.

Je connais un médecin qui peut m'aider.
I know a doctor who can help me.
Je cherche un médecin qui puisse m'aider.
I am looking for a doctor who can help me. (But I haven't found one yet.)

Je connais un homme qui sait parler français.
I know a man who knows how to speak French.
Je cherche un homme qui sache parler français.
I am looking for a man who knows how to speak French. (But I haven't found him yet.)

307. Complete the following sentences with the correct form of each indicated expression.

1. Je connais une secrétaire qui _____.
   (parler français, écrire bien, savoir faire le traitement de texte)
2. J'ai besoin d'une secrétaire qui _____.
   (parler français, écrire bien, savoir faire le traitement de texte)

308. Rewrite the following sentences according to the model.

Je connais une fille. Elle sait parler français.
Je connais une fille qui sait parler français.

Je cherche une fille. Elle sait parler français.
Je cherche une fille qui sache parler français.

1. Je cherche un homme. Il connaît la route.
2. J'ai trouvé un homme. Il connaît cette chanson.

3. Je veux acheter une blouse. Elle me va bien.
4. J'ai une blouse. Elle me va bien.
5. Je cherche un poste. Il est intéressant.
6. J'ai un poste. Il est intéressant.

*After **rien, personne, quelqu'un***

The subjunctive is also used after **rien, personne** or **quelqu'un** when doubt is implied.

> **Il n'y a personne qui puisse m'aider.**
> **Il n'y a rien qu'il puisse faire.**
> **Y a-t-il quelqu'un qui puisse le faire?**

But:

> **Voici quelqu'un qui peut le faire.**

309. Complete the following sentences with the correct form of the indicated verb.

1. Y a-t-il quelqu'un qui _____ la réponse? *savoir*
2. Il n'y a personne qui _____ le faire. *vouloir*
3. Il n'y a rien qui _____ m'aider. *pouvoir*
4. Voici quelqu'un qui _____ le français. *lire*
5. Il n'y a personne qui _____ aider cet enfant. *pouvoir*

*With the superlative and **seul, unique***

The subjunctive is used in a relative clause after a superlative expression, and after **seul** and **unique** when the superlative expression implies judgment or is considered to be an exaggeration.

> **C'est le plus beau poème qu'il connaisse.**
> *It is the most beautiful poem that he knows.*
> **C'est le seul livre que je comprenne.**
> *It is the only book that I understand.*

310. Complete the following sentences with the appropriate form of the indicated verb.

1. C'est le meilleur livre que j'_____. *avoir*
2. C'est le seul livre que je _____. *vouloir*
3. Pierre est le plus gentil garçon que je _____. *connaître*
4. C'est la ville la plus cosmopolite qui _____ dans le monde. *exister*
5. C'est la seule chose que je _____. *comprendre*

**Subjunctive after indefinite words such as *si... que, quelque... que,
quel... que, qui que...*, etc.**

The subjunctive is used after certain indefinite words.

Si... que	*However*
Quelque	*However*
Quelque(s)... que	*Whatever*
Quel(le)(s)(les) que	*Whatever*
Qui que	*Whoever*
Quoi que	*Whatever*
Où que	*Wherever*
Soit que... soit que	*Whether ... or*
De quelque manière que	*However*

Si intelligent qu'il soit, il ne pourra pas comprendre.
However intelligent he may be, he will not understand.
Quelque fort qu'il soit, il ne pourra pas le faire.
However strong he is, he won't be able to do it.
Quelques fautes que les élèves fassent, il faut les encourager.
Whatever mistakes the students make, you must encourage them.
Quels que soient vos problèmes, vous pourrez les résoudre.
Whatever your problems are, you can resolve them.
Qui que vous soyez, je ne vous connais pas.
Whoever you may be, I don't know you.
Quoi que tu dises, je te croirai.
Whatever you say, I'll believe you.
Où que vous alliez, je vous suivrai.
Wherever you go, I'll follow.
Soit qu'il vienne, soit qu'il ne vienne pas, j'irai quand même.
Whether he comes or not, I'll go.
De quelque manière qu'elle agisse, vous l'aimerez.
However she acts, you will like her.

311. Complete the following sentences with the appropriate form of the indicated verb.

1. Quelque difficulté que vous _____, persévérez.   *avoir*
2. Qui que vous _____, travaillez bien.   *être*
3. Quoi qu'il _____, il le fait bien.   *faire*
4. Où que nous _____, nous vous téléphonerons.   *aller*
5. Quels que _____ vos problèmes, je vous aiderai.   *être*
6. Quoi qu'on _____, vous êtes gentille.   *dire*
7. Si bon que je _____, elle ne m'aime pas.   *être*
8. Quelque méchamment qu'il _____, il a beaucoup d'amis.   *agir*
9. De quelque manière qu'il _____, on ne le comprend pas.   *parler*
10. Soit qu'elle _____, soit qu'elle ne _____ pas, nous commencerons la conférence.   *venir*

Avoiding the Subjunctive

When there is no change of subject in the relative clause, the infinitive is usually used.

Il est content qu'il vienne.
Il est content de venir.

Verbs indicating a command, permission or refusal of permission (see pages 201–202) are usually not used with a subjunctive clause. The clause is normally replaced by an indirect object introduced by **à** and followed by an infinitive introduced by **de**.

Il permet que son fils parte.
Il permet à son fils de partir.
He permits his son to leave.

You can also avoid the subjunctive by replacing a clause with a noun.

Je vais le voir **avant qu'il ne parte.**
I'm going to see him before he leaves.
Je vais le voir **avant son départ.**
I'm going to see him before his departure.

312. Rewrite the following sentences using an infinitive construction or a noun instead of the subjunctive.

1. Il se dépêche afin qu'il arrive à l'heure.
2. Il est content qu'il soit ici.
3. Il ordonne que son fils parte.
4. Il permet que l'avocat parle.
5. J'attends jusqu'à ce qu'il arrive.
6. Nous ferons cela avant que nous partions.

Review

313. Complete the following sentences with the appropriate form of the indicated verb.

1. Je veux que vous y _____ aussi. *aller*
2. Je n'ai rien qui leur _____. *plaire*
3. Je crois qu'il _____ . *venir*
4. Il va attendre jusqu'à ce que nous _____. *revenir*
5. Je connais quelqu'un qui _____ le faire. *pouvoir*
6. Il permet que je _____ du vin. *boire*
7. Il regrette que je ne _____ pas le faire. *pouvoir*
8. Il vaut mieux qu'il _____ de bonne heure. *partir*
9. Il est probable qu'il _____ la réponse. *savoir*
10. C'est le plus beau livre que je _____. *connaître*
11. Il faut que nous _____ le travail. *faire*
12. Il est certain qu'il _____ la vérité. *dire*
13. Croyez-vous qu'il _____ demain? *pleuvoir*
14. Si malades que nous _____, nous travaillerons. *être*
15. Je le ferai à moins que vous n'_____ le temps de le faire. *avoir*
16. Il se dépêche afin d'_____ à l'heure. *arriver*

314. Complete each of the following with three endings.

1. Je regrette que...
2. Je pense que...
3. J'irai au cinéma à moins que...
4. Je suis content(e) que...
5. Je suis désolé(e) que...
6. Il est étonnant que...
7. J'étudierai tous les jours afin de...
8. Il est sûr que...
9. C'est le plus beau (la plus belle)...
10. Il n'y a personne qui...
11. Je veux que...
12. Je connais quelqu'un qui...
13. Je doute que...
14. Il est certain que...
15. Je suis heureux de...
16. Que mon professeur...

The Past Subjunctive

The past subjunctive is formed by using the subjunctive of the verb **avoir** or **être** and the past participle.

parler	venir
j'aie parlé	je sois venu(e)
tu aies parlé	tu sois venu(e)
il, elle, on ait parlé	il, on soit venu
nous ayons parlé	elle soit venue
vous ayez parlé	nous soyons venu(e)s
ils, elles aient parlé	vous soyez venu(e)(s)(es)
	ils soient venus
	elles soient venues

Je regrette qu'il n'ait pas attendu.
I am sorry that he didn't wait.
Je suis content qu'elle soit venue.
I am happy that she came.

315. Complete the following sentences with the correct form of the past subjunctive of the indicated verb.

1. Elle est contente que tu _____. *arriver*
2. Elle a peur que nous _____ cela à tout le monde. *dire*
3. Il est possible qu'elles vous _____. *reconnaître*
4. Je ne crois pas qu'elle _____. *venir*
5. Il est possible que vous _____. *rester*
6. Nous doutons qu'elle _____. *souffrir*
7. Je ne crois pas qu'ils _____ leurs devoirs. *faire*
8. Bien qu'il _____, il n'a pas réussi. *étudier*
9. Nous sommes heureux qu'elle _____. *s'amuser*
10. Quoique les enfants _____ de bonne heure, ils étaient fatigués le matin. *se coucher*

316. Rewrite the following sentences, putting the action of the dependent clause in the past.

1. Elle doute que nous comprenions.
2. Je regrette que tu arrives.
3. Il est possible que vous finissiez à l'heure.
4. Je ne crois pas qu'elles viennent.
5. Je doute qu'elle fasse le travail.
6. Pensez-vous qu'il se rase?

317. Comment on the following, using the indicated expression. Follow the model.

Elle est arrivée à l'heure.   *Je doute que*
Je doute qu'elle soit arrivée à l'heure.

1. Nous avons reconnu cet homme.   *Il doute que*
2. Ils sont partis.   *Je ne crois pas que*
3. Vous avez fait vos devoirs.   *Il est important que*
4. Elle est revenue de bonne heure.   *Il se peut que*
5. Il a su la réponse.   *Je doute que*

318. React to the following, using one of the expressions below. There may be more than one possibility as long as the expression is logical.

C'est dommage que   Je suis heureux (heureuse) que
Il est bon que   Je suis surpris(e) que
Je suis désolé(e) que

Il a fait du soleil le jour du pique-nique.
Il est bon (Je suis heureux [heureuse]) qu'il ait fait du soleil le jour du pique-nique.

1. Il a plu le jour du pique-nique.
2. Nous avons apporté des parapluies.
3. J'ai trouvé un emploi d'été.
4. Nous avons réussi à nos examens.
5. Il est tombé malade le jour de son anniversaire.
6. Elle a gagné à la loterie.
7. Notre équipe a perdu le match.
8. Il s'est fait mal au pied.

The Imperfect Subjunctive

The imperfect subjunctive is formed by dropping the **s** from the second person singular form of the *passé simple* (literary past tense) and adding the endings -sse, -sses, -^t, -ssions, -ssiez, -ssent.

parler	**finir**	**attendre**
Base: **tu parlas**	**tu finis**	**tu attendis**
je parla**sse**	je fini**sse**	j'attendi**sse**
tu parla**sses**	tu fini**sses**	tu attendi**sses**
il, elle, on parl**ât**	il, elle, on fin**ît**	il, elle, on attend**ît**
nous parla**ssions**	nous fini**ssions**	nous attendi**ssions**
vous parla**ssiez**	vous fini**ssiez**	vous attendi**ssiez**
ils, elles parla**ssent**	ils, elles fini**ssent**	ils, elles attendi**ssent**

avoir	**être**
Base: **tu eus**	**tu fus**
j'eu**sse**	je fu**sse**
tu eu**sses**	tu fu**sses**
il, elle, on e**ût**	il, elle, on f**ût**
nous eu**ssions**	nous fu**ssions**
vous eu**ssiez**	vous fu**ssiez**
ils, elles eu**ssent**	ils, elles fu**ssent**

Study the following. For other verbs which have irregular forms in the *passé simple*, see pages 169–172.

Infinitive	*Passé simple*	*Imperfect subjunctive*
partir	tu partis	**je partisse, il partît**
rire	tu ris	**je risse, il rît**
dire	tu dis	**je disse, il dît**
prendre	tu pris	**je prisse, il prît**
boire	tu bus	**je busse, il bût**
connaître	tu connus	**je connusse, il connût**
courir	tu courus	**je courusse, il courût**
croire	tu crus	**je crusse, il crût**
devoir	tu dus	**je dusse, il dût**
lire	tu lus	**je lusse, il lût**
paraître	tu parus	**je parusse, il parût**
plaire	tu plus	**je plusse, il plût**
pouvoir	tu pus	**je pusse, il pût**
recevoir	tu reçus	**je reçusse, il reçût**
savoir	tu sus	**je susse, il sût**
se taire	tu te tus	**je me tusse, il se tût**
vivre	tu vécus	**je vécusse, il vécût**
vouloir	tu voulus	**je voulusse, il voulût**
battre	tu battis	**je battisse, il battît**
rompre	tu rompis	**je rompisse, il rompît**
offrir	tu offris	**j'offrisse, il offrît**
ouvrir	tu ouvris	**j'ouvrisse, il ouvrît**
couvrir	tu couvris	**je couvrisse, il couvrît**

souffrir	tu souffris	**je souffrisse, il souffrît**
vaincre	tu vainquis	**je vainquisse, il vainquît**
écrire	tu écrivis	**j'écrivisse, il écrivît**
conduire	tu conduisis	**je conduisisse, il conduisît**
traduire	tu traduisis	**je traduisisse, il traduisît**
naître	tu naquis	**je naquisse, il naquît**
voir	tu vis	**je visse, il vît**
craindre	tu craignis	**je craignisse, il craignît**
joindre	tu joignis	**je joignisse, il joignît**
peindre	tu peignis	**je peignisse, il peignît**
faire	tu fis	**je fisse, il fît**
mourir	tu mourus	**je mourusse, il mourût**
tenir	tu tins	**je tinsse, il tînt**
venir	tu vins	**je vinsse, il vînt**

Use of the Imperfect Subjunctive

The imperfect subjunctive is used only in written language when the verb in the main clause is in the past of the indicative or in the conditional. In spoken language, the present subjunctive replaces the imperfect subjunctive.

Spoken and written:	**Je veux qu'il vienne me voir.**
	I want him to come to see me.
Written:	**Je voulais qu'il vînt me voir.**
Spoken:	**Je voulais qu'il vienne me voir.**
	I wanted him to come to see me.

319. Complete the following sentences with the correct form of the imperfect subjunctive of the indicated verb.

  1. Je doutais qu'il _____ me voir.   *venir*
  2. Elle cherchait quelqu'un qui _____ le faire.   *pouvoir*
  3. Je voudrais qu'il _____ à l'heure.   *être*
  4. Je ne croyais pas qu'ils _____ à l'heure.   *finir*
  5. Il doutait que nous _____ malades.   *être*
  6. Elle était heureuse que vous _____ la vérité.   *savoir*
  7. Il était content que nous _____ le travail.   *faire*
  8. Elle était heureuse qu'il _____ la lettre.   *écrire*
  9. Elle voulait que vous _____ tout de suite.   *venir*
10. On craignait que les enfants ne _____ pas à l'heure.   *rentrer*
11. Il avait peur que tu ne _____ fâché.   *devenir*
12. Il fallait que les enfants _____ de bonne heure.   *se coucher*

320. Rewrite the following sentences in spoken language.

  1. Il voulait que nous vinssions.
  2. J'étais heureux qu'elles fussent à l'heure.
  3. Il fallait qu'elle le fît.
  4. Elle était trop fatiguée pour que la soirée fût agréable.
  5. Je cherchais quelqu'un qui pût le faire.
  6. Je craignais que l'équipe ne gagnât pas le prix.

The Pluperfect Subjunctive

The pluperfect subjunctive is formed by using the imperfect subjunctive of **avoir** or **être** and the past participle.

parler	partir
j'eusse parlé	je fusse parti(e)
tu eusses parlé	tu fusses parti(e)
il, elle, on eût parlé	il, on fût parti
nous eussions parlé	elle fût partie
vous eussiez parlé	nous fussions parti(e)s
ils, elles eussent parlé	vous fussiez parti(e)(s)(es)
	ils fussent partis
	elles fussent parties

Use of the Pluperfect Subjunctive

The pluperfect subjunctive is a literary tense. In conversation, the past subjunctive replaces the pluperfect subjunctive.

Spoken and Written: **Il regrette que nous ne soyons pas venus.**
He is sorry we didn't come.

Written: **Il regrettait que nous ne fussions pas venus.**
Spoken: **Il regrettait que nous ne soyons pas venus.**
He was sorry we didn't come.

If the subjunctive is obligatory, the sentence can usually be rewritten to avoid it.

Bien qu'il eût déjà mangé, il alla au restaurant.
Il avait déjà mangé, mais il est allé au restaurant.

321. Complete the following sentences with the correct form of the pluperfect subjunctive of the indicated verb.

1. Il doutait qu'elle _____ malade. *être*
2. Je regrettais qu'elles ne _____ pas _____. *venir*
3. Elle était heureuse que vous _____ la vérité. *savoir*
4. Elle était triste qu'il _____. *partir*
5. J'étais heureux qu'il _____ la lettre. *écrire*
6. Il était content que tu _____. *réussir*
7. Il était possible qu'elles _____ cela. *savoir*
8. Elles ne croyaient pas que j' _____ tant de chance. *avoir*
9. Nous préférions attendre jusqu'à ce qu'ils _____. *revenir*
10. Elle avait peur qu'il n' _____ pas _____ le travail. *finir*
11. Il semblait que nous _____ des efforts inutiles. *faire*
12. Elle était contente que nous _____. *se débrouiller*

322. Rewrite the following sentences in spoken language.

1. Je regrettais qu'elle ne fût pas venue à l'heure.
2. Bien qu'elles eussent déjà compris, ils continuaient à leur expliquer.
3. J'étais contente qu'il eût connu mon ami.
4. Il fallait que vous eussiez dit cela.
5. Il semblait que nous eussions fait des efforts.
6. Il avait peur que le pain ne fût devenu trop dur.

Si *Clauses in the Subjunctive*

The subjunctive is used in *if* clauses in literary style. The pluperfect subjunctive can be used in the *if* clause to replace the pluperfect indicative and in the main clause to replace the past conditional. It is in reality "a literary past conditional."

Spoken:	**S'il l'avait cru, il serait parti.**
Written:	**S'il l'eût cru, il fût parti.**
	S'il l'avait cru, il fût parti.
	S'il l'eût cru, il serait parti.

323. Rewrite the following sentences, putting all verbs in literary style.

1. S'il avait eu assez d'argent, il serait allé au cinéma.
2. Si vous étiez venu, vous auriez vu Paul.
3. S'il avait été prêt, il serait parti.
4. Si vous étiez venu, vous auriez appris la nouvelle.
5. S'il avait fait beau, nous serions partis.
6. Si elle était revenue, elle serait venue nous revoir.

324. Rewrite the following sentences in spoken language.

1. Le nez de Cléopâtre s'il eût été plus court, toute la face de la terre eût changé.
2. Si elle eût eu assez d'argent, elle fût venue nous voir.
3. Si nous eussions su cela, nous l'eussions dit.
4. S'il eût fait beau, elle fût partie.
5. S'il eût plu, elles ne fussent pas venues.
6. Si j'eusse su cela, je ne vous eusse pas répondu.

Sequence of Tenses in Indirect Discourse

Direct discourse *directly cites* someone's words.

Il me dit: « Viens chez moi samedi. »
Il me dit: « Je le ferai dans une heure. »

Indirect discourse *indirectly reports* someone's words.

Il me dit de venir chez lui samedi.
Il me dit qu'il le fera dans une heure.

When the verb in the principal introductory phrase is in the present or the future tense, there is no tense change in indirect discourse. When the principal verb is in the past tense, the following changes of tense occur.

	Direct discourse		*Indirect discourse*
	imperfect		imperfect
	present		imperfect
	passé composé		pluperfect
il dit	future	**il a dit**	present conditional
il dira	present conditional		past conditional
	futur antérieur		past conditional
	imperative		infinitive or subjunctive
	subjunctive		subjunctive

Pierre dit: « **Il faisait** beau hier. »
Pierre **dit** qu'il **faisait** beau hier.
Pierre **a dit** qu'il **faisait** beau hier.

Elle dit: « **Je pars** tout de suite. »
Elle **dit** qu'**elle part** tout de suite.
Elle **a dit** qu'**elle partait** tout de suite.

Anne répond: « **J'ai vu** le film hier. »
Anne **répond** qu'**elle a vu** le film hier.
Anne **a répondu** qu'**elle avait vu** le film hier.

Il déclare: « **Je viendrai** ici demain. »
Il **déclare** qu'**il viendra** ici demain.
Il **a déclaré** qu'**il viendrait** ici demain.

André dit: « **Je voudrais** faire sa connaissance. »
André **dit** qu'**il voudrait** faire sa connaissance.
André **a dit** qu'**il aurait voulu** faire sa connaissance.

Marie dit: « **Pierre aura fini** à trois heures. »
Marie **dit** que **Pierre aura fini** à trois heures.
Marie **a dit** que **Pierre aurait fini** à trois heures.

Elle lui dit: « **Attends** un moment. »
Elle lui **dit d'attendre** un moment.
Elle lui **a dit d'attendre** un moment.

Il lui suggère: « **Allons** au cinéma. »
Il lui **suggère** qu'**ils aillent** au cinéma.
Il lui **a suggéré** qu'**ils aillent** au cinéma.

Le professeur dit: « **Je veux que vous fassiez** le travail. »
Le professeur **dit** qu'**il veut que nous fassions** le travail.
Le professeur **a dit** qu'**il voulait que nous fassions** le travail.

Note that the first and second persons are generally replaced by the third person in indirect discourse.

Indirect Discourse in Sentences with an Interrogative Word

After the verbs **demander, se demander, ignorer, savoir, comprendre** and **chercher**, certain interrogative words change in form and in order.

A direct question related to a verb and **est-ce que** becomes **si** in indirect discourse. **Si** means *whether* or *if*.

Direct discourse

Il demande: « **Les Leblanc seront ici bientôt?** »
                          « **Est-ce que les Leblanc seront ici bientôt?** »
                          « **Les Leblanc seront-ils ici bientôt?** »

Indirect discourse

Il demande si les Leblanc seront ici bientôt.
He asks whether the Leblancs will be here soon.

Interrogative Pronouns in Indirect Discourse

Qui is used in all cases for people.

Direct discourse	*Indirect discourse*
Il demande: « Qui est-ce que tu vois? »	**Il demande qui tu vois.**
Il demande: « Qui vois-tu? »	**Il demande qui est-ce que tu vois.** *(spoken)*
Il demande: « Avec qui va-t-elle à la surprise-partie? »	**Il demande avec qui elle va à la surprise-partie.**
	Il demande avec qui est-ce qu'elle va à la surprise-partie. *(spoken)*

For things, the subject pronoun **ce qui** and the object pronoun **ce que** are used. **Quoi** is the object of the preposition.

Je me demande **ce qui** se passe, **ce que** vous dites, **avec quoi** elle peint.

In spoken language, the long forms of **ce qui** and **ce que**, **qu'est-ce qui** and **qu'est-ce que** and **avec quoi est-ce que** are used.

See *Interrogative Pronouns*, pages 236–237.

Inversion of the Subject in Indirect Discourse

In indirect discourse, there is never inversion of the pronoun subject and the verb but there can be simple inversion of the noun subject and the verb.

Direct discourse	*Indirect discourse*
Je me demande: « Quand se mariera-t-il? »	**Je me demande quand il se mariera.**
Je lui demande: « Où travaille ta femme? »	**Je lui demande où travaille sa femme (où sa femme travaille).**

Inversion can be used only if the verb stands alone without a direct object.

There can never be inversion with **pourquoi.**

Elle demande pourquoi ils sont toujours en retard.

Inversion is used with **ce que, avec qui, avec quoi.**

Je ne sais pas ce que fait son enfant.

There is never inversion after **qui** as a direct object.

J'ignore qui Marie va épouser.

325. Put the following sentences in indirect discourse. Then put the answers in the past tense. Follow the model.

Pierre dit: « Je veux acheter une bicyclette. »
Pierre *dit* qu'*il veut* acheter une bicyclette.
Pierre *a dit* qu'*il voulait* acheter une bicyclette.

1. André dit: « Je ne peux pas le faire. »
2. Marie dit: « Je n'ai jamais vu rien de si beau. »
3. Jean promet: « Je ferai tout pour vous aider. »
4. Ils disent: « Nous pouvons aider la nouvelle étudiante. »
5. Mes parents me promettent: « Nous te donnerons une auto si tu reçois de meilleures notes. »

6. Monsieur Leblanc dit: « Nous irons en Afrique cet été. »
7. Claire répond: « J'ai déjà lu ce livre. »
8. Anne dit: « J'aimerais voir ce film. »
9. Pierre dit: « Il faisait beau hier. »
10. Roger dit: « Elle aura fini à trois heures. »
11. Marie demande: « Ont-ils gagné le match? »
12. Le professeur demande: « Serez-vous à la réunion? »

326. Madame Leclerc was a witness to a crime. She is being interrogated by the lawyer in a courtroom. Relate the following interview between the lawyer and Madame Leclerc, using indirect discourse.

L'avocat	Où étiez-vous à deux heures du matin le 8 octobre?
Mme Leclerc	J'étais dans la cuisine.
L'avocat	Avez-vous l'habitude d'être dans la cuisine si tard?
Mme Leclerc	Non, mais ce soir-là je ne pouvais pas dormir et donc, je suis descendue dans la cuisine pour chercher un verre de lait.
L'avocat	Avez-vous entendu ou vu quelque chose d'étrange?
Mme Leclerc	Oui, j'ai entendu des cris dans la maison de ma voisine et j'ai vu un homme attaquer ma voisine avec un couteau.
L'avocat	Pourriez-vous identifier cet homme?
Mme Leclerc	Oui, je pourrais l'identifier clairement, car la lumière était allumée dans sa maison.
L'avocat	Cet homme, est-il dans cette salle?
Mme Leclerc	Oui, c'est l'accusé.
L'avocat	Merci, vous pouvez quitter la barre des témoins.

L'avocat lui a demandé où elle était à deux heures du matin le 8 octobre.
Mme Leclerc a répondu qu'elle...

Continue.

Uses of the Infinitive

After Prepositions

The infinitive is used after most prepositions, such as **avant de, pour, afin de** and **sans.** The present participle is sometimes used in English.

avant de partir	*before leaving*
pour aller	*in order to go*
afin de venir	*in order to come*
sans comprendre	*without understanding*

Je lui ai parlé **avant de partir.**
I spoke to him before leaving.

En is followed by the present participle.

en parlant	*while speaking*
en sortant	*upon leaving*

En sortant, il nous a dit au revoir.
Upon leaving, he told us good-bye.
En faisant ses courses, elle a vu son ami.
While shopping, she saw her friend.

See the use of the present participle, page 140–141.

After the preposition **après,** the infinitive of **avoir** or **être** plus the past participle of the verb is used.

après avoir parlé	*after having spoken*
après être parti(e)(s)(es)	*after having left*
après s'être habillé(e)(s)(es)	*after having gotten dressed*

As a Noun

Vouloir c'est pouvoir.
Where there's a will, there's a way.
Voter est un droit.
Voting is a right.

As an Imperative

Ne pas marcher sur le gazon.
Do not walk on the grass.
Laisser cuire pendant trente minutes.
Cook for thirty minutes.

In an Interrogative Phrase Expressing Deliberation

Que faire?
What shall I (we) do?
Où aller?
Where shall I (we) go?

In an Exclamatory Phrase

Oh! être jeune encore!
Oh, to be still young!

327. Substitute each indicated infinitive in the following sentences. Make all necessary changes.

1. Je lui parlerai avant de partir. (manger, chanter, danser, décider, revenir, finir, commencer)
2. Que faut-il faire afin de comprendre? (venir, réussir, finir à l'heure, savoir la leçon)
3. Il part sans dire au revoir. (manger, attendre, faire ses devoirs, parler)
4. Après avoir chanté, il est parti. (parler, finir, manger, dire au revoir)
5. Après être arrivé, il est venu me voir. (rentrer, entrer, retourner, descendre)

328. Combine the following sentences according to the model.

Il a fini la leçon. Ensuite, il est allé au théâtre.
Avant d'aller au théâtre, il a fini la leçon.
Après avoir fini la leçon, il est allé au théâtre.

1. Il a mangé. Ensuite, il est parti.
2. Nous avons déjeuné. Ensuite, nous sommes allés au musée.
3. Nous avons fait le ménage. Ensuite, nous avons joué au tennis.
4. Elle s'est habillée. Ensuite, elle a lu le journal.

329. Translate the following into French, using an infinitive or a present participle.

1. before arriving
2. after arriving
3. upon arriving
4. while eating
5. after eating
6. before eating
7. Do not translate.
8. Beat three eggs.
9. What shall we do?
10. Oh, to be rich!

330. Answer the following personalized questions.

1. Qu'est-ce que tu fais avant dc tc coucher?
2. Qu'est-ce que tu fais afin de réussir aux examens de français?
3. Qu'est-ce que tu fais après t'être réveillé(e) samedi matin?
4. Écoutes-tu de la musique en faisant tes devoirs?
5. Qu'est-ce que tu fais avant de prendre tes repas?

331. Complete the following to describe your typical day.

1. Après (se réveiller)...
2. Avant de (prendre le petit déjeuner)...
3. Après (s'habiller)...
4. Avant de (sortir)...
5. Après (manger)...
6. Avant de (se coucher)...

Faire in Causative Construction

An important use of the verb **faire** is in causative construction. In this construction, the subject causes an action to bc donc by someone or something else. **Faire** is followed by the infinitive.

Je fais chanter les enfants.
I have (make) the children sing.
J'ai fait réciter les élèves.
I had (made) the students recite.
Il fait faire ce travail.
He has this work done.
Il a fait faire ce travail.
He had this work done.

When there is one object, it is a direct object. If it is a noun, it follows the infinitive. If it is a pronoun, it precedes **faire** in the negative imperative and in declarative sentences.

Ne faites pas descendre les valises maintenant.
Don't have the suitcases brought down now.
Ne les faites pas descendre maintenant.
Don't have them brought down now.

Il fait chanter la fille.
He has the girl sing.
Il la fait chanter.
He has her sing.

Elle fait faire une robe.
She has a dress made.
Elle la fait faire.
She has it made.

Elle a fait construire une maison.
She had a house built.
Elle l'a fait construire.
She had it built.

In the above sentence, the object of **faire** is **construire**. **Faire** does not agree with the direct object pronoun.

In the affirmative imperative, the direct object noun follows the infinitive, but the direct object pronoun precedes the infinitive.

> **Faites laver la voiture.**
> *Have the car washed.*
> **Faites-la laver.**
> *Have it washed.*

When there are two noun or pronoun complements, one will be the direct object and the other will be the indirect object. The person or thing doing the action is the indirect object. Again, all pronoun objects precede **faire** except in the affirmative imperative.

> **Il fait réciter le poème aux étudiants.**
> *He has the students recite the poem.*
> **Il le fait réciter aux étudiants.**
> *He has the students recite it.*
> **Il leur fait réciter le poème.**
> *He has them recite the poem.*
> **Il le leur fait réciter.**
> *He has them recite it.*
> **Ne le leur fais pas réciter.**
> *Don't have them recite it.*
>
> *But:*
>
> **Fais-le-leur réciter.**
> *Have them recite it.*

The past participle of **faire** is always invariable when followed by an infinitive.

> la maison que nous avons **fait** construire
> *the house we had built*

If necessary, review object pronouns in Chapter 8.

To avoid possible ambiguity with the indirect object, the person or thing doing the action can be introduced by **par** instead of **à**. For example, **Il fait chanter une chanson à Marie** can mean (1) *He has Mary sing a song* or (2) *He has a song sung to Mary*. If the first meaning is intended, **par** can replace **à**.

> **Il fait chanter une chanson par Marie.**
> *He has Mary sing a song.*

A reflexive pronoun can be used with the verb **faire** in causative construction.

> **Elle s'est fait faire une robe.**
> *She had a dress made (for herself).*
> **Je me fais couper les cheveux.**
> *I have my hair cut.*
> **Je me suis fait couper les cheveux.**
> *I had my hair cut.*
> **Je me les suis fait couper.**
> *I had it cut.*

332. Madame Dupont is having a house built. Tell who is responsible for various aspects of construction. Follow the model.

> **Qui construit la maison?** *la Compagnie Leclerc*
> **Elle fait construire la maison à la Compagnie Leclerc.**

1. Qui fait les dessins? *l'architecte*
2. Qui peint les murs? *le peintre*
3. Qui installe les salles de bains? *le plombier*
4. Qui pose des fils électriques? *les électriciens*
5. Qui bâtit les étagères à livres? *le charpentier*

333. Rewrite the following sentences, substituting **par** for **à** in order to make the sentences less ambiguous.

1. Le professeur a fait écrire le devoir à la classe.
2. Elle fait chanter la chanson aux garçons.
3. Nous faisons écrire une lettre à notre ami.
4. Je fais jouer du piano à l'enfant.

334. Rewrite the following sentences, replacing the direct object by a pronoun, according to the model.

> **Le professeur fait expliquer la leçon.**
> **Le professeur la fait expliquer.**

1. Le professeur fera réciter les élèves.
2. La fille a fait faire la robe.
3. Nous ferons faire les portraits.
4. Il fera construire la maison.
5. Vous avez fait venir le médecin.
6. Elle s'est fait laver les cheveux.
7. Fais entrer les invités.
8. Faites venir le médecin.

335. The Leblanc family purchased an old house and there was a lot of work to do so they needed help. Say what they had others do. Follow the model.

> **Ont-ils fait faire les dessins pour la rénovation?** / *l'architecte*
> **Ils ont fait faire les dessins pour la rénovation par l'architecte.**
> **Ils les lui ont fait faire.**

1. Ont-ils repeint la maison eux-mêmes? / le peintre
2. Ont-ils redécoré les chambres eux-mêmes? / le décorateur
3. Ont-ils remplacé les tuyaux eux-mêmes? / le plombier
4. Ont-ils planté les fleurs eux-mêmes? / les jardinières
5. Ont-ils lavé les fenêtres eux-mêmes? / le laveur de vitres
6. Ont-ils réparé le toit? / le couvreur
7. Ont-ils construit la nouvelle cuisine? / les ouvriers
8. Ont-ils mis l'électricité? / l'électricien

336. Rewrite the following sentences, replacing the direct and indirect objects by pronouns, according to the model.

> **Il fait lire le poème aux étudiants.**
> **Il le leur fait lire.**

1. Il fera écrire la lettre à son fils.
2. Elle s'est fait faire un chandail.
3. Il fait écrire le résumé aux élèves.
4. Il fera faire la robe par la couturière.
5. Il fait apprendre les verbes à Marie.
6. On a fait jouer le jeu aux enfants.
7. Fais réparer le garage au charpentier.
8. Faites chanter la chanson aux enfants.

337. Answer the following personalized questions.

> **Qu'est-ce qui te fait rire?**
> **Un film comique me fait rire.**

1. Qu'est-ce qui te fait rire?
2. Qu'est-ce qui te fait pleurer?
3. Qu'est-ce qui te fait courir?
4. Qu'est-ce qui te fait crier?
5. Qu'est-ce qui te fait sourire?

Laisser and Verbs of Perception plus the Infinitive

After the verb **laisser** and after the verbs of perception **entendre, voir, écouter, regarder** and **sentir,** the infinitive is used. Unlike in English, the infinitive precedes the noun. The pronoun precedes the main verb. These verbs function similarly to the verb **faire** in causative construction.

> **Je laisse Marie finir le travail.**
> *I let Mary finish the work.*
> **Je la (lui) laisse finir le travail.**
> *I let her finish the work.*
> **Je la laisse le finir.**
> *or*
> **Je le lui laisse finir.**
> *I let her finish it.*
>
> **Je vois coudre Hélène.**
> *I see Helen sewing.*
> **Je la vois coudre.**
> *I see her sewing.*
>
> **J'ai entendu chanter Marie.**
> *I heard Mary singing.*
> **Je l'ai entendue chanter.**
> *I heard her singing.*
>
> **J'ai entendu chanter la chanson.**
> *I heard the song sung.*
> **Je l'ai entendu chanter.**
> *I heard it sung.*

Note that the past participle agrees with the preceding direct object if the object performs the action expressed by the infinitive. In the expression **la femme que j'ai entendue chanter,** the woman did the singing and, therefore, the past participle agrees. However, in the expression **la chanson que j'ai entendu chanter,** the past participle does not agree since **chanson** is the object of **chanter.**

338. Translate the following sentences into French.

1. I saw Mary walking on the boulevard.
2. I see her arriving.
3. I let Peter leave.
4. I let him play.
5. I heard the baby cry.
6. I heard them (f.) sing.
7. I listen to them singing.
8. He looks at the painters painting.

339. Complete the following sentences, using a noun + an infinitive.

1. J'ai laissé...
2. J'ai vu...
3. J'ai entendu...
4. Je laisse...

The Use of the Prepositions *à* and *de* before an Infinitive

à

The following verbs are followed by the preposition **à** before an infinitive.

s'amuser à	se décider à	passer (du temps) à	réussir à
apprendre à	demander à (de)	penser à	servir à
arriver à	destiner à	persister à	songer à
s'attendre à	engager à	se plaire à	suffire à
avoir à	enseigner à	se préparer à	tarder à
chercher à	s'habituer à	recommencer à (de)	tendre à
commencer à (de)	hésiter à	renoncer à	tenir à
consentir à	se mettre à	se résigner à	travailler à
continuer à (de)	parvenir à	se résoudre à	trouver à

The following verbs have a direct object before **à** + infinitive.

aider quelqu'un à	**forcer** quelqu'un à
autoriser quelqu'un à	**inviter** quelqu'un à
condamner quelqu'un à	**obliger** quelqu'un à
encourager quelqu'un à	**pousser** quelqu'un à

de

The following verbs are followed by the preposition **de** before an infinitive.

accepter de	dispenser de	interdire de	regretter de
(s')accuser de	douter de	jurer de	se réjouir de
achever de	écrire de	manquer de	se repentir de
s'agir de	s'efforcer de (à)	mériter de	résoudre de
s'arrêter de	s'ennuyer de (à)	négliger de	rêver de
cesser de	entreprendre de	offrir de (à)	rire de
choisir de	envisager de	ordonner de	risquer de
commander de	essayer de	oublier de	souhaiter de
se contenter de	s'étonner de	parler de	soupçonner de
continuer de (à)	éviter de	se passer de	se souvenir de
convenir de	s'excuser de	permettre de	supplier de
craindre de	feindre de	plaindre de	supporter de
décider de (à)	finir de	se plaindre de	tâcher de
défendre de	se garder de	promettre de	tenter de
demander de (à)	se hâter de	proposer de	trembler de
se dépêcher de	s'indigner de	refuser de	venir de
dire de	inspirer de		

Demander à is used when there is no indirect object.

Il **demande à** venir.
He asks to come.

Demander de is used when there is an indirect object.

> Il **me demande de** venir.
> *He asks me to come.*

See pages 130 and 148 for uses of **venir de.**

The following verbs have direct objects before **de.**

accuser quelqu'un de	**forcer*** quelqu'un de
avertir quelqu'un de	**menacer** quelqu'un de
blâmer quelqu'un de	**obliger*** quelqu'un de
charger quelqu'un de	**persuader** quelqu'un de
empêcher quelqu'un de	**prier** quelqu'un de
féliciter quelqu'un de	**remercier** quelqu'un de

The following group of verbs have an indirect object complement and are followed by **de** plus an infinitive.

commander à quelqu'un de	**ordonner** à quelqu'un de
conseiller à quelqu'un de	**permettre** à quelqu'un de
défendre à quelqu'un de	**promettre** à quelqu'un de
demander à quelqu'un de	**proposer** à quelqu'un de
dire à quelqu'un de	**refuser** à quelqu'un de
écrire à quelqu'un de	**reprocher** à quelqu'un de
interdire à quelqu'un de	**suggérer** à quelqu'un de
offrir à quelqu'un de	**téléphoner** à quelqu'un de

The following verbs are followed directly by an infinitive.

aimer	devoir	paraître	revenir
affirmer	écouter	partir	savoir
aller	entendre	penser	sembler
assurer	envoyer	pouvoir	sentir
avouer	espérer	préférer	souhaiter
compter	faire	prétendre	supposer
courir	falloir	se rappeler	valoir mieux
croire	laisser	reconnaître	venir
déclarer	mener	regarder	voir
descendre	monter	rentrer	vouloir
désirer	oser	retourner	

Some transitive verbs that are intransitive in English are not followed by a preposition.

attendre	*to wait for*	**espérer**	*to hope for*
chercher	*to look for*	**payer**	*to pay for*
demander	*to ask for*	**regarder**	*to look at*
envoyer chercher	*to send for*		

> Il **a attendu** l'autobus pendant un quart d'heure.
> *He waited for the bus for a quarter of an hour.*

---

*The use of **de** after **forcer** and **obliger** is practically confined to the past participle of these verbs:
> **Je suis obligé de le faire.**
> But:
> **Il m'oblige à le faire.**

Il **paie** les billets.
He pays for the tickets.

Some verbs have a thing as a direct object and a person as an indirect object.

acheter quelque chose à quelqu'un   **enseigner** quelque chose à quelqu'un
apprendre quelque chose à quelqu'un   **ôter** quelque chose à quelqu'un
arracher quelque chose à quelqu'un   **pardonner** quelque chose à quelqu'un
cacher quelque chose à quelqu'un   **prendre** quelque chose à quelqu'un
dire quelque chose à quelqu'un   **refuser** quelque chose à quelqu'un
emprunter quelque chose à quelqu'un   **souhaiter** quelque chose à quelqu'un
enlever quelque chose à quelqu'un   **voler** quelque chose à quelqu'un

For infinitives following a noun or an adjective, see Chapter 3, *Prepositions*, pages 82–83.

340. Complete the following sentences with the correct preposition when it is necessary.

1. Il apprend _____ chanter.
2. Elle lui a dit _____ le faire.
3. Je vous demande _____ venir me voir.
4. Nous avons essayé _____ faire du ski.
5. Savez-vous _____ jouer de la guitare?
6. Il a commencé _____ neiger.
7. Tu veux _____ parler avec moi.
8. Il refuse _____ m'aider.
9. Elle a peur _____ voir ce film.
10. Il préfère _____ rester ici.
11. Je vous prie _____ m'aider.
12. Nous espérons _____ réussir.
13. Tu réussis _____ le faire.
14. Il faut _____ commencer le travail.
15. Nous envoyons _____ chercher le médecin.
16. Elle m'a empêché _____ venir.
17. Je vous invite _____ aller au cinéma.
18. Venez _____ voir le spectacle!
19. Je dois _____ rentrer à la maison.
20. Il vous permet _____ l'aider.
21. Je le persuade _____ ne pas partir.
22. Il me promet _____ être sage.
23. J'espère _____ voir ce film bientôt.
24. Regardez _____ ce beau tableau.

341. Complete the following, using a preposition plus an infinitive.

Je me dépêche...
Je me dépêche de finir.

1. Je rêve...   7. Je m'amuse...
2. J'apprends...   8. Je me permets...
3. Je passe du temps...   9. Mes parents m'empêchent...
4. Je songe...   10. Mon professeur me conseille...
5. Je crains...   11. J'écris à mes parents...
6. J'essaie...   12. Mon ami(e) m'invite...

Passive Voice

Forms of the Passive Voice

Infinitive	**être aimé(e) / avoir été aimé(e)**
Present participle	**étant aimé(e)**
Past participle	**aimé(e) / ayant été aimé(e)**
Present	**je suis aimé(e)**
Present subjunctive	**que je sois aimé(e)**
Imperfect	**j'étais aimé(e)**
Future	**je serai aimé(e)**
Conditional	**je serais aimé(e)**
Imperative	**sois aimé(e), soyons aimé(e)s, soyez aimé(e)(s)(es)**
Passé composé	**j'ai été aimé(e)**
Pluperfect	**j'avais été aimé(e)**
Conditional past	**j'aurais été aimé(e)**
Past subjunctive	**que j'aie été aimé(e)**
Literary past	**je fus aimé(e)**
Imperfect subjunctive	**que je fusse aimé(e)**
Past anterior	**j'eus été aimé(e)**
Pluperfect subjunctive	**que j'eusse été aimé(e)**
Passé surcomposé	**j'ai eu été aimé(e)**

True Passive with *être*

The passive voice is used less frequently in French than in English. When the true passive voice is used, however, it is formed by using a form of the verb **être** plus the past participle.

Passive:	**Les lettres ont été distribuées par le facteur.**
	The letters were delivered by the mailman.
Active:	**Le facteur a distribué les lettres.**
	The mailman delivered the letters.

The agent or person who performed the action is usually introduced by the preposition **par**.

Cette lettre a été envoyée par Marie.
This letter was sent by Mary.

De is used with verbs expressing condition or emotion.

Le professeur est aimé de ses étudiants.
The teacher is liked by his students.
La montagne est couverte de neige.
The mountain is covered with snow.

The passive voice should be avoided, if possible. If the agent is expressed, simply rewrite the sentence actively.

Passive:	**Ce livre sera écrit par un grand auteur.**
Active:	**Un grand auteur écrira ce livre.**

When the agent is not expressed, the passive voice can be replaced by **on** and an active verb.

Passive:	**La lettre a été envoyée.**
Active:	**On a envoyé la lettre.**
Passive:	**J'ai été admiré.**
Active:	**On m'a admiré.**

The passive voice cannot be used with intransitive verbs. In English we can say:

The letter was answered.

But in French, we must say:

On a répondu à la lettre.

In English, an indirect object can be the subject of a passive verb. This cannot be done in French.

English:	*John was given a present.*
French:	**Un cadeau a été donné à Jean.**
	On a donné un cadeau à Jean.

342. Rewrite the following sentences in the active voice, according to the models.

La carte a été envoyée par Marie.
Marie a envoyé la carte.
La carte a été envoyée.
On a envoyé la carte.

1. Le roman a été écrit par Balzac.
2. Ce monument a été construit par les Romains.
3. La chanson a été chantée par Céline Dion.
4. Cette peinture a été peinte par Cézanne.
5. Cette maison sera construite par un grand architecte.
6. J'ai été aimé.
7. Le travail a été fini.
8. Cette ville a été détruite pendant la guerre.

The Passive Voice with *se*

A common way to form the passive voice in French is by using the reflexive pronoun **se** with the third person singular or plural form of the verb. This construction is most common when the action is habitual or normal or when the person by whom the action is carried out (the agent) is unimportant.

Les cravates se vendent ici.
Ties are sold here.
Le gouvernement se compose de trois parties.
The government is composed of three parts.
Le français se parle ici.
French is spoken here.
Cela ne se fait pas.
That is not done.

343. Rewrite the following sentences in the passive voice, using the reflexive form.

1. On parle français au Québec.
2. On n'écrit pas ce mot sans *s*.
3. On verra le plus beau monument au centre de la ville.
4. Autrefois, on faisait cela à la main.
5. On a modernisé la ville.
6. On ouvrira les portes à huit heures.
7. On fabriquait ces autos dans cette usine.
8. On ne dit pas cela.

CHAPTER 6

Interrogative Words and Constructions

Forming Questions

Questions are formed in French in the following ways:

1. by changing the period of a statement to a question mark and using a rising intonation.

Statement	*Question*
Marie parle français.	**Marie parle français?**
Vous avez bien dormi.	**Vous avez bien dormi?**
Il se réveille.	**Il se réveille?**

2. by adding **n'est-ce pas?** to an affirmative sentence. An affirmative answer is usually expected.

Statement	*Question*
Tu vas au musée.	**Tu vas au musée, n'est-ce pas?**
Il est arrivé.	**Il est arrivé, n'est-ce pas?**
Elle se débrouille.	**Elle se débrouille, n'est-ce pas?**

3. by adding **est-ce que** or **est-ce qu'** (before vowels) at the beginning of the statement and changing the period to a question mark.

Statement	*Question*
Pierre nous parlera.	**Est-ce que Pierre nous parlera?**
Il se rase.	**Est-ce qu'il se rase?**
Elle s'est bien habillée.	**Est-ce qu'elle s'est bien habillée?**

1. Form questions about the students in the class. Follow the model.

Elle parle français.
Elle parle français, n'est-ce pas?
Est-ce qu'elle parle français?

1. Marie travaille bien.
2. Il fait ses devoirs chaque soir.
3. Pierre se couche de bonne heure.
4. Elle s'habillait bien tous les jours.

5. Ils viendront à l'école à l'heure.
6. Ils sont allés au cinéma hier soir.

7. Ces étudiants ont lu ce livre.
8. Pierre s'est reposé hier soir.

Interrogative Forms by Inversion—Simple Tenses

Questions may be formed by inverting a pronoun subject and the verb of declarative sentences. The subject is connected to the verb with a hyphen.

Statement	Question
Tu vas à Londres.	**Vas-tu à Londres?**
Vous parlez français.	**Parlez-vous français?**
Nous nous levons.	**Nous levons-nous?**
Vous vous débrouillez bien.	**Vous débrouillez-vous bien?**

When inverting a third person singular subject and a verb, a **t** must be inserted between the inverted verb and the subject if the verb ends in a vowel. The **t** is connected to the verb with hyphens.

Statement	Question
Il parle français.	**Parle-t-il français?**
Il se lève.	**Se lève-t-il?**

But:

Il écrit.	**Écrit-il?**

Inversion is usually not used with **je**. Instead, use **est-ce que**.

Est-ce que je parle bien?

When inversion is used with the first person singular verb that ends in a mute **e**, the **e** is replaced by **é**.

Je parle français.	**Parlé-je français?**
J'ose le faire.	**Osé-je le faire?**

Inversion with **je** is permitted with certain often-used verbs.

Suis-je intelligent?
Ai-je raison?
Que sais-je?
Puis-je vous aider?

Note that **peux** becomes **puis** in inversion with **je**.

When inverting with a noun subject, state the noun, then the verb, then the pronoun.

Statement	Question
Marie parle français.	**Marie parle-t-elle français?**
Pierre s'habille.	**Pierre s'habille-t-il?**

After interrogative adverbs, either simple or complex inversion can be used.

Quand viendront les invités?
Quand les invités viendront-ils?

Complex inversion is obligatory

1. after **pourquoi** when the subject is a noun.

> **Pourquoi les élèves font-ils du bruit?**

2. when the verb is followed by an adjective or direct object.

> **Pourquoi Pierre est-il paresseux?**
> **À qui la fille doit-elle donner l'argent?**

2. Form questions according to the model.

> **Tu regardes le film.**
> **Regardes-tu le film?**

1. Tu regardes la peinture.
2. Vous allez à Paris.
3. Nous savons la réponse.
4. Ils écoutent la radio.
5. Elle court.

6. Tu te dépêches.
7. Nous nous lèverons de bonne heure.
8. Elles se couchent à dix heures.
9. Je suis amusant.
10. Je peux le faire.

3. Ask if the people do the following. Form questions according to the model.

> **Il parle français.**
> **Parle-t-il français?**

1. Elle pleure beaucoup.
2. Il ouvre la porte pour les gens âgés.
3. Elle rencontre des amis au café.

4. Il se dépêche toujours.
5. Elle se lève de bonne heure.
6. Elle s'amuse bien le samedi.

4. Ask if the people will do the following for the party. Form questions according to the model.

> **Marie invitera les amis.**
> **Marie, invitera-t-elle les amis?**

1. Hélène et Pierre feront les décorations.
2. Marie fera les sandwichs.
3. Anne et Gisèle apporteront les CD.
4. André préparera les boissons.
5. Nicole mettra la table.
6. Les amis se reposeront l'après-midi.
7. Le soir, tout le monde se retrouvera chez Marie.
8. Les amis s'amuseront à la fête.

Interrogative Forms by Inversion—Compound Tenses

In compound tenses, the subject pronoun and the auxiliary verb are inverted.

Statement	*Question*
Il a travaillé.	**A-t-il travaillé?**
Vous êtes arrivé.	**Êtes-vous arrivé?**
Ils se sont rasés.	**Se sont-ils rasés?**
Elle s'est couchée.	**S'est-elle couchée?**

5. Rewrite the following in the interrogative form, according to the model.

Il a chanté.
A-t-il chanté?

1. Nous avons fait nos devoirs.
2. Elle a dit la vérité.
3. Louise est vite montée.
4. Nous sommes arrivés à l'heure.
5. Ils se sont couchés.
6. Elles se sont moquées de vous.
7. Nous nous sommes dépêchées.
8. Hélène s'est lavée.

6. Ask if the people did the following for the party. Form questions according to the model.

Marie / inviter les amis
Marie, a-t-elle invité les amis?

1. Hélène et Pierre / faire les décorations
2. Marie / faire les sandwichs
3. Anne et Gisèle / apporter les CD
4. André / préparer les boissons
5. Nicole / mettre la table
6. Les amis / se reposer l'après-midi
7. Le soir / tout le monde / se retrouver chez Marie
8. Les amis / s'amuser à la fête

Interrogative Adverbs and Adverbial Expressions

Following are common interrogative words used to introduce questions.

Où?	*Where?*	**Combien?**	*How many?*
Quand?	*When?*	**Pourquoi?**	*Why?*
Comment?	*How?*	**À quelle heure?**	*At what time?*

Study the following.

Où va-t-elle?	*Where is she going?*
Quand arrivera-t-elle?	*When is she arriving?*
Comment va-t-il?	*How is he?*
Combien de livres y a-t-il sur la table?	*How many books are there on the table?*
Combien coûte le bifteck?	*How much does the steak cost?*
Combien de temps allez-vous passer ici?	*How much time are you going to spend here?*
Pourquoi pleure-t-elle?	*Why is she crying?*
À quelle heure vient-il?	*At what time is he coming?*

7. Complete the following with an appropriate question word.

1. Elles partent demain. _____ partent-elles?
2. L'auto coûte deux mille dollars. _____ coûte l'auto?
3. Marie va au musée. _____ va Marie?
4. L'église est moderne. _____ est l'église?
5. Elle arrivera à trois heures. _____ arrivera-t-elle?
6. Elle met un chandail parce qu'elle a froid. _____ met-elle un chandail?
7. Elles vont à la plage en été. _____ vont-elles à la plage?
8. Elles vont à la plage en été. _____ vont-elles en été?
9. Elle a trois CD. _____ de CD a-t-elle?
10. Elle est heureuse. _____ est-elle?

8. Ask questions of Pierre, the foreign exchange student. Follow the model.

Ask him how he is.
Comment vas-tu?

Ask him:

1. where he lives in France.
2. when he arrived here.
3. how he arrived here.
4. why he came to this university.
5. how much time he is going to stay here.
6. how many classes he has.
7. at what time his last class ends.

Interrogative Pronouns

The interrogative pronouns are:

Subject

Qui?	} *Who?*	**Qui** vient?	*Who is coming?*
Qui est-ce qui?		**Qui est-ce qui** vous parle?	*Who is speaking to you?*
Qu'est-ce qui?	*What?*	**Qu'est-ce qui** se passe?	*What is happening?*
		Qu'est-ce qui est arrivé?	*What happened?*

Note that there is no short form for **qu'est-ce qui.**

Object

Qui?	} *Whom?*	
Qui est-ce que?		
Que?	} *What?*	
Qu'est-ce que?		
Qui voyez-vous?	*Whom do you see?*	
Qui est-ce que vous voyez?	*Whom do you see?*	
Que voyez-vous?	*What do you see?*	
Qu'est-ce que vous voyez?	*What do you see?*	

Qui is never joined to a following word beginning with a vowel. **Que** becomes **qu'** before a word beginning with a vowel.

Qui avez-vous vu?	*Whom did you see?*
Qu'avez-vous vu?	*What did you see?*

Que can be used as a predicate.

Qu'est-il sans sa famille?
What is he without his family?
Qu'est-ce qu'un dîner sans vin?
What's a dinner without wine?

Object of a preposition

qui?	*whom?*
quoi?	*what?*

Avec qui avez-vous parlé?	*With whom did you speak?*
Avec quoi écrit-il?	*With what does he write?*

À qui, meaning *whose*, is used to denote ownership for persons.

À qui sont ces livres?   *Whose books are these?*

De qui is used to denote relationship to someone.

De qui est-il le fils?   *Whose son is he?*

Quoi can be used without a verb in certain idiomatic expressions.

Quoi de neuf?
Quoi de nouveau? } *What's new?*

Quoi can also be used alone.

Quoi? Vous voulez me voir?
What? You want to see me?

The third person singular form of the verb is usually used with **qui, qui est-ce qui** and **qu'est-ce qui** even when a plural answer is expected.

Qui vient?
Paul et Marie viennent.

When **qui** is a predicate nominative, the verb can be in the plural.

Qui êtes-vous?

9. Complete the following with an appropriate question word.

1. Marie est venue nous voir.
   _____ est venu nous voir? (short form)
   _____ est venu nous voir? (long form)
2. Le tonnerre a fait ce bruit.
   _____ a fait ce bruit?
3. C'est Pierre que je vois.
   _____ vous voyez?
   _____ voyez-vous?
4. C'est Marie qu'il a vue.
   _____ il a vu?
   _____ a-t-il vu?

5. Elle fait une promenade.
   _____ elle fait?
   _____ fait-elle?
6. Il a cherché un hôtel.
   _____ il a cherché?
   _____ a-t-il cherché?
7. Il a parlé de Marie.
   De _____ a-t-il parlé?
8. Il a parlé de ses livres.
   De _____ a-t-il parlé?

10. Form questions, using the interrogative word that will elicit the italicized element in the response.

Marie vient.
Qui vient?   Qui est-ce qui vient?

1. *Quelqu'un* parle.
2. Elle est la sœur d'*Hélène*.

3. Il a vu *le film*.
4. Il écrit sa composition sur *l'architecture moderne*.
5. *Le vent* a fermé la porte.
6. Il parle à *Marie*.
7. *Quelque chose* se passe.
8. Elle parle de *ses peintures*.
9. Il regarde *son amie*.
10. Il fait *une promenade*.
11. Ces livres sont à *Pierre*.
12. Elle est la fille de *Madame Leblanc*.
13. *Marie et Pierre* vont à la bibliothèque.
14. *Les avions* font ce bruit.

11. Translate the following into French.

1. Whose paintings are these?
2. Whose son is he?
3. Whose books are these?
4. Whose mother is she?
5. What's new?

Qu'est-ce que c'est? Qu'est-ce que?

Qu'est-ce que c'est or **qu'est-ce que** are used in explanations or definitions and mean *what is or what's*.

Qu'est-ce que c'est?	*What's that?*
Qu'est-ce que c'est que cela?	*What's that?*
Qu'est-ce que c'est que le jeu de boules?	*What's the game of boules?*
Qu'est-ce qu'un dîner sans vin?	*What's a dinner without wine?*

12. Translate the following into French.

1. What's the Louvre?
2. What's the *Tour de France?*
3. What's a symbol?
4. What's the Sorbonne?

Interrogative Adjective Quel

The interrogative adjective **quel** (*what*) agrees with the noun it modifies.

	Masculine	Feminine
Singular	quel	quelle
Plural	quels	quelles

Quel est votre nom?	*What is your name?*
Quels livres lisez-vous?	*What books are you reading?*
Quelle heure est-il?	*What time is it?*
Quelles sont vos idées?	*What are your ideas?*

The interrogative adjective can be the subject of the verb **être** except when it refers to a person. Then **qui** is used.

Quelle est votre adresse?	*What is your address?*
Qui est votre amie?	*Who is your friend?*

Quel can be used with persons when meaning *what kind of*.

> **Quels** sont ces hommes? Ce sont des médecins.
> *What kind of men are they? They are doctors.*
> **Quel** est cet homme? C'est un écrivain.
> *What kind of man is he? He is a writer.*

Quel can be used in indirect address.

> Je voudrais savoir **quel** livre vous lisez.
> *I want to know what book you are reading.*

The interrogative adjective can also mean *what a . . . !*

> **Quel garçon!** *What a boy!*
> **Quelle fille!** *What a girl!*

13. Write mini-dialogues, using **quel**. Use the cues provided or provide your own details.

> — **J'aime les restaurants. (italiens)**
> — **Quels restaurants aimes-tu?**
> — **J'aime les restaurants italiens.**

1. J'aime les restaurants. (français)
2. J'aime les films. (d'aventure)
3. Les peintures sont bonnes. (impressionnistes)
4. Ce livre est intéressant. (de photos)
5. Cette robe est jolie. (bleue)

14. Complete the following with the correct form of **quel** or **qui**.

1. _____ heure est-il?
2. _____ sont ces hommes? Ce sont des avocats.
3. _____ est cette fille?
4. _____ livres lisez-vous?
5. _____ est votre adresse?
6. _____ robes préférez-vous?

15. You are on a safari and your companion is pointing out things. React, using **quel**, according to the model.

> **Regarde le garçon!**
> **Quel garçon!**

1. Regarde le paysage!
2. Regarde la girafe!
3. Regarde l'arbre!
4. Regarde les éléphants!

Interrogative Pronoun Lequel

Lequel is the interrogative word which corresponds to the English *which one*.

	Singular		Plural	
Masculine	**lequel**	*which one*	**lesquels**	*which ones*
Feminine	**laquelle**	*which one*	**lesquelles**	*which ones*

The forms of **lequel** must agree with the noun to which they refer.

> **Lequel** de ces livres voulez-vous?
> *Which one of these books do you want?*
> **Lesquels** de ces livres voulez-vous?
> *Which (ones) of these books do you want?*

Laquelle de ces peintures préférez-vous?
Which one of these paintings do you prefer?
Lesquelles de ces peintures préférez-vous?
Which (ones) of these paintings do you prefer?

The forms of **lequel** make the normal contractions with **à** or **de**.

à + lequel = auquel   de + lequel = duquel
à + lesquels = auxquels   de + lesquels = desquels
à + lesquelles = auxquelles de + lesquelles = desquelles
à + laquelle do not contract. de + laquelle do not contract.

Auquel de ces garçons parlez-vous?
To which one of these boys are you speaking?
Desquelles a-t-il parlé?
Of which ones did he speak?

16. Complete the following with the correct form of **lequel**.

    1. Marie a deux livres. _____ des deux voulez-vous?
    2. Hélène a deux peintures. _____ des deux voulez-vous?
    3. Voilà des livres. _____ voulez-vous? (plural)
    4. Voilà des robes. _____ voulez-vous? (plural)

17. Complete the following with the correct form of **à** plus **lequel**.

    1. Il parle à une fille. _____ parle-t-il?
    2. Elle parle à un garçon. _____ parle-t-elle?
    3. Il parle aux filles. _____ parle-t-il?
    4. Elles parlent aux garçons. _____ parlent-elles?

18. Complete the following with the correct form of **de** plus **lequel**.

    1. Il a parlé d'un garçon. _____ a-t-il parlé?
    2. Elle a parlé d'une fille. _____ a-t-elle parlé?
    3. Il a parlé des filles. _____ a-t-il parlé?
    4. Elle a parlé des garçons. _____ a-t-elle parlé?

Review

19. Complete the following questions with the appropriate expressions based on the answers given to the questions.

    1. _____ de ces lettres la vedette va-t-elle répondre?
       À toutes!
    2. _____ d'États y a-t-il aux États-Unis?
       Il y en a 50.
    3. _____ des deux sacs à main préfères-tu?
       Je préfère celui qui est en cuir.
    4. _____ a découvert le radium?
       Madame Curie.

5. _____ est-il le fils? C'est le fils de M. Dupont.

6. Des trois candidats, pour _____ as-tu voté?
Pour la plus honnête.

7. _____ est ton film préféré?
Casablanca.

8. _____ parle-t-il?
De ses amis.

9. _____ a-t-on besoin pour changer le pneu?
D'un cric, d'une manivelle et d'une clé en croix.

10. _____ part-elle en vacances?
Le 25 juin.

11. _____ le Tour de France?
C'est une course à bicyclette autour de la France.

12. _____ faut-il faire pour réussir?
Il faut étudier.

13. _____ sont ces livres?
Ils sont à Marie et à Anne.

14. _____ arrive le train de Lyon?
À dix heures précises.

15. _____ étudie-t-elle le japonais?
Parce qu'elle va au Japon cet été.

16. _____ s'est passé?
Rien.

17. Vous pouvez en choisir deux. _____ voulez-vous?
Je voudrais celui-ci et celui-là.

18. _____ va-t-elle pendant les vacances?
En Chine.

20. Ask questions of a new student. Use inversion.

Demande-lui d'où il (elle) vient?
D'où viens-tu?

1. Demande-lui comment il (elle) s'appelle.
2. Demande-lui son âge.
3. Demande-lui quand il (elle) est né(e).
4. Demande-lui où il (elle) est né(e).
5. Demande-lui pourquoi il (elle) a déménagé.
6. Demande-lui combien de frères et de sœurs il (elle) a.
7. Demande-lui à quelle heure il (elle) part pour l'école.
8. Demande-lui avec qui il (elle) sort.
9. Demande-lui avec quoi il (elle) vient en classe.
10. Demande-lui quels sports il (elle) aime.
11. Demande-lui quelle sorte de musique il (elle) aime.
12. Demande-lui ce qu'il (elle) fait pour s'amuser.
13. Demande-lui où il (elle) va pendant les vacances d'été.
14. Demande-lui où il (elle) est allé(e) l'été dernier.

CHAPTER 7

Negative Words and Constructions

Negation of Simple Tenses

Verbs in simple tenses are made negative by placing **ne** before the verb and **pas** after it. Note that **ne** becomes **n'** before words beginning with a vowel.

Affirmative	*Negative*
Il parle français.	Il **ne** parle **pas** français.
Nous lisons beaucoup.	Nous **ne** lisons **pas** beaucoup.
Elle écrira le poème.	Elle **n'**écrira **pas** le poème.
Dans ce cas-là, elle viendrait.	Dans ce cas-là, elle **ne** viendrait **pas**.

To form the negative of reflexive verbs in simple tenses, **ne** is placed before the reflexive pronoun and **pas** is placed after the reflexive verb.

Affirmative	*Negative*
Je me réveille.	Je **ne** me réveille **pas.**
Il s'habillera bien.	Il **ne** s'habillera **pas** bien.
Nous nous couchions de bonne heure.	Nous **ne** nous couchions **pas** de bonne heure.

In sentences with verbs followed by a complementary infinitive, **ne** is placed before and **pas** after the main verb.

Affirmative	*Negative*
Il veut venir.	Il **ne** veut **pas** venir.
Je vais me lever.	Je **ne** vais **pas** me lever.

See page 139 for the negative imperative.

1. Rewrite the following sentences in the negative.

1. Il va au théâtre.
2. Vous lirez le roman.

3. Je crains cet homme.
4. J'écoute le professeur.
5. Tu habitais à Paris en ce temps-là.
6. Vous arriveriez en retard.
7. Je me reposerai dimanche.
8. Elles se couchaient à onze heures tous les soirs.
9. Vous vous retrouverez à la gare.
10. Ils se moquent de lui.
11. Nous nous débrouillons bien.
12. Il s'habille bien.

2. Rewrite the following sentences in the negative, according to the model.

Je veux travailler.
Je ne veux pas travailler.

1. Nous voulons partir.
2. Elle aime chanter.
3. Elle veut se lever.
4. Tu vas t'habiller.

Negation of Compound Tenses

Verbs in compound tenses are made negative by adding **ne** before and **pas** after the auxiliary verb **avoir** or **être**.

Affirmative	*Negative*
J'ai fini.	Je **n'**ai **pas** fini.
Elle est venue.	Elle **n'**est **pas** venue.
Nous serons arrivés.	Nous **ne** serons **pas** arrivés.
Elles étaient venues.	Elles **n'**étaient **pas** venues.
Nous aurions fait cela.	Nous **n'**aurions **pas** fait cela.

To form the negative of reflexive verbs in compound tenses, **ne** is added before the reflexive pronoun and **pas** is added after the auxiliary verb.

Affirmative	*Negative*
Elle s'est levée.	Elle **ne** s'est **pas** levée.
Je me serai bien habillé.	Je **ne** me serai **pas** bien habillé.

3. Rewrite the following sentences in the negative.

1. J'ai acheté la robe.
2. Vous aviez compris la situation.
3. Ils ont écrit leurs devoirs.
4. Nous sommes restés ici.
5. Elle est tombée du cheval.
6. Ils seront venus à l'heure.
7. Elle s'est bien reposée.
8. Nous nous serons dépêchées.
9. Elles se sont plaintes de tout.
10. Vous vous êtes levés de bonne heure.

4. Answer the following questions in the negative.

1. Avez-vous reçu la lettre?
2. A-t-il lu l'histoire?
3. Êtes-vous allée au cinéma hier?
4. Sont-elles parties de bonne heure?
5. Vous êtes-vous levé de bonne heure?
6. S'est-elle endormie?

The Negative Interrogative

The negative interrogative is formed by placing **ne** before the verb and **pas** after it when using intonation, **est-ce que** or **n'est-ce pas.**

Affirmative	*Negative*
Marie travaille?	Marie **ne** travaille **pas**?
Est-ce qu'Hélène se réveille?	Est-ce qu'Hélène **ne** se réveille **pas**?
Pierre se rasera, n'est-ce pas?	Pierre **ne** se rasera **pas,** n'est-ce pas?

In compound tenses, **ne** is placed before the auxiliary verb and **pas** after it.

Affirmative	*Negative*
Est-ce qu'il a parlé?	Est-ce qu'il **n'a pas** parlé?
Elle s'est amusée, n'est-ce pas?	Elle **ne** s'est **pas** amusée, n'est-ce pas?

In interrogative sentences by inversion, **ne** is placed before the verb and **pas** is placed after the pronoun.

Affirmative	*Negative*
Travaille-t-il?	**Ne** travaille-t-il **pas**?
Georges va-t-il à Paris?	Georges **ne** va-t-il **pas** à Paris?

In compound tenses, **ne** is placed before the auxiliary verb and **pas** is placed after the subject pronoun.

Affirmative	*Negative*
A-t-il fini?	**N'a**-t-il **pas** fini?
Es-tu parti?	**N'es**-tu **pas** parti?

For reflexive verbs, **ne** precedes the reflexive pronoun and **pas** follows the subject pronoun.

Affirmative	*Negative*
Vous couchez-vous?	**Ne** vous couchez-vous **pas**?
Se lève-t-il?	**Ne** se lève-t-il **pas**?
Vous êtes-vous réveillé?	**Ne** vous êtes-vous **pas** réveillé?

5. Rewrite the following in the negative.

1. Est-ce que Georges vous parlera?
2. Lit-il le livre?
3. Ouvre-t-elle la fenêtre?
4. Se dépêche-t-il?
5. Vous réveillez-vous?
6. Avez-vous fini?
7. Ont-elles craint cet homme?
8. Sont-elles rentrées de bonne heure?
9. Se sont-ils couchés?
10. T'es-tu blessé?

6. Rewrite the following sentences in the inverted interrogative form.

1. Tu ne vis pas bien ici.
2. Il ne saura pas la vérité.
3. Nous ne nous dépêchons pas.
4. Vous ne vous levez pas de bonne heure.
5. Elle n'a pas cru l'histoire.
6. Elles ne sont pas revenues de bonne heure.
7. Il ne s'est pas rasé.
8. Vous ne vous êtes pas bien débrouillé.

Si *in Answer to a Negative Question*

When answering a negative question in the affirmative, **si** is used instead of **oui**.

Ne parles-tu pas français?	*Don't you speak French?*
Si, je parle français.	*Yes, I speak French.*
Tu ne viendras pas, n'est-ce pas?	*You won't come, will you?*
Si, je viendrai.	*Yes, I will come.*

If the answer is affirmative to an affirmative question, **oui** is used.

Parles-tu français?	*Do you speak French?*
Oui, je parle français.	*Yes, I speak French.*

7. Answer the following questions, using **si** or **oui**.

1. Parlez-vous français?
2. Ne parlez-vous pas français?
3. Viendront-ils à l'heure?
4. Ne viendront-ils pas à l'heure?
5. A-t-il fini?
6. Il n'a pas fini, n'est-ce pas?
7. Se réveille-t-elle?
8. Elle ne se réveille pas, n'est-ce pas?

8. Answer the following questions, using **si** or **oui**.

1. Vit-il bien ici?
2. Ne sont-ils pas venus?
3. Elle ne prendra pas le déjeuner ici?
4. A-t-il lu ce roman?
5. N'ont-ils pas craint le criminel?

Omission of **Pas**

Pas may be omitted in the negative after **savoir, pouvoir, oser** and **cesser** when they are accompanied by an infinitive.

Il ne sait que faire.	*He doesn't know what to do.*
Il ne peut la comprendre.	*He can't understand her.*
Il n'ose le faire.	*He doesn't dare do it.*
Il ne cesse de neiger.	*It doesn't stop snowing.*

9. Rewrite the following sentences, putting the first verb in the negative, omitting **pas.**

1. Il sait le réparer.
2. Il cesse de pleuvoir.
3. Elle ose le dire.
4. Elle peut le faire.

Negation of the Infinitive

To make an infinitive negative, place **ne pas** before the infinitive.

Il me dit de **ne pas pleurer.**	*He tells me not to cry.*

When there is a pronoun, **ne pas** precedes the pronoun.

Il m'a dit de **ne pas le faire.**	*He told me not to do it.*
Il m'a dit de **ne pas me coucher.**	*He told me not to go to bed.*
Il m'a dit de **ne pas y aller.**	*He told me not to go there.*

With the past infinitive, **pas** can come before or after the auxiliary.

Elle affirme **ne pas** avoir fait ses devoirs.
Elle affirme **n'**avoir **pas** fait ses devoirs.
Elle affirme **ne pas** les avoir faits.
Elle affirme **ne** les avoir **pas** faits.

10. Rewrite the following sentences, making the infinitive negative.

1. Il vous dit d'avoir peur.
2. Elle vous demande de venir.
3. Elle vous dit d'être heureux.
4. Je vous demande de leur parler.
5. Elle vous dit de le faire.
6. Elle affirme avoir vu ce film.

Negative Words and Phrases

Many negative expressions function like **ne... pas.**

1. **ne... pas du tout**   *not at all*

   Il **n'**est **pas du tout** bête.
   He is not at all stupid.

2. **ne... point**   *not* (emphatic)

   Il **ne** le dit **point.**
   He does not say it.

3. **ne... plus**   *no longer, no more*

   Je **ne** travaille **plus.**
   I am no longer working.
   Je **n'**ai **plus** de livres.
   I have no more books.

4. **ne... jamais**   *never*

   Il **n'**oubliera **jamais** ce film.
   He will never forget this film.

   Jamais without **ne** means *ever.*

   Êtes-vous **jamais** allé à Paris?
   Did you ever go to Paris?

   It can also stand alone, meaning *never.*

   Avez-vous vu ce film?   **Jamais!**
   Have you (ever) seen this film?   *Never!*

5. **ne... guère**   *hardly*

   Il **n'**a **guère** le temps.
   He hardly has the time.

6. **ne... aucun(e)**   *no not any*

   Il **n'**a **aucun** livre.
   He hasn't a single book.
   Je **n'**ai **aucune** idée.
   I have no idea.

Ne... aucun(e) is the negative of **quelque(s)**.

> Elle a **quelques** peintures.
> *She has some paintings.*
> Elle **n'a aucune** peinture.
> *She has no paintings.*

7. **aucun(e)... ne**   *none*

> **Aucun n'**est vrai.
> *None is true.*

8. **ne... plus aucun(e)**   *no longer any*

> Il **n'**a **plus aucun** livre.
> *He no longer has any books.*

9. **ne... que**   *only*

> Il **n'a que** deux chambres.
> *He has only two rooms.*
> Il **n'**a lu **que** des journaux.
> *He has read only newspapers.*

Note that **que** follows the past participle in compound tenses.

10. **ne... rien**   *nothing, not anything*

> Il **ne** voit **rien.**
> *He sees nothing.   (He doesn't see anything.)*
> Qu'est-ce qu'il voit?   **Rien.**
> *What does he see?   Nothing.*

Rien is the negative expression for **quelque chose**.

> Je vois **quelque chose.**
> *I see something.*
> Je **ne** vois **rien.**
> *I see nothing. (I don't see anything.)*

Note that **rien** precedes the past participle in compound tenses.

> Il **n'a rien** vu.
> *He saw nothing.   (He didn't see anything.)*

11. **Rien ne...**   *nothing*

> **Rien ne** peut m'aider.
> *Nothing can help me.*

12. **ne... personne**   *no one, not anyone*

> Elle **ne** regarde **personne.**
> *She is not looking at anyone.   (She is looking at no one.)*
> Elle **n'a** vu **personne.**
> *She saw no one.   (She didn't see anyone.)*

Note that **personne** follows the past participle in compound tenses.

13. **Personne ne...**   *no one*

> **Personne n'**est venu.
> *No one came.*
> Qui est arrivé?   **Personne.**
> *Who arrived?   No one.*

Note that **personne** and **rien** can stand alone.

14. nul (nulle) ne...   *no one*

> **Nul ne** sait la vérité.
> *No one knows the truth.*

15. ne... nul(le)   *no, not any*

> **Nul** film **ne** l'intéresse.
> *No film interests him (her).*

16. ne... nulle part   *nowhere, not anywhere*

> Elle **ne** va **nulle part.**
> *She is not going anywhere. (She is going nowhere.)*

17. ne... ni... ni   *neither ... nor*

> Il **n'**a **ni** père **ni** mère.
> *He has neither a father nor a mother.*
> Il **n'**a écrit **ni** à son père **ni** à sa mère.
> *He wrote neither to his father nor to his mother.*

Ni may be used more than twice.

> Il **ne** veut **ni** lire, **ni** écrire, **ni** étudier.
> *He wants neither to read, nor to write, nor to study.*

18. ni l'un(e) ni l'autre ne...   *neither one*

> **Ni l'un ni l'autre n'**est venu.
> *Neither one came.*

When used as a direct object, **ni l'un(e) ni l'autre** means *either one.*

> Il **ne** veut **ni l'un ni l'autre.**
> *He doesn't want either one.*

19. non plus   *neither, either*

Non plus is the negative expression which replaces **aussi.**

> Il le sait. Je le sais **aussi.**
> *He knows it. I know it too.*
> Il ne le sait pas. Je **ne** le sais **pas non plus.**
> *He doesn't know it. I don't know it either.*

> Elle travaille beaucoup. **Moi aussi.**
> *She works a lot. Me too (also). (So do I.)*
> Elle ne travaille pas beaucoup. **Ni moi non plus.**
> *She doesn't work much. Neither do I.*

Note that the pronoun used is the disjunctive pronoun.

> **Ni lui non plus.**
> *Nor he either.*

Note that **de** is used instead of the partitive article after **ne... pas, ne... plus** and **ne... jamais.**

>Je **n'ai pas de** livres.
>*I don't have any books.*
>Elle **n'a plus** d'argent.
>*She doesn't have any more money.*
>Il **ne** mange **jamais de** tomates.
>*He never eats tomatoes.*

The partitive is used after **ne... que.**

>Je **n'ai que des** livres.
>*I have only books.*

No article or partitive is used after **ne... ni... ni.**

>Il **n'a ni** frères **ni** sœurs.
>*He has neither brothers nor sisters.*

When **jamais** and **personne** are in conditional or interrogative sentences, they may appear without the **ne. Jamais** then means *ever* and **personne** means *anyone.*

>A-t-elle **jamais** fait du ski?
>*Has she ever skied?*
>Y a-t-il **personne** d'intéressant ici?
>*Is there anyone interesting here?*

Study the following:

Affirmative	*Negative*
Elle y va **toujours.**	Elle **n'**y va **jamais.**
Toujours, je le ferai.	**Jamais,** je **ne** le ferai.
Il a **quelque** problème.	Il **n'a aucun** problème.
Je vois **quelque chose.**	Je **ne** vois **rien.**
Quelque chose arrive.	**Rien n'**arrive.
Je vois **quelqu'un.**	Je **ne** vois **personne.**
Quelqu'un est venu.	**Personne n'**est venu.

Avez-vous **un** dictionnaire ou **un** roman?	Je n'ai **ni** dictionnaire **ni** roman.
Tous les deux sont venus.	**Ni l'un ni l'autre** n'est venu.

Unlike English, many negative words can be used in the same sentence.

>Il **ne** dit **jamais rien** à **personne.**
>*He never says anything to anyone.*

11. Rewrite the following sentences, replacing the italicized word with a negative phrase.

1. Elle dit *toujours* la même chose.
2. *Toujours*, elle le fait.
3. Elle a *toujours* chanté.
4. J'ai *quelque* espoir.
5. Marie trouve *quelque chose*.
6. Marie a perdu *quelque chose*.
7. *Quelque chose* est dans la cuisine.

8. *Quelque chose* s'est passé.
9. Il y a *quelqu'un* dans la boutique.
10. Il a vu *quelqu'un.*
11. *Quelqu'un* frappe à la porte.
12. *Quelqu'un* est arrivé.
13. J'ai *un* crayon et *un* stylo.
14. Il parle *à* son père et *à* sa mère.
15. Elle veut *du* pain et *du* beurre.
16. *Tous les deux* sont partis.
17. Pierre parle *toujours* de *quelque chose* à *quelqu'un.*
18. Il va *quelque part.*

12. Rewrite the following sentences, adding the French equivalent of the English words.

1. J'ai vu ce film.   *never*
2. Nous avons dansé.   *not at all*
3. Il oubliera cette leçon.   *never*
4. Il prend du vin.   *hardly*
5. Est-ce qu'il va étudier?   *ever*
6. Il a un CD.   *no longer any*
7. Elle a des amis et des ennemis.   *neither . . . nor*
8. Il a écrit des poèmes.   *only*
9. Il a du temps.   *hardly*
10. Elle a deux frères.   *only*
11. Elle chante des chansons.   *no longer*

13. Answer the following questions, using the cue provided.

1. Est-ce qu'il y a quelque chose d'intéressant à faire?   *ne . . . rien*
2. Va-t-elle travailler?   *ne . . . jamais*
3. Y a-t-il quelqu'un ici?   *ne . . . personne*
4. Qui est venu?   *Personne ne . . .*
5. A-t-il des livres?   *ne . . . aucun*
6. A-t-il des livres ou des journaux?   *ne . . . ni . . . ni*
7. Avez-vous le temps de le faire?   *ne . . . guère*
8. Est-elle riche?   *pas du tout*

14. Replace **aussi** with **non plus** in the following sentences and make necessary changes.

1. Il est riche aussi.
2. Elles aussi, elles ont beaucoup d'argent.
3. Marie le sait aussi.
4. Moi aussi, je viens.
5. Lui aussi, il la verra.
6. Elles mangent ici aussi.
7. Il l'a fait aussi.

Review

15. Say that John never does what Peter does. Follow the models.

Pierre boit du lait.
Jean *ne boit pas* de lait.

Pierre va *toujours* au cinéma.
Jean *ne* va *jamais* au cinéma.

1. Pierre mange des épinards.
2. Pierre aime jouer au tennis.
3. Pierre sait quoi faire.
4. Pierre se lève *toujours* de bonne heure.
5. Pierre est allé au cinéma hier.
6. Pierre s'est couché de bonne heure hier soir.
7. Pierre a *une* auto et *une* bicyclette.
8. Pierre a acheté *quelques* chemises hier.
9. Pierre achète *toujours quelque chose* quand il est en vacances.
10. Pierre parle à *tout le monde*.

16. Write if you do the following often, sometimes, never, or no longer. Then write if you did or did not do the following last year.

jouer au football
Je joue souvent au football.
Je joue quelquefois au football.
Je ne joue jamais au football.
Je ne joue plus au football.
J'ai joué au football l'année dernière.
Je n'ai pas joué au football l'année dernière.

1. jouer au baseball
2. jouer du piano
3. aller au cinéma
4. faire des voyages
5. dîner au restaurant

17. Complete the following.

1. Je ne bois (mange) pas...
2. Je n'aime ni... ni...
3. Je n'ai aucun(e)...
4. Aucun(e)... ne me plaît.
5. Je ne fais jamais de...
6. Personne ne (n')...
7. Rien ne (n')...
8. Je n'ai jamais...
9. Je n'ose...

CHAPTER 8

Pronouns

Subject Pronouns

The subject pronouns in French are as follows.

je	*I*	**nous**	*we*
tu	*you*	**vous**	*you*
il	*he, it*	**ils**	*they*
elle	*she, it*	**elles**	*they*
on	*one, they, people, we*		

There are three ways to express *you* in French. **Tu** is used to address a friend, relative or close associate. **Vous** is used to address someone you do not know well, or someone older than yourself. To address two or more people, whatever their relation to you, **vous** is used.

> **Tu** es gentil, **Pierre.**
> **Vous** êtes gentil, **Monsieur Leclerc.**
> **Vous** êtes gentils, **Pierre et Marie.**
> **Vous** êtes gentils, **Monsieur et Madame Leclerc.**

Il is used for a person or thing when referring to a masculine noun. **Elle** is used for a person or thing when referring to feminine nouns. **Ils** is used to refer to more than one masculine noun or a combination of masculine and feminine nouns. **Elles** refers to more than one feminine noun.

> **Le journal** est sur la table.
> **Il** est sur la table.
>
> **Ces hommes** sont distingués.
> **Ils** sont distingués.
>
> **La fleur** est jolie.
> **Elle** est jolie.
>
> **Les assiettes** sont dans le placard.
> **Elles** sont dans le placard.

Pierre et Marie vont au cinéma.
Ils vont au cinéma.

The pronoun **on** is used with the **il / elle** form of the verb and can mean *one, people, you, they*.

Si on étudie, on reçoit de bonnes notes.
If one (people, you, they) studies (study), one (people, you, they) gets (get) good grades.

In spoken language, the pronoun **on** can replace the pronoun **nous**. When **on** replaces **nous,** the adjective is usually in the plural.

Nous sommes contents ici.
On est contents ici.

See pages 230-231 for the uses of **on** to replace a passive voice.

1. Change the italicized words to a pronoun.

1. *Marie* parle français.
2. *Pierre* chante bien.
3. *Georges et André* jouent de la guitare.
4. *Hélène et Anne* étudient à la Faculté de Médecine.
5. *Yvonne et Georges* vont en vacances.
6. *Ces livres* sont intéressants.
7. *Ces peintures* sont belles.
8. *Le garçon et la fille* jouent dans le jardin.

2. Follow the model. Use **tu** or **vous**.

heureux / Pierre
Es-tu heureux, Pierre?

1. content / Monsieur
2. malheureuse / Marie
3. paresseux / Jean et Georges
4. fatigué / Jean
5. contents / Monsieur et Madame Leblanc

3. Qu'est-ce qu'on fait samedi soir? Tell what you and your friends do and how you feel on Saturdays. Follow the model.

regarder la télévision
On regarde la télévision.

1. aller au cinéma
2. manger une pizza
3. discuter politique
4. écouter des chansons
5. être content
6. s'amuser bien

Direct Object Pronouns

Le, la, l', les

The third person direct object pronouns in French are **le** (*it, him*), **la** (*it, her*), **l'** (*it, him, her*) and **les** (*them*). The direct object pronoun **le** replaces masculine singular nouns; **la** replaces feminine singular nouns; **l'** is used before verbs beginning with a vowel; **les** replaces plural nouns. **Les** connects with a **z** sound to a word beginning with a vowel. Note that the pronouns can refer to either persons or things and that they immediately precede the conjugated form of the verb.

Jean lit **le livre.**   *John reads the book.*
Jean **le** lit.   *John reads it.*

Pierre regarde **les nuages.**   *Peter looks at the clouds.*
Pierre **les** regarde.   *Peter looks at them.*

Marie voit **Pierre**.	*Mary sees Peter.*
Marie **le** voit.	*Mary sees him.*
Le garçon voit **l'arbre**.	*The boy sees the tree.*
Le garçon **le** voit.	*The boy sees it.*
Pierre regarde **les enfants**.	*Peter looks at the children.*
Pierre **les** regarde.	*Peter looks at them.*
André écoute **la chanson**.	*Andrew listens to the song.*
André **l'**écoute.	*Andrew listens to it.*
Hélène achète **les livres**.	*Helen buys the books.*
Hélène **les** achète.	*Helen buys them.*
Jacques cherche **la photo**.	*James looks for the photo.*
Jacques **la** cherche.	*James looks for it.*
Georges regarde **les peintures**.	*George looks at the paintings.*
Georges **les** regarde.	*George looks at them.*
Nous lisons **l'histoire**.	*We are reading the story.*
Nous **la** lisons.	*We are reading it.*
Jean regarde **Marie**.	*John is looking at Mary.*
Jean **la** regarde.	*John is looking at her.*
Pierre regarde **les peintures**.	*Peter is looking at the paintings.*
Pierre **les** regarde.	*Peter is looking at them.*
Claire achète **la voiture**.	*Claire buys the car.*
Claire **l'**achète.	*Claire buys it.*
Pierre aide **les filles**.	*Peter helps the girls.*
Pierre **les** aide.	*Peter helps them.*

4. What do the people do with the following? Complete the following sentences with the appropriate object pronoun. Follow the model.

La radio?   Je _____ écoute.
La radio?   Je *l*'écoute.

1. La télévision? Je _____ regarde deux heures par jour.
2. Les élèves? Le professeur _____ enseigne.
3. Le maillot de bain? Elle _____ porte en été.
4. Les chansons? Ils _____ écoutent.
5. Les pommes? Je _____ mange.
6. Le journal? Elle _____ achète chaque matin.
7. Les romans policiers? Nous _____ lisons.
8. La lettre? Il _____ écrit à son amie.
9. L'argent? Elle _____ met à la banque.
10. L'histoire? Nous _____ croyons.

5. The following people are good students. Rewrite the following sentences, substituting the italicized object with a pronoun.

1. Pierre résout *les problèmes de mathématiques*.
2. J'écris *la composition*.
3. Anne lit *le livre*.
4. Ils font *les devoirs* chaque soir.
5. Nous aimons *nos cours*.
6. Tu comprends *la leçon*.

7. Vous aidez *les autres élèves*.
8. Tu étudies *le français* cinq fois par semaine.
9. Anne et Marie préparent bien *les examens*.
10. Elles reçoivent *le prix d'honneur*.

Special Use of the Pronoun *le*

Le can be used to replace a complete idea.

Croyez-vous qu'il arrive ce soir?
Oui, je **le** crois. *Yes, I think so.*

Je suis content et elle **l**'est aussi.
I am happy and she is (happy) too.

Le can also replace an adjective. The pronoun **le** never changes, regardless of the gender and number of the adjective it replaces.

Je suis heureux et ils **le** sont aussi.
I am happy and they are too.

Je suis heureuse et elles **le** sont aussi.
I am happy and they are too.

Il est moins intelligent que je **ne le** pensais.
He is more intelligent than I thought (he was).

The **ne** in the above sentence is not negative. It is used, particularly in careful speech, in sentences with comparisons and in subjunctive clauses.

6. Answer the following questions according to the model.

Pensez-vous qu'il va inviter Marie? *Oui*
Oui, je le pense.

1. Pensez-vous qu'il aime l'art moderne?   *Oui*
2. Croyez-vous qu'il fasse le travail?   *Non*
3. Pensez-vous qu'il arrive à l'heure?   *Oui*
4. Croyez-vous qu'il vienne?   *Non*
5. Savez-vous qu'il pleut?   *Oui*

7. Complete the following sentences with the correct object pronoun.

1. Pierre est content et Marie _____ est aussi.
2. Je suis fatigué et elles _____ sont aussi.
3. Elle est heureuse et il _____ est aussi.
4. Je suis triste et ils _____ sont aussi.

Direct and Indirect Object Pronouns

Me, te, nous, vous

The pronouns **me** (*me*), **te** (*you*, familiar), **nous** (*us*) and **vous** (*you*, formal, [singular] and plural) can be used as both direct and indirect object pronouns. The position is the same as for the object pronouns **le, la, l'** and **les**.

Direct: Il **me** voit.   *He sees me.*
Indirect: Il **me** parle.   *He speaks to me.*

Direct:	Elle **te** regarde.	*She looks at you.*
Indirect:	Elle **te** répond.	*She answers you.*
Direct:	Elle **nous** comprend.	*She understands us.*
Indirect:	Elle **nous** donne le livre.	*She gives us the book.*
Direct:	Je **vous** regarde.	*I am looking at you.*
Indirect:	Je **vous** parle.	*I am speaking to you.*

Me becomes **m'** and **te** becomes **t'** before a vowel.

Il **m'**aime.
Il **t'**écoute.

There is a liaison between **nous** or **vous** and a word beginning with a vowel.

Il nous‿écoute.
Il vous‿aime.

8. Answer the following questions in the affirmative.

1. Est-ce que Paul te parle?
2. Est-ce que Jean t'écoute?
3. Est-ce qu'il me dit bonjour?
4. Est-ce qu'il m'invite?
5. Est-ce qu'elle nous voit?
6. Est-ce qu'elle nous appelle?
7. Pierre, est-ce qu'elle vous répond?
8. Hélène, est-ce qu'il vous écoute?
9. Pierre et André, est-ce qu'ils vous regardent?
10. Marie et Anne, est-ce qu'ils vous écrivent?

9. Paul is nice. Say what nice things he does. Follow the model.

répondre gentiment / toi et moi
Il *nous* répond gentiment.

1. apporter des fleurs / moi
2. inviter à dîner / ma mère et moi
3. aider / toi et ton fils
4. donner des cadeaux / toi
5. respecter / mes amies et moi
6. téléphoner souvent / moi
7. prêter ses outils / toi et ton père
8. écouter toujours / toi

Indirect Object Pronouns

Lui, leur

The third person indirect object pronouns are **lui** (*to him, to her*) in the singular and **leur** (*to them*) in the plural. They refer only to people. Note that in the third person there is a difference between the direct and indirect object pronouns. The direct object pronouns are **le (l'), la (l')** and **les.** With the indirect object pronouns, there is no gender differentiation.

Je parle **à Pierre.**	*I speak to Peter.*
Je **lui** parle.	*I speak to him.*
Je donne le livre **à Marie.**	*I give the book to Mary.*
Je **lui** donne le livre.	*I give the book to her. (I give her the book.)*
Je parle **aux garçons.**	*I speak to the boys.*
Je **leur** parle.	*I speak to them.*
Je donne la lettre **aux filles.**	*I give the letter to the girls.*
Je **leur** donne la lettre.	*I give the letter to them. (I give them the letter.)*

10. What gifts does Nicole give her friends and relatives? Follow the model.

> **à ses amis / des biscuits**
> **Elle *leur* donne des biscuits.**

1. à son frère / un livre
2. à ses parents / des photos
3. à sa sœur / un collier
4. à Georges et à André / des cravates
5. à son amie / un bracelet
6. à Pierre / des livres

11. Complete the following sentences with the appropriate direct or indirect object pronoun.

1. Marie visite la tour Eiffel. Marie _____ visite.
2. Le père lit le conte à son fils. Le père _____ lit le conte.
3. Marie voit Charles à la plage. Marie _____ voit à la plage.
4. La fille sait les verbes. La fille _____ sait.
5. L'enfant répond à ses parents. L'enfant _____ répond.
6. Pierre dit bonjour à Marie. Pierre _____ dit bonjour.
7. Le garçon voit son amie et il donne la main à son amie. Le garçon _____ voit et il _____ donne la main.

The Pronoun Y

The pronoun **y** can replace a prepositional phrase beginning with any preposition other than **de** when the object of the preposition is a thing. When **y** replaces a phrase telling the name of a place, it means *there*.

Je vais **à la gare.**	*I am going to the railroad station.*
J'**y** vais.	*I am going there.*
Elle est **dans le salon.**	*She is in the living room.*
Elle **y** est.	*She is there.*
Elle met l'argent **sur la table.**	*She puts the money on the table.*
Elle **y** met l'argent.	*She puts the money there.*

When **y** stands for a thing or idea and follows a verb which requires **à**, it is translated by *it* or *them*.

Il répond **à la lettre.**	*He answers the letter.*
Il **y** répond.	*He answers it.*
Il obéit **aux lois.**	*He obeys the laws.*
Il **y** obéit.	*He obeys them.*

Remember that **lui** and **leur** are used when the object of the preposition is a person.

> Elle dit bonjour à **Marie.**
> Elle **lui** dit bonjour.

12. Rewrite the following sentences, replacing the italicized words by a pronoun.

1. Il va *à la gare.*
2. Le livre est *sur l'étagère.*
3. Elle sera *devant le cinéma.*
4. Il montera *dans le train.*
5. Il répond *à la lettre.*
6. Il obéit *aux lois.*

13. Answer that you do the following. Use **y, lui** or **leur** in your answers.

1. Réponds-tu aux invitations?   4. Réponds-tu au professeur?
2. Obéis-tu à tes parents?   5. Réfléchis-tu à l'avenir?
3. Obéis-tu aux lois?

The Pronoun En

The pronoun **en** replaces a prepositional phrase introduced by **de.** It means *of it, of them, from it, from them, from there, some* or *any*. It is used:

1. in a prepositional sense.

Nous venons **de New York.**   *We come from New York.*
Nous **en** venons.   *We come from there.*

2. in the partitive sense.

J'ai **du pain.**   *I have some bread.*
J'**en** ai.   *I have some.*

3. with expressions followed by **de.**

Elle parle **de ce livre.**   *She speaks about this book.*
Elle **en** parle.   *She speaks about it.*

Elle est fière **de sa robe.**   *She is proud of her dress.*
Elle **en** est fière.   *She is proud of it.*

4. with expressions of quantity.

Il a **beaucoup d'argent.**   *He has a lot of money.*
Il **en** a **beaucoup.**   *He has a lot of it.*

Elle a **trop de livres.**   *She has too many books.*
Elle **en** a **trop.**   *She has too many of them.*

Elle a **dix livres.**   *She has ten books.*
Elle **en** a **dix.**   *She has ten of them.*

Elle a **plusieurs CD.**   *She has several CDs.*
Elle **en** a **plusieurs.**   *She has several (of them).*

J'ai **quelques livres.**   *I have several (a few) books.*
J'**en** ai **quelques-uns.**   *I have several (a few) (of them).*

J'ai **quelques peintures.**   *I have several (a few) paintings.*
J'**en** ai **quelques-unes.**   *I have several (of them).*

14. Rewrite the following sentences, replacing the italicized words by a pronoun.

1. Nous sortons *du théâtre.*   9. Elles ont beaucoup *de livres.*
2. Elle vient *de Paris.*   10. Il a un peu *d'argent.*
3. Ils sortiront *de ce restaurant.* 11. Elle achète une douzaine *de poires.*
4. Il a *du pain.*   12. Il prend quatre *billets.*
5. Elle choisit *des fleurs.*   13. Il a plusieurs *CD.*
6. Elle achète *de la viande.*   14. Elle a quelques *livres.*
7. Il parle *de son travail.*   15. Il a quelques *cravates.*
8. Il est fier *de son appartement.*

15. Rewrite the following sentences, replacing the italicized objects with the correct pronoun, **y, en, lui** or **leur.**

    1. Nous allons *à l'aéroport.*
    2. Il répond *à ses amis.*
    3. Nous avons besoin *de ces journaux.*
    4. Les valises sont *sous le lit.*
    5. Elle répond *aux questions.*
    6. J'ai plusieurs *robes.*
    7. Il parle *au professeur.*
    8. Elle a quelques *fleurs.*
    9. Il y a beaucoup *de peintures* ici.

Double Object Pronouns

When two pronouns are used, both precede the verb in the following order except in the affirmative command.

me te se nous vous	precede	le la les	precede	lui leur	precede	y	precede	en

Il **me le** donne.	*He gives it to me.*
Il **te la** dit.	*He tells it to you.*
Elle **se le** rappelle.	*She remembers it.*
Elle **se le** fait faire.	*She has it made.*
Il **nous les** montre.	*He shows them to us.*
Je **vous l'**écris.	*I write it to you.*
Je **le lui** donne.	*I give it to him.*
Elle **la leur** apporte.	*She brings it to them.*
Il **m'en** donne.	*He gives some to me.*
Elle **lui en** donne.	*She gives some to him.*
Il **nous y** rencontre.	*He meets us there.*
Il **y en** a beaucoup.	*There are a lot of them.*

16. Rewrite the following sentences, substituting the direct object with a pronoun.

    1. Elle me montre les photos.
    2. Il nous sert le déjeuner.
    3. Elle t'envoie la lettre.
    4. Il nous dit la vérité.
    5. Il vous apporte le bifteck.
    6. Il lui envoie le cadeau.
    7. Elle leur donne les billets.
    8. Elle te donne du pain.
    9. Il vous pose des questions.
    10. Il lui donne plusieurs livres.
    11. Il m'apporte de la soupe.
    12. Elle m'attend sur le boulevard.
    13. Il nous rencontre au théâtre.
    14. Il y a quatre livres.

17. Rewrite the following sentences, substituting noun objects with pronouns.

    1. Elle se rappelle la leçon.
    2. Il se brosse les dents.
    3. Vous vous lavez la figure.
    4. Elles se lavent les cheveux.
    5. Elle se souvient du concert.
    6. Il se fait faire la chemise.

18. Rewrite the following sentences, replacing noun objects with object pronouns.

    Qu'est-ce que ces gens font dans leur travail?

    1. Le médecin me donne des piqûres chaque semaine.
    2. Le vendeur rencontre le client devant la maison.

3. Le professeur explique la leçon aux étudiants.
4. Le banquier prête de l'argent au fermier.
5. Le bijoutier te vend ce bracelet en or.
6. Le garçon apporte trois cafés à nos amis.
7. L'avocat donne les contrats aux clients.
8. Le biologiste fait des recherches dans un laboratoire.
9. Le facteur nous apporte le courrier chaque matin.
10. Le pharmacien donne le médicament au malade.
11. L'épicier vous vend des provisions.
12. Le marchand de fruits vend les pommes à Madame Durand.
13. Le chauffeur de taxi rencontre les touristes à l'aéroport.
14. Le conducteur vend les billets aux voyageurs.

Position of Object Pronouns

With Conjugated Verbs

The object pronouns always precede the conjugated form of the verb. If the sentence is negative, **ne** precedes the object pronoun and **pas** follows the verb or auxiliary. In compound tenses the pronoun precedes the auxiliary verb.

Affirmative sentence:	Je **la** regarde.
	Je **le lui** dis.
	Il **l'**a regardé.
Negative sentence:	Je ne **l'**écoute pas.
	Je ne **le lui** donne pas.
	Je ne **le lui** ai pas donné.
Affirmative question:	**Les** voyez-vous? Est-ce que vous **les** voyez?
	Leur en parlez-vous? Est-ce que vous **leur en** parlez?
	Leur en avez-vous parlé? Est-ce que vous **leur en** avez parlé?
Negative question:	Ne **l'**entendez-vous pas? Est-ce que vous ne **l'**entendez pas?
	Ne **l'**avez-vous pas attendu? Est-ce que vous ne **l'**avez pas attendu?
	Ne **la lui** apportez-vous pas? Est-ce que vous ne **la lui** apportez pas?
	Ne **la lui** avez-vous pas apportée? Est-ce que vous ne **la lui** avez pas apportée?
Negative command:	Ne **le** regarde pas!
	Ne **la lui** donne pas!

With semiauxiliary verbs and verbs of perception followed by an infinitive, object pronouns are placed before the verb.

Je **l'**ai fait venir.
Nous ne **les** entendons pas chanter.

The pronouns always precede **voici** and **voilà.**

Les voici.
Le voilà.

Remember that when a direct object precedes the verb in compound tenses, the past participle agrees with the preceding direct object. See pages 154–155.

Il a écrit la lettre.
Il **l'**a écrit**e**.

The past participle does not agree with **en.**

Elle lui a donné des livres.
Elle lui **en** a donné.

19. Rewrite the following sentences, substituting pronouns for the direct and indirect objects.

   1. Il ne fait pas le travail.
   2. Cherchez-vous vos amis à la gare?
   3. N'entend-il pas ce bruit?
   4. Ne mange pas la pomme dans le salon!
   5. Voilà les livres.
   6. Elle m'expliquera la situation.
   7. Il ne nous répète pas la question.
   8. J'avais donné des livres à Jean
   9. N'a-t-elle pas attendu son ami devant le cinéma?
   10. Elle écrivait des cartes à ses parents.
   11. Il n'aurait pas lu ce roman.
   12. Il a cru l'histoire.
   13. As-tu écrit les devoirs?
   14. Elles ont pris les photos devant la statue.
   15. Elle aura dit la vérité au professeur.
   16. Il a écouté le chanteur chanter.
   17. J'ai fait venir le médecin.

With an Infinitive

When a pronoun is the direct or indirect object of the infinitive, it always precedes the infinitive.

Je vais acheter **le CD.**
Je vais **l'**acheter.

Je vais parler **de cela à Jean.**
Je vais **lui en** parler.

Il me dit d'acheter **le CD.**
Il me dit de **l'**acheter.

Il me demande de ne pas faire **le travail.**
Il me demande de ne pas **le** faire.

20. Rewrite the following, substituting pronouns for the direct and indirect objects.

   1. Je voudrais acheter la peinture.
   2. Je voudrais donner le cadeau à Marie.
   3. Je vais parler aux bouquinistes.
   4. Je vais mettre les livres sur l'étagère.
   5. Elle va avoir honte de ses actions.
   6. Il me dit de ne pas acheter cette robe.
   7. Il me demande de ne pas parler de cela à Georges.

With Infinitive Constructions: Causative *faire* **(*faire faire*),** *laisser* **and Verbs of Perception**

(See Chapter 5, pages 223–224)

In the causative **faire (faire faire)** construction all pronouns precede the conjugated form of the verb **faire** except in the affirmative command.

> **Elle fait construire une maison.**
> *She is having a house built.*
> **Elle la fait construire.**
> *She is having it built.*
> **Elle l'a fait construire par Monsieur Dupont.**
> *She is having Mr. Dupont build it.*
> **Elle la lui fait construire.**
> *She is having him build it.*

In compound tenses the past participle does not agree with the direct object pronoun.

> **Elle a fait construire une maison.**
> *She had a house built.*
> **Elle l'a fait construire.**
> *She had it built.*

> **Elle a fait construire une maison par Monsieur Dupont.**
> *She had Mr. Dupont build a house.*
> **Elle l'a fait construire par Monsieur Dupont.**
> *She had Mr. Dupont build it.*
> **Elle la lui a fait construire.**
> *She had him build it.*

After the verb **laisser** and verbs of perception plus an infinitive, the direct object precedes the conjugated verb.

> **Je laisse Marie finir le travail.**
> *I let Mary finish the work.*
> **Je la laisse finir le travail.**
> *I let her finish the work.*
> **J'entends chanter la chanson.**
> *I hear the song being sung.*
> **Je l'entends chanter.**
> *I hear it being sung.*

When there are two direct noun objects, the person doing the action follows the conjugated verb and the noun object follows the infinitive. When there are two pronoun objects, one pronoun object precedes the conjugated verb and the pronoun object of the infinitive precedes the infinitive.

> **Je vois Hélène coudre la robe.**
> *I see Helen sewing the dress.*
> **Je la vois coudre la robe.**
> *I see her sewing the dress.*
> **Je vois Hélène la coudre.**
> *I see Helen sewing it.*
> **Je la vois la coudre.**
> *I see her sewing it.*

In compound tenses the past participle agrees with the preceding pronoun object only if this pronoun is the subject of the infinitive, that is, the object performs the action expressed by the infinitive.

J'ai entendu Hélène chanter la chanson.
I heard Helen sing the song.
Je l'ai entendue chanter la chanson.
I heard her singing the song.
Je l'ai entendue la chanter.
I heard her singing it.

But:

J'ai entendu chanter la chanson.
I heard the song being sung.
Je l'ai entendu chanter.
I heard it being sung.

In the sentence **je l'ai entendue la chanter,** a woman **(Hélène)** is singing and, therefore, the past participle agrees. In the expression **je l'ai entendu chanter,** the past participle does not agree since **chanson** is the object of **chanter.**

21. Rewrite the following sentences, substituting pronouns for the italicized words.

1. Je regarde *ma fille* jouer du piano.
2. J'ai entendu *le bébé* pleurer.
3. Je regarde *le chef* préparer *le repas*.
4. Je laisse *Marie* finir *le travail*.
5. J'ai laissé *Marie* finir *le travail*.
6. J'ai entendu *le chansonnier* chanter *la chanson*.
7. Il fait faire *ce travail*.
8. Il a fait construire *la maison*.
9. Il a fait construire *la maison par l'architecte*.

With Affirmative Commands

In affirmative commands, the pronouns follow the verb and are attached to it and to each other with a hyphen. **Le, la, les** precede **me, te, nous, vous, lui** and **leur.** All precede **y** and **y** precedes **en.**

Donne le jouet à l'enfant!
Donne-le-lui!

Donne de la soupe à l'enfant!
Donne-lui-en!

Va au cinéma!
Vas-y!

Note that **me** becomes **moi** and **te** becomes **toi** in an affirmative command.

Donne-la-moi!   *But:*   **Donnez-m'en!**
Achète-le-toi!   *But:*   **Achète-t'en!**

Note that all commands that end in a vowel add **s** when followed by the pronouns **y** or **en.**

Donne du pain. **Donnes-en.**
Va au parc. **Vas-y.**

22. Rewrite the following in the affirmative.

1. Ne me parlez pas!
2. Ne la lisez pas!
3. Ne le lui donne pas!
4. Ne lui en parle pas!
5. N'y allez pas!
6. Ne te l'achète pas!

23. Follow the model.

> **J'ai l'intention de nettoyer la chambre.**
> **D'accord, nettoyez-la!**

1. J'ai l'intention de lire l'histoire.
2. J'ai l'intention de vous parler de ce sujet.
3. J'ai l'intention d'écrire les lettres à Pierre.
4. J'ai l'intention de répondre à la lettre.
5. J'ai l'intention d'aller au parc.
6. J'ai l'intention de leur parler de ce problème.
7. J'ai l'intention de vous donner des livres.

Review

24. Rewrite the following sentences, replacing the italicized words with pronouns.

1. Il n'obéit pas *à sa mère*.
2. Il a trop *de livres*.
3. Elle est allée *à l'aéroport*.
4. Elle a mis *les livres sur la table*.
5. Il ne dit pas *la vérité à ses parents*.
6. Elle ne répond pas *à la lettre*.
7. N'écoute pas *cet homme*!
8. Il se rappelle *le film*.
9. Il y a beaucoup *de gens*.
10. Elle a mis douze *pommes dans son panier*.
11. Donnez-moi *du beurre*!
12. Parlez-vous *de cela à votre ami*?
13. Je vais donner *les livres à Marie*.
14. Donnez *les jouets aux enfants*.
15. As-tu donné *la montre à Marie*?
16. Ne parle-t-elle pas *de son voyage à Jean*?

25. Say that the Leblanc family members are procrastinators. Use object pronouns. Follow the model.

> **Pierre / réparer la voiture**
> **Pierre ne l'a pas réparée.**
> **Il ne la répare pas maintenant.**
> **Il va la réparer plus tard.**

1. Pierre / laver les voitures
2. Anne / écrire la lettre à sa grand-mère
3. M. Leblanc / peindre la maison
4. M. et Mme Leblanc / acheter des provisions au supermarché
5. Anne et Pierre / ranger la vaisselle dans les placards
6. Mme Leblanc / jeter les ordures dans la poubelle
7. Marie / donner de la nourriture aux chiens
8. Mme Leblanc / planter les fleurs dans le jardin

26. Answer the following personalized questions. Use pronouns in your answers.

> **Envoies-tu des cartes d'anniversaire à tes ami(e)s?**
> **Oui, je leur en envoie.**
> **Non, je ne leur en envoie pas.**

1. Écris-tu des lettres à tes parents?
2. As-tu écrit une lettre à tes parents cette semaine?
3. As-tu acheté tes livres à la librairie de l'université?
4. Vas-tu souvent au cinéma?
5. Es-tu allé(e) au cinéma hier?
6. Achètes-tu des vêtements au grand magasin?
7. As-tu donné un cadeau d'anniversaire à ton ami(e)?
8. Aimes-tu les épinards?
9. Est-ce que ton professeur te donne beaucoup de devoirs?
10. Te rappelles-tu la leçon d'hier?
11. Dis-tu la vérité à tes parents?
12. Habiteras-tu en ville l'année prochaine?
13. Réfléchis-tu à l'avenir?
14. Achèteras-tu plusieurs CD samedi prochain?
15. Vas-tu faire le ménage ce week-end?

Reflexive Pronouns

Reflexive pronouns are used when the action in the sentence is both executed and received by the subject. For a complete review of reflexive verbs, see Chapter 5.

The reflexive pronouns are:

Singular	Plural
me	nous
te	vous
se	se

Reflexive pronouns can be direct or indirect objects.

> *Direct:* Je **me** lève.
> *Indirect:* Je **me** lave les cheveux.

Me, te and **se** become **m', t'** and **s'** before verbs beginning with a vowel. There is a liaison between **nous** or **vous** and a word beginning with a vowel or silent **h.**

> Il **se** lève.
> Il **s'**habille.
> Nous **nous** débrouillons.
> Nous **nous** habillons.

27. Complete the following sentences with the appropriate reflexive pronoun.

1. Je _____ appelle Marie.
2. Nous _____ lavons la figure.
3. À quelle heure _____ lèves-tu?
4. Pourquoi est-ce qu'elle ne _____ peigne pas?
5. Elles _____ débrouillent bien.
6. Vous _____ asseyez ici.
7. Je _____ dépêche pour arriver à l'heure.
8. Nous _____ couchons tard.
9. Elle _____ habille bien.
10. Tu _____ arrêtes un moment.

Disjunctive Pronouns

The disjunctive pronouns or stress pronouns are the same as the subject pronouns **elle, elles, nous** and **vous.** The other forms change.

Singular		*Plural*	
Subject	*Disjunctive*	*Subject*	*Disjunctive*
je	moi	nous	nous
tu	toi	vous	vous
il	lui	ils	eux
elle	elle	elles	elles
on	soi		

The pronouns occur:

1. after **c'est** and **ce sont.**

C'est is used with all the disjunctive pronouns except **eux** and **elles,** which use **ce sont.** Note that the verb in the **qui** clause must agree with the subject.

> **C'est moi. C'est moi** qui parle.
> *It is I. It is I who am speaking.*
> **C'est nous. C'est nous** qui l'avons fait.
> *It is we. It is we who did it.*
> **Ce sont eux. Ce sont eux** qui mentent.
> *It is they. It is they who are lying.*
> **Ce sont elles. Ce sont elles** qui arrivent.
> *It is they. It is they who are arriving.*

2. after a preposition.

> Elle parle **de lui.**   *She speaks about him.*
> Nous allons **avec elle.**   *We are going with her.*

Remember that when the object of a preposition is a thing rather than a person, **y** or **en** must be used.

> Je pense **à Marie.** Je pense **à elle.**
> *I am thinking about Mary. I am thinking about her.*
> Je pense **aux examens.** J'**y** pense.
> *I am thinking about the examinations. I am thinking about them.*
> Je parle **de Pierre.** Je parle **de lui.**
> *I am speaking about Peter. I am speaking about him.*
> Je parle **de ce livre.** J'**en** parle.
> *I am speaking about this book. I am speaking about it.*

When the direct object pronoun is **me, te, se, nous** or **vous,** the indirect object is expressed by **à** plus a disjunctive pronoun.

> Il **se** présente **à elle.**
> *He presents himself to her.*
> Vous **me** recommandez **à lui.**
> *You recommend me to him.*

3. after a comparison.

> Elle est **plus** intelligente **que lui.**
> *She is more intelligent than he.*
> Il est **plus** beau **que moi.**
> *He is more handsome than I.*

4. alone for emphasis.

> Qui est là? **Moi.**   *Who's there? I am.*
> Qui regarde-t-elle? **Lui.** *Whom is she looking at? Him.*

5. to add emphasis to a non-accentuated pronoun.

> **Moi,** je prépare la salade, **toi,** tu prépares les sandwichs.

6. after **ne... que.**

> Elle **n'**aime **que lui.**   *She likes only him.*

7. as a part of a compound subject.

> **Vous et moi,** nous le ferons.   *You and I will do it.*
> **Pierre et lui,** ils arrivent.   *Peter and he arrive.*

8. as part of a compound object.

> Il nous regarde, **elle et moi.**   *He sees her and me.*

9. in combination with **même.**

moi-même	*myself*	**nous-mêmes**	*ourselves*
toi-même	*yourself*	**vous-même(s)**	*yourself, yourselves*
lui-même	*himself*	**eux-mêmes**	*themselves*
elle-même	*herself*	**elles-mêmes**	*themselves*

> Je le ferai **moi-même.**   *I'll do it myself.*

Soi is used when the subject is general: **on, chacun, nul, personne.**

> Chacun pour **soi.**   *Each one for himself.*

28. Complete the following paragraph with the appropriate disjunctive pronoun.

Nous aimons tous un sport différent!

_____, je préfère jouer au tennis mais _____, tu préfères jouer au badminton. Et Philippe?
₍₁₎ _____ et _____, nous préférons jouer au football, mais Pierre, _____, il préfère jouer au football nord-américain. André et Marc, _____, ils préfèrent jouer au hockey. Hélène et _____ deux, vous préférez nager. Martine et Anne, _____, elles préfèrent faire du ski nautique.

29. Everyone helps prepare for a birthday party for Nicole. Follow the model.

> **Qui fera le menu?** *Marie, je*
> **C'est nous qui ferons le menu.**
> **Elle et moi, nous ferons le menu.**

1. Qui a envoyé les invitations? *je*
2. Qui a acheté le cadeau? *Martine, je*
3. Qui s'occupe de la musique? *Nicole et Jeannette*
4. Qui prépare les sandwichs? *Georges et André*
5. Qui va faire le gâteau? *il*
6. Qui va chercher les boissons? *il, tu*
7. Qui va faire les décorations? *Anne*
8. Qui va faire la présentation du cadeau? *tu*

30. Translate the following sentences into French.

1. I'll do it myself.
2. He'll do it himself.
3. The boys will do it themselves.
4. We'll do it ourselves.
5. Each one for himself.

31. Answer the following questions in the affirmative, using the disjunctive pronoun, **y** or **en**.

1. Pensez-vous à ce livre?
2. Avez-vous peur de cet homme?
3. Partirez-vous sans vos camarades?
4. Avez-vous honte de vos actions?
5. Pensez-vous à Hélène?
6. Allez-vous à la gare?
7. Est-ce que ce sont Hélène et Marie qui parlent?
8. Vont-ils chez Marianne?
9. Va-t-elle avec Pierre?
10. Avez-vous besoin de votre argent?
11. Je me présente à Pierre.

Possessive Pronouns

A possessive pronoun is used to replace a possessive adjective plus a noun. The possessive pronoun must agree with the noun it replaces and is accompanied by the appropriate definite article or one of its contracted forms, **au, aux, du, des.**

Masculine			Feminine	
Singular	Plural		Singular	Plural
le mien	**les miens**	*mine*	**la mienne**	**les miennes**
le tien	**les tiens**	*yours (fam.)*	**la tienne**	**les tiennes**
le sien	**les siens**	*his, hers, its*	**la sienne**	**les siennes**
le nôtre	**les nôtres**	*ours*	**la nôtre**	**les nôtres**
le vôtre	**les vôtres**	*yours*	**la vôtre**	**les vôtres**
le leur	**les leurs**	*theirs*	**la leur**	**les leurs**

J'ai **mon livre** et non pas **le tien.**
I have my book and not yours.
J'aime **ma blouse** et non pas **la tienne.**
I like my blouse and not yours.
Voici **tes billets.** Où sont **les miens**?
Here are your tickets. Where are mine?
Voici **vos valises.** Où sont **les miennes**?
Here are your suitcases. Where are mine?

Je préfère **mon livre au tien.**
I prefer my book to yours.
J'ai expliqué la situation **à ma mère.** As-tu expliqué la situation **à la tienne**?
I explained the situation to my mother. Did you explain the situation to yours?
J'ai besoin **de mes livres.** Ont-ils besoin **des leurs**?
I need my books. Do they need theirs?
Je parle **de mon professeur.** Parle-t-il **du sien**?
I am speaking about my teacher. Is he speaking about his?

When the possessor is an indefinite pronoun subject such as **on, personne, tout le monde, chacun,** the pronouns **le sien, la sienne, les siens, les siennes** are used.

On aime sa **famille. On** aime **la sienne.**
Tout le monde a ses **valises. Tout le monde** a **les siennes.**

If a plural subject is modified by **chacun,** the possessive pronoun agrees with the subject.

Nous avons apporté **chacun les nôtres.**

In the masculine plural, the possessive pronoun designates relatives, friends, allies, etc.

Il est **des nôtres.**
He's one of us.

32. Replace the italicized phrase with the appropriate possessive pronoun.

1. Ce sont *mes livres*. Où sont *tes livres*?
2. Je n'aime pas *ma voiture*. Aimez-vous *votre voiture*?
3. Il a pensé à *ses amis* et elles ont pensé à *leurs amis*.
4. J'ai besoin de *mes livres* et vous avez besoin de *vos livres*.
5. *Notre piscine* est plus petite que *ta piscine*.
6. Nous avons *nos billets*. Avez-vous *vos billets*?
7. Il a parlé de *sa situation* et tu as parlé de *ta situation*.
8. J'ai besoin de *leur voiture*.
9. Pierre va chercher *ses valises* et *mes valises*.
10. Vous mettez *votre manteau* et je mets *mon manteau*.
11. Nous sommes fiers de *notre pays* et ils sont fiers de *leur pays*.
12. Elle préfère *nos meubles* à *vos meubles*.
13. Il a cherché *son passeport* et les filles ont cherché *leur passeport*.
14. *Ton appareil photographique* est meilleur que *mon appareil photographique*.
15. Il a téléphoné à *sa mère* et nous avons téléphoné à *notre mère*.

33. To whom do the objects belong? Follow the model.

À qui sont ces livres?   *à moi*
Ce sont les miens.

1. À qui sont ces CD?   *à vous*
2. À qui est ce livre?   *à moi*
3. À qui est cette bicyclette?   *à toi*
4. À qui est cette maison?   *à nous*
5. À qui est cette pomme?   *à lui*
6. À qui est ce parapluie?   *à elle*
7. À qui sont ces robes?   *à moi*
8. À qui sont ces peintures?   *à eux*

34. Make comparisons between you and your friends. Follow the models, using possessive pronouns in your answers.

Mes cours
Mes cours sont difficiles. Les siens sont faciles.
Ton ordinateur
Ton ordinateur est tout neuf. Le mien est vieux.

1. Mon professeur de français
2. Ton ordinateur
3. Mes amis
4. Ma sœur / Mon frère
5. Ton frère / Ta sœur
6. Mes amies

Demonstrative Pronouns

The French forms of demonstrative pronouns *this one, that one, these, those* are as follows:

	Singular	Plural
Masculine	**celui**	**ceux**
Feminine	**celle**	**celles**

When followed by a relative pronoun, the demonstrative pronouns mean *the one, the ones, he (she) who, these* or *those.*

Celui qui travaille ici est mon ami.
The one who works here is my friend.

The demonstrative pronouns followed by **de** can indicate possession.

La bicyclette de Pierre et **celle** de Marie
Peter's bicycle and Mary's

To distinguish between *this one* and *that one* and between *these* and *those,* the suffixes **-ci** (*this*) and **-là** (*that*) are added.

J'aime **celui-ci.**   *I like this one.*
J'aime **celle-là.**   *I like that one.*

When two things are mentioned, **celui-ci** means *the latter* and **celui-là** means *the former.*

J'ai parlé avec M. Dupont et M. Leclerc.
Celui-ci (M. Leclerc) est médecin et **celui-là** (M. Dupont) est homme d'affaires.
The latter is a doctor and the former is a businessman.

Celui-ci can be replaced by **ce dernier** and **celui-là** by **le premier.**

Ce dernier est médecin et **le premier** est homme d'affaires.

35. You are explaining who owns the lost objects. Answer the following questions, using a demonstrative pronoun according to the model.

C'est ton livre? *mon frère*
Non, c'est celui de mon frère.

1. C'est ta bicyclette?   *ma sœur*
2. C'est ton chien?   *mon ami*
3. Ce sont tes livres?   *mon frère*
4. Ce sont tes photos?   *ma mère*
5. C'est ton cahier?   *mon amie*
6. C'est ta montre?   *mon oncle*

36. Complete the following sentences with the appropriate demonstrative pronoun, according to the model.

Les légumes? _____ sont plus frais que _____.
Les légumes? *Ceux-ci* sont plus frais que *ceux-là*.

Au supermarché

1. Les tomates? _____ sont plus rouges que _____.
2. Le bifteck? _____ est plus tendre que _____.
3. Les oranges? _____ sont plus sucrées que _____.
4. Le fromage? _____ est plus crémeux que _____.
5. La pomme? _____ est meilleure que _____.
6. Les haricots verts? _____ sont plus frais que _____.
7. Le vin? _____ est plus sec que _____.
8. La crème? _____ est plus douce que _____.

Indefinite Demonstrative Pronouns

Ce, ceci, cela (ça)

Ce

Ce (c') is used mainly with the verb **être** and sometimes with the verbs **aller, devoir** and **pouvoir**. Sometimes **ce** may be replaced by **cela**.

It is used with the verb **être**:

1. before a noun that is modified.

   Regardez cet homme. **C'**est un grand pianiste.
   Look at this man. He's a great pianist.
   Qui est cette fille? **C'**est ma sœur.
   Who is this girl? She's my sister.

2. before a proper noun.

   Voilà un jeune homme. **C'**est André Pierron.
   There is a young man. It is André Pierron.

3. before a pronoun.

   J'ai trouvé ce paquet. Est-**ce** le vôtre?
   I found this package. Is it yours?

4. before a superlative.

   Ce sont les meilleures cerises de la ville.
   These are the best cherries in the city.

5. before an infinitive.

   Le problème **c'**est de savoir où commencer.
   The problem is to know where to begin.

6. before an adverb.

   C'est aujourd'hui un jour de congé.
   Today is a holiday.
   C'est maintenant ou jamais.
   It's now or never.

7. as a neuter subject.

> **Il** est vrai que deux et deux font quatre. Oui, **c'**est vrai.
> *It is true that two and two are four. Yes, it's true.*

Note that **ce** is used to represent something that has preceded. The pronoun **il** is used to announce something that follows.

37. Complete the following sentences with **ce (c'), il** or **elle.**

    1. _____ est inutile de me parler.
    2. Manger _____ est vivre.
    3. Voilà mon amie. _____ est intelligente.
    4. Voilà mon amie. _____ est une grande artiste.
    5. Ne me parlez pas. _____ est inutile.
    6. _____ sont les meilleures peintures de l'artiste.

Ceci, cela (ça)

When the demonstrative pronoun replaces an indefinite expression or an idea, **ceci** or **cela** is used. **Ça** is used in familiar style. **Cela** is used when the expression has already been mentioned. **Ceci** is used to introduce the expression.

> **Ceci** est bon. Vous avez bien réussi.
> *This is good. You have succeeded well.*
> Vous avez réussi. **Cela** est bon.
> *You have succeeded. That is good.*

Like **celui-ci** and **celui-là**, **ceci** refers to the closest thing mentioned and **cela** to the farthest thing.

> Du cinéma ou du théâtre, **ceci** me plaît plus que **cela.**

38. Complete the following sentences with **ce, c', ceci** or **cela.**

    1. _____ est bon. Vous avez bien fait.
    2. Vous avez bien fait. _____ est bon.
    3. _____ est mon ami.
    4. J'ai un gant. Est-_____ le vôtre?
    5. _____ m'est égal.
    6. Ne touchez pas au feu! _____ ne se fait pas.
    7. Retenez bien _____.

Relative Pronouns

The relative pronoun is used to introduce a clause that modifies a noun.

Qui who, which, that

Qui functions as the subject of the clause and may refer to either a person or a thing.

> La femme **qui** parle est ma mère.
> *The woman who is speaking is my mother.*
> Le livre **qui** est sur la table est bon.
> *The book which is on the table is good.*

Qui is used in proverbs to replace **celui qui.**

Rira bien qui rira le dernier.
He who laughs last laughs best.

Qui can also be used in certain archaic idiomatic expressions to replace **ce qui.**

Qui plus est	*What's more*
Qui pis est	*What's worse*
Qui mieux est	*What's better*

Il est désagréable et **qui pis est** méchant.
He is disagreeable and what's worse he's naughty.

Que **whom, which, that**

Que functions as the direct object of a clause and may refer to either persons or things. Note that **que** becomes **qu'** before a vowel.

Le garçon **que** nous avons vu hier est mon frère.
The boy whom we saw yesterday is my brother.
Les livres **qu'**elle écrit sont intéressants.
The books she writes are interesting.

Que is sometimes used to replace **où** after certain expressions of time.

L'année **que** je reviendrai
The year when I will return

39. Complete the following sentences with **qui** or **que.**

1. La fille _____ parle est intelligente.
2. Le film _____ j'ai vu est merveilleux.
3. Les livres _____ il regarde sont les miens.
4. Le restaurant _____ est au coin de la rue est excellent.
5. L'homme _____ nous avons vu hier est avocat.
6. Les garçons _____ viennent d'entrer sont mes amis.
7. Les poèmes _____ elle a écrits sont beaux.
8. Les tableaux _____ sont dans le salon sont jolis.

40. Combine the following pairs of sentences, according to the model.

L'homme fait un discours. Il est avocat.
L'homme qui fait un discours est avocat.

1. Voilà un garçon. Il est sportif.
2. La dame entre. Elle est la femme de mon professeur.
3. L'église est au centre de la ville. Elle est grande.
4. La jeune fille danse. Elle est très intelligente.
5. Je connais cette femme. Elle donne de bons discours.

41. Combine the following pairs of sentences, according to the model.

Il écrit les livres. Les livres sont intéressants.
Les livres qu'il écrit sont intéressants.

1. Voilà le restaurant. Pierre préfère le restaurant.
2. Je lis le journal. Le journal est parisien.

3. Elle a acheté cette robe. La robe est très chère.
4. Nous avons vu le film. Le film est américain.
5. C'est un médecin. Je connais ce médecin.

42. Complete the following sentences.

1. J'aime les restaurants qui...
2. Je connais quelqu'un qui...
3. J'aime les films qui...
4. _____ est un acteur que...
5. _____ est une actrice que...
6. J'aime les gens qui...

Ce qui and *ce que*

Ce qui   *What, that which*

Ce qui is used as the subject of the clause when there is no antecedent.

Comprenez-vous **ce qui** se passe?
Do you understand what is happening?
Ce qui est arrivé est presque impossible.
What happened is almost impossible.

Ce que   *What, that which*

Ce que is used as the object of a verb in a relative clause when there is no antecedent.

Je ne comprends pas **ce que** vous dites.
I don't understand what you are saying.
Ce qu'il écrit est difficile à comprendre.
What he writes is difficult to understand.

Ce qui and **ce que** can be combined with **tout.**

Tout ce qui est bon est beau.
All that is good is beautiful.
Tout ce qu'elle fait est bon.
All that she does is good.

43. Say that you do not know or do not understand something. Complete the following sentencees with **ce qui** or **ce que (ce qu').**

1. Je ne comprends pas _____ il dit.
2. Je ne comprends pas _____ se passe.
3. Je nc sais pas _____ va avoir lieu.
4. Je ne sais pas _____ Pierre fait.
5. Je ne comprends pas _____ est arrivé.
6. Je ne comprends pas _____ on dit.

44. You are interviewing another student. Rephrase the following questions, using **ce qui** or **ce que.**

Qu'est-ce qui t'amuse?
Dis-moi ce qui t'amuse.
Qu'est-ce que tu trouves bizarre?
Dis-moi ce que tu trouves bizarre.

1. Qu'est-ce qui t'intéresse?
2. Qu'est-ce que tu trouves amusant?
3. Qu'est-ce qui te fait peur?

4. Qu'est-ce que tu fais les samedis?
5. Qu'est-ce que tu penses des politiciens?
6. Qu'est-ce qui te rend heureux (heureuse)?

Relative Pronouns with Prepositions Other than *de*: *Qui, lequel*

Qui

Qui as object of a preposition refers to persons only.

La fille **à qui** vous parlez est gentille.
The girl to whom you are speaking is nice.
La femme **pour qui** je travaille est intelligente.
The woman for whom I work is intelligent.

Lequel, laquelle, lesquels, lesquelles Which

Lequel is the relative pronoun used after a preposition and refers to things or to persons. **Lequel** must agree with the antecedent.

La maison **dans laquelle** Pierre habite est grande.
The house in which Peter lives is big.
Le restaurant **devant lequel** j'ai attendu mon ami est merveilleux.
The restaurant in front of which I waited for my friend is marvelous.
Les raisons **pour lesquelles** je fais cela sont évidentes.
The reasons why I do that are evident.

After **parmi** and **entre,** the forms of **lequel** are obligatory when referring to persons. The pronoun **qui** cannot be used.

Les gens **parmi lesquels** il vit sont gentils.
The people among whom he lives are nice.
Les femmes **entre lesquelles** elle se tient debout sont ses amies.
The women between whom she stands are her friends.

When preceded by the preposition **à, lequel** contracts with it to form **auquel, auxquels, auxquelles. À** plus **laquelle** do not contract.

Le concert **auquel** il a assisté a été bon.
The concert which he attended was good.
L'école **à laquelle** elle va est vieille.
The school where (to which) she goes is old.
Les bâtiments **auxquels** nous allons sont vieux.
The buildings where we are going are old.
Les villes **auxquelles** nous allons sont intéressantes.
The cities where we are going are interesting.

45. Complete the following sentences with the correct relative pronoun.

1. La fille à _____ je parle est une bonne artiste.
2. L'homme avec _____ je sors est intelligent.
3. La boutique derrière _____ se trouve un arbre est une boutique moderne.
4. Le bâtiment dans _____ je travaille est un gratte-ciel.
5. Les villes vers _____ nous nous dirigeons sont de véritables musées.
6. Voilà les pinceaux avec _____ il a peint ce tableau.
7. Les garçons entre _____ il est assis sont gentils.

46. Combine the two sentences into one, according to the models.

J'ai parlé à l'homme. Il est intéressant.
L'homme à qui j'ai parlé est intéressant.

Je pense à ce travail. Il est difficile.
Le travail auquel je pense est difficile.

1. Voilà le garçon. Je suis sorti avec le garçon.
2. Voilà la maison. J'ai habité dans cette maison.
3. J'ai écrit à ces hommes. Ils sont mes anciens professeurs.
4. C'est le pinceau. L'artiste travaille avec le pinceau.
5. Voilà un morceau de papier. Il a dessiné sur ce morceau de papier.
6. Paul entre dans le restaurant. Le restaurant est très petit.
7. Nous allons chez cette fille. Elle est gentille.
8. Voilà les tables. Marie a mis des fleurs sur les tables.
9. Il attend son ami devant le musée. Le musée est formidable.
10. Nous sommes allés au théâtre. Le théâtre est très vieux.
11. Elle a assisté à la conférence. La conférence était intéressante.
12. Il a répondu à ces lettres. Elles étaient urgentes.
13. Il a écrit à ces hommes. Ces hommes sont avocats.
14. Je suis allée aux musées. Les musées sont grands.

Où

A relative clause referring to a place or time is usually introduced by **où** to avoid using a preposition plus a form of **lequel.**

Voilà la maison **dans laquelle** Georges habite.
Voilà la maison **où** habite Georges.
There is the house where George lives.
Le siècle **pendant lequel** il vécut était intéressant.
Le siècle **où** il vécut était intéressant.
The century in which he lived was interesting.

47. Rewrite the following sentences according to the model.

L'école à laquelle nous allons est vieille.
L'école où nous allons est vieille.

1. L'appartement dans lequel j'habite est très petit.
2. La boulangerie dans laquelle j'entre est bonne.
3. Le bureau auquel je vais se trouve au centre de la ville.
4. Les restaurants dans lesquels nous dînons ne sont pas chers.
5. Les églises auxquelles nous allons sont vieilles.

Relative Pronouns with the Preposition *de*: *Dont, duquel*

While the forms **de qui,** referring to persons, and **duquel, desquels, de laquelle, desquelles,** referring to things do occur, most French-speakers use **dont.**

Dont may refer to persons or things and means *whose, of (about) which, of (about) whom.*

La femme **de qui** nous parlons est Marie Dupont.
La femme **dont** nous parlons est Marie Dupont.
The woman about whom we are speaking is Marie Dupont.

Le film **duquel** nous parlons est bon.
Le film **dont** nous parlons est bon.
The movie of which we are speaking is good.

Je connais une fille **dont** la mère est médecin.
I know a girl whose mother is a doctor.
L'homme **dont** le fils parle est avocat.
The man whose son is speaking is a lawyer.
Voilà un tableau **dont** j'admire la beauté.
There is a painting whose beauty I admire.

Dont cannot be followed by a possessive adjective.

Voilà la fille. Je connais **ses** parents.
Voilà la fille **dont** je connais **les** parents.

Dont can be used only when it immediately follows the noun to which it refers. If the noun is followed by a prepositional phrase, the appropriate form of **de** plus **lequel** must be used.

C'est le garçon avec la sœur **duquel** je suis sorti.
He is the boy whose sister I went out with.
Voilà la fille à la mère **de laquelle (de qui)** vous avez parlé.
There is the girl whose mother you spoke to.

48. Rewrite the following sentences, replacing **de qui** and the forms of **duquel** by **dont**.

1. Le garçon de qui le père est mort est mon ami.
2. Le musée duquel le nom m'échappe est célèbre.
3. La dame de qui nous cherchons le chien est une amie de ma mère.
4. L'homme de qui les usines sont à Lyon habite à Paris.
5. J'aime ce jardin duquel les fleurs l'embellissent.
6. Le crayon duquel vous vous servez n'est pas bon.
7. Les livres desquels vous m'avez parlé sont intéressants.
8. La peinture de laquelle vous avez envie est très chère.

49. Follow the model.

Voilà le garçon. Je connais ses parents.
Voilà le garçon dont je connais les parents.

1. Voilà une fille. Son père est médecin.
2. Voilà le mannequin. Ses robes sont jolies.
3. Voilà les garçons. Vous connaissez leur sœur.
4. Voilà un professeur. Sa fille est chimiste.
5. Voilà un garçon. Son père est mort.
6. Voilà une femme. J'admire la beauté de cette femme.
7. Voilà un peintre. Le tableau de ce peintre est cher.
8. C'est un beau tableau. Nous avons parlé de ce tableau.
9. C'est un livre. Vous avez envie de ce livre.
10. As-tu étudié le poème? Il a parlé du poème.
11. C'est un livre. J'ai besoin de ce livre.
12. J'ai vu la jeune fille. Ils ont parlé de cette jeune fille.
13. C'est un beau poème. Nous avons lu quelques passages de ce poème.

50. Follow the model.

> **C'est le garçon. Je suis sorti avec sa sœur.**
> **C'est le garçon avec la sœur duquel je suis sorti.**

1. C'est la fille. J'ai parlé à sa mère.
2. C'est un homme. Je suis sorti avec sa fille.
3. Il y a une boutique ici. Près de la boutique se trouve un bureau de tabac.
4. Il a fait un discours. À cause de ce discours j'ai pleuré.
5. Voilà les jeunes filles. Je suis sortie avec leur frère.

Quoi, ce dont

Quoi (*what*) is used after a preposition.

> Je sais **de quoi** il s'agit.
> *I know what it is about.*
> Je sais **à quoi** vous avez pensé.
> *I know what you thought about.*
> Je sais **sur quoi** il écrit.
> *I know what he is writing about.*

Ce dont (*what*) can be used before expressions requiring the preposition **de.**

> Il sait **ce dont** vous avez besoin.
> *He knows what you need.*

51. Complete the following sentences with **quoi, à quoi** or **ce dont.**

1. Elle comprend _____ je m'étonne.
2. Il sait de _____ il parle.
3. Je sais _____ vous pensez.
4. Elles savent de _____ il s'agit.
5. Elle comprend _____ vous avez peur.

Review

52. Complete the following sentences with the appropriate relative pronoun. Include prepositions when necessary.

1. _____ vous voulez est impossible à avoir.
2. Voilà un homme _____ est avocat.
3. C'est une fille _____ je connais le frère.
4. Voilà la maison _____ nous demeurons.
5. Voilà les livres _____ Pierre cherche.
6. Avez-vous trouvé la lettre _____ j'ai besoin?
7. Savez-vous _____ est dans le tiroir?
8. Dites-moi _____ il vous a dit.
9. C'est l'homme avec la fille _____ je suis sorti.
10. Les femmes _____ ils parlent sont jolies.
11. Je comprends de _____ il s'agit.
12. Un boucher est un homme _____ vend de la viande.
13. C'est un politicien _____ je suis d'accord.
14. Ce sont des idées _____ je suis d'accord.

53. Complete the following, choosing an appropriate completion from the second column. Then make up your own completions.

1. Je connais un homme qui	vous dites
2. Je connais une femme que	Pierre habite
3. Je connais un garçon dont	tout le monde admire
4. Je sais de quoi	sont intelligents
5. Je comprends ce que	la mère est médecin
6. Nous arrivons à la ville où	il s'agit
7. Les étudiants auxquels nous parlons	parle arabe

Indefinite Pronouns

Following are some indefinite pronouns.

1. **aucun(e)**   *anyone, none*
   aucun(e)...   *none*

   Aucun d'eux **n'**est arrivé.
   None of them arrived.
   Aucune d'elles **n'**est arrivée.
   None of them arrived.
   Y a t il **aucun** de vous qui puisse le faire?
   Is there anyone of you who can do it?
   Avez-vous des peintures?   **Aucune.**
   Do you have any paintings?   None.

2. **l'autre**   *the other, the other one*
   les autres   *the others, the other ones*

   Deux filles sont restées. **Les autres** sont parties.
   Two girls stayed. The others left.
   J'ai perdu un foulard, mais j'en ai **d'autres**.
   I lost a scarf, but I have others (other ones).

3. **l'un (l'une)... l'autre**   *the one ... the other*
   les uns (les unes)... les autres   *the ones (some) ... the others*

   Les uns dansaient; **les autres** bavardaient.
   Some danced; others talked.

4. **l'un (l'une) et l'autre**   *both, both of them*
   l'un (l'une) ou l'autre   *either one*
   ni l'un (l'une) ni l'autre   *neither one*
   l'un (l'une) à l'autre   *to each other*
   l'un (l'une) pour l'autre   *one for the other*

   Elles sont venues **l'une et l'autre**.
   Both of them came.
   Vous avez deux livres. Donnez-moi **l'un ou l'autre**.
   You have two books. Give me either one. (It makes no difference.)
   Ni l'un ni l'autre n'est venu.
   Neither one came.
   Ils s'écrivent **l'un à l'autre**.
   They write to each other.
   Elles travaillent **l'une pour l'autre**.
   They work for each other.

5. **autre(s)**   *other(s)*

> Voici deux livres: je prends celui-ci; prenez **l'autre.**
> *Here are two books: I'll take this one; take the other.*

6. **autre chose**   *something else*

> Je voudrais **autre chose** de sucré.
> *I would like something else sweet.*

When an adjective modifies **autre chose,** the adjective is always masculine and is always preceded by **de.**

Note also the fixed expression **quelque chose d'autre** (something else).

> Il a quelque chose **d'autre.**
> *He has something else.*

7. **autrui**   *others, other people*

> Il ne faut pas convoiter le bien d'**autrui.**
> *You must not covet the property of others.*

8. **certain, certaine**   *a certain one*
   certains, certaines   *certain ones, some*

> **Certains** d'entre eux voulaient danser.
> *Some of them wanted to dance.*

9. **chacun, chacune**   *each one, everyone*

> **Chacun** à son goût.
> *Each to his own taste.*
> **Chacun** des garçons apportera un cadeau.
> *Each one of the boys will bring a gift.*

10. **pas grand-chose**   *not much*

> Il n'a **pas grand-chose** à me dire.
> *He does not have much to say to me.*

Grand-chose is always used in the negative.

11. **Je ne sais qui**   *I don't know who*
    Je ne sais quoi   *I don't know what*

> **Je ne sais qui** a téléphoné.
> *I don't know who telephoned.*
> Elle a **je ne sais quoi** d'élégant.
> *She has somewhat of an elegant air.*

12. **le même, la même**   *the same (one)*
    les mêmes   *the same (ones)*

> C'est **la même.**
> *It's the same one.*

13. **n'importe qui**   *anyone*

> **N'importe qui** pourra le faire.
> *Anyone will be able to do it.*
> Je parlerai à **n'importe qui.**
> *I will speak to anyone.*

14. **n'importe quoi** *anything*

> Il peut faire **n'importe quoi.**
> *He can do anything.*

15. **nul** *no one*

> **Nul** ne sait la réponse.
> *No one knows the answer.*

Nul is used in the sense of **personne.**

16. **on** *one, they, people*

> **On** a construit ce pont.
> *They built this bridge.*
> **On** n'emploie pas le passé simple dans la langue parlée.
> *One doesn't use the* passé simple *in spoken language.*

On can be replaced by **l'on** after **et, ou, où, que, qui, quoi** and **si** if not close to another **l**.

> Si **l'on** veut, on peut tout faire.
> *If one wants, one can do everything.*

But:

> Le livre qu'**on** lit.
> *The book one reads.*

17. **Personne ne...** *no one*
    ne... personne *not... anyone, no one*

> **Personne** n'est venu.
> *No one came.*
> Je **ne** vois **personne.**
> *I don't see anyone.*

18. **plusieurs** *several*

> Il en a **plusieurs.**
> *He has several.*
> **Plusieurs** d'entre eux sont gentils.
> *Several of them are nice.*

19. **qui que** *whoever, whomever*
    qui que ce soit qui *whoever*
    quoi que *whatever*
    quoi que ce soit que *whatever*

> **Qui que** vous voyiez, ne me trahissez pas.
> *Whomever you see, don't betray me.*
> **Qui que ce soit qui** vous parle, ne dites rien.
> *Whoever speaks to you, don't say anything.*
> **Quoi que** vous disiez, je ne vous croirai pas.
> *Whatever you say, I won't believe you.*

Note that these expressions are followed by the subjunctive.

20. **quelqu'un**   *someone*

> **Quelqu'un** frappe à la porte.
> *Someone is knocking at the door.*

Quelqu'un does not have a feminine form.

21. **quelqu'un d'autre**   *someone else*

> **Quelqu'un d'autre** peut le faire.
> *Someone else can do it.*

22. **quelques-uns, quelques-unes**   *some*

> Avez-vous des livres? Oui, j'en ai **quelques-uns.**
> *Do you have any books? Yes, I have some.*

> Avez-vous acheté des pommes? Oui, j'en ai acheté **quelques-unes.**
> *Did you buy any apples? Yes, I bought some.*

Note that **en** is used when **quelques-uns** and **quelques-unes** are used as direct objects.

23. **quelque chose**   *something*

quelque chose d'autre   *something else*

> Voulez-vous **quelque chose?**
> *Do you want something?*

> Je voudrais **quelque chose** de joli.
> *I want something pretty.*

> Voulez-vous **quelque chose d'autre?**
> *Do you want something else?*

Note that **de** precedes the adjective which refers to **quelque chose.** The adjective is always masculine.

24. **quiconque**   *whoever, anyone who*

> **Quiconque** travaille mangera.
> *Whoever works will eat.*

25. **Rien ne...**   *nothing*
    ne... rien   *not... anything*

> **Rien ne** se passe.
> *Nothing is happening.*
> Je **ne** vois **rien.**
> *I don't see anything.*

26. **tel, telle**   (designates an undetermined person)

> M. **un tel**   *Mr. So-and-so*
> Mme **une telle**   *Mrs. So-and-so*
> Mlle **une telle**   *Miss So-and-so*

The form **un tel** is used when one doesn't want to or is unable to name the person.

> **Tel** qui rit vendredi dimanche pleurera.
> *He who laughs today cries tomorrow.*

27. **tout, toute, tous, toutes**   *all, everything*

  Tout est bien ici.
  Everything is fine here.
  J'ai tous les billets. Je les ai **tous.**
  I have all the tickets. I have all of them.
  Il a vu toutes les peintures. Il les a **toutes** vues.
  He saw all the paintings. He saw all of them.

    Note that **de** is never used with **tout,** although in English we say *all of them* or *all.* Note too that the **s** is pronounced in the pronoun form **tous.** Also, the pronoun **tout** precedes the past participle in compound tenses.

  Il les a **tous** lus.
  He read them all.

28. **tout ce qui, tout ce que**   *everything, all that*

  On a vu **tout ce qui** est dans cette ville.
  We saw everything in this city.
  Tout ce que nous faisons est intéressant.
  Everything we do is interesting.

  Tout ce qu'elle dit est intéressant.
  Everything she says is interesting.

29. **tout le monde**   *everyone*

  Tout le monde est ici.
  Everyone is here.

  Tout le monde is used with a singular verb.

  See Chapter 7 for more study on negative indefinite pronouns.

54. Complete the following sentences with the correct French words for the English words in parentheses.

  1. _____ (Anyone) peut le faire.
  2. _____ (Someone) le fera.
  3. _____ (Everyone) aime la beauté.
  4. _____ (One) peut venir ici.
  5. Voudriez-vous _____ (something) de bon?
  6. Il a _____ (everything) compris.
  7. _____ (The others) viendront plus tard.
  8. Je comprends les verbes. Je les comprends _____ (all).
  9. As-tu des disques? Oui, j'en ai _____ (some).
  10. Elles viendront _____ (both of them).
  11. Je n'aime _____ (either one).
  12. _____ (Certain ones) d'entre elles voudraient bavarder.
  13. Il dira _____ (anything).
  14. Voudriez-vous _____ (something else)?
  15. _____ (All that) Pierre fait est intéressant.
  16. Il en a _____ (several).
  17. Avez-vous des blouses? Oui, j'en ai _____ (some).
  18. _____ (Each one) des mères apportera quelque chose.

19. _____ (Someone else) pourra le faire.
20. _____ (Some) voulaient danser; _____ (the others) voulaient aller au cinéma.
21. Ils parlent _____ (to each other).
22. Vous avez deux robes. Donnez-moi _____ (either one).
23. _____ (Anyone) le dira.
24. Est-ce que c'est une autre robe? Non, c'est _____ (the same).
25. _____ (None) d'elles ne viendra.
26. _____ (No one) ne sait la réponse.
27. _____ (Everything) est bien ici.
28. _____ (Nothing) n'est arrivé.
29. Allez voir _____ (Mr. So-and-so).
30. _____ (Whoever) essaiera, réussira.
31. Il ne faut pas dire du mal d' _____ (others).
32. Avez-vous _____ (something else)?

CHAPTER 9

Special Meanings of Certain Verbs

Expressions with Aller

Some idiomatic expressions with the verb **aller** are:

aller à la pêche   *to go fishing*
aller à la chasse   *to go hunting*
aller à pied   *to go on foot, to walk*
aller à bicyclette   *to go by bicycle*
aller en voiture, en avion, par le train   *to go by car, by plane, by train*
aller loin   *to succeed*
    Elle est intelligente. Elle ira loin.
aller trop loin   *to go too far*
    Il va trop loin. Je suis très fâché.
aller bien, mal, mieux   *to feel (be) well (fine), bad, better*
    Je vais bien.
aller à quelqu'un   *to suit, to become*
    Cette robe vous va très bien.
Allez-y! Vas-y! (fam.)   *Go ahead*
Comment allez-vous?
Comment vas-tu?   ⎫ *How are you?*
Comment ça va? (fam.) ⎭
Comment va-t-il?   *How is he?*
Ça va? (informal)   *How are you?*

1. Translate the following sentences into French, using the verb **aller.**

1. He is going by car.
2. He will succeed.
3. I feel bad.
4. He feels better today.
5. This hat is becoming to you.
6. How are you?
7. I am fine.
8. He is going fishing.

Expressions with Avoir

The verb **avoir** is used in many idiomatic expressions.

avoir chaud   *to be warm*
    Elle a chaud en été.
avoir froid   *to be cold*
    Il a froid en hiver.
avoir faim   *to be hungry*
    J'ai très faim.
avoir soif   *to be thirsty*
    Elle a très soif.
avoir sommeil   *to be sleepy*
    Elle va se coucher. Elle a sommeil.
avoir peur de   *to be afraid of*
    Il a peur du lion.
avoir honte de   *to be ashamed of*
    Il a honte de ses actions.
avoir raison   *to be right*
    Elle a raison.
avoir tort   *to be wrong*
    Cet élève a tort.
avoir mal à   *to have an ache in*
    Elle a mal à la tête.
    Elle a mal aux dents.
avoir lieu   *to take place*
    L'action a eu lieu dans une grande ville.
avoir beau   *to do something in vain*
    Il avait beau étudier; il n'a pas réussi à l'examen.
    He studied in vain; he didn't pass the exam.
avoir l'air...   *to look, to seem*
    Elle a l'air contente.
avoir de la chance   *to be lucky*
    Marie a de la chance.
avoir de la patience   *to be patient*
    Les mères ont de la patience.
avoir... de retard   *to be late by ...*
    L'avion a quinze minutes de retard.
avoir... d'avance   *to be early by ...*
    Ils ont dix minutes d'avance.
avoir envie de   *to want to*
    Il a envie d'aller au cinéma.
avoir besoin de   *to need*
    Il a besoin d'étudier.
avoir l'habitude de   *to be in the habit of*
    Elle a l'habitude de prendre du thé à quatre heures.

    avoir l'occasion de   *to have the chance to*
        Il a l'occasion d'aller à Paris.
    avoir l'intention de   *to intend to*
        J'ai l'intention d'étudier davantage.
    avoir le temps de   *to have the time to*
        J'ai le temps de le faire.
    avoir quelque chose   *to have something wrong*
        Vous avez quelque chose?
    avoir... ans   *to be ... years old*
        Quel âge avez-vous?
        J'ai vingt ans.
    avoir à   *to have to*
        J'ai à faire ce travail.
    avoir... de longueur, de hauteur, d'épaisseur   *to be ... long, tall, thick*
        La boîte a dix mètres de longueur.
        La tour a cent mètres de hauteur.
        Le mur a trente centimètres d'épaisseur.

2. Follow the model. Use an expression with the verb **avoir** in your answer.

    Je voudrais un sandwich.
    J'ai faim.

    1. Je voudrais boire.
    2. Je voudrais manger.
    3. Je voudrais dormir.
    4. Je vais porter un manteau.
    5. J'ouvre la fenêtre.
    6. Je prends de l'aspirine.
    7. Je vais chez le dentiste.
    8. Je demande pardon.
    9. Je pense que Tokyo est la capitale du Japon.
   10. Je pense qu'il y a 52 États aux États-Unis.

3. Translate the following sentences into French, using the verb **avoir**.

    1. I came in vain. No one was there.
    2. She is afraid of this man.
    3. He is ashamed of his work.
    4. We were right.
    5. I have a headache.
    6. The girls look tired.
    7. Peter is lucky.
    8. The train is a half hour late.
    9. The plane is ten minutes early.
   10. He has the chance to go to Martinique.
   11. What's wrong with you?
   12. How old are you?
   13. He is fifty years old.
   14. She needs the book.
   15. The house is twenty meters high.
   16. We are warm.
   17. The children are sleepy.

Expressions with Être

    être en train de   *to be in the act of*
        Je suis en train de travailler.
    être à   *to belong to*
        Ces livres sont à moi.

être de   *to be from*
     Elle est de New York.

être égal à   *to make no difference to*
     Cela m'est égal.

être de retour   *to be back*
     Elle sera de retour lundi.

Ça y est   *It's all right. It's done. That's it!*
     Vous avez terminé? Oui, ça y est.

4. Translate the following sentences into French, using the verb **être**.

1. She's in the act of studying.
2. The boys are from Paris.
3. It makes no difference to me.
4. We will be back tomorrow.
5. These books belong to her.
6. It's all right.

Expressions with Faire

The verb **faire** is used in many weather expressions.

Il fait chaud.	*It is warm.*
Il fait froid.	*It is cold.*
Il fait frais.	*It is cool.*
Il fait mauvais.	*The weather is bad.*
Il fait bon (beau).	*The weather is good (nice).*
Il fait du soleil.	*The sun is shining.*
Il fait du vent.	*It is windy.*
Il fait du brouillard.	*It is foggy.*

Some other idiomatic expressions with the verb **faire** are:

Il fait nuit.	*It is night.*
Il fait jour.	*It is daylight.*

faire l'impossible	*to do the impossible*
faire de son mieux	*to do one's best*
faire son possible	*to do one's best*

faire du bien   *to produce a good effect*
     Le soleil vous fera du bien.

faire fortune   *to become rich*

faire des économies   *to save money*

faire plaisir   *to give pleasure*

faire mal   *to hurt*
     Ma jambe me fait mal.   *My leg hurts.*

faire mal à   *to harm*

se faire du mal   *to hurt oneself*
     Elle s'est fait du mal.   *She hurt herself.*
     Elle s'est fait mal au bras.   *She hurt her arm.*

faire attention à   *to pay attention to*

faire peur à   *to scare*
     Le tigre leur fait peur.   *The tiger scares them.*

faire confiance à   *to trust*
     Faites-moi confiance.   *Trust me.*

faire la connaissance de quelqu'un   *to meet someone*

faire les courses   *to run errands, to go shopping*

faire le ménage   *to do housework*
faire la vaisselle   *to do the dishes*
faire la cuisine   *to cook*
faire les devoirs   *to do homework*
faire sa toilette   *to prepare oneself, to dress*
faire du sport   *to play sports*
faire du jogging   *to jog*
faire la queue   *to wait in line*
faire un voyage   *to take a trip*
faire une promenade   *to take a walk*
faire exprès   *to do something on purpose*
    Je ne l'ai pas fait exprès.
faire semblant   *to pretend*
    Elle fait semblant de dormir.
Ça ne fait rien.   *It doesn't matter.*

5. Complete each sentence with an expression using **faire.**

    Le soleil brille, le ciel est bleu et la température est de 25° Celsius. Il...
    Il fait beau.

    1. Elle ne dépense pas d'argent. Elle...
    2. Nous écoutons bien en classe. Nous...
    3. Il donne un coup de chiffon aux meubles et il balaye le plancher. Il...
    4. J'aime marcher. Je... tous les jours.
    5. Tu deviens riche. Tu...
    6. Ils vont chez le boulanger, chez le boucher, chez l'épicier. Ils...
    7. Je ne dépense pas d'argent. Je...
    8. Elle étudie la leçon pour demain. Elle...
    9. Il nettoie les verres et les assiettes. Il...
    10. Ils vont en France. Ils...
    11. Tu nettoies ta chambre. Tu...

6. Translate the following sentences into French, using the verb **faire.**

    1. It is warm.   7. This medicine will do you good.
    2. The weather is cool.   8. I hurt my arm.
    3. The sun is shining.   9. We waited in line for an hour.
    4. It is foggy.   10. I did it on purpose.
    5. It is night.   11. It doesn't matter.
    6. He does his best.   12. They pretended not to hear.

Special Uses of Other Verbs

Devoir, pouvoir, savoir, vouloir

    The verbs **devoir, pouvoir, savoir** and **vouloir** have special meanings in different tenses.

Devoir

    present tense   *to owe*
    je dois   *I owe*

        Je **dois** dix francs à Jean.   *I owe John ten francs.*

    devoir plus infinitive   *must, to have to*
    je dois   *I must, I have to*

Il **doit** travailler.	*He must work.*
Je **devrai** travailler.	*I shall have to work.*
Elle **a dû** travailler.	*She had to work.*

present and imperfect tenses   *to be supposed to, to be scheduled to*

Elle **doit** partir demain.
She is supposed to (is scheduled to) leave tomorrow.
Il **devait** partir lundi.
He was supposed to leave on Monday.

present, *passé composé* and imperfect tenses — to express probability — *must be*

Il **doit** être malade.
He must be (is probably) sick.
Il **a dû** être malade.
He must have been (was probably) sick.
Le film **devait** être bon.
The movie was probably good.

present and past conditional to express advice or reproach—*should, ought to*
je devrais   *I should, I ought to*
j'aurais dû   *I should have, I ought to have*

Vous **devriez** travailler.
You should (ought to) work.
Vous **auriez dû** travailler.
You should have (ought to have) worked.

Pouvoir

present tense   *to be able to*
je peux   *I can, I am able*

Je peux le faire maintenant.	*I can do it now.*

passé composé – for a single event
j'ai pu   *I was able, I could (I succeeded)*

J'ai pu m'échapper.	*I was able to escape (succeeded in escaping).*
Je **n'ai pas pu** le faire.	*I couldn't do it. (But I tried.)*

imperfect tense – usually the past tense of the present tense for events that are repeated.

Je **pouvais** vous aider tous les vendredis.	
I was able to help you every Friday.	

conditional
je pourrais   *I could, I would be able*

Je **pourrais** vous aider.	*I could help you.*

conditional perfect
j'aurais pu   *I could have, I would have been able*

Elle **aurait pu** le faire.	*She could have done it (would have been able to do it).*

Savoir

present   *to know (a fact), to know how to (do something), to be able to*
je sais   *I know, I know how to, I can*

Je **sais** qu'il a vingt ans.	*I know he is twenty years old.*
Je **sais** jouer du piano.	*I know how to (I can) play the piano.*

imperfect tense – past tense of the present tense

Je **savais** jouer du piano.
I used to know how to play the piano.

passé composé
j'ai su   *I knew, I found out*

J'**ai su** la vérité.	*I found out the truth.*

conditional
je saurais   *I would be able to, I could*

Je ne **saurais** pas cacher ma colère.	*I wouldn't be able to hide my anger.*

Vouloir

present   *to want*
je veux   *I want*

Je **veux** ce livre.	*I want this book.*
Je **veux** le voir.	*I want to see him.*

imperfect tense – past tense of the present tense

Je **voulais** ce livre. *I wanted this book.*	
Je **voulais** le voir.	*I wanted to see him.*

passé composé
j'ai voulu   *I tried*

J'**ai voulu** le faire.	*I tried to do it.*

je n'ai pas voulu   *I refused*

Je **n'ai pas voulu** le faire.	*I refused to do it.*

conditional
je voudrais   *I want, I would like*

Je **voudrais** du beurre.	*I want some butter.*
Je **voudrais** aller au cinéma.	*I would like to go to the movies.*

7. Translate the following sentences into French, using **devoir, pouvoir, savoir** or **vouloir.**

1. I owe Mary five dollars.
2. He must come.
3. She was supposed to leave for New York.
4. He must be sick.
5. You should have come.
6. He ought to study.
7. I can do it.
8. We couldn't finish. (But we tried.)
9. I could have helped you.
10. He succeeded in doing it.
11. We found out the truth.
12. She tried to open the door.
13. He refused to go there.

Habiter, demeurer, vivre

Habiter, demeurer and **vivre** all mean *to live*. **Habiter** and **demeurer** mean *to live, to dwell* and are used with names of places.

Il **demeure** à Paris.	*He lives in Paris.*
Elle **habite** à Paris.	*She lives in Paris.*

Habiter is sometimes used without a preposition.

Il **habite** l'Angleterre.	*He lives in England.*
Il **habite** Paris.	*He lives in Paris.*

Vivre means *to live, to be alive*.

Il **vivra** longtemps.	*He'll live a long time.*

8. Complete the following sentences with the correct form of the present tense of **demeurer** or **vivre**.

1. Elle _____ bien.
2. Nous _____ en Suisse.
3. Mon père _____ toujours.
4. Vous _____ en Espagne.
5. Ils _____ longtemps.

9. Rewrite the following sentences according to the model.

Ils habitent en Angleterre.
Ils habitent l'Angleterre.

1. Elle habite à Paris.
2. Ils habitent en Suisse.
3. Vous habitez à New York.
4. Nous habitons au Mexique.

Jouer, jouer à, jouer de

Jouer means *to play*. **Jouer à** means *to play (a game)*. **Jouer de** means *to play (a musical instrument)*.

Ils **jouent** dans le jardin.
They are playing in the garden.
Elle **joue** un morceau de Beethoven.
She is playing a piece by Beethoven.
Il **joue au** football.
He plays soccer.
Elle **joue du** piano.
She plays the piano.

10. Complete the following sentences with the correct form of the present tense of **jouer, jouer à** or **jouer de.**

1. Il _____ le rôle de Rodrigue.
2. Nous _____ violon.
3. Ils _____ cartes.
4. Vous _____ la clarinette.
5. Ils _____ dans le parc.
6. Vous _____ football.

Manquer, manquer à, manquer de

The verb **manquer** means *to miss*. **Manquer de** means *to be lacking*. Study the following:

Il a **manqué** son train.	*He missed his train.*
André **manque à** Marie.	*Mary misses Andrew.*

André **lui manque.**	*She misses Andrew.*
Il **lui manque.**	*She misses him.*
Cette ville **me manque.**	*I miss this city.*
Nous **manquons** d'argent.	*We are lacking money.*
Il **manque** d'intelligence.	*He is lacking in intelligence.*

11. Complete the following sentences with the correct form of the present tense of **manquer, manquer à** or **manquer de.**

1. Il _____ l'autobus.
2. Marie _____ Paul.
3. Vous _____ patience.

4. Elles _____ le concert.
5. Les cafés _____ ces étudiants.

12. Translate the following sentences into French.

1. He missed the train.
2. I miss her.

3. She misses me.
4. They are lacking in patience.

Penser à, penser de

Penser à and **penser de** both mean *to think about.* **Penser de** is used when *to think about* means *to have an opinion about something or someone.*

Elle **pense à** ses amis.
She is thinking about her friends.
Que **pensez-vous de** mes amis?
What do you think about (What is your opinion about) my friends?

After **penser à,** a stress pronoun is used when talking about a person. When the object is a thing, **y** is used to replace **à** plus the noun.

Il pense **à sa mère.**
Il pense **à elle.**

Il pense **à cette lettre.**
Il **y** pense.

After **penser de,** a stress pronoun is used when talking about a person. When talking about a thing, **en** replaces **de** plus the noun.

Que pensez-vous **de Pierre?**
Que pensez-vous **de lui?**

Que pensez-vous **du tableau?**
Qu'**en** pensez-vous?

13. Complete the following sentences with the correct form of the preposition **à** or **de.**

1. Que pensez-vous _____ projet?
2. Il pense toujours _____ Marie.
3. Que pense-t-elle _____ ce roman?

4. Elle pense _____ examens.
5. Nous pensons _____ cette fille.

14. Rewrite the following sentences, replacing the nouns with pronouns.

1. Je pense à Hélène.
2. Que pense-t-il du film?
3. Elle pense à Georges.

4. Que pense-t-elle de l'auteur?
5. Nous pensons à ces problèmes.
6. Que pensent-elles de mes amis?

Partir, sortir, s'en aller, laisser, quitter

Partir, sortir, s'en aller, laisser and **quitter** all mean *to leave*.

Partir means *to leave, to go away*.

Nous **partons** pour Paris.	*We are leaving for Paris.*
Nous **partons** de Paris.	*We are leaving Paris.*

Note that **de** is used with **partir** in the above sentence.

Sortir means *to leave, to go out, to go out of a place, to come out, to go out with someone, to take out.*

Elle **sort** souvent.	*She goes out often.*
Elle **sort** de la salle.	*She leaves (goes out of) the room.*
Elle **sort** avec Pierre.	*She goes out with Peter.*
Elle **sort** du sucre.	*She takes out some sugar.*

S'en aller means *to leave, to go away*.

Je **m'en vais.**	*I'm going away.*

Laisser means *to leave, to leave a thing or person behind*.

Elle **a laissé** le livre à la bibliothèque.
She left the book in the library.
Elle **a laissé** sa sœur au cinéma.
She left her sister at the movies.

Quitter means *to leave, to leave a place or person*.

Elle **quitte** la maison à huit heures.
She leaves the house at eight o'clock.
Je vous **quitte** maintenant.
I am leaving you now.

15. Complete the following sentences, choosing the correct form of the present tense of one of the indicated verbs.

1. Paul _____ avec Hélène.   *sortir / quitter*
2. Il _____ ce soir.   *s'en aller / laisser*
3. Elle _____ ses livres dans le tiroir.   *sortir / laisser*
4. Je _____. Je suis fatigué.   *s'en aller / quitter*
5. Il _____ son appartement à sept heures.   *quitter / laisser*
6. Il _____ de la salle.   *s'en aller / sortir*
7. Je _____ pour New York.   *partir / quitter*

Passer, se passer, se passer de

Passer means *to pass (someone or something), to spend (time), to go across*.

Passez-moi le poivre, s'il vous plaît.
Please pass me the pepper.
Il **a passé** deux semaines à Paris.
He spent two weeks in Paris.
Elle **a passé** la frontière.
She went across the border.

Se **passer** means *to take place, to happen.*

> L'action **s'est passée** dans une rue déserte.
> *The action took place in a deserted street.*
> Qu'est-ce qui **se passe**?
> *What is happening?*

Se passer de means *to do without.*

> Il **s'est passé de** viande.
> *He did without meat.*

16. Complete the following sentences with the correct form of the *passé composé* of **passer, se passer** or **se passer de.**

   1. Il _____ trois semaines dans le Midi.
   2. Qu'est-ce qui _____?
   3. Nous _____ dessert.
   4. D'étranges choses _____ ici.
   5. Elle _____ la nuit chez Hélène.
   6. L'accident _____ au coin de la rue.
   7. Il _____ beurre.

Plaire

When **plaire** is used in place of **aimer**, an indirect object is used. Note the following.

> **Paris me plaît.**
> *I like Paris. (Paris is pleasing to me.)*
> **Les peintures me plaisent.**
> *I like the paintings. (The paintings are pleasing to me.)*

17. Rewrite the following sentences according to the model.

> **Elle aime le concert.**
> **Le concert lui plaît.**

   1. J'aime le film.
   2. Elle aime les peintures modernes.
   3. Il aime le cinéma.
   4. Elles aiment la pièce.
   5. Tu aimes le livre.

Se rappeler, se souvenir de

Both **se rappeler** and **se souvenir de** mean *to remember.*

Il **se rappelle** la leçon.	*He remembers the lesson.*
Il **se la rappelle.**	*He remembers it.*
Il **se souvient de** la leçon.	*He remembers the lesson.*
Il **s'en souvient.**	*He remembers it.*

Note that when the direct object is replaced by a pronoun, the direct object pronouns are used with **se rappeler** while **en** is used with **se souvenir de.**

18. Rewrite the following sentences, substituting **se souvenir de** for **se rappeler.**

   1. Je me rappelle cette occasion.
   2. Je me rappelle cette fille.
   3. Ils se rappellent cette soirée.
   4. Vous vous rappelez la guerre.
   5. Nous nous le rappelons.

Servir, se servir de

Servir means *to serve, to serve as, to be of use as.*

Elle **sert** le déjeuner.   *She serves lunch.*
Elle nous **sert** de guide.   *She serves as a guide for us.*

Se servir de means *to use.*

Je **me sers d'**un stylo pour écrire.
I use a pen to write with.

19. Complete the following sentences with the appropriate form of the present tense of **servir** or **se servir de.**

    1. Ce papier _____ à écrire.   4. Elle ne lui _____ à rien.
    2. Le petit _____ une petite cuiller.   5. Elle _____ ce livre.
    3. Il _____ le dîner.

Savoir **versus** *connaître*

Savoir and **connaître** both mean *to know.*

Savoir means *to know a fact, a reason* or *a learning discipline.* Used with an infinitive, it means *to know how to.*

Il **sait** les résultats.   *He knows the results.*
Il **sait** jouer du piano.   *He knows how to play the piano.*

Connaître is used with persons, places, works of art, literature, countries, etc. It has the meaning of *to be acquainted with.*

Je **connais** Marie.   *I know Mary.*
Nous **connaissons** ce poème. *We know this poem.*

Study the meanings of **savoir** and **connaître** in the imperfect and the *passé composé.*

Elle **connaissait** cet homme. *She knew this (that) man.*
Elle **a connu** cet homme.   *She met this (that) man.*
Elle **savait** la réponse.   *She knew the answer.*
Elle **a su** la réponse.   *She found out the answer.*

20. Complete the following sentences with the correct form of the present tense of the verb **savoir** or **connaître.**

    1. Nous _____ jouer du piano.
    2. Elle _____ Robert.
    3. Je _____ que vous avez raison.
    4. _____-vous l'heure?
    5. Ils _____ cette partie de la ville.
    6. Elle _____ son adresse.
    7. Vous _____ la littérature canadienne.
    8. _____-tu cette maison? Oui, je _____ qu'elle est en bon état.

21. Translate the following sentences using **savoir** or **connaître** in the *passé composé* or the imperfect tense as necessary.

    1. He found out the truth.   3. She knew the truth.
    2. He has met this woman.   4. She knew these children.

Venir de

The present tense of **venir de** followed by an infinitive means *to have just (done something)*. The imperfect tense of **venir de** followed by an infinitive means *had just (done something)*.

> Il **vient d'**arriver.
> *He has just arrived.*
> Il **venait d'**arriver quand nous sommes sortis.
> *He had just arrived when we left.*

22. Complete the following sentences with the correct form of **venir de** in the present tense.

1. Je _____ chanter cette chanson.
2. Elles _____ sortir.
3. Vous _____ arriver.
4. Nous _____ rentrer d'Espagne.
5. Tu _____ manger.
6. Il _____ entrer.

23. Rewrite the sentences of the above exercise in the imperfect tense.

Answers to Exercises

Chapter 1

1.
1. Le, la, le
2. Le, le, la
3. Le, l', l', la, la
4. L', la
5. La, le, la
6. L', le
7. L', la
8. La, la, le
9. L', le, le
10. La, la, le

2.
1. La, l' (f.), l' (f.)
2. le, le, le, la
3. la, la
4. l' (m.), la
5. la, la
6. Le, le
7. La, la
8. Le, le
9. la

3.
1. Le professeur
2. la cousine
3. L'informaticienne
4. L'Anglais
5. La danseuse
6. la chatte (la chienne)

4.
1. Le, la
2. le, la
3. le, la
4. Le, La
5. Le, la
6. le
7. La
8. le, la
9. La, Le
10. le

5.
1. tables
2. vers
3. noyaux
4. sous
5. poux
6. festivals
7. Messieurs, mesdames, mesdemoiselles
8. genoux
9. feux
10. amis
11. nez
12. vœux
13. animaux
14. vitraux
15. choux
16. éventails

6.
1. Les lois sont justes.
2. Les voix sont jolies.
3. Regardez les feux!
4. Les trous sont grands.
5. Les repas sont bons.
6. Les journaux expliquent les travaux.
7. Les écoles sont modernes.
8. Les châteaux sont jolis.
9. Les détails des dessins sur les chandails sont magnifiques.
10. Les prix sont élevés.
11. Les jeux sont amusants.
12. Voilà les clous.
13. Les bijoux sont jolis.
14. Les cailloux sont petits.
15. Les bateaux sont grands.
16. Les musées sont grands.
17. Les yeux sont grands.
18. Les chevaux sont les animaux que vous aimez.
19. Messieurs, regardez les peintures.
20. Les bals ont lieu samedi.
21. Les gentilshommes sont grands.
22. Voici des bonshommes de neige.

7.
1. Le roi habite dans le château.
2. Le nez est grand.
3. Le joujou est intéressant.
4. Le carnaval est amusant.
5. Le ciel est bleu.
6. L'ami est aimable.
7. La peau de vison est chère.
8. Le journal est intéressant.
9. L'aïeul est célèbre.
10. L'œil est brun.
11. Le bras est fort.
12. Le clou est long.
13. Le vitrail est joli.
14. Le vœu est compréhensible.
15. Le chandail est chaud.
16. Le hibou est noir.
17. La voix du chanteur est jolie.
18. Le jeu de cartes est intéressant.

8.
1. Les
2. Les
3. Les
4. La

9.
1. Les après-midi les grands-pères dorment.
2. Les réveille-matin sonnent à huit heures du matin.
3. Les grands-mères mettent les choux-fleurs dans les paniers pour les pique-niques.
4. Il lit les chefs-d'œuvre de Racine.
5. Il y a des gratte-ciel à New York.
6. Les timbres-poste sont dans les coffres-forts.
7. Il faut nettoyer les pare-brise.
8. Pour ouvrir les bouteilles de vin, prenez des tire-bouchons.
9. Les beaux-frères mangent les hors-d'œuvre.
10. Les belles-sœurs aiment les arcs-en-ciel.

10.
1. Les
2. La
3. La
4. Les
5. Les
6. Les
7. L'
8. Le
9. les
10. les
11. La
12. Les
13. L'

11.
1. Le
2. Le
3.
4. —
5. —
6. —
7. —
8. le
9. Le
10. La

12.
1. —
2. le
3. la
4. Le
5. —
6. —
7. —

13.
1. —
2. le
3. L'
4. le (—)
5. —
6. —
7. le
8. —
9. —
10. Le
11. le
12. le, l'

14.
1. C'est aujourd'hui lundi.
2. Demain, c'est mardi.
3. Mon jour préféré est le samedi.
4. Je vais au cours le lundi, le mardi, le mercredi, le jeudi et le vendredi.
5. Je fais les courses le samedi.
6. Les jours de la fin de semaine sont samedi et dimanche.
7. Je vais au cinéma le samedi.
8. J'ai mon cours de français le lundi, le mercredi et le vendredi.

15.
1. La
2. L'
3. Les
4. Le
5. —
6. La
7. le
8. L'
9. l'
10. —

16.
1. Les, la
2. le
3. Les, la
4. Le, le

17.
1. les
2. la
3. la
4. la
5. les

18.   1 —   3. de   4. Le, le
     2. — (la)

19.   1. au, du   3. à l', de l'   4. à la, de la, aux, des
     2. à la, de la

20.   1. On va au cinéma pour regarder un film.
     2. On va à la confiserie pour acheter des bonbons.
     3. On va à la crémerie pour acheter du lait.
     4. On va aux musées pour regarder des peintures.
     5. On va à la boucherie pour acheter de la viande.
     6. On va au stade pour regarder un match de football.
     7. On va à la pâtisserie pour acheter des gâteaux.
     8. On va à la pharmacie pour acheter des cachets d'aspirine.
     9. On va au théâtre pour regarder un spectacle.
    10. On va à la bibliothèque pour lire des livres.

21.   1. un, un, des   5. un, un
     2. un, une   6. un, un, un, des, des
     3. une, un, une, des   7. un, un
     4. une, des, un   8. une, une, un

22.   1. —, un   4. une   7. un
     2. —   5. —   8. un
     3. un   6. —

23.   1. —   4. —   7. —
     2. —   5. —   8. —,—
     3. un   6. des

24.   1. du   7. du   13. du
     2. de la   8. du   14. du
     3. des   9. de la   15. des
     4. des   10. de la   16. du
     5. du   11. de la   17. de l'
     6. du   12. du   18. du

25.   1. Il aime beaucoup l'eau minérale et il va prendre de l'eau minérale maintenant.
     2. Il aime beaucoup la soupe aux pois et il va prendre de la soupe aux pois maintenant.
     3. Il aime beaucoup les artichauts et il va prendre des artichauts maintenant.
     4. Il aime beaucoup la salade et il va prendre de la salade maintenant.
     5. Il aime beaucoup le pain italien et il va prendre du pain italien maintenant.
     6. Il aime beaucoup le thé et il va prendre du thé maintenant.

26.   1. le, du, du, Le   3. le, le, un, du
     2. La, la, la, la, une   4. du, le, le, un

27.   1. Il n'a pas de courage.   4. Je ne bois pas d'eau.
     2. Il n'y a pas de soupe.   5. Elle ne fume pas de cigarettes.
     3. Je n'ai pas de bonbons.

28.   1. Il y a de belles peintures ici.   4. Elle mange des petits pains.
     2. Nous lisons des livres intéressants.   5. Ce sont des jeunes filles.
     3. Ce sont de grandes villes.   6. J'ai de grandes armoires.

29.
1. d'
2. d'
3. de
4 —
5. de
6. —
7. des
8. de
9. de
10. d'
11. de
12. du

30.
1. Le, au
2. l'
3. La, la
4. Les, la
5. La
6. La, des
7. La, à la
8. L', le
9. le, du
10. Les, à l'
11. les, aux
12. Le, de l', les

31.
1. Les repas sont bons.
2. Les chevaux sont des animaux.
3. J'aime les carnavals.
4. Ouvrez les yeux.
5. Les bateaux sont petits.
6. Les prix des clous ne sont pas chers.
7. Les choux sont dans les trous.
8. Les eaux entourent les châteaux.
9. Les jeux sont intéressants.
10. Les après-midi, il prépare les hors-d'œuvre et les choux-fleurs pour les pique-niques.
11. Messieurs, ne prenez pas ces bijoux.
12. Les grands-pères vont acheter des abat-jour.

32.
1. —, une, une, la, Les, un,—
2. —, un,—, une
3. —, un, un, La, une
4. un, un, l',—, le, le, le, le, le,—

33.
1. À la, de la, du, du, une, d', du, le, un
2. de la, à la, de la, du, du, de l'
3. À la, de, de, Le, le, le
4. Au, d',—, des, de la, du, du, de la, d', des
5. de, du, de, à l', de, de la, la, une, une, des, de la (une)

34.
1. Il attend l'arrivée du professeur.
2. Il entend les cris de l'enfant.
3. Il parle à l'ami de Jean.
4. Elle aime la voix du chanteur.
5. Il cherche les jouets des enfants.
6. Il va au supermarché du village.
7. Il aime le vitrail de l'église.
8. Il regarde les peintures du musée.
9. Elle veut aller à la bibliothèque de la ville.
10. Il achète du sucre, des gâteaux et de la glace.

35. Answers will vary.
Examples:
1. D'habitude, je mange des œufs pour le petit déjeuner, un sandwich pour le déjeuner et du bifteck pour le dîner.
2. Quand je fais les courses au supermarché, j'achète du lait, des légumes, des œufs, etc. (use partitive).
3. J'aime le football, le baseball, etc.
4. Je porte un jean quand je vais aux cours. Quand je vais au théâtre, je porte une robe, un habit, etc. Quand je vais à une noce, je porte un habit de cérémonie, une robe du soir, etc.
5. J'ai un lit, un micro-ordinateur, etc.
6. J'aime le français, les sciences, etc. (use definite article).
7. J'ai mon cours de français le lundi, le mercredi et le vendredi (use definite article with days of the week).
8. Mon jour préféré est samedi (no definite article with day of the week).
9. C'est aujourd'hui lundi (no definite article with day of the week).
10. Demain c'est mardi (no definite article with day of the week).

36. Answers will vary.
Examples:
1. J'aime le pain et je mange souvent du pain.
2. Je n'aime pas les épinards et je ne mange pas d'épinards.
3. J'aime le lait et je bois souvent du lait.
4. Je n'aime pas le café et je ne bois pas de café.
5. J'achète du pain, de la soupe, etc., à l'épicerie.
6. J'achète des vêtements au grand magasin.
7. Je vais à la pâtisserie pour acheter un gâteau, des brioches, etc.
8. Dans ma ville, il y a une banque, un musée, une bibliothèque, etc.

Chapter 2

1.
1. L'idée est mauvaise.
2. La cathédrale est grande.
3. La tour est haute.
4. La cuisine est parfaite.
5. La sorcière est laide.
6. La peinture est jolie.
7. La femme est honnête.
8. La chemise est rouge.
9. La pierre est dure.
10. La réponse est claire.

2.
1. mauvais
2. française
3. grand
4. poli
5. noir
6. faible
7. noire
8. fantastique
9. formidable
10. compliquée

3. Marie est française. Elle est très jeune et très petite. Elle n'est pas grande. Elle est agréable et amusante. Et, elle est très polie aussi.

4.
1. cruelle
2. parisienne
3. bonne
4. muette
5. épaisse
6. discrète
7. prête
8. sotte
9. chère
10. fière

5.
1. Le film est sensationnel.
2. La peinture est ancienne.
3. Ce paquet est gros.
4. Cette étudiante est lasse.
5. Cette histoire est secrète.
6. L'homme est inquiet.
7. Madame Leclerc est étrangère.
8. Pierre est premier en math.
9. Cette phrase est pareille.

6.
1. heureuse
2. sérieuse
3. furieux
4. doux
5. douce
6. rousse
7. fausse
8. menteuse
9. protectrice
10. meilleure
11. créatrice
12. majeure

7.
1. attentive
2. neuve
3. sportif
4. brève
5. blanche
6. franc
7. sèche
8. grecque
9. publique

8.
1. aiguë
2. longue
3. favorite
4. maligne
5. malin
6. fraîche

9.
1. nouveau
2. belle
3. vieil
4. nouvelle
5. nouvel
6. vieux
7. belle
8. vieille
9. bel
10. beau
11. beau
12. vieux
13. nouveau

10.
1. Les films sont incroyables.
2. Les films sont merveilleux.
3. Les robes sont bleues.
4. Les notes sont mauvaises.
5. Les lois sont légales.
6. Les châteaux sont beaux.
7. Les chandails sont bleus.
8. Les hommes sont gros.
9. Les coups sont fatals.
10. Les maisons sont nouvelles.
11. Les tomates sont parfaites.
12. Les mots sont finals.

11.
1. intéressants
2. merveilleuses
3. médiévaux
4. nouveaux
5. finals
6. grands
7. bleus
8. frais
9. fatals
10. épais
11. sociaux
12. belles
13. légales
14. intelligentes
15. bleues
16. heureux
17. beaux

12.
1. nu
2. vieilles
3. demie
4. demi
5. nue
6. mi
7. ci-jointes
8. demi
9. Haut
10. âgés
11. marron
12. brun foncé
13. joyeuses
14. belles

13.
1. tragi-comique
2. sourde-muette
3. nouveau-nés
4. sud-américains
5. sous-développés
6. grandes ouvertes

14.
1. Il y a un joli tableau.
2. Il y a une vieille chaise.
3. Il y a une peinture intéressante.
4. Il y a un bon livre.
5. Il y a un gros divan-lit.
6. Il y a une petite lampe.
7. Il y a un fauteuil confortable.
8. Il y a une grande cheminée.
9. Il y a un tapis oriental.
10. Il y a une chaise rouge.

15.
1. Ce sont des livres intéressants.
2. Ce sont des films formidables.
3. Ce sont des conférences importantes.
4. Ce sont de bons amis.
5. Ce sont d'autres histoires.
6. Ce sont de bonnes écoles.
7. Ce sont de vieux amis.
8. Ce sont de beaux écrivains.
9. Ce sont de vieilles amies.
10. Ce sont de grandes maisons.
11. Ce sont de nouveaux hôtels.
12. Ce sont des jeunes filles.
13. Ce sont des petits pois.

16.
1. Elle achète un grand stéréo japonais.
2. Elle achète une longue robe bleue.
3. Elle achète un gentil petit chien amusant.
4. Elle achète de beaux meubles français.
5. Elle achète de nouvelles chaussures italiennes.
6. Elle achète de beaux gants noirs.
7. Elle achète un nouvel ordinateur fantastique.
8. Elle achète un gros diamant brillant.
9. Elle achète un petit jeune chat.
10. Elle achète de jolies vieilles peintures.

17. Answers will vary. Following are some possibilities.

1. Je suis beau (belle) et intelligent (intelligente).
2. Mon père est un gentil homme magnifique.
3. Ma mère est une jolie femme formidable.
4. Ma sœur est sérieuse. Mes sœurs sont sérieuses.
5. Mon frère est sportif. Mes frères sont sportifs.
6. Ma tante est célèbre.
7. Mon oncle est intéressant et intelligent.

8. Mon cousin (ma cousine) est gentil (gentille).
   Mes cousins (mes cousines) sont gentils (gentilles).
9. Mon ami(e) est généreux (généreuse).
10. Mes ami(e)s sont généreux (généreuses)

18.
1. C'est un monument ancien.
   Monsieur Dupont est (C'est) mon ancien professeur.
2. C'est un homme brave.
   C'est un brave homme.
3. C'est un chandail cher.
   C'est un cher ami.
4. La semaine dernière il est allé au cinéma.
   C'est la dernière semaine du trimestre.
5. Différentes personnes sont venues.
   Des personnes différentes sont venues.

6. C'est un grand écrivain.
   C'est un écrivain grand.
7. C'est un pauvre garçon.
   C'est un garçon pauvre.
8. C'est une chambre propre.
   C'est ma propre chambre
9. C'est une femme maigre.
   C'est une maigre vie.

19.
1. C'est une histoire incroyable.
   C'est une vraie histoire.
   Ce film raconte la vie de Van Gogh.
   C'est une histoire vraie.
2. Tu vas sûrement tout perdre. C'est un risque certain.
   Si tu joues à la Bourse, tu vas courir un certain risque.
3. Elle est arrivée le jour même comme prévu.
   Maintenant, même le professeur va être d'accord avec vous.
   Marcher et *aller à pied* sont presque la même chose.
4. Je viens d'acheter cette robe; c'est une nouvelle robe.
   Au printemps, les maisons de haute couture vont présenter une collection de robes nouvelles.
5. Une personne seule ne peut pas tout faire. Mon seul souci, c'est ma famille.
6. Ce garçon est désagréable. C'est un vilain garçon.
   Ce garçon n'est pas beau. C'est un garçon vilain.
7. Le piano ne marche pas bien. J'entends une fausse note.
   Il faut chanter la note *b*, pas la note *c*. C'est une note fausse.
8. C'est un manteau sale.
   Cet homme n'est pas gentil. C'est un sale homme.
9. Cette histoire ne vaut rien. C'est une triste histoire.
   Cette histoire me fait pleurer. C'est une histoire triste.
10. Un homme qui extorque de l'argent aux autres est un malhonnête homme.
    Un homme qui dit des grossièretés est un homme malhonnête.
11. Je vous verrai la semaine prochaine.
    La prochaine fois, dites la vérité.
12. À la réunion, diverses personnes discutent des circonstances diverses.
13. Ce thé a un goût amer. C'était une amère expérience.

20.
1. Elle chante doucement.
2. Il a prononcé parfaitement.
3. Elle étudie sérieusement.
4. Elle danse naturellement.
5. Il a compris finalement.

6. Il est parti soudainement.
7. Il agit dangereusement.
8. Il parle rapidement.
9. Elle répond franchement.
10. Il écoute attentivement.

21.
1. Il agit hardiment.
2. Elle agit résolument.
3. Elles chantent gaîment (gaiement).

4. Il parle continûment.
5. Il parle crûment.

22.
1. confusément
2. profondément
3. exquisément

4. aveuglément
5. précisément
6. opportunément

23.
1. couramment
2. fréquemment
3. patiemment
4. brillamment
5. décemment
6. Évidemment
7. prudemment
8. patiemment
9. constamment
10. lentement
11. véhémentement
12. abondamment

24.
1. brièvement
2. gentiment
3. bien
4. mal
5. peu
6. clair
7. bas
8. cher
9. dur
10. bien
11. court
12. fort

25.
1. Il court rapidement.
2. La situation est absolument impossible.
3. Elle a beaucoup voyagé.
4. Il a bien étudié.
5. Nous avons déjà mangé.
6. Nous y sommes souvent allés.
7. Elle est arrivée hier.
8. Elle a travaillé patiemment.
9. Elle va trop travailler. (Elle va travailler trop.)
10. J'ai assez mangé.

26.
1. Naturellement, je suis content.
2. Certainement, il va être à l'heure.
3. Évidemment, il est triste.
4. Finalement, elle est arrivée.
5. Heureusement, elle est arrivée à l'heure.

27.
1. Anne est plus intelligente que sa sœur.
2. Cet enfant est aussi poli que sa sœur.
3. Elle est moins patiente que sa sœur.
4. Annette est plus sérieuse que sa sœur.
5. Il est aussi gentil que sa sœur.
6. Hélène parle plus intelligemment que sa sœur.
7. Cet homme conduit aussi dangereusement que sa sœur.
8. Vous chantez moins doucement que votre (sa) sœur.
9. Judith attend plus patiemment que sa sœur.
10. Vous agissez aussi poliment que votre (sa) sœur.

28.
1. Georges est plus grand que lui.
2. Pierre est plus intelligent que moi.
3. Les autres travaillent plus patiemment que nous.
4. Hélène danse aussi gaiement qu'elle.
5. Pierre écoute aussi attentivement qu'eux.
6. Marc est moins intelligent qu'elles.

29.
1. Il ne parle pas plus vite que moi.
2. Il ne répond pas si (aussi) intelligemment que Georges.
3. Il ne chante pas moins doucement que Pierre.
4. Elle n'est pas plus belle que Babeth.
5. Elle n'est pas si (aussi) gentille que sa sœur.

30.
1. Il est moins bête que vous ne le croyez.
2. Elle est plus intelligente que vous ne le trouvez.
3. Il est moins drôle que vous ne le pensez.
4. Il est plus méchant qu'il n'en a l'air.
5. Cette chanson est moins compliquée qu'elle n'en a l'air.

31.
1. Anne a autant d'argent que moi.
2. Elle a moins de robes que moi.
3. Il a plus d'autos que moi.
4. Elle a autant de gâteaux que moi.
5. Vous avez plus de peintures que moi.
6. Vous avez autant de CD que moi.
7. Il a mangé plus de tartes que moi.
8. Elle a pris moins de livres que moi.

32.
1. Oui, c'est la fille la plus intéressante du village.
2. Oui, c'est la plus petite rue du village.
3. Oui, ce sont les enfants les plus amusants du village.
4. Oui, c'est le plus joli jardin du village.
5. Oui, c'est le garçon le plus honnête du village.
6. Oui, c'est le professeur le plus exigeant du village.
7. Oui, c'est la plus vieille église du village.
8. Oui, ce sont les filles les plus intelligentes du village.
9. Oui, c'est le plus grand musée du village.
10. Oui, c'est la plus belle peinture du village.

33.
1. Oui, il chante le plus fort de tous.
2. Oui, elle travaille le plus sérieusement de toutes.
3. Oui, elle danse le plus exquisément de toutes.
4. Oui, il parle le plus profondément de tous.
5. Oui, elle chante le plus brillamment de toutes.

34.
1. meilleur
2. mieux
3. meilleure
4. mieux
5. pire (plus mauvais)
6. plus mal (pis)
7. plus
8. moins
9. les meilleures
10. le plus mal
11. la plus petite
12. la moindre

35.
1. Ce gâteau-ci est aussi bon que ce gâteau-là.
   Ce gâteau-ci est moins bon que ce gâteau-là.
   Ce gâteau-ci est meilleur que ce gâteau-là.
   Ce gâteau-ci est le meilleur de tous.
2. Ces fromages-ci sont aussi bons que ces fromages-là.
   Ces fromages-ci sont moins bons que ces fromages-là.
   Ces fromages-ci sont meilleurs que ces fromages-là.
   Ces fromages-ci sont les meilleurs de tous.
3. Cette orange-ci est aussi bonne que cette orange-là.
   Cette orange-ci est moins bonne que cette orange-là.
   Cette orange-ci est meilleure que cette orange-là.
   Cette orange-ci est la meilleure de toutes.
4. Ces tomates-ci sont aussi bonnes que ces tomates-là.
   Ces tomates-ci sont moins bonnes que ces tomates-là.
   Ces tomates-ci sont meilleures que ces tomates-là.
   Ces tomates-ci sont les meilleures de toutes.
5. Ce beurre-ci est aussi mauvais que ce beurre-là.
   Ce beurre-ci est moins mauvais que ce beurre-là.
   Ce beurre-ci est plus mauvais (pire) que ce beurre-là.
   Ce beurre-ci est le plus mauvais (le pire) de tous.
6. Cette tarte-ci est aussi mauvaise que cette tarte-là.
   Cette tarte-ci est moins mauvaise que cette tarte-là.
   Cette tarte-ci est plus mauvaise que cette tarte-là.
   Cette tarte-ci est la plus mauvaise (la pire) de toutes.

7. Elle chante aussi bien que vous.
   Elle chante moins bien que vous.
   Elle chante mieux que vous.
   Elle chante le mieux de toutes.

8. Il écrit aussi bien que vous.
   Il écrit moins bien que vous.
   Il écrit mieux que vous.
   Il écrit le mieux de tous.

9. Il travaille aussi mal que vous.
   Il travaille moins mal que vous.
   Il travaille plus mal (pis) que vous.
   Il travaille le plus mal de tous.

36.
1. L'enfant parle de plus en plus chaque jour.
2. Plus il travaille, plus il comprend.
3. Tant mieux!
4. L'économie va de mal en pis.
5. Il est d'autant plus heureux qu'il habite à la campagne.
6. Le malade mange de mieux en mieux.
7. Marie est ma sœur aînée.

37.
1. ma, mes, mon
2. ton, ta, tes
3. sa, son, ses
4. notre, nos
5. vos, votre
6. leurs, leur

38.
1. C'est son cahier.
2. C'est son livre.
3. C'est sa photo.
4. Ce sont ses amies.
5. C'est son amie.
6. Ce sont ses lettres.
7. C'est leur école.
8. C'est son adresse.
9. Ce sont ses livres.
10. C'est leur auto.
11. Ce sont leurs amis.
12. Ce sont leurs livres.

39.
1. nos
2. son
3. mon
4. leurs
5. ta
6. sa
7. notre
8. votre
9. mes
10. tes
11. leur
12. ma
13. ses
14. ton
15. vos

40.
1. Mon
2. Ton
3. ma
4. sa
5. son
6. leur
7. son
8. leurs
9. son
10. sa
11. son
12. nos
13. vos
14. ta
15. Votre
16. Mes
17. ses
18. ses
19. notre
20. les
21. la
22. ses
23. tes
24. la
25. vos
26. son

41.
1. C'est son père à elle.
2. C'est sa sœur à lui.
3. C'est mon livre à moi.
4. C'est leur propriété à eux.
5. Ce sont ses stylos à elle.
6. C'est ton chien à toi.
7. Ce sont nos enfants à nous.
8. C'est votre bicyclette à vous.

42. Answers will vary.

43.
1. ce
2. cette
3. Cet
4. ces
5. Ces
6. cet

7. Cette   9. ce
8. Ces   10. Cette

44. 1. Je voudrais cette orange-ci, pas cette orange-là.
     2. Je voudrais cet abricot-ci, pas cet abricot-là.
     3. Je voudrais ces cerises-ci, pas ces cerises-là.
     4. Je voudrais cette pomme-ci, pas cette pomme-là.
     5. Je voudrais ce pamplemousse-ci, pas ce pamplemousse-là.
     6. Je voudrais ces fraises-ci, pas ces fraises-là.

45. 1. quelque   10. aucune   21. Quelques
     2. quelques   11. Même   22. quelconque
        (plusieurs)   12. même   23. si
     3. plusieurs   13. même   24. quelque
        (quelques)   14. une telle   25. même
     4. certaines   15. Telle, telle   26. d'autres
     5. diverses   16. Tel   27. Nul (Aucun)
     6. Chaque (Tout)   17. Quelle que   28. Tout
     7. Chaque   18. quelconque   29. Maintes
     8. Tous   19. Autres, autres
     9. autre   20. toute, tout

46. 1. Marie est intelligente aussi.   9. Marie est discrète aussi.
     2. Marie est forte aussi.   10. Marie est fière aussi.
     3. Marie est sûre d'elle-même aussi.   11. Marie est sérieuse aussi.
     4. Marie est honnête aussi.   12. Marie est rousse aussi.
     5. Marie est gentille aussi.   13. Marie est créatrice aussi.
     6. Marie est bonne aussi.   14. Marie est sportive aussi.
     7. Marie n'est pas sotte non plus.   15. Marie est franche aussi.
     8. Marie n'est pas grosse non plus.   16. Marie n'est pas maligne non plus.

47. 1. une grande maison blanche, aux volets bleu foncé
     2. un très joli jardin, aux couleurs vives
     3. de beaux vieux meubles, une belle chaise noir et blanc, une vieille lampe marron, un vieil abat-jour
        marron
     4. des fleurs fraîches cueillies, une belle petite photo
     5. une petite jeune fille rousse, aux yeux bleu clair, aux joues ivoire, un bel homme blond (et) sérieux, aux
        cheveux châtains, des gens royaux, ma photo favorite
     6. une autre table, une grande statue merveilleuse, une grosse chatte maligne, aux longues griffes
     7. de grosses peintures, de nos villages natals (et) nord-africains
     8. une grande cuisine, un vieil évier, une vieille cuisinière, un vieux réfrigérateur, l'odeur douce, fenêtres
        grandes-ouvertes
     9. une grande table ancienne, de style français
    10. de nouveaux meubles élégants, une belle armoire nouvelle (une belle nouvelle armoire), un bon lit, une
        grande commode nouvelle (une grande nouvelle commode)

48. 1. C'est une chaise chère.   4. C'est une robe propre.
     2. C'est un homme brave.   5. Il est parti le jour même.
     3. C'est une fille pauvre.   6. Ce sont de nouvelles bottes.

49. Answers will vary.

50. Answers will vary. The adjectives in the second column will precede the noun. All other adjectives will follow. *Long* and *court* could also follow. Following are some possibilities.

1. Je préfère les grandes autos japonaises.
2. J'aime les restaurants italiens.
3. J'aime les restaurants italiens et français.
4. Je préfère les petits hôtels fantastiques.
5. J'ai les cheveux châtains.

51.
1. Il parle résolument.
2. Il vient fréquemment.
3. Il parle couramment.
4. Elle travaille continûment.
5. Il a bien dormi.
6. Il est parti tard.
7. Finalement, il a fini.
   (Il a fini finalement.)
8. Heureusement, il a bien mangé.
   (Il a bien mangé, heureusement.)
9. Elle a fini hier.
10. Elle chante bien.
11. Il parle haut.
12. Il voit clair.
13. Il crie fort.

52.
1. Pierre est sérieux.
   Il travaille sérieusement.
2. Anne est précise.
   Elle parle précisément.
3. Yvette est attentive.
   Elle écoute attentivement.
4. Jean est franc.
   Il répond franchement.
5. Jacques et Charles sont intelligents.
   Ils répondent intelligemment.
6. Marie et Jeanne sont gentilles.
   Elles agissent gentiment.
7. André et Marc sont patients.
   Ils écoutent patiemment.
8. Diane est brillante.
   Elle résout le problème brillamment.
9. Paul et Philippe sont véhéments.
   Ils agissent véhémentement.
10. David et Georges sont loyaux.
    Ils agissent loyalement.
11. Éric et Roger sont lents.
    Ils marchent lentement.
12. Nicole est naturelle.
    Elle agit naturellement.

53.
1. Les attractions de la ville A sont aussi bonnes que les attractions de la ville B.
   Les attractions de la ville A sont moins bonnes que les attractions de la ville C.
   Les attractions de la ville A ne sont pas si bonnes que les attractions de la ville C.
   Les attractions de la ville A sont meilleures que les attractions de la ville D.
   Les attractions de la ville C sont les meilleures de toutes.
2. Les restaurants de la ville A sont aussi bons que les restaurants de la ville B.
   Les restaurants de la ville A sont moins bons que les restaurants de la ville C.
   Les restaurants de la ville A ne sont pas si bons que les restaurants de la ville C.
   Les restaurants de la ville A sont meilleurs que les restaurants de la ville D.
   Les restaurants de la ville C sont les meilleurs de tous.
3. Les magasins de la ville A sont aussi chics que les magasins de la ville B.
   Les magasins de la ville A sont moins chics que les magasins de la ville C.
   Les magasins de la ville A ne sont pas si chics que les magasins de la ville C.
   Les magasins de la ville A sont plus chics que les magasins de la ville D.
   Les magasins de la ville C sont les plus chics de tous.
4. La pollution de la ville A est aussi mauvaise que la pollution de la ville B.
   La pollution de la ville A est moins mauvaise que la pollution de la ville C.
   La pollution de la ville A n'est pas si mauvaise que la pollution de la ville C.
   La pollution de la ville A est pire (plus mauvaise) que la pollution de la ville D.
   La pollution de la ville C est la pire (la plus mauvaise) de toutes.
5. Les habitants de la ville A marchent aussi vite que les habitants de la ville B.
   Les habitants de la ville A marchent moins vite que les habitants de la ville C.
   Les habitants de la ville A ne marchent pas si vite que les habitants de la ville C.

Les habitants de la ville A marchent plus vite que les habitants de la ville D.
Les habitants de la ville C marchent le plus vite de tous.

6. Les habitants de la ville A vivent aussi bien que les habitants de la ville B.
Les habitants de la ville A vivent moins bien que les habitants de la ville C.
Les habitants de la ville A ne vivent pas si bien que les habitants de la ville C.
Les habitants de la ville A vivent mieux que les habitants de la ville D.
Les habitants de la ville C vivent le mieux de tous.

7. La ville A a plus de théâtres que la ville B.
La ville A a moins de théâtres que la ville C.
La ville A a autant de théâtres que la ville D.

8. La ville A a plus de cafés que la ville B.
La ville A a moins de cafés que la ville C.
La ville A a autant de cafés que la ville D.

54. 1. Marie est la fille la plus intelligente de la classe.
2. Hélène est la plus jolie fille de la classe.
3. Pierre est le plus bel homme de la classe.
4. Henri est le garçon le plus intéressant de la classe.

55.

1. Ce, mon	6. Ces, vos	11. Ce, votre
2. Ces, ses	7. Ces, nos	12. Cette, ma
3. Cette, ta	8. Ces, mes	13. Ces, leurs
4. Cette. son	9. Cet. ton	14. Ces, tes
5. Cette, sa	10. Ce, leur	15. Cette, notre

56.

1. les	3. sa	4. la
2. vos		

57. 1. Je veux cette robe-ci, pas cette robe-là.
2. Je veux cet appareil photographique-ci, pas cet appareil photographique-là.
3. Je veux ce disque compact-ci, pas ce disque compact-là.
4. Je veux ces cravates-ci, pas ces cravates-là.

58.

1. Marie a quelques journaux.	10. J'ai mange tous les gâteaux.
2. Hélène a plusieurs amis.	11. Même son ennemi le croit.
3. Il a quelque temps.	12. Je n'ai jamais vu une telle pièce.
4. Certains problèmes sont difficiles à résoudre.	13. Tel est mon choix.
5. Nous avons parlé à diverses personnes.	14. Tout homme veut être heureux.
6. Chaque homme veut réussir.	15. D'autres livres sont intéressants.
7. Avez-vous d'autres CD?	16. Il a couru quelque cent mètres.
8. J'ai vu toutes les maisons.	17. Elle est toute grande.
9. Il n'y a aucun livre ici.	18. Prenez un livre quelconque.

Chapter 3

1.

1. au, dans la	5. dans	9. sur
2. à l', en, dans la	6. au, chez	10. en
3. dans	7. dans	
4. chez	8. du, à la	

2.

1. en	4. en, dans l'	7. pour, par
2. en, à la	5. à	8. en, en
3. à (de), de	6. au, dans l'	9. en, dans le, au

10. aux
11. du, d'
12. au, à
13. à, en
14. d' (pour l'), de (pour le)

3.
1. La Maison Blanche se trouve à Washington aux États-Unis.
2. Le Taj Mahal se trouve en Inde.
3. Les Pyramides se trouvent en Égypte.
4. Le Parthénon se trouve en Grèce.
5. On parle allemand en Allemagne.
6. On parle chinois en Chine.
7. On parle japonais au Japon.
8. On parle anglais en Angleterre et aux États-Unis.

4.
1. à
2. en, en
3. en
4. à
5. par le
6. en
7. en
8. en
9. à (en), à (en)
10. par, par

5. Answers will vary. Following are some possibilities:
1. Je vais à l'école à bicyclette.
2. Je vais à la banque à pied.
3. J'envoie ce colis par avion.
4. Je vais au théâtre en taxi.
5. Je vais au restaurant en auto.

6.
1. en, à
2. en
3. à
4. avant, après

7.
1. en
2. dans
3. dans
4. Dans
5. dans
6. dans
7. en
8. en

8.
1. à
2. de
3. de, de
4. de, de
5. aux, aux, au
6. à, à
7. d'
8. de
9. à la, aux
10. en (d'), en (de), en (de)
11. de
12. de

9.
1. avec
2. d'
3. à
4. d'
5. avec
6. à

10.
1. à
2. à
3. de
4. à, à
5. de
6. à
7. d'
8. à
9. à
10. de

11.
1. une tasse de the
2. une tasse à thé
3. un verre d'eau
4. un verre à eau
5. une cuiller à soupe
6. une tarte aux cerises
7. de la glace au chocolat
8. une bicyclette à vendre
9. l'homme aux yeux bruns
10. la soupe aux tomates
11. une agence de voyage
12. un professeur de géographie
13. une robe en soie
14. une robe de soie

12.
1. de, en, en
2. de, à, par le
3. au, en
4. à l', à
5. par, par
6. chez le, en
7. à, en
8. sur, à, au, au
9. du, en
10. de l', dans l', en
11. chez le, en (à)
12. dans le, aux
13. en, à la
14. à, en, dans

13.
1. à l'	13. à	25. en
2. de	14. à	26. à
3. à	15. à	27. d'
4. en	16. à	28. avec
5. du	17. à	29. à
6. à	18. à	30. avant
7. à l'	19. dans	31. en
8. en	20. aux	32. dans
9. de	21. au	33. dans
10. au	22. aux	34. à
11. à	23. au	35. Chez
12. dans	24. devant	36. d'

Chapter 4

1.
1. dix
2. dix-neuf
3. vingt
4. vingt et un
5. vingt-sept
6. trente et un
7. soixante et un
8. soixante-dix
9. soixante-douze
10. quatre-vingts
11. quatre-vingt-quatre
12. quatre-vingt-dix
13. quatre-vingt-dix-neuf
14. cent
15. deux cents
16. cinq cent soixante-cinq
17. sept cent quatre-vingt-dix-huit
18. mille cent vingt-quatre (onze cent vingt-quatre)
19. un million cent quarante-cinq mille sept cent quatre-vingt-douze
20. deux mille neuf cent cinquante-quatre
21. deux à deux
22. tous les quinze jours
23. une personne sur dix
24. tous les deux ans
25. toutes les dix minutes

2.
1. premier
2. neuvième
3. cinquième
4. première
5. deuxième
6. cent unième
7. deuxième (seconde)
8. tierce

3.
1. Napoléon premier
2. Louis quinze
3. les deux premières années
4. les deux derniers jours

4.
1. Je voudrais une dizaine de pêches.
2. Je voudrais une vingtaine de poires.
3. Je voudrais une trentaine de pommes.
4. Il y a un million de gens dans cette salle.
5. Elle gagne dans les trente mille dollars par an.

5.
1. un demi (la moitié)
2. une demi-bouteille
3. vingt et un et demi
4. un tiers
5. trois quarts
6. sept seizièmes
7. dix et un quart

6.
1. Dix et cinq font quinze.
2. Dix-huit moins six font douze.
3. Huit fois douze font quatre-vingt-seize.
4. Cinquante divisé par cinq fait dix.
5. Cette boîte a quinze centimètres (15 cm) de long (de longueur) sur dix centimètres (10 cm) de large (de largeur) sur huit centimètres (8 cm) de haut (de hauteur).

7. Answers will vary.

8.
1. le lundi vingt-cinq juin
2. le mardi quatre décembre
3. au mois de janvier
4. en juin
5. le premier avril
6. Quel jour est-ce aujourd'hui? (Quel jour sommes-nous aujourd'hui?)
7. C'est aujourd'hui le vendredi vingt-deux décembre deux mille dix-huit.
8. au printemps
9. en été
10. en hiver

9.
1. Il est une heure du matin.
2. Il est quatre heures moins le quart de l'après-midi. (Il est quatre heures moins un quart de l'après-midi.)
3. Il est huit heures et demie du matin.
   (Il est huit heures trente du matin.)
4. Il est midi.
5. Il est minuit.
6. Il est neuf heures et quart du soir.
   (Il est neuf heures quinze du soir.)
7. Il est midi et demi.
8. Il est minuit et demi.
9. Il est dix heures vingt-cinq du soir.
10. Il est dix heures moins vingt du matin.

10.
1. Il est une heure.
2. Il est quinze heures quarante-cinq.
3. Il est huit heures trente.
4. Il est douze heures. (Il est midi.)
5. Il est zéro heure. (Il est minuit.)
6. Il est vingt et une heures quinze.
7. Il est douze heures trente. (Il est midi et demi.)
8. Il est zéro heure trente. (Il est minuit et demi.)
9. Il est vingt-deux heures vingt-cinq.
10. Il est neuf heures quarante.

11.
1. On célèbre l'Hallowe'en (la veille de la Toussaint) le 31 octobre en automne. Octobre est le dixième mois de l'année.
2. On célèbre Noël le 25 décembre en hiver.
   Décembre est le douzième mois de l'année.
3. On célèbre la fête nationale en France le 14 juillet en été.
   Juillet est le septième mois de l'année.
4. On célèbre la fête du travail en France le 1ᵉʳ mai au printemps.
   Mai est le cinquième mois de l'année.
5. On célèbre le jour de l'An le premier janvier en hiver.
   Janvier est le premier mois de l'année.
6. On célèbre la fête du Saint-Patrice le 17 mars en hiver.
   Mars est le troisième mois de l'année.

12.
1. Soixante-dix-huit et vingt font quatre-vingt-dix-huit.
2. Un tiers et deux tiers font un.
3. Mille et mille cinq cents (quinze cents) font deux mille cinq cents (vingt-cinq cents).
4. Trois quarts moins un demi font un quart.
5. Mille fois mille font un million.
6. Quatre-vingts pour cent de cent font quatre-vingts.
7. Mille deux cents (Douze cents) divisé par cent fait douze.
8. Un milliard divisé par un million fait mille.
9. Deux fois vingt-cinq font cinquante.
10. Mille neuf cent cinquante-cinq (Dix-neuf cent cinquante-cinq) moins mille huit cent cinquante (dix-huit cent cinquante) font cent cinq.

13.
1. Elle se lève à sept heures moins le quart (six heures quarante-cinq) du matin.
2. Elle prend le petit déjeuner à sept heures du matin.
3. Elle part pour l'université à sept heures et demie (sept heures trente) du matin.
4. Elle a son cours de français à huit heures du matin.
5. Elle prend un café à neuf heures moins dix (huit heures cinquante) du matin.
6. Elle a son cours d'histoire à neuf heures et quart (neuf heures quinze) du matin.
7. Elle prend le déjeuner à la cafétéria à midi et quart (midi quinze).
8. Elle travaille dans la bibliothèque à une heure de l'après-midi.
9. Elle rentre chez elle à cinq heures moins le quart (cinq heures moins quinze, quatre heures quarante-cinq) de l'après-midi.
10. Elle prend le dîner à six heures et demie (six heures trente) du soir.
11. Elle va au cinéma à huit heures dix du soir.
12. Elle se couche à minuit.

14.
1. Ma date de naissance est le _____ (date).
2. Le lundi, je vais à (au, chez) _____ (place).
3. Lundi dernier, je suis allé(e) à (à la, au) _____ (place).
4. Le samedi, je vais à (à la, au) _____ (place).
5. Samedi prochain, je vais à (à la, au) _____ (place).
6. Je me lève à _____ heures.
7. Je me couche à _____ heures.
8. Il y a à peu près _____ habitants dans ma ville.

Chapter 5

1.
1. e	6. es	11. ons
2. e	7. es	12. ez
3. e	8. ent	13. ez
4. e	9. ent	14. ez
5. e	10. ons	

2.
1. loue	6. tombent	11. cherchez
2. parlons	7. traverses	12. dessine
3. regardent	8. raconte	13. télécharges
4. restez	9. rencontrent	14. commandons
5. travaille	10. posons	15. dînent

3.
1. cache	3. déjeunons	5. fermez
2. fréquentes	4. gardent	6. fouille

4. travaillons, préparons, passons, travaillons, gagnons, jouons, parlons, dansons

5.
1. Elle danse à la discothèque.	4. Tu goûtes le vin.
2. Nous louons un appartement.	5. Je raconte une histoire.
3. Ils jouent dans le parc.	6. Vous fermez la fenêtre.

6.
1. Je prépare mes leçons à _____ dans _____.
2. Oui, je passe (Non, je ne passe pas) beaucoup de temps à étudier.
3. Oui, je travaille. Je travaille à _____. Je travaille _____ (l'après-midi, le soir, etc.). Oui, je gagne (Non je ne gagne pas) beaucoup d'argent.
4. Oui, je passe (Non, je ne passe pas) beaucoup de temps avec mes ami(e)s. Je passe beaucoup de temps avec mes ami(e)s _____.

5. Oui, je parle français et anglais.
6. Je déjeune à _____ (place) à _____ (time).
7. Je dîne à _____ (place) à _____ (time).

7.
1. J'allume la lampe.
2. J'oublie son nom.
3. J'attire une foule.
4. J'arrive en retard.
5. J'apporte le déjeuner.

8.
1. J'aime la peinture moderne.
2. Nous arrivons à l'heure.
3. Tu oublies le livre.
4. J'aide mes amis.
5. Vous enseignez le français.
6. Ils étudient l'histoire.
7. Elles habitent à Paris.
8. J'écoute des CD.
9. Le garçon apporte le bifteck.
10. Nous avouons nos défauts.

9. habite, étudie, échoue, invite, écoutons, aimons

10.
1. J'admire _____.
2. Oui, j'écoute la radio. J'écoute la station _____. (Non, je n'écoute pas la radio.)
3. J'emporte mes livres dans _____.
4. J'étudie à _____.
5. J'habite à _____.
6. J'écoute les CD de _____. J'aime _____.

11.
1. commençons
2. recommençons
3. avançons
4. mangeons
5. changeons
6. nageons

12.
1. commençons, commencent
2. voyages, voyageons
3. mangent, mangeons
4. commence, commencez
5. nage, nagez
6. lance, lancent

13.
1. Je mange _____ au petit déjeuner. Je mange _____ au déjeuner. Je mange _____ au dîner.
2. Quand je sors avec mes ami(e)s, nous mangeons _____.
3. Oui, nous nageons. (Non, nous ne nageons pas.)
4. Mon cours de français commence à _____.

14.
1. Tu cèdes ta place.
2. Je considère ce poste.
3. Je célèbre la fête.
4. Tu répètes les exercices.
5. Tu préfères partir de bonne heure.

15.
1. Nous espérons le voir.
2. Nous cédons à ses demandes.
3. Vous préférez venir à huit heures.
4. Vous interprétez le poème.

16.
1. interprétez
2. complètent
3. protégeons
4. préfère
5. considèrent
6. cèdes

17.
1. Je célèbre _____. Mes ami(e)s célèbrent _____.
2. Oui, je possède (Non, je ne possède pas) beaucoup de livres.
3. Je préfère _____.
4. J'espère devenir _____.
5. Oui, je considère (Non, je ne considère pas) les deux côtés d'une question.

18.
1. Je lève le rideau.
2. Tu pèses cinquante kilos.
3. Je gèle en hiver.
4. Tu mènes une vie tranquille.
5. J'appelle un taxi.
6. Tu jettes la balle.

19. 1. Nous achetons des livres.
2. Vous levez le rideau.
3. Nous enlevons les ordures.
4. Vous emmenez le chien dans de longues promenades.
5. Nous appelons Pierre.
6. Vous jetez le livre.

20. 1. mène
2. jettent
3. jetez
4. appellent
5. enlevons
6. pèsent
7. appelles
8. menez
9. achète
10. appelons

21. 1. Je pèse _____.
2. J'achète _____ au supermarché.
3. Oui, je mène (Non, je ne mène pas) une vie intéressante.
4. Je jette les ordures _____.

22. 1. nettoie
2. envoies
3. paie (paye)
4. essuient
5. ennuient
6. employons
7. payez

23. 1. Je paie (paye) ces dettes.
2. Tu emploies une femme de ménage.
3. Tu essaies (essayes) de réussir.
4. J'envoie des messages (des textos).
5. Il nettoie les meubles.
6. Elle essaie (essaye) de le faire.

24. 1. J'emploie _____ pour écrire.
2. Oui, je nettoie (Non, je ne nettoie pas) ma chambre. Oui, je balaie (Non, je ne balaie pas) le plancher.
3. Oui, j'envoie des messages (des textos) (Non, je n'envoie pas de messages (de textos)) à mes ami(e)s.
4. Oui, j'essaie (Non, je n'essaie pas) de parler français.

25. 1. it
2. it
3. is
4. is
5. is
6. is
7. issent
8. issent
9. issons
10. issons
11. issez
12. issez

26. 1. remplis
2. réunissons
3. obéissent
4. choisit
5. réfléchis
6. agrandissez
7. envahissent
8. punit
9. finissons
10. réussissez

27. 1. saisis
2. remplit
3. punissez
4. applaudissent
5. accomplissons
6. réussis

28. 1. Nous bâtissons une maison à la campagne.
2. Les enfants grandissent chaque année.
3. Il réussit à l'examen.
4. Vous choisissez votre programme d'études.
5. Je finis le travail.
6. Tu obéis aux lois.

29. 1. Oui, j'accomplis (Non, je n'accomplis pas) tout ce que je veux.
2. J'applaudis _____.
3. Oui, je finis (Non, je ne finis pas) mes devoirs avant de sortir avec mes ami(e)s.
4. Je réfléchis à _____.
5. Oui, j'obéis (Non, je n'obéis pas) aux lois.

30.
1. défend
2. fond
3. réponds
4. descends
5. pends
6. entends
7. fendent
8. répandent
9. vendons
10. rendons
11. perdez
12. tendez

31.
1. Elles vendent l'auto.
2. Vous descendez sur la place.
3. Nous entendons le professeur.
4. Ils fendent du bois.

32.
1. Il entend du bruit.
2. Tu attends le train.
3. Elle perd le match.
4. Je défends cet homme.

33.
1. Vous tendez un piège pour la souris.
2. J'entends la chanson.
3. Elles descendent la rue.
4. Nous perdons l'espoir.
5. Il rend les devoirs au professeur.
6. J'attends un copain devant le cinéma.
7. Tu vends la maison.
8. Ils répondent à la question.

34.
1. Oui, je défends (Non, je ne défends pas) mes ami(e)s.
2. Je perds souvent _____.
3. Oui, je rends (Non, je ne rends pas) mes devoirs à l'heure qu'il faut.
4. Oui, je réponds (Non, je ne réponds pas) aux questions en classe.
5. Oui, je vends _____. (Non, je ne vends rien.)

35.
1. cueillent
2. ouvre
3. accueille
4. offrez
5. souffres
6. ouvrons
7. découvre
8. recouvre
9. recouvrons
10. souffrent

36.
1. Oui, je souffre (Non, je ne souffre pas) d'un rhume de temps en temps.
2. Je découvre _____ en faisant des voyages.
3. Oui, j'accueille (Non, je n'accueille pas) mes invité(e)s à bras ouverts.
4. J'offre _____ comme cadeaux d'anniversaire à mes ami(e)s.
5. Oui, j'ouvre (Non, je n'ouvre pas) la fenêtre quand il fait chaud.

37.
1. Il rit aux éclats.
2. Elle court vite.
3. Il conclut l'accord.
4. Elle sourit beaucoup.
5. Il rompt les liens.
6. Elle interrompt le professeur.

38.
1. court
2. rient
3. corrompt
4. secourez
5. conclus
6. romps
7. ris
8. parcourons
9. rit
10. sourions
11. interrompons
12. cours
13. concluent
14. interrompent
15. riez

39. Answers will vary. Following are some possibilities.
1. quand je regarde un film comique.
2. quand je suis en retard.
3. quand je suis heureux (heureuse).
4. quand je veux une réponse.
5. les liens.

40.
1. Je mets les vêtements dans l'armoire.
2. Tu bats le tapis.
3. Il remet le travail à demain.
4. Elle promet d'aller avec moi.

41.
1. Ils admettent le crime.
2. Les armées soumettent les rebelles.
3. Vous mettez la nappe sur la table.
4. Nous battons le linge pour le nettoyer.

42.
1. battent
2. soumets
3. promet
4. remettons
5. combattez
6. bats
7. mets
8. soumettent
9. admettez
10. permet
11. transmettons
12. promets

43.
1. Oui, je promets (Non, je ne promets pas) de dire toujours la vérité.
2. Oui, je remets (Non, je ne remets pas) mes vêtements dans l'armoire.
3. Oui, je l'admets (Non, je ne l'admets pas) quand j'ai tort.
4. Je remets _____ à demain.

44.
1. ment
2. sort
3. sers
4. pars
5. dors
6. sens
7. partent
8. sortent
9. servons
10. mentons
11. sortez
12. dormez

45.
1. Je pars à huit heures.
2. Tu dors bien.
3. Tu sers des apéritifs.
4. Elle sert un bon repas.
5. Il sent l'odeur fraîche.
6. Elle dort huit heures.

46.
1. Nous sortons de la classe.
2. Ils mentent au professeur.
3. Elles dorment sur le divan.
4. Vous partez de bonne heure.

47. Answers will vary. Following are some possibilities.

1. huit
2. samedi soir
3. du poisson

48.
1. Nous vainquons le rival.
2. Vous vainquez la difficulté.
3. Ils convainquent le sceptique.
4. Elles convainquent l'homme de sa culpabilité.

49. Je vaincs l'ennemi.
Vous vainquez l'ennemi.
Elles vainquent l'ennemi.

Nous vainquons l'ennemi.
Tu vaincs l'ennemi.

50.
1. connaissent
2. reconnaissent
3. apparaît
4. naît
5. disparaît
6. hait
7. paraît
8. reconnaissons
9. connaissons
10. haïssez
11. reconnaissez
12. connais
13. disparais
14. hais
15. connais

51.
1. L'invité paraît à la porte.
2. Je connais les Leclerc.
3. Tu reconnais le criminel.
4. Il hait la bureaucratie.
5. Il disparaît souvent.

52.
1. Nous reconnaissons cet enfant.
2. Vous connaissez le poète.
3. Elles haïssent l'injustice.
4. Ces hommes paraissent malades.
5. Les chiens disparaissent derrière l'arbre.

53. Answers will vary. Following are some possibilities.

1. les Leblanc.
2. cette route.
3. l'injustice.

54.
1. Il plaît à tout le monde.
2. Elle se tait pendant le concert.
3. Je plais à Marie.
4. Tu te tais pendant la conférence.

55.
1. Ils plaisent à cette femme.
2. Elles se taisent pendant le spectacle.
3. Vous plaisez à tout le monde.
4. Nous nous taisons maintenant.
5. Ces livres déplaisent à Pierre.

56. Answers will vary. Following are some possibilities.
1. Cette peinture
2. Ces vêtements
3. le professeur entre dans la salle de classe.

57.
1. La troupe détruit la ville.
2. Il élit un président.
3. Tu dis la vérité.
4. Tu traduis la phrase.
5. Je lis un roman.
6. Je conduis une Citroën.

58.
1. Elles lisent *le Monde* tous les jours.
2. Ils conduisent une Renault.
3. Nous disons la vérité.
4. Nous détruisons le livre.
5. Vous produisez un nouveau jouet.
6. Vous dites bonjour.

59.
1. lit
2. dites
3. suffit
4. conduis
5. reconstruisent
6. détruit
7. traduisons
8. interdit
9. reconstruis
10. construit

60.
1. Oui, je lis (Non, je ne lis pas) souvent.
2. Je lis _____.
3. Oui, je dis (Non, je ne dis pas) toujours la vérité.
4. Oui, je conduis une auto. Je conduis _____.

61.
1. suivent
2. écrivent
3. décrivons
4. suivons
5. écrivez
6. vivez
7. suit
8. écrit
9. décris
10. poursuis
11. suis
12. vis

62.
1. Nous vivons bien ici.
2. Vous suivez ce cours.
3. Elles écrivent un poème.
4. Ils décrivent le match.

63.
1. Elle survit à l'accident.
2. Il écrit les devoirs.
3. Je vis bien.
4. Tu suis un cours de français.

64.
1. J'écris des cartes d'anniversaire à _____.
2. Oui, j'écris des (Non, je n'écris pas de) cartes postales quand je suis en vacances.
3. Oui, je vis une vie intéressante.
4. Je suis des cours de _____.

65.
1. croyons
2. voyons
3. nous enfuyons
4. croyez
5. croyez
6. voyez

66.
Vous mourez de faim.
Il meurt de faim.
Je meurs de faim.
Tu meurs de faim.
Elles meurent de faim.

67.
1. Elle le voit.
2. Je crois en Dieu.
3. Tu fuis sa présence.
4. Il croit cette histoire.
5. Il meurt de fatigue.
6. Je meurs de peur.

68. 1. Nous voyons qu'il a tort.
2. Elles croient que vous êtes fatigué.
3. Ils s'enfuient de la salle précipitamment.
4. Vous mourez de faim.
5. Vous croyez l'histoire.

69. 1. Oui, je crois (Non, je ne crois pas) à la chance.
2. Je crois à (à l', au, aux) _____.
3. Je prévois _____.
4. Je meurs de _____.

70.
1. craignent
2. joignent
3. éteignons
4. atteignons
5. plaignez
6. peignez
7. craint
8. peint
9. plains
10. rejoins
11. crains
12. peins

71. 1. Nous craignons cet homme.
2. Vous rejoignez Pierre à l'heure.
3. Ils peignent un paysage.
4. Elles se plaignent de tout.
5. Elles joignent les deux bouts.

72. 1. Elle craint de répondre.
2. Je peins le mur.
3. Tu éteins la lumière.
4. Il vous plaint.
5. Je joins les deux bouts.

73.
1. rejoignez
2. craignons
3. peignent
4. éteins
5. plains
6. atteint

74. Answers will vary. Following are some possibilities.

1. le tonnerre, les éclairs
2. un portrait de mon ami(e)
3. mes ami(e)s, huit
4. tout

75. 1. Nous prenons le déjeuner à midi.
2. Nous apprenons les verbes.
3. Vous reprenez le CD.
4. Vous surprenez l'enfant.
5. Ils comprennent le français.
6. Ces nouvelles nous surprennent.

76.
1. comprends
2. surprend
3. prenons
4. comprennent
5. apprends
6. prenez
7. reprend

77. 1. J'apprends _____.
2. Oui, je comprends (Non, je ne comprends pas) mes ami(e)s.
3. Je surprends mes ami(e)s _____.
4. Je prends le dîner à _____ heures.

78.
1. viennent
2. retiennent
3. convient
4. appartient
5. reviens
6. deviens
7. obtiens
8. parviens
9. revenons
10. tenons
11. maintenez
12. obtenez

79. 1. Il vient tout de suite.
2. Tu deviens riche.
3. Je maintiens ma position.
4. La boîte contient des papiers.
5. Je parviens à un âge avancé.

80. 1. Ils tiennent à vous voir.
2. Elles viennent tout de suite.
3. Ces livres vous appartiennent.
4. Vous obtenez le prix.
5. Nous venons maintenant.

81. 1. Oui, avec l'âge, je deviens plus patient(e), plus libéral(e), plus optimiste. (Non, avec l'âge, je ne deviens pas plus patient(e), plus libéral(e), plus optimiste.)
2. En général, je reviens des vacances _____.

3. Je viens de _____.

4. Oui, mes ami(e)s viennent (Non, mes ami[e]s ne viennent pas) souvent chez moi.

82. 1. J'acquiers de l'expérience.
2. Je conquiers son affection.
3. Tu acquiers une maison.
4. Tu conquiers l'ennemi.

83.
1. acquiers	3. acquiers	5. conquiert
2. conquièrent	4. acquérez	6. conquérons

84.
1. peuvent	3. peux	5. voulons
2. veux	4. veut	6. pouvez

85. 1. Je peux partir maintenant.
2. Je veux revenir demain.
3. Tu peux sortir maintenant.
4. Tu veux rester ici.
5. Il peut venir ce soir.
6. Elle veut savoir la réponse.

86. 1. Nous pouvons attendre une minute.
2. Nous voulons sortir maintenant.
3. Ils veulent jouer au football samedi.
4. Elles peuvent rester ici si elles le veulent.

87. 1. Je peux partir et je veux partir maintenant.
2. Vous pouvez jouer au football et vous voulez jouer au football maintenant.
3. Nous pouvons sortir ce soir et nous voulons sortir ce soir.
4. Il peut voir ce film et il veut voir ce film maintenant.
5. Tu peux aller au cinéma et tu veux aller au cinéma maintenant.
6. Elles peuvent réussir et elles veulent réussir maintenant.

88. Answers will vary. Following are some possibilities.
1. acheter beaucoup de vêtements (chaussures, CD, etc.)
2. faire un voyage, (acheter une peinture, etc.)

89.
1. boivent	8. reçois
2. reçoivent	9. aperçois
3. doivent	10. reçois
4. reçoit	11. buvons
5. doit	12. recevons
6. déçoit	13. décevez
7. bois	14. buvez

90.
1. bois, buvez	4. buvez, boivent
2. reçois, recevons	5. devons, doivent
3. dois, devez	

91. 1. Nous devons de l'argent.
2. Nous recevons une carte postale.
3. Vous buvez du vin.
4. Vous recevez la lettre.
5. Ils déçoivent le professeur.
6. Elles reçoivent de l'argent.

92. 1. Si je suis malade, je dois aller chez le médecin, etc.
2. Je bois _____ au petit déjeuner. Je bois _____ au déjeuner. Je bois _____ au dîner.
3. Oui, je reçois des (Non, je ne reçois pas de) cadeaux d'anniversaire. Je reçois _____.
4. Je reçois des cadeaux _____.

93.
1. a	5. ai	9. avez
2. a	6. ai	10. avez
3. as	7. avons	11. ont
4. as	8. avons	12. ont

94.
1. Les amies (Elles) ont les billets aussi.
2. J'ai de l'argent aussi.
3. Vous avez vos passeports aussi.
(Nous avons nos passeports aussi.)
4. Les autres (Ils) ont les billets aussi.
5. Pierre (Il) a des cartes de crédit aussi.
6. Nous avons nos visas aussi.

95.
1. J'ai les sandwichs.
2. Vous avez le couvert.
3. Nous avons le dessert.
4. Anne a le panier.
5. Michel et André ont les boissons.
6. Pierre a les serviettes.
7. Tu as le tire-bouchon.

96.
1. Oui, j'ai beaucoup (Non, je n'ai pas beaucoup) d'ami(e)s.
2. Oui (Non), quand j'ai tort, je l'admets (je ne l'admets pas).
3. Oui, j'ai des (Non, je n'ai pas de) cartes de crédit.
4. Oui, j'ai (Non, Je n'ai pas) beaucoup d'ami(e)s sur Facebook.

97.
1. est	5. suis	9. sommes
2. est	6. suis	10. sommes
3. es	7. sont	11. êtes
4. es	8. sont	12. êtes

98.
1. Je suis française.
2. Ils sont heureux.
3. Elle est malade.
4. Tu es loyal.
5. Nous sommes forts.
6. Vous êtes grands.

99.
1. Je suis de la France
Je suis français(e).
2. Il est de l'Italie.
Il est italien.
3. Tu es des États-Unis.
Tu es américain(e).
4. Nous sommes de l'Allemagne.
Nous sommes allemand(e)s.
5. Elles sont de la Russie.
Elles sont russes.
6. Vous êtes de la Chine.
Vous êtes chinois(e)(es).

100.
1. Elle est journaliste.
2. Il est avocat.
3. Elles sont dentistes.
4. Nous sommes ingénieurs.
5. Tu es chirurgien.
6. Je suis professeur.

101.
1. Je suis _____. Mes parents sont _____.
2. Je suis petit(e) or Je suis grand(e).
3. Je suis optimiste (pessimiste).
4. Je suis (Je ne suis pas) heureux (heureuse).

102.
1. va	5. vais	9. allons
2. va	6. vais	10. allons
3. vas	7. vont	11. allez
4. vas	8. vont	12. allez

103.
1. Nous allons très bien.
2. Vous allez bien.
3. Ils vont très mal.
4. Tu vas assez bien.
5. Elle va mieux.
6. Je vais mal.

104.
1. Elle va à la discothèque.
2. Tu vas à la bibliothèque.
3. Nous allons au cinéma.
4. Je vais à la piscine.
5. Vous allez au restaurant.
6. Anne et Michèle vont à la boulangerie.

105.
1. Je vais _____.
2. Je vais à l'école _____.
3. Nous allons _____.
4. Je vais bien, assez bien, très bien, etc.

106.
1. fait
2. fait
3. fais
4. fais
5. fais
6. fais
7. font
8. font
9. faisons
10. faisons
11. faites
12. faites

107. Tu fais fortune.
Nous faisons fortune.
Ils font fortune.
Elle fait fortune.
Vous faites fortune.

108.
1. fait des réparations à l'auto
2. faisons la vaisselle
3. fais le ménage
4. font une promenade
5. faites attention
6. fais du ski

109.
1. Je fais attention _____.
2. Oui, je fais (Non, je ne fais pas) le ménage. Je fais _____.
3. Je fais des promenades _____.
4. Je fais _____.

110.
1. sait
2. sait
3. sais
4. sais
5. sais
6. sais
7. savent
8. savent
9. savons
10. savons
11. savez
12. savez

111.
1. Nous savons qu'elle est malade.
2. Vous savez où elle habite.
3. Ils savent faire du ski.
4. Elles savent faire la cuisine.

112.
1. Nous savons guérir les maladies.
2. Elle sait réparer les autos.
3. Je sais jouer du piano.
4. Vous savez faire la cuisine.
5. Ils savent parler espagnol.
6. Tu sais bien conduire.

113. Answers will vary. Following are some possibilities.

1. Je sais faire du patinage (jouer du violon, parler français, etc.)

114.
1. vaut
2. faut
3. valent
4. valez

115. Il faut arriver de bonne heure.
Il vaut mieux arriver de bonne heure.
Il vaut mieux venir de bonne heure.

116. Answers will vary. Following are some possibilities.

1. étudier et travailler
2. étudier
3. être optimiste
4. être gentil(le)
5. travailler

117.
1. connaissons
2. est
3. demeure
4. apprenons
5. écrivez

118.
1. Il y a une heure que je lis ce poème.
   Ça fait une heure que je lis ce poème.
   Voilà une heure que je lis ce poème.
2. Il y a cinq minutes que j'attends l'autobus.
   Ça fait cinq minutes que j'attends l'autobus.
   Voilà cinq minutes que j'attends l'autobus.
3. Il y a deux semaines qu'elle cherche ce livre.
   Ça fait deux semaines qu'elle cherche ce livre.
   Voilà deux semaines qu'elle cherche ce livre.
4. Il y a longtemps qu'ils dorment.
   Ça fait longtemps qu'ils dorment.
   Voilà longtemps qu'ils dorment.

119. 1. Je travaille (Nous travaillons) depuis une heure.
2. Il y a deux ans qu'il habite ici.
3. Ça fait 15 minutes que j'attends le train.
4. Je conduis (Nous conduisons) une auto depuis l'âge de 18 ans.
5. Voilà dix minutes que j'attends (nous attendons) un taxi.
6. Il y a longtemps qu'il étudie le français.
7. Ils lisent depuis une heure.
8. Il y a un mois que je joue (nous jouons) de la guitare.
9. Oui, elle vient d'arriver il y a deux minutes.
10. Oui, je viens (nous venons) de finir le travail il y a une heure.

120. 1. J'étudie le français depuis _____.
2. J'habite ici depuis _____.
3. Ma famille habite à _____ depuis _____.
4. Je suis à l'université depuis _____.

121. Answers will vary. Following are some possibilities.

2. Je viens d'acheter du lait, des œufs, etc.
3. Je viens de voir mon ami(e), etc.

122.
1. préfère	12. plaît	22. peuvent
2. envoies	13. met	23. voulez
3. commençons	14. faites	24. reçoit
4. appelle	15. dort	25. devez
5. choisissez	16. traduisons	26. buvons
6. offres	17. suit	27. sait, vient
7. rit	18. craignez	28. avons
8. vainquent	19. peint	29. êtes
9. croyons	20. comprenons	30. vais
10. meurt	21. reviennent	31. faut
11. connaît		

123. 1. Vous mangez au restaurant
2. Les garçons nagent dans le lac.
3. Nous appelons la police quand nous voyons un crime.
4. Je réussis aux examens.
5. Les hommes rompent les liens.
6. Ils vendent leur maison.
7. Nous ouvrons les fenêtres quand il fait chaud.
8. Les chefs mettent du sel dans le ragoût.
9. J'attends mon ami devant le cinéma.
10. Les bébés dorment tout le temps.
11. Marie mène une vie tranquille.
12. Georges convainc cet homme de partir.
13. Nous connaissons cette chanson.
14. Vous lisez beaucoup de journaux (beaucoup de lettres).
15. Angèle apprend sa leçon (cette chanson).
16. Les Pierron viennent ici souvent.
17. Les enfants voient un bon film au cinéma.
18. Je peux le faire.
19. David reçoit beaucoup de lettres (beaucoup de journaux).
20. Nous savons toujours les réponses.

124. Answers will vary. Following are some possibilities.
1. J'achète des provisions au grand magasin.
2. Je regarde un film au cinéma.

3. Je bois du café (du thé) au café.
4. Je mange un repas au restaurant.
5. J'achète une robe (une chemise, un pantalon, etc.) au magasin de vêtements.
6. Je suis des cours de français à l'université.
7. Je prépare le dîner dans la cuisine.
8. Je joue au parc.
9. Je lis des livres à la bibliothèque.
10. Je fais attention en classe.
11. Je plante des fleurs dans le jardin.
12. J'écoute les musiciens au concert.
13. Le matin, je me lève (je me rase, etc.). L'après-midi, j'ètudie. Le soir, je sors avec des ami(e)s.
14. Le samedi, je sors avec des ami(e)s. Le dimanche, je vais à l'église. Le lundi, je vais au cours.
15. Je m'amuse en vacances.

125.
1. s'
2. me
3. se
4. t'
5. nous
6. vous
7. m'
8. te
9. se
10. nous

126.
1. se réveille
2. me dépêche
3. te laves
4. nous retrouvons
5. vous débrouillez
6. se rasent
7. s'habillent
8. m'appelle
9. t'amuses
10. se marie
11. nous promenons
12. vous moquez

127.
1. Je me lève tout de suite.
Ma sœur se lève tout de suite aussi.
Mes parents se lèvent tout de suite aussi.
Oui, nous nous levons tous tout de suite.
2. Je me lave dans la salle de bains.
Ma sœur se lave dans la salle de bains aussi.
Mes parents se lavent dans la salle de bains aussi.
Oui, nous nous lavons tous dans la salle de bains.
3. Je me brosse les dents.
Ma sœur se brosse les dents aussi.
Mes parents se brossent les dents aussi.
Oui, nous nous brossons tous les dents.
4. Je me peigne.
Ma sœur se peigne aussi.
Mes parents se peignent aussi.
Oui, nous nous peignons tous.
5. Je m'habille.
Ma sœur s'habille aussi.
Mes parents s'habillent aussi.
Oui, nous nous habillons tous.

128.
1. Je m'appelle Marie.
2. L'action se passe dans une rue déserte.
3. La pharmacie se trouve à côté du bureau de poste.
4. Nous nous demandons si nous recevrons une bonne note.
5. Je m'ennuie (Nous nous ennuyons) parce que le film n'est pas intéressant.
6. Il s'en va parce qu'il est fatigué.
7. Elles se couchent à dix heures.
8. Oui, ils se fâchent souvent.
9. Je me porte (Nous nous portons) bien.
10. Je me souviens de mes vacances. (Nous nous souvenons de nos vacances.)
11. Il se tait parce que la conférence commence.
12. L'enfant s'endort sur le divan.

129.
1. Je me lève à _____.
2. Oui, je me lave dans la salle de bains.
3. Oui, je me brosse les dents.
4. Oui, je m'habille (Non, je ne m'habille pas) tout de suite.
5. Je me couche à _____.
6. Je m'amuse _____.
7. Je me repose _____.

130.
1. s'assied
2. s'assied
3. m'assieds
4. m'assieds
5. t'assieds
6. t'assieds
7. s'asseyent
8. s'asseyent
9. nous asseyons
10. nous asseyons
11. vous asseyez
12. vous asseyez

131.
1. Ils s'asseyent devant vous.
2. Nous nous asseyons devant le feu.
3. Vous vous asseyez dans le fauteuil.
4. Elles s'asseyent au premier rang.

132.
1. Je m'assieds.
2. Tu t'assieds à table.
3. Il s'assied devant le bureau.
4. Elle s'assied sur le balcon.

133.
1. la
2. les
3. les
4. la

134. Answers will vary. Some possibilities:
Je me réveille à _____ heures.
Je me lève tout de suite.
Je me lave la figure, les mains.
Je me brosse les dents, les cheveux, etc.
Je me coupe les ongles, etc.

135.
1. me
2. —
3. —
4. se
5. nous
6. —
7. —
8. t'

136.
1. Nous nous écrivons.
2. Ils s'aiment.
3. Ils se regardent.
4. Nous nous cherchons.

137.
1. m'asseoir
2. te raser
3. nous peigner
4. se réveiller
5. s'habiller
6. vous endormir

138.
1. Samedi, Mme Dupont va se lever à neuf heures.
2. Samedi, vous allez vous coucher tard.
3. Samedi, nous allons nous habiller après le petit déjeuner.
4. Samedi, Pierre et Marie vont se parler une heure au téléphone.
5. Samedi, je vais me laver les cheveux.
6. Samedi, tu vas te réveiller à dix heures.

139.
1. Parle français! Parlons français! Parlez français!
2. Écoute le professeur! Écoutons le professeur! Écoutez le professeur!
3. Choisis un livre! Choisissons un livre! Choisissez un livre!
4. Réfléchis à ces idées! Réfléchissons à ces idées! Réfléchissez à ces idées!
5. Attends le train! Attendons le train! Attendez le train!
6. Vends l'auto! Vendons l'auto! Vendez l'auto!
7. Prends le déjeuner! Prenons le déjeuner! Prenez le déjeuner!
8. Ouvre la porte! Ouvrons la porte! Ouvrez la porte!
9. Bois du lait! Buvons du lait! Buvez du lait!
10. Écris la lettre! Écrivons la lettre! Écrivez la lettre!
11. Pars maintenant! Partons maintenant! Partez maintenant!
12. Viens tout de suite! Venons tout de suite! Venez tout de suite!
13. Sois honnête! Soyons honnêtes! Soyez honnête(s)!
14. Aie du courage! Ayons du courage! Ayez du courage!
15. Sache le poème par cœur! Sachons le poème par cœur! Sachez le poème par cœur!

140.
1. Fais les devoirs. Faites les devoirs.
2. Étudie chaque jour. Étudiez chaque jour.
3. Prends de bonnes notes en classe.
   Prenez de bonnes notes en classe.

ANSWERS TO EXERCISES

4. Viens en classe à l'heure.
           Venez en classe à l'heure.
        5. Lis des livres. Lisez des livres.
        6. Écoute le professeur.
           Écoutez le professeur.

        7. Sois attentif (attentive).
        8. Sache les leçons. Sachez les leçons.
        9. Aie de la patience. Ayez de la patience.

141. 1. D'accord, faisons des projets pour le week-end.
        2. D'accord, allons au cinéma.
        3. D'accord, faisons une promenade dans le parc.
        4. D'accord, partons à dix heures.
        5. D'accord, prenons un verre au café.
        6. D'accord, écoutons la musique.
        7. D'accord, mangeons au restaurant.

142. 1. Sois toujours honnête!
        2. Soyons toujours en avance!
        3. Soyez toujours heureux!
        4. Aie toujours de la patience!
        5. Ayons toujours du courage!
        6. Ayez toujours de la pitié!
        7. Sache toujours la vérité!
        8. Sachons toujours la réponse!
        9. Sachez toujours le poème par cœur!

143. 1. Lève-toi!
        2. Amusez-vous!
        3. Habille-toi vite!
        4. Dépêchons-nous!

144. 1. Ne parlez pas!
        2. Ne travaille pas!
        3. Ne soyez pas en retard!
        4. Ne restons pas ici!
        5. N'aie pas de courage!
        6. N'écoutez pas la conversation.
        7. N'arrivons pas à l'heure!

145. 1. Ne touche pas la peinture.
        2. Ne mange pas la corde.
        3. Ne sois pas méchant.
        4. Ne va pas trop près de la piscine.
        5. Ne bois pas le café.

146. 1. Ne te couche pas!
        2. Ne t'habille pas!
        3. Ne vous dépêchez pas!
        4. Ne vous promenez pas dans le parc!
        5. Ne nous réveillons pas!

147. 1. J'écoute la radio en faisant mes devoirs.
        2. Pierre regarde la télévision en mangeant.
        3. Anne écoute la musique en s'habillant.
        4. Nous écoutons les nouvelles à la radio en conduisant.
        5. Vous lisez en attendant l'autobus.
        6. Le chef chante en préparant le repas.

148. 1. En se promenant, il rencontre son ami Paul.
        2. En descendant la rue, elle tombe.
        3. En racontant une histoire amusante, elle rit.
        4. En regardant la télévision, il s'endort.
        5. En se levant, les spectateurs crient bravo.

149. 1. C'est en étudiant qu'on reçoit de bonnes notes.
        2. C'est en jouant du piano tous les jours qu'on apprend à bien jouer.
        3. C'est en ayant de l'ambition qu'on devient chef d'entreprise.
        4. C'est en courant tous les jours qu'on reste en forme.
        5. C'est en étant généreux qu'on a de bons amis.
        6. C'est en sachant les verbes qu'on réussit à l'examen de français.
        7. C'est en mangeant moins qu'on maigrit.
        8. C'est en travaillant qu'on gagne de l'argent.

150. 1. Il se brûle la main en faisant la cuisine.
        2. Elle s'ennuie en faisant ce travail.
        3. Nous nous amusons (Je m'amuse) à nager.
        4. Elles entrent en courant.
        5. Il parle en dormant.
        6. Elle finit par dormir.
        7. Il commence par remercier les invités.

151.
1. Étant chirurgien, il veut travailler à l'hôpital.
2. Ayant de l'argent, elle peut voyager partout.
3. Voulant réussir, nous travaillons.
4. Disant au revoir, il part.
5. Sachant la leçon, (maintenant) je peux jouer avec mes amis (maintenant).

152. Answers will vary. Use the present participle in your answers. Following are some possibilities.
1. faisant les exercices.
2. étudiant.
3. regardant la télévision.
4. conduisant.

153.
1. Nous travaillions beaucoup.
2. Nous prenions le petit déjeuner à huit heures.
3. Nous pouvions le faire.
4. Nous attendions longtemps.
5. Nous écrivions beaucoup de lettres.
6. Nous lisions des romans policiers.
7. Nous voyions clair.
8. Nous riions souvent.
9. Nous craignions de partir.
10. Nous venions souvent.
11. Nous nous débrouillions.
12. Nous nous couchions de bonne heure.

154.
1. changeais
2. vendais
3. parlais
4. préférais
5. employait
6. suivait
7. prenaient
8. voulaient
9. disions
10. buvions
11. faisiez
12. lisiez
13. mangeaient
14. étudiions
15. se levaient

155.
1. J'étais content.
2. Tu étais heureux.
3. Elle était fatiguée.
4. Nous étions malades.
5. Vous étiez triste.
6. Ils étaient enfants.

156.
1. Ils pouvaient chanter.
2. Nous apprenions le français.
3. Je sortais souvent.
4. Tu avais beaucoup de temps.
5. Elle venait nous voir.
6. Vous buviez du lait.
7. Il mentait souvent.
8. Elle croyait ses amis.
9. Nous étions heureuses.
10. Elle se dépêchait.
11. Vous vous habilliez bien.
12. Ils se promenaient dans le parc.

157. J'avais 40 ans. Tous les jours je me levais à six heures et demie. Je me lavais et puis je me brossais les dents. Je m'habillais avec soin. Je prenais le train pour aller en ville. Je travaillais dur pendant la journée. Je rentrais tard le soir. Je mangeais le dîner. Je jouais avec les enfants et ensuite, je me couchais tôt. Ah! Métro, boulot, dodo!

158. étais, avais, sortais, nous amusions, allions, jouions, gagnait, invitait, apportaient, préparaient, mangions, buvions, écoutions, dansions (mangions, buvions, dansions can be interchanged.)

159.
1. Chaque année, elle allait en vacances.
2. Nous lisions souvent.
3. Nous rentrions toujours à la même heure.
4. Elle faisait des courses tous les jours.
5. Chaque matin, elles achetaient des baguettes.
6. D'habitude, je mangeais des croissants au petit déjeuner.
7. Bien des fois, vous saviez comment vous débrouiller.
8. Tu voyageais fréquemment.
9. Elle allait en Europe chaque été.
10. Il craignait le tonnerre.
11. Il faisait du ski quelquefois.
12. De temps en temps, vous disiez des bêtises.

160.
1. Pas maintenant, mais en ce temps-là, je lisais souvent.
2. Pas maintenant, mais quand j'étais jeune, je riais.
3. Pas maintenant, mais autrefois je chantais bien.
4. Pas maintenant, mais quand j'étais jeune, je me couchais de bonne heure.

161. Answers will vary. Verbs should be in the imperfect tense. Following are some possibilities.
  1. je jouais au tennis.
  2. j'allais à la plage.
  3. je me levais de bonne heure.
  4. je regardais la télévision.
  5. je sortais avec des ami(e)s.

162.
  1. Je ne voulais pas partir.
  2. Vous regrettiez les jours passés.
  3. Nous pouvions venir tous les samedis.
  4. Il ne savait pas les réponses.
  5. Elles croyaient que vous aviez raison.
  6. Nous espérions recevoir de bonnes notes.
  7. À quoi pensais-tu?
  8. Nous étions désolés de ne pas pouvoir venir.
  9. Elle préférait voyager en auto.
  10. Je le désirais beaucoup.

163. Answers will vary. Following are some possibilities:
  1. faire un voyage en Italie.
  2. jouer au tennis.
  3. les films comiques.
  4. réparer le téléviseur.
  5. mentir.
  6. la situation.
  7. sortir avec mes ami(e)s.

164.
  1. Il était huit heures du soir.
  2. Il faisait froid.
  3. Les étoiles brillaient dans le ciel.
  4. Il y avait beaucoup de monde sur la patinoire.
  5. Il y avait un homme qui avait à peu près soixante ans.
  6. Une fille faisait du patinage avec son ami.
  7. Elle était blonde et lui, il était brun.
  8. Ils portaient de beaux patins.
  9. Ils étaient heureux.

165. passions, avions, faisait, portions, faisait, était, brillaient, étions, voulions

166.
  1. Si on jouait aux cartes?
    Si nous jouions aux cartes?
  2. Si on faisait du ski?
    Si nous faisions du ski?
  3. Si on allait au cinéma?
    Si nous allions au cinéma?
  4. Si on dînait au restaurant?
    Si nous dînions au restaurant?
  5. Si on achetait une nouvelle voiture?
    Si nous achetions une nouvelle voiture?

167.
  1. travailliez
  2. écrivait
  3. voulait
  4. connaissait
  5. étudiais
  6. construisaient
  7. savions
  8. habitiez
  9. veniez de
  10. venait de

168.
  1. J'ai oublié ma valise.
  2. Elle a préparé un bon repas.
  3. Nous avons ramassé les papiers.
  4. Vous avez sauté de joie.
  5. Elles ont goûté le vin.
  6. Tu as porté une nouvelle robe.
  7. Le petit a frappé à la porte.
  8. Ils ont appelé leurs amis.
  9. J'ai payé l'addition.
  10. J'ai vite mangé.
  11. Elle a toujours gardé le secret.
  12. Elle a déjà acheté des cadeaux pour Noël.
  13. J'ai vite travaillé.
  14. Le conférencier a quitté la salle.
  15. Il a jeté les ordures.
  16. Tu as cherché partout.
  17. J'ai chassé le gibier.
  18. Nous avons dîné au restaurant.
  19. Vous avez fermé la porte.
  20. Elles ont loué l'appartement.

169. Answers will vary. Past participles will end in **-é.**
Examples:
  1. J'ai mangé au restaurant samedi dernier.
  2. J'ai acheté un livre récemment.
  3. J'ai travaillé dur hier.
  4. J'ai étudié à la bibliothèque hier soir.
  5. J'ai regardé une bonne émission à la télé récemment.
  6. J'ai dansé à la discothèque avec mes ami(e)s.

170. 1. Ils ont applaudi le concert.
2. J'ai choisi un beau tapis.
3. Elle a rempli la tasse de café.
4. Nous avons réfléchi aux problèmes.
5. La police a saisi le criminel.

6. Vous avez bien dormi.
7. Tu as obéi aux lois.
8. Vous avez déjà accompli la tâche.
9. Les écoliers ont fini leurs devoirs.
10. Les ouvriers ont bâti une maison.

171. avons fini, avons saisi, avons choisi, a applaudi

172. 1. Le bûcheron a fendu du bois.
2. Nous avons entendu du bruit.
3. Ils ont rompu les liens.
4. Vous avez vaincu le problème.
5. Il a battu le tapis.

6. Elle a vite répondu.
7. La marchande a vendu des légumes.
8. La glace a fondu.
9. Tu as attendu tes amis.
10. L'avocat a défendu son client.

173. Answers will vary. All answers will have past participles ending in **-u.** Following are some possibilities.
1. J'ai attendu trop longtemps samedi dernier l'arrivée de Marie.
2. Oui, j'ai répondu (Non, je n'ai pas répondu) aux questions en classe.
3. J'ai vendu ma bicyclette.
4. Oui, j'ai défendu mon amie Carole.
5. J'ai perdu mon stylo cette année.

174.
1. été	7. mis	13. cuit
2. fait	8. pris	14. détruit
3. souri	9. compris	15. traduit
4. suffi	10. surpris	16. dit
5. suivi	11. conduit	17. écrit
6. acquis	12. construit	18. décrit

175. 1. Elle a suivi un cours d'histoire.
2. L'élève a appris l'alphabet.
3. Vous avez écrit vos devoirs.
4. Nous avons fait des progrès.
5. J'ai dit la vérité.

6. Ils ont surpris leurs amis.
7. Tu as ri aux éclats.
8. Elle a suivi ce boulevard.
9. Ils ont construit un pont.
10. Elle a mis le couvert.

176. 1. André et Sylvie ont écrit les invitations.
2. Anne et Suzette ont mis la table.
3. Pierre a produit les décorations.
4. Solange et Jean ont acquis les provisions.

5. Le jour de la fête tout le monde a surpris Marie.
6. Tout le monde a dit « Bon anniversaire ».

177.
1. disparu	7. reçu	13. vu
2. reconnu	8. bu	14. voulu
3. retenu	9. eu	15. valu
4. couru	10. cru	16. lu
5. déplu	11. su	17. vécu
6. dû	12. pu	

178. 1. J'ai connu les LeBlanc.
2. Cette décision a déplu à ces gens.
3. Elle a cru le professeur.
4. Il a survécu à ses parents.
5. Tu as vu tes amis.
6. Elles ont reçu le prix.
7. Elle a retenu une chambre à l'hôtel.
8. Nous avons vite couru.

9. Ils ont maintenu un air calme.
10. Vous avez aperçu quelque chose d'étrange.
11. Tu as dû répondre.
12. Cet homme a paru étrange.
13. Elle a lu les romans de Proust.
14. Cette conférence a plu à tout le monde.
15. Il a eu de l'argent.
16. Vous avez tenu votre promesse.

17. Ils ont élu un président.
18. Nous avons reconnu cette peinture.
19. Nous avons bu du lait.
20. Il a voulu faire ce devoir.

179. Answers will vary. Following are some possibilities.
1. J'ai bu du café pour le petit déjeuner.
2. Oui, j'ai su (Non, je n'ai pas su) répondre aux questions du professeur hier.
3. J'ai vu (name of film). Oui, le film m'a plu. (Non, le film ne m'a pas plu.)
4. Oui, j'ai eu (Non, je n'ai pas eu) l'occasion de voir mes ami(e)s samedi dernier.
5. J'ai lu (name of the book).
6. J'ai voulu oublier une mauvaise note (les événements d'hier soir, etc.).
7. Oui, j'ai couru (Non, je n'ai pas couru) aujourd'hui.
8. J'ai élu (name of person) comme président(e) de ma classe.

180.
1. Il a ouvert la fenêtre.
2. Le biologiste a découvert un microbe.
3. Vous avez souffert d'un rhume.
4. Nous avons ouvert les cadeaux.
5. La mère a couvert l'enfant.
6. Il a offert un cadeau à son ami.
7. Tu as couvert le mur de peintures.
8. J'ai souffert de maux de tête.

181. Answers will vary.
1. J'ai offert un livre à mon père, un chandail à ma mère, un CD à mon ami(e) pour son anniversaire.
2. Oui, j'ai souffert d'une maladie. J'ai souffert d'asthme.
3. J'ai couvert mon lit d'une couverture en laine.
4. Oui, j'ai découvert quelque chose récemment. J'ai découvert une autre façon de préparer la dinde.

182.
1. Il a atteint son but.
2. Elle a craint cet homme.
3. Nous avons rejoint nos amis.
4. Vous avez éteint la lumière.
5. L'artiste a peint un portrait.
6. Nous avons plaint cet homme.
7. Vous avez craint les rues désertes.
8. Nous avons rejoint nos amis par téléphone.

183. Answers will vary. Following are some possibilities.
1. Oui, j'ai atteint mes buts. J'ai réussi (à) mon examen de français.
(J'ai appris à jouer du piano, etc.)
2. J'ai éteint les lumières hier soir à onze heures (à vingt-trois heures).
3. J'ai rejoint mes amis par téléphone hier soir.
4. Oui, j'ai peint un portrait de _____.

184.
1. prise
2. pris
3. peinte
4. peint
5. craintes
6. craints
7. endurées
8. endurés
9. vue
10. vu

185.
1. Quelle leçon avez-vous apprise?
2. Quel livre avez-vous compris?
3. Quels CD avez-vous mis?
4. Quels murs avez-vous couverts?
5. Quelle phrase avez-vous dite?
6. Quelle auto avez-vous conduite?
7. Quelles blouses avez-vous prises?
8. Quelles fenêtres avez-vous ouvertes?
9. Quel poème avez-vous lu?
10. Quel criminel avez-vous craint?
11. Quelles pièces avez-vous vues?
12. Quelle histoire avez-vous crue?

186.
1. es
2. —
3. —
4. —
5. —
6. es

187. 1. Je l'ai déjà mangé.
2. Je les ai déjà faits.
3. Je l'ai déjà écrite.
4. Je les ai déjà apprises.
5. Je les ai déjà achetés.

188. 1. Le président a fait le tour de l'Afrique.
2. Les habitants ont élu un nouveau président.
3. La femme du président a visité les écoles.
4. Le président a accueilli les représentants des autres pays.
5. Le président a répondu aux questions des journalistes.
6. Deux savants américains ont découvert une nouvelle étoile.
7. Les athlètes américains ont reçu trois médailles d'or aux Jeux olympiques.
8. Tout le monde a ri au spectacle hier soir.
9. La police a surpris un voleur à la banque.

189.
1. est allée
2. est entré
3. sont arrivées
4. sont montés
5. est née
6. est retourné
7. sont tombées
8. sont restés
9. est rentrée
10. est sorti
11. sont parties
12. sont venus
13. est descendue
14. est revenu
15. sont devenues
16. sont morts

190. 1. Elle est montée dans le wagon.
2. Nous sommes arrivées de bonne heure.
3. Monsieur, vous êtes rentré tard.
4. Pierre et Georges, vous êtes devenus ennuyeux.
5. Marie et Lucille, vous êtes revenues trop tard.
6. Nous sommes restés chez nous.
7. Vous êtes morte de faim.
8. Nous sommes parties de bonne heure.
9. Je suis rentrée chez moi.
10. Tu es descendu dans la rue.
11. Vous êtes entrées dans l'atelier.
12. Les bonnes sont venues à l'heure.
13. Les enfants sont tombés dans l'escalier.
14. Je suis allé au bureau.
15. Tu es allée au restaurant.
16. Il est parti à l'heure.

191. 1. Ils sont partis pour Paris le 24 juin à huit heures du soir.
2. Ils sont arrivés à l'aéroport Charles de Gaulle à neuf heures du matin.
3. Ils sont restés deux semaines à l'hôtel.
4. Ils sont sortis tous les soirs pour dîner et pour aller aux spectacles.
5. Ils sont montés dans le train pour aller en Provence.
6. Ils sont descendus quatre heures plus tard à Aix-en-Provence.
7. Ils sont retournés à Paris une semaine plus tard.
8. Ils sont revenus aux États-Unis.

192. 1. Je suis né(e) (date).
2. Oui, je suis sorti(e) [Non, je ne suis pas sorti(e)] samedi dernier. Je suis parti(e) à (time). Je suis allé(e) à (place).
3. Je suis revenu(e) chez moi (time).
4. Je suis venu(e) en classe aujourd'hui à pied, en auto, etc.
5. Oui, je connais quelqu'un (Non, je ne connais personne) qui est devenu célèbre.
6. Nous sommes allé(e)s (place).

193. 1. Elle est vite montée.
2. Elle a monté l'escalier.
3. Nous sommes descendues du train.
4. Nous avons descendu la valise.
5. Elles sont sorties samedi.
6. Elles ont sorti l'argenterie du tiroir.
7. Il est monté dans sa chambre.
8. Ils ont descendu les valises.
9. Nous avons sorti de l'argent.
10. Elles sont descendues de l'autobus.
11. Nous avons passé nos vacances au bord de la mer.

12. Nous sommes passé(e)s près d'ici samedi.
13. Il est entré dans la salle de classe.
14. Il a entré les notes dans son cahier.

15. Elle est rentrée très tard.
16. Elle a rentré le courrier.

194.
1. s'est dépêchée
2. s'est rasé
3. se sont ennuyées
4. se sont souvenus

5. me suis assis
6. me suis trompée
7. t'es réveillé
8. t'es lavé

9. vous êtes amusés
10. vous êtes habillées
11. nous sommes réposés
12. nous sommes endormies

195.
1. Il s'est bien débrouillé.
2. Elle s'est levée de bonne heure.
3. Nous nous sommes bien amusées.
4. Hélène et Marie, vous vous êtes trompées.
5. Elles se sont retrouvées devant le musée.
6. Elle s'est lavé les mains.
7. Ils se sont brossé les dents.
8. Je me suis assise devant le feu.

9. Elles se sont couchées dans le lit.
10. Tu t'es réveillé à huit heures.
11. Vous vous êtes peignée.
12. Je me suis trompé.
13. Nous nous sommes dépêchés.
14. Pierre et Jean, vous vous êtes rasés.
15. Elles se sont téléphoné.

196.
1. Jean et Marie se sont levés à huit heures.
2. Marie s'est maquillée avec soin.
3. Elle s'est habillée en blanc.
4. Jean s'est rasé avec soin.
5. Les demoiselles d'honneur se sont habillées en rose.
6. Les placeurs se sont dépêchés pour arriver à l'église à l'heure.
7. Les invités se sont rencontrés à l'église.
8. Marie et Jean se sont mariés à onze heures.
9. Tout le monde s'est réuni pour la réception.
10. Les invités se sont parlé et ils se sont amusés à la réception.

197.
1. sommes allé(e)s
2. a bâti
3. a vu
4. sont venus

5. avez voyagé
6. s'est couchée
7. avons loué

8. a découvert
9. a dit
10. s'est rasé

198. Answers will vary.
1. J'ai mangé au restaurant...
2. Je suis allé(e) au cinéma...
3. J'ai joué au tennis...
4. J'ai fait la cuisine...

5. Je me suis couché(e) très tard...
6. Je me suis réveillé(e) très tard...
7. J'ai reçu un cadeau...
8. J'ai vu mon grand-père...

199.
1. Elle venait me voir bien des fois.
2. Tu le voyais bien des fois.
3. Pierre disait cela bien des fois.

4. Nous recevions des lettres bien des fois.
5. Vous l'appeliez bien des fois.

200.
1. Elle est venue me voir l'année passée.
2. Je suis allé(e) à Paris l'année passée.
3. J'ai vu Marie l'année passée.

4. Nous avons voyagé en Europe l'année passée.
5. Elle a joué ce rôle l'année passée.

201.
1. Ils regardaient la télévision chaque soir.
2. L'autre jour il a joué au tennis.
3. Elle a répété cette phrase une fois.
4. Pierre venait ici tous les dimanches.
5. Nous sommes allé(e)s à ce restaurant samedi dernier.
6. Souvent nous discutions politique.

    7. Ta mère a été malade pendant deux ans.

    8. Pendant tous ses voyages, elle payait par cartes de crédit.

    9. Nous y allions de temps en temps.

   10. Ce matin, il a dormi jusqu'à sept heures.

202. 1. Oui, j'ai reçu la carte hier.

    2. Oui, j'ai habité à New York l'année dernière.

    3. Oui, j'allais au concert tous les dimanches.

    4. Oui, en ce temps-là, je travaillais beaucoup.

    5. Oui, j'ai beaucoup dormi hier soir.

    6. Oui, je conduisais toujours cette auto.

    7. Oui, j'ai beaucoup nagé l'été dernier.

    8. Oui, je suis allé(e) à la plage la semaine dernière.

203. Answers will vary. Numbers 1, 2, 3, and 6 should be in the *passé composé*. Numbers 4 and 5 should be in the imperfect. Following are some possibilities.

    1. Hier soir, j'ai regardé la télévision.

    2. La semaine dernière, je suis allé(e) au théâtre.

    3. L'année dernière, je suis allé(e) en France.

    4. Tous les samedis, je jouais au tennis.

    5. Habituellement, j'allais au cinéma tous les samedis.

    6. Un samedi, je suis allé(e) à un match de football.

204. 1. J'allais souvent au théâtre. Je suis allé(e) souvent au théâtre.

    2. Je jouais souvent au tennis. J'ai joué souvent au tennis.

    3. Je lisais souvent des romans. J'ai lu souvent des romans.

    4. Je mangeais souvent au restaurant. J'ai mangé souvent au restaurant.

    5. Je faisais souvent des excursions à bicyclette. J'ai fait souvent des excursions à bicyclette.

205. 1. lisais, a frappé

    2. faisait, a découvert

    3. mangeaient, as téléphoné

    4. avons fait, étions

    5. parlait, suis entré(e)

    6. ai vu(e)(s)(es), sortiez (êtes sorti[e][s][es])

    7. prenait, a entendu

    8. dormais, a sonné

    9. discutaient, a annoncé

   10. étions, sont entrés

206. 1. a mangé, a bu

    2. est entrée, est parti

    3. a fait, a pris

    4. a pleuré, a aboyé

    5. a préparé, ai mis

207. 1. Un homme mangeait et un autre buvait du vin.

    2. La police entrait et le voleur partait.

    3. Pierre faisait les valises et Marie prenait les billets.

    4. Le bébé pleurait et le chien aboyait.

    5. Ma mère préparait le repas pendant que je mettais le couvert.

208. Answers will vary. Verbs will be in the imperfect tense. Following are some possibilities.

    1. Je dormais quand il a commencé à pleuvoir.

    2. Je regardais la télévision quand quelqu'un a frappé à la porte.

    3. Tu faisais du patinage quand tu es tombé(e).

    4. Tu faisais une promenade dans le parc quand tu as entendu le tonnerre.

    5. Tu lisais quand les lumières se sont éteintes.

209. 1. Pierre est allé chez le médecin parce qu'il était malade.

    2. Monsieur et Madame Dupont sont allés en vacances parce qu'ils avaient besoin de repos.

3. Nicole a mangé parce qu'elle avait faim.

4. Nous nous sommes dépêché(e)s parce que nous étions en retard.

5. Vous avez mis un imperméable parce qu'il pleuvait.

6. Tu as nagé parce que tu voulais être en forme.

210. C'était le sept juillet. Il était quatre heures de l'après-midi. Il faisait très chaud. Je faisais des courses. Pendant que je me promenais le long du boulevard, j'ai rencontré mon amie. Nous avons décidé d'aller chez le bijoutier. Pendant que nous regardions les bracelets et les colliers, un homme est entré dans le magasin. Il avait à peu près 25 ans. Il avait les cheveux noirs. Il portait un pantalon noir, une chemise verte et un masque au visage. Il a tiré un révolver et il a demandé de l'argent au caissier. Le caissier avait (a eu) peur et il lui a donné de l'argent. Mais heureusement, un autre employé a vu le vol et a appelé la police. La police est arrivée et a arrêté le voleur.

211.
1. Savais-tu (Est-ce que tu savais, Saviez-vous, Est-ce que vous saviez) le nom du professeur?
   Non, mais j'ai su son nom hier soir.

2. As-tu (Est-ce que tu as, Avez-vous, Est-ce que vous avez) connu mon mari?
   Je le connaissais déjà.

3. Voulait-elle (Est-ce qu'elle voulait) passer la soirée au cinéma?
   Oui, mais elle n'a pas pu le faire.

4. Voulais-tu (Est-ce que tu voulais, Vouliez-vous, Est-ce que vous vouliez) partir à cinq heures?
   Non, je ne voulais pas partir à cinq heures.

5. Voulais-tu (Est-ce que tu voulais, Vouliez-vous, Est-ce que vous vouliez) partir à cinq heures?
   Non, je n'ai pas voulu partir à cinq heures.

6. Je pouvais jouer, mais je n'ai pas voulu jouer cela.

7. Avais-tu (Est-ce que tu avais, Aviez-vous, Est-ce que vous aviez) faim à trois heures?
   Non, mais j'ai eu faim à cinq heures.

212.
1. Tu as beaucoup parlé.
2. Elles ont bien dormi.
3. Ils ont répondu à la question.
4. Elles ont suivi les instructions.
5. Elle a descendu l'escalier.
6. Nous nous sommes levées de bonne heure.
7. Nous sommes allés au musée.
8. Elle est montée dans le wagon.
9. Nous avons pris les billets.
10. Il a fait la leçon.
11. Elles ont monté les bagages.
12. J'ai reconnu cet homme.
13. Il est revenu tout de suite.
14. Elles ont écrit les devoirs.
15. Elles se sont promenées dans le parc.
16. Cette peinture m'a plu.
17. Vous avez reçu la lettre.
18. Tu as lu le roman.
19. Ils ont bien vécu ici.
20. Vous avez peint ce paysage.
21. Elle a ouvert la fenêtre.
22. Voilà les photos que je vous ai offertes.
23. Voilà les pièces que j'ai lues.
24. Elles se sont bien débrouillées.

213.
1. Non, mais j'ai appris cette leçon hier.
2. Non, mais il a voulu aller au cinéma hier.
3. Non, mais je l'ai comprise (nous l'avons comprise) hier.
4. Non, mais je me suis souvenu(e) (nous nous sommes souvenu[e]s) de la réponse hier.
5. Non, mais il a valu le prix hier.
6. Non, mais elle a ri hier.
7. Non, mais j'ai souffert (nous avons souffert) d'un rhume hier.
8. Non, mais vous avez dit la vérité hier.
9. Non, mais elle est revenue à huit heures hier.
10. Non, mais j'ai mis (nous avons mis) un imperméable hier.
11. Non, mais il est resté jusqu'à dix heures hier.
12. Non, mais j'ai vu Pierre hier.

214. Answers will vary. Verbs will be in the *passé composé* and a time expression will complete the sentence.
Examples:

1. Je suis allé(e) au cinéma...
2. J'ai téléphoné à mes parents...
3. J'ai dansé à la discothèque...
4. J'ai joué d'un instrument de musique...
5. J'ai fait un voyage...
6. J'ai pris des vacances...

215. Answers will vary.
Examples:

1. Je suis allé(e) (place).
2. Je suis parti(e) (time).
3. Je suis arrivé(e) (place, time).
4. Je suis resté(e) à (hotel, etc.).
5. J'ai pris des repas (place).
6. J'ai visité (museums, sights, etc.).
7. J'ai vu (sights, etc.).
8. J'ai acheté...
9. Je suis revenu(e) (place, time).

216.
1. allait, assistait, voyait
2. nous sommes levé(e)s, avons travaillé, avons passé
3. allait, travaillait, rentrait
4. ont joué, ont regardé, ont écouté, se sont couchés
5. prenions, nous amusions
6. avons fait, avons vu, nous sommes amusé(e)s

217. Il était sept heures du matin. Je suis allé(e) dans les montagnes parce que je voulais faire du ski. Il faisait froid et il faisait du vent mais le soleil brillait. Je portais un beau costume de ski. Je suis arrivé(e) au chalet. J'ai acheté mon billet pour les remonte-pentes et j'ai fait la queue pour monter la montagne. J'ai remarqué qu'il y avait beaucoup de monde sur les pistes de ski. Je montais. Je descendais. J'étais très content(e). Je savais bien faire du ski. Mais malheureusement, à la quatrième descente, je suis tombé(e). Je me suis cassé la jambe. On m'a emmené(e) à l'hôpital où on a mis ma jambe dans du plâtre. La journée qui a commencé bien a fini mal.

218. Answers will vary. Verbs will be in the *passé composé*. Following are some possibilities.

1. le téléphone a sonné.
2. mon ami(e) est arrivé(e).
3. quelqu'un a frappé à la porte.
4. j'ai rencontré mon professeur.
5. ma mère est entrée.

219. Anne avait de la chance. Elle a passé l'été chez une famille française qui habitait dans la banlieue de Paris. Elle a fait ses valises une semaine à l'avance. Le jour de son départ, elle s'est réveillée tôt parce qu'elle ne pouvait pas dormir. Pour le petit déjeuner, elle a pris seulement des rôties et elle a bu un peu de café. Pour le déjeuner elle a mangé seulement un sandwich. L'après-midi, elle a pris l'avion pour Paris. Le voyage semblait être long. La famille avec qui elle allait vivre l'a rencontrée à l'aéroport. Elle a passé un été formidable avec cette famille française. Elle s'entendait bien avec la fille de la famille. Toutes les deux ont fait beaucoup de choses ensemble. Elles ont fait des promenades dans le jardin du Luxembourg; elles ont vu les monuments historiques; elles ont monté la tour Eiffel; elles ont regardé les peintures au Louvre et au musée d'Orsay; elles ont pris des repas formidables dans de bons restaurants; elles ont fait les courses. Anne s'est acheté un beau chandail et une robe. La robe qu'elle a achetée était très chic. Tous les samedis les deux filles sortaient avec un groupe d'amis et ils s'amusaient à la discothèque. C'était un été formidable.

220. Answers will vary. Verbs will be in the imperfect or the *passé composé*.
Examples:

Je me suis réveillé(e)...
Je me suis levé(e)...
J'avais soif, faim.
J'ai pris... pour le petit déjeuner.

J'ai bu...
Je me suis habillé(e)
Je me suis rasé...
Je me suis maquillée...

J'ai rencontré des ami(e)s à...
Nous nous sommes promené(e)s...
Nous sommes allé(e)s au cinéma...
Nous avons mangé au restaurant.

Nous avons dansé toute la nuit.
Nous étions fatigué(e)s.
Je me suis couché(e) à... heures.

221.
1. On publia le livre en 1973.
2. On brûla Jeanne d'Arc en 1431 à Rouen.
3. Tu achetas ce CD.
4. Tu appelas ton père.
5. J'emmenai mes amis avec moi.
6. J'envoyai le télégramme.
7. Nous allâmes à Paris.
8. Nous trouvâmes ce livre.
9. Vous célébrâtes la fête.
10. Vous arrivâtes à l'heure.
11. Les Américains débarquèrent en Normandie en 1944.
12. Ils commencèrent la construction de la cathédrale en 1150.

222.
1. Il a cherché son père.
2. Nous avons donné de l'argent à nos amis.
3. Elles ont médité sur l'avenir.
4. J'ai frappé à la porte.
5. Vous avez deviné les résultats.
6. Tu es vite monté(e).
7. Nous avons compté notre argent.
8. Ils ont marché dans les rues désertes.
9. Je suis retourné(e) chez moi.
10. Elle est allée à l'église.

223.
1. découvrit
2. attendit
3. embellis
4. défendis
5. applaudis
6. partis
7. perdîmes
8. finîmes
9. réussîtes
10. vendîtes
11. choisirent
12. répondirent

224.
1. Ils ont découvert la vérité.
2. Nous avons réfléchi aux problèmes.
3. Il a agrandi le palais.
4. Vous avez répandu la nouvelle.
5. J'ai vendu des timbres.
6. Tu as rendu tes devoirs.
7. Elles ont fini leurs devoirs.
8. Vous avez descendu le boulevard.

225.
1. Elle suivit la route.
2. Tu partis.
3. Je sortis.
4. Nous mentîmes.
5. Vous dormîtes huit heures.
6. Ils rirent aux éclats.
7. Elle acquit les peintures.
8. Je mis le couvert.
9. Tu dis la vérité.
10. Nous prîmes le déjeuner.
11. Vous apprîtes la vérité.
12. Ils comprirent la situation.

226.
1. Nous sommes sorti(e)s ce soir-là.
2. Elle a suivi la route pour Dijon.
3. Elles ont pris les livres.
4. Vous avez mis votre manteau.
5. Tu as servi un bon repas.
6. J'ai souri en entrant.

227.
1. Elle but trop de vin.
2. Il courut vite.
3. Tu voulus venir.
4. Tu pus le faire.
5. Je crus l'histoire.
6. Je reconnus cet homme.
7. Nous lûmes *Les Misérables*.
8. Nous reçûmes la lettre.
9. Vous dûtes travailler.
10. Vous eûtes des difficultés.
11. Ce livre parut chez un grand éditeur.
12. Ils vécurent à Londres.

228.
1. bûmes
2. reconnurent
3. reçus
4. vécus
5. lûtes
6. purent
7. plut
8. crûmes

229.
1. rompit
2. battîmes
3. offrîtes
4. conduisit
5. traduisirent
6. convainquis
7. écrivîmes
8. naquit
9. vîtes

10. peignit	14. fîmes	18. vint
11. craignîtes	15. fus	19. retînmes
12. rejoignîmes	16. furent	20. revinrent
13. fit	17. mourut	

230.
1. Il a traduit le livre.
2. Ils ont écrit des romans.
3. Il a été roi de France.
4. Je suis venu(e) te voir.
5. Elles ont rejoint leurs amis.
6. Ils sont venus de Paris.
7. Nous avons ouvert la porte.
8. Vous avez beaucoup souffert.
9. Elle est née à Paris.
10. Nous avons vu le film.

231.
1. Samuel de Champlain a fondé Québec en 1608.
2. Pierre et Marie Curie ont découvert le radium.
3. Edgar Degas a peint des portraits et des scènes de danse.
4. Napoléon a vaincu l'ennemi dans beaucoup de batailles.
5. Albert Camus est mort dans un accident de voiture.
6. Le peuple de Paris a détruit la Bastille.
7. Charles de Gaulle a été président de la Cinquième République.
8. Le Corbusier a fait bâtir beaucoup de bâtiments célèbres.
9. Jean Anouilh a écrit *Antigone*.
10. Louis XIV est devenu roi de France en 1643.

232.
1. Les Acadiens furent agriculteurs.
2. Un fermier, Bénédict Bellefontaine, eut une fille.
3. La fille s'appela Évangéline.
4. Évangéline tomba amoureuse de Gabriel Lajeunesse.
5. Mais elle n'épousa pas Gabriel.
6. Les Anglais chassèrent les Acadiens de leur pays.
7. Ils brûlèrent leurs maisons.
8. Ils déportèrent les Acadiens.
9. Évangéline essaya de retrouver Gabriel.
10. Un jour en Pennsylvanie, elle alla dans un hôpital pour soigner les malades.
11. Là, elle retrouva Gabriel, vieux et malade.
12. Gabriel mourut et il partit de la vie d'Évangéline pour toujours.

233.
1. vais
2. allons
3. va
4. allez
5. vont
6. vas

234.
1. Nous allons faire les valises.
2. Je vais regarder la télévision.
3. Elle va parler au professeur.
4. Vous allez sortir de bonne heure.
5. Ils vont habiter à New York.
6. Tu vas venir tout de suite.
7. Nous allons boire du café.
8. Vous allez lire le journal.
9. Il va savoir les résultats.
10. Vous allez finir le travail.

235. Answers will vary. Following are some possibilities.
1. Demain, je vais aller au cinéma, faire les devoirs, etc.
2. Dans trois heures, je vais manger, etc.
3. Cet après-midi, mon ami(e) et moi, nous allons jouer au tennis, etc.
4. Ce soir, mes ami(e)s vont aller à la discothèque.

236.
1. discutera
2. finira
3. vendras
4. parleras
5. mangerai
6. remplirai

7. obéirez

8. répondrez

9. voyagerons

10. suivrons

11. se réveilleront

12. rendront

237.
1. Nous regarderons la télévision.
2. Vous étudierez davantage.
3. J'écrirai des cartes postales.
4. Il plaira à cette fille.
5. Elles dormiront huit heures.
6. L'artiste peindra un portrait.
7. Tu conduiras prudemment.
8. Elle dira la vérité.
9. Elles rejoindront leurs amis.
10. Vous suivrez les instructions.
11. Je prendrai le déjeuner à midi.
12. Elle se couchera à dix heures.

238.
1. Elle nettoiera sa chambre.
2. Il paiera ses dettes.
3. Elle essaiera de partir.
4. Il ennuiera ses amis.
5. On achètera des bonbons.
6. Elle mènera une vie tranquille.
7. Elle lèvera le rideau.
8. Il appellera ses amis.
9. Elle jettera la lettre dans la corbeille.

239.
1. nettoierons
2. appellerez
3. emmèneront
4. pèserai
5. enlèveras
6. jettera
7. achètera
8. essaierons

240.
1. Maman paiera les factures.
2. Papa jettera les ordures.
3. Les enfants nettoieront leur chambre.
4. Anne achètera du pain à l'épicerie.
5. Maman enlèvera la tache sur le divan.
6. Elle emploiera un nouveau produit pour l'enlever.
7. Papa emmènera le chien chez le vétérinaire.
8. Ma sœur appellera une amie pour l'inviter à dîner.
9. Nous essaierons de finir nos tâches avant six heures.

241.
1. cueilleront
2. s'assiéront
3. irons
4. aura
5. serez
6. ferons
7. saurez
8. faudra
9. vaudra
10. voudrons
11. apercevrons
12. décevra
13. devras
14. pleuvra
15. recevra
16. courras
17. secourront
18. mourra
19. pourra
20. verront
21. enverras
22. viendront
23. retiendra
24. reviendrons

242.
1. Non, mais la prochaine fois, ils pourront finir à l'heure.
2. Non, mais la prochaine fois, je ferai (nous ferons) le voyage en avion.
3. Non, mais la prochaine fois, ils sauront la vérité.
4. Non, mais la prochaine fois, j'irai voir ce film.
5. Non, mais la prochaine fois, il aura confiance en son ami.
6. Non, mais la prochaine fois, j'enverrai la lettre par avion.
7. Non, mais la prochaine fois, elle verra Pierre.
8. Non, mais la prochaine fois, je retiendrai (nous retiendrons) une chambre.
9. Non, mais la prochaine fois, elle viendra avec André.
10. Non, mais la prochaine fois, il recevra une bonne note.
11. Non, mais la prochaine fois, je secourrai (nous secourrons) les pauvres.
12. Non, mais la prochaine fois, il vaudra la peine d'y aller.
13. Non, mais la prochaine fois, je ferai de mon mieux (nous ferons de notre mieux).
14. Non, mais la prochaine fois, je cueillerai des fleurs.
15. Non, mais la prochaine fois, ils seront à l'heure.
16. Non, mais la prochaine fois, je voudrai sortir.
17. Non, mais la prochaine fois, il faudra le faire.

18. Non, mais la prochaine fois, je devrai le faire.
19. Non, mais la prochaine fois, j'apercevrai (nous apercevrons) l'incendie.
20. Non, mais la prochaine fois, je m'assiérai (nous nous assiérons) au premier rang.
21. Non, mais la prochaine fois, il pleuvra.
22. Non, mais la prochaine fois, il mourra.
23. Non, mais la prochaine fois, nous courrons (je courrai).

243. 1. Ma famille partira le 22 juin.
2. Elle prendra le vol 476 sur Air France.
3. Nous serons en France pendant un mois.
4. D'abord, nous irons à Paris.
5. Ma sœur fera des courses sur le boulevard Haussmann.
6. Mon petit frère courra dans le jardin du Luxembourg.
7. Mes parents regarderont les peintures au Louvre et au musée d'Orsay.
8. Nous irons au théâtre plusieurs fois.
9. Je ferai une excursion aux châteaux de la Loire.
10. Nous pourrons aller en Normandie pour visiter le Mont Saint-Michel.
11. Il vaudra la peine d'y aller.
12. Nous aurons aussi l'occasion d'aller en Provence.
13. J'enverrai beaucoup de cartes postales à mes ami(e)s.
14. Malheureusement, nous devrons rentrer avant la fin du mois de juillet.

244. 1. arrivera, mangerons   5. dormira, lirai   8. voudrez
2. verrai, donnerai   6. feront, mettront   9. voyagerez
3. finira, paierai   7. pourrez   10. partirons, arriveront
4. terminerons, sortirons

245. 1. Quand il sera astronaute, il ira à la lune.
2. Dès que Marie obtiendra son doctorat, elle enseignera à l'université.
3. Aussitôt que nous réussirons à nos examens, nous pourrons travailler.
4. Dès qu'elle sera présidente, elle changera le système.
5. Quand elle deviendra médecin, elle découvrira un nouveau médicament contre le cancer.
6. Dès qu'il aura de l'argent, il ira en Europe.
7. Lorsqu'elle le verra, elle lui dira « Bon anniversaire. »

246. 1. Je pense qu'elle étudiera.   4. Je crois qu'ils viendront.
2. Je sais qu'il viendra.   5. Je ne sais pas s'il voudra y aller.
3. J'espère que nous arriverons à l'heure.   6. Je ne sais pas si elle pourra venir.

247. 1. Il dit qu'il sortira.   3. Elles disent qu'elles travailleront.
2. Elle dit qu'elle pourra le faire.   4. Ils disent qu'ils sauront le poème par cœur.

248. Answers will vary. Following are some possibilities.
1. Mon ami(e) dit qu'il (qu'elle) ira en France cet été (apprendra à jouer du piano, etc.)
2. Je dis que je réussirai (que je ferai le travail maintenant, etc.)
3. Mes ami(s) disent qu'ils (qu'elles) joueront au tennis samedi (iront au cinéma samedi, etc.)

249. 1. sera   3. aura
2. sera   4. auront

250. 1. Elle n'est pas dans sa chambre. Elle sera avec Pierre.
2. Regardez ce qu'ils achètent. Ils auront de l'argent à jeter.
3. Comme elle court! Elle aura peur.

    4. Elles viennent me voir. Elles auront besoin de moi.

    5. Elle ne mange pas. Elle sera malade.

251. 1. Il aura peur.   3. Il sera malade.   4. Elle aura froid.

        2. Il sera chez lui.

252.
1. attendront	6. mènerez	11. aura
2. sera	7. réfléchiras	12. faudra
3. viendra, ferons	8. saura	13. nous assiérons
4. viendront, irons	9. verront	14. mourront
5. nettoiera	10. pourrons	15. voudrez

253. 1. Pierre gagnera à la loterie et il achètera une villa.

        2. Anne deviendra millionnaire et elle fera le tour du monde.

        3. Nicole sera chirurgienne et elle saura guérir les gens malades.

        4. Martine et Sylvie découvriront un remède contre le cancer et elles obtiendront le prix Nobel.

        5. Monique se mariera et elle aura trois enfants.

        6. Georges et Nicole seront astronautes et ils pourront voyager en fusée.

        7. Tu courras dans le marathon et tu recevras une médaille d'or.

        8. Nous pourrons voyager partout et nous verrons beaucoup de sites historiques.

        9. Vous serez écrivain et vous écrirez un roman.

     10. Paul ira habiter à la campagne et il mènera une vie tranquille.

254. Answers will vary. Following are some possibilities.

    Je me réveillerai à neuf heures.

    Je me lèverai à neuf heures et quart.

    Je prendrai des œufs, des toasts et du café pour le petit déjeuner.

    Je lirai le journal.

    Je m'habillerai.

    Je me raserai (me maquillerai).

    J'aurai du temps pour voir mes ami(e)s.

    Je rencontrerai des ami(e)s au parc.

    Nous nous promènerons dans le parc.

    Ensuite, nous irons au cinéma.

    Nous mangerons au restaurant.

    Ensuite, nous danserons toute la nuit.

    Je serai fatigué(e).

    Je me coucherai dès que j'arriverai chez moi.

255. Answers will vary. Following are some possibilities.

     1. Demain, j'irai au cinéma (je ferai les devoirs).

     2. L'année prochaine, je recevrai mon diplôme.

     3. Dans dix ans, j'aurai trois enfants.

     4. Dans vingt ans, je serai riche.

     5. Dans 50 ans, je serai vieux (vieille),

     6. Quand il fera beau, je ferai une promenade dans le parc.

     7. Quand il pleuvra, je resterai à la maison.

     8. Lorsque j'aurai beaucoup d'argent, je ferai le tour du monde.

     9. Mes ami(e)s disent que j'aurai du succès.

    10. Je sais que j'atteindrai tous mes buts.

256. 1. Je dînerais en ville.   4. Nous paierions nos dettes.

      2. Tu resterais à la maison.   5. Vous viendriez à trois heures.

      3. Elle prendrait l'avion.   6. Il serait de retour à huit heures.

7. Elle aurait faim.
8. Nous le ferions.
9. Elle enverrait la lettre par avion.
10. Il mourrait de remords.

11. Elles verraient leurs amis.
12. Vous pourriez voir ce film.
13. Ils secourraient les pauvres.
14. Nous nous assiérions devant le feu.

257.
1. nageraient
2. écrirais
3. paierait
4. iriez
5. viendraient
6. serions
7. ferait

8. enverrait
9. saurions
10. vous coucheriez
11. m'assiérais
12. recevrais
13. pourriez
14. devrions

15. achèteraient
16. emploierais
17. verrait
18. voudrais
19. aurions
20. mourrait

258.
1. À votre place, j'étudierais.
2. À votre place, je viendrais.

3. Dans ce cas-là, j'irais à Paris.
4. Dans ce cas-là, j'écrirais.

259.
1. Ah! non, ils ne feraient jamais de bêtises.
2. Ah! non, il ne mentirait jamais.
3. Ah! non, tu n'échouerais (vous n'échoueriez) pas à ton (votre) examen de français.

4. Ah! non, elle ne rentrerait pas tard.
5. Ah! non, vous n'oublieriez jamais de payer les factures.

260.
1. finirait, reviendrait
2. lirait, aurait
3. comprendrait, expliqueriez

4. pourrait, donneriez
5. rentrerait
6. reviendraient

261. Answers will vary. Verbs will be in the conditional. Following are some possibilities.
1. Je mangerais dès que mes ami(e)s arriveraient et elles nettoieraient avec moi.
2. J'écrirais quand j'obtiendrais son adresse et puis nous nous verrions plus souvent.
3. Je resterai ici au cas où mon ami(e) viendrait.

262.
1. Pourriez-vous venir tout de suite?
2. Pourriez-vous me conduire à l'aéroport?
3. Pourriez-vous me donner ce livre?
4. Pourriez-vous m'aider?
5. Voudriez-vous dîner en ville?
6. Voudriez-vous assister à la conférence?

7. Voudriez-vous aller voir ce film?
8. Voudriez-vous prendre le train?
9. Je voudrais du vin rouge.
10. Je voudrais deux billets aller et retour.
11. Je voudrais ce livre.
12. Je voudrais ces chaussures.

263.
1. Serait-il huit heures? Ils sont arrivés.
2. Elle aurait bien 50 ans!

3. Comme il court! Il saurait les résultats.
4. Il ferait sa médecine à Paris maintenant.

264.
1. Il habiterait à Paris.
2. Elle aurait une peinture de Picasso.

3. Le président serait à New York.
4. Il serait deux heures.

265.
1. Il m'a dit qu'il sortirait ce soir.
2. Elle m'a assuré qu'elle serait heureuse.
3. Il m'a demandé si je mènerais une vie tranquille.
4. Elle a dit qu'elle m'écrirait.

266.
1. écrira
2. viendrais
3. fera

4. auraient
5. mettrions
6. pourra

7. serait
8. serai

267.
1. paierait
2. irions
3. boirais

4. faudrait
5. mourrais
6. ferait

7. auriez
8. sauraient
9. verrions

10. enverrais	12. serait	14. achèteriez
11. pourrait	13. viendraient	

268. Answers will vary. Verbs in answers for numbers 1–4 and 7 will be in the conditional. Numbers 5 and 6 will have an infinitive or a direct object. Following are some possibilities.

1. Dans ce cas-là, je dirais la vérité.
2. À votre place, je refuserais.
3. Je mangerais quand mes ami(e)s arriveraient.
4. Je sortirais quand ils (elles) reviendraient.
5. J'aimerais aller en France l'année prochaine.
6. Je voudrais faire sa connaissance.
7. Il (Elle) m'a dit qu'il (elle) comprendrait quand vous expliqueriez.

269.

1. étions, arrivées	5. étions, descendus	8. étiez revenus
2. avait lu	6. avaient mangé	9. s'était couchée
3. avais fait	7. étais, partie	10. nous étions levées
4. avait cassé		

270.

1. J'étais déjà revenu quand elle est entrée.
2. Elles avaient déjà déjeuné quand je suis arrivé.
3. J'avais déjà fini mes devoirs quand le téléphone a sonné.
4. Elle avait déjà écrit la lettre quand son ami a frappé à la porte.
5. Les voleurs étaient déjà partis quand la femme a crié.
6. Nous nous étions déjà couchés quand il est revenu.

271.

1. Non, j'avais déjà regardé la télévision quand on a annoncé le dîner.
2. Non, ils avaient déjà fait leurs devoirs quand le professeur est entré.
3. Non, nous étions déjà sorti(e)s (j'étais déjà sorti[e]) quand elles sont arrivées.
4. Non, elles étaient déjà rentrées quand il a commencé à pleuvoir.
5. Non, elle avait déjà lu le journal quand il est arrivé.
6. Non, il s'était déjà rasé quand je suis parti.
7. Non, vous vous étiez déjà moqué(e)s du politicien quand il est arrivé sur la scène.

272.

1. J'ai pris le petit déjeuner parce que je m'étais levé(e) de bonne heure. *or*
   Je n'ai pas pris le petit déjeuner parce que je m'étais levé(e) tard.
2. J'avais faim parce que je n'avais pas pris le déjeuner. *or*
   Je n'avais pas faim parce que j'avais pris le déjeuner.
3. J'ai réussi à l'examen de français parce que j'avais étudié. *or*
   J'ai échoué à l'examen de français parce que je n'avais pas étudié.
4. Je suis arrivé(e) à l'heure parce que j'étais parti(e) tôt. *or*
   Je suis arrivé(e) en retard parce que j'étais parti(e) tard.
5. Je suis allé(e) au cinéma parce que j'avais fini mes devoirs à cinq heures. *or*
   Je ne suis pas allé(e) au cinéma parce que j'avais fini mes devoirs à onze heures.

273.

1. aurons, parlé	5. aura acheté	9. aurez écrit
2. serez rentré(e)(s)(es)	6. sera rentrée	10. vous serez couché(e)(s)(es)
3. auront fait	7. serai, parti(e)	11. aurez lu
4. auras appris	8. aurons vu	12. aurai acheté

274.

1. Je partirai quand ils seront rentrés.
2. Ils iront mieux quand ils auront pris le médicament.
3. Vous vous coucherez quand vous aurez éteint les lumières.
4. Tu auras un diplôme quand tu auras étudié pendant quatre ans.

5. Nous résoudrons le problème quand le professeur aura expliqué une chose.

6. Elle mangera quand elle sera allée au supermarché.

275. 1. Il arrivera quand je serai sorti(e).

2. Elle viendra nous voir quand nous nous serons couché(e)s.

3. Nous arriverons quand le restaurant sera fermé.

4. Il apportera les hors d'œuvres quand elles auront fini le dîner.

5. Il répondra à la question quand j'aurai rendu mes devoirs.

276.

1. auraient fini	5. aurais vu	8. aurait pu
2. aurions mangé	6. auriez bu	9. me serais couché(e)
3. serions rentré(e)s	7. aurait pris	10. te serais habillé(e)
4. aurait accompagné		

277. 1. Il se serait rasé, mais il n'avait pas de rasoir.

2. Elles auraient mangé au restaurant, mais elles n'avaient pas d'argent.

3. Vous auriez fait un voyage, mais vous n'aviez pas le temps.

4. Nous aurions écrit la lettre, mais nous n'avions pas de papier.

5. Je serais parti(e), mais je n'avais pas de parapluie.

6. Tu aurais ouvert le paquet, mais tu n'avais pas de couteau.

278. 1. À sa place, j'aurais pris l'avion.

2. À sa place, nous aurions mangé du poisson.

3. À sa place, Marie se serait couchée avant minuit.

4. À sa place, Anne et Georges auraient fait des économies.

5. À sa place, tu serais resté(e) chez toi.

279. 1. Quand il a eu mangé, il est parti.

2. Lorsqu'elles ont été réunies, elles ont élu un président.

3. Lorsque le professeur a eu fini le discours, il est descendu de l'estrade.

4. À peine a-t-il eu fini que nous sommes arrivé(e)s.

5. Après qu'ils ont été guéris, ils sont retournés au travail.

6. Quand il a été arrivé, la conférence a commencé.

280. 1. Dès qu'elle eut appris la nouvelle, elle décida de partir.

2. À peine eut-elle reçu l'invitation qu'elle y répondit.

3. À peine fut-elle entrée qu'elle comprit la situation.

4. Aussitôt qu'ils furent partis, ils soupirèrent.

281. 1. Papa était allé au supermarché.
Papa sera allé au supermarché.
Papa serait allé au supermarché.

2. Pierre avait nettoyé le salon.
Pierre aura nettoyé le salon.
Pierre aurait nettoyé le salon.

3. Marie avait préparé les hors d'œuvres.
Marie aura préparé les hors d'œuvres.
Marie aurait préparé les hors d'œuvres.

4. Marie et Pierre avaient mis les couverts.
Marie et Pierre auront mis les couverts.
Marie et Pierre auraient mis les couverts.

5. Maman avait fait les apéritifs.
Maman aura fait les apéritifs.
Maman aurait fait les apéritifs.

6. J'avais mis la viande dans le four.
J'aurai mis la viande dans le four.
J'aurais mis la viande dans le four.

7. Nous nous étions lavé(e)s.
Nous nous serons lavé(e)s.
Nous nous serions lavé(e)s.

8. Nous nous étions habillé(e)s.
Nous nous serons habillé(e)s.
Nous nous serions habillé(e)s.

282. Answers will vary. Completions for number 1 will be in the imperfect or the pluperfect. Number 2 will be in the future perfect. Number 3 will be in the conditional or past conditional. Number 4 will be in the future or future perfect. Numbers 5 and 7 will be in the imperfect or *passé composé*. Number 6 will be in the future. Following are some possibilities.

1. j'étais malade (je n'avais pas le temps).
2. ma femme de chambre sera arrivée.
3. je ferais les devoirs (j'aurais dit la vérité).
4. je serai avocat (j'aurai terminé mes etudes à la faculté de médecine).
5. Je n'avais pas assez d'argent.
6. je chercherai un poste (j'irai en Europe).
7. mon ami(e) m'a laissé un message au téléphone.

283.

1. ont	5. avaient	9. avait pris
2. êtes	6. avait	10. étiez venu(e)(s)(es)
3. partirai	7. ferais	11. aurait mis
4. ferons	8. resterions	12. seriez arrivé

284.
1. Si Anne a de l'argent, elle achètera une Mercedes.
   Si Anne avait de l'argent, elle achèterait une Mercedes.
   Si Anne avait eu de l'argent, elle aurait acheté une Mercedes.
2. Si nous avons de l'argent, nous irons en Europe.
   Si nous avions de l'argent, nous irions en Europe.
   Si nous avions eu de l'argent, nous serions allé(e)s en Europe.
3. Si tu as de l'argent, tu t'habilleras bien.
   Si tu avais de l'argent, tu t'habillerais bien.
   Si tu avais eu de l'argent, tu te serais bien habillé(e).
4. Si Marie et Nicole ont de l'argent, elles viendront nous voir plus souvent.
   Si Marie et Nicole avaient de l'argent, elles viendraient nous voir plus souvent.
   Si Marie et Nicole avaient eu de l'argent, elles seraient venues nous voir plus souvent.
5. Si Georges a de l'argent, il ne travaillera pas.
   Si Georges avait de l'argent, il ne travaillerait pas.
   Si Georges avait eu de l'argent, il n'aurait pas travaillé.
6. Si j'ai de l'argent, je ferai un long voyage.
   Si j'avais de l'argent, je ferais un long voyage.
   Si j'avais eu de l'argent, j'aurais fait un long voyage.
7. Si les Dupont ont de l'argent, ils vivront bien.
   Si les Dupont avaient de l'argent, ils vivraient bien.
   Si les Dupont avaient eu de l'argent, ils auraient bien vécu.
8. Si vous avez de l'argent, vous aurez une grande maison.
   Si vous aviez de l'argent, vous auriez une grande maison.
   Si vous aviez eu de l'argent, vous auriez eu une grande maison.

285.
2. Si elle se casse la jambe, elle ira à la salle d'urgence à l'hôpital.
   Si elle se cassait la jambe, elle irait à la salle d'urgence à l'hôpital.
   Si elle s'était cassé la jambe, elle serait allée à la salle d'urgence à l'hôpital.
3. S'il accepte ce poste, il gagnera beaucoup d'argent.
   S'il acceptait ce poste, il gagnerait beaucoup d'argent.
   S'il avait accepté ce poste, il aurait gagné beaucoup d'argent.
4. Si nous rentrons trop tard, nos parents se fâcheront.
   Si nous rentrions trop tard, nos parents se fâcheraient.
   Si nous étions rentré(e)s trop tard, nos parents se seraient fâchés.

5. Si tu vas en Égypte, tu verras les Pyramides.
Si tu allais en Égypte, tu verrais les Pyramides.
Si tu étais allé(e) en Égypte, tu aurais vu les Pyramides.
6. S'il fait beau, les enfants joueront dans le parc.
S'il faisait beau, les enfants joueraient dans le parc.
S'il avait fait beau, les enfants auraient joué dans le parc.
7. Si vous arrivez à l'aéroport à temps, vous pourrez prendre l'avion de 10 heures.
Si vous arriviez à l'aéroport à temps, vous pourriez prendre l'avion de 10 heures.
Si vous étiez arrivé(e)(s)(es) à l'aéroport à temps, vous auriez pu prendre l'avion de 10 heures.
8. Si les étudiants étudient, ils réussiront à l'examen.
Si les étudiants étudiaient, ils réussiraient à l'examen.
Si les étudiants avaient étudié, ils auraient réussi à l'examen.
9. Si j'ai sommeil, je dormirai.
Si j'avais sommeil, je dormirais.
Si j'avais eu sommeil, j'aurais dormi.
10. Si nous sommes en retard, nous nous dépêcherons.
Si nous étions en retard, nous nous dépêcherions.
Si nous avions été en retard, nous nous serions dépêché(e)s.

286. Answers will vary. Verbs will be in the future tense or in the conditional. Following are some possibilities.

Si je vais en France, je regarderai les peintures au Louvre (je ferai le tour du pays, je goûterai la cuisine française, etc.)
Si j'allais en France, je regarderais les peintures au Louvre (je ferais le tour du pays, je goûterais la cuisine française, etc.)

287.
1. Si je voulais voir un film, j'irais au cinéma.
2. Si j'avais besoin d'argent, je travaillerais.
3. Si je voulais recevoir de bonnes notes, j'étudierais.
4. Si je me sentais mal, j'appellerais le médecin.
5. Si je gagnais à la loterie, je voyagerais partout dans le monde.
6. Si j'avais faim, je mangerais un sandwich.
7. S'il pleuvait, je resterais chez moi.
8. S'il faisait du soleil, je me promènerais dans le parc.

288. Answers will vary. Verbs will be in the pluperfect in the *si* clause and the past conditional in the other clause. Following are some possibilities.
1. Si je n'avais pas fait mes devoirs, j'aurais dit au professeur que mon chien les avait mangés.
2. Si j'avais eu assez d'argent, je serais allé(e) en France.
3. Si j'avais vécu au dix-neuvième siécle, j'aurais voulu être Victor Hugo.
4. Si j'avais eu le temps, je serais allé(e) au cinéma vendredi dernier.
5. Si j'avais eu l'occasion d'aller en France l'année dernière, j'aurais fait le tour du pays.

289.
1. parlent, entrent, finissent, réussissent, attendent, répondent
2. parte, sorte, mente, se repente, dorme
3. rompe les liens, vainque mes passions, craigne cet homme, peigne ce portrait
4. écrives la lettre, suives la route, vives ici, décrives la vue, serves le déjeuner
5. parlions, lisions, dormions, disparaissions, nous asseyions
6. souriiez, étudiiez, riiez, oubliiez ceci

290.
1. envoient
2. nettoyions
3. croient
4. voyiez
5. considèrent
6. cédions
7. achètent
8. levions
9. appellent
10. jetiez

291.
1. prennent
2. preniez
3. vienne
4. reteniez

5. meure
6. mouriez
7. reçoivent

8. recevions
9. boives
10. buvions

292.
1. vous soyez, ils soient, elle soit, tu sois, je sois
2. j'aie, il ait, elles aient, nous ayons, vous ayez
3. nous puissions, vous puissiez, ils puissent, tu puisses, elle puisse
4. je fasse, il fasse, elles fassent, nous fassions, vous fassiez
5. vous sachiez, nous sachions, ils sachent, elle sache, je sache
6. nous voulions, vous vouliez, tu veuilles, elles veuillent, je veuille
7. tu ailles, ils aillent, elle aille, nous allions, vous alliez
8. elle vaille, elles vaillent, il vaille, ils vaillent

293.
1. parlent, mangent, écrivent, dorment, viennent, sortent, conduisent
2. payions, cédions, appelions le garçon, venions, buvions, allions, soyons ici
3. travaille, lise, vienne, finisse, sorte
4. veniez, compreniez, mangiez, attendiez

294. *A.*
1. Le professeur veut que tu lises le livre.
2. Le professeur veut que vous étudiiez la leçon.
3. Le professeur veut que nous complétions nos devoirs.
4. Le professeur veut qu'elles sachent les réponses.
5. Le professeur veut que je fasse attention en classe.
6. Le professeur veut qu'il soit à l'heure.

B.
1. Je doute que le politicien dise la vérité.
2. Je doute que tu partes à l'heure.
3. Je doute qu'il pleuve demain.
4. Je doute que vous achetiez cette maison.
5. Je doute qu'ils meurent de faim.
6. Je doute que nous prenions nos vacances sur la lune.

C.
1. Pierre est heureux que ses amis puissent aller en Europe en été.
2. Pierre est heureux que Babeth vienne le voir.
3. Pierre est heureux que Jeanne et Anne reçoivent de bonnes notes.
4. Pierre est heureux que Claire peigne un beau portrait.
5. Pierre est heureux que nous considérions son offre.
6. Pierre est heureux que vous receviez le prix.

D.
1. Le médecin ordonne que vous preniez les pilules quatre fois par jour.
2. Le médecin ordonne que tu aies de la patience.
3. Le médecin ordonne que la patiente se repose.
4. Le médecin ordonne que nous buvions huit verres d'eau par jour.
5. Le médecin ordonne que je suive un régime.
6. Le médecin ordonne que vous soyez calme.

E.
1. Anne regrette que vous ne vouliez pas venir à la surprise-partie.
2. Anne regrette que tu ne veuilles pas le faire.
3. Anne regrette que son amie n'obtienne pas la médaille d'or.
4. Anne regrette que nous ne puissions pas aller au cinéma avec elle.
5. Anne regrette que sa sœur ne soit pas à la maison.

295.
1. conduises
2. arriviez
3. fume
4. connaisse
5. soyez
6. fasse
7. allions
8. sachiez
9. veuillent
10. traduisions
11. rentre
12. vienne
13. comprenne
14. aille
15. sortiez

296. Answers will vary. Following are some logical possibilities.
1. Je suis désolé(e) (Je regrette) que tu sois (vous soyez) malade.
2. Je suis fâché(e) (Je suis furieux [furieuse]) que tu ne fasses pas (vous ne fassiez pas) tes (vos) devoirs.
3. Je suis content(e) (Je suis heureux [heureuse]) que vous receviez de bonnes notes.
4. Je suis content(e) (Je suis heureux [heureuse]) qu'ils aillent en Europe cet été.
5. Je suis furieux (furieuse) qu'elle ne fasse pas attention en classe.
6. Je suis surpris(e) (Je crains, J'ai peur) qu'il prenne des risques.

297.
1. prépare, lise, reçoive, fasse, sache, perde
2. finissions, mangions, comprenions, suivions, fassions, répétions, retenions
3. compreniez, veniez, finissiez, sortiez, sachiez la réponse
4. réussisse, comprenne, arrive, finisse, réponde

298.
1. Il est essentiel que nous recevions ces lettres.
2. Il suffit que je te le dise.
3. Il vaut mieux que tu sois ici.
4. Il est bon que vous vouliez venir.
5. Il est important qu'elle écrive ses devoirs.
6. Il faut qu'ils aillent au marché.
7. Il est temps que vous veniez.
8. C'est dommage que vous soyez malade.
9. Il vaut mieux qu'elles partent tout de suite.
10. Il est heureux que tu réussisses à l'examen.
11. Il est douteux que Paul puisse venir.
12. Il est honteux que tu mentes.
13. Il est bon qu'ils sachent la vérité.
14. Il est possible qu'on le craigne.
15. Il convient qu'ils viennent demain.

299.
1. Il faut que tu ailles (vous alliez) chez le médecin.
2. Il est important que tu étudies (vous étudiiez) davantage.
3. Il est urgent que vous vous dépêchiez.
4. Il vaudrait mieux qu'elle fasse ses devoirs.
5. Il est important qu'ils boivent de l'eau. (Impersonal expressions can vary.)

300.
1. sera
2. fasse
3. viennent
4. viendront
5. sachions
6. alliez
7. fait (fera)
8. obtienne
9. finissions
10. a
11. sache
12. croie
13. veut (voudra)
14. veuillent
15. puissions

301.
1. Non, je ne crois pas que Jean le sache.
2. Non, je ne suis pas certain que Pierre le sache.
3. Non, il n'est pas probable qu'il conduise une auto.
4. Non, il n'est pas sûr qu'ils viennent.
5. Non, je ne crois pas (nous ne croyons pas) qu'elles arrivent demain.
6. Non, il n'est pas sûr qu'elle parte tout de suite.

    7. Non, il n'est pas probable qu'il vienne.

    8. Non, je ne suis pas certain que Jean vienne.

302. Answers will vary. With expressions in the first column, the verbs will be in the indicative. With expressions in the second column, verbs will be in the subjunctive.

    1. ... les astronautes iront (aillent) sur la lune.

    2. ... nous atteindrons (atteignions) (j'atteindrai, j'atteigne) l'âge de 50 ans.

    3. ... tu recevras (reçoives) (vous recevrez, vous receviez) de bonnes notes.

    4. ... mes professeurs sont (soient) trop exigeants.

    5. ... j'aurai (j'aie) dix enfants.

    6. ... mes amis feront (fassent) le tour du monde.

    7. ... mes amis seront (soient) toujours fidèles.

    8. ... vous prendrez (preniez) vos vacances sur Mars.

    9. ... je deviendrai (devienne) professeur.

    10. ... vous mourrez (mourriez).

303. 1. saches la leçon, fasses tes devoirs, lises le roman, écrives la composition

    2. neige, fasse froid, pleuve

    3. sera fatigué, arrivera, rentrera, reviendra

304.

1. parte	7. compreniez	13. étudient
2. sorte	8. puisse	14. neige
3. vienne	9. soyons	15. arrivicz
4. reçoive	10. pleuve	16. fasse
5. reviennent	11. arrivent	17. saches
6. dise	12. soit	

305.

1. arrivera	3. viendra	5. jouais
2. attende	4. compreniez	6. parte

306.

1. Qu'elle vienne tout de suite!	5. Qu'elle apprenne la leçon!
2. Qu'il conduise sagement!	6. Qu'elles disent la vérité!
3. Qu'il réponde au professeur!	7. Qu'il sache la réponse!
4. Qu'ils obéissent à leurs parents!	8. Qu'elles finissent leurs devoirs!

307. 1. parle français, écrit bien, sait faire le traitement de texte

    2. parle français, écrive bien, sache faire le traitement de texte

308.

1. Je cherche un homme qui connaisse la route.	4. J'ai une blouse qui me va bien.
2. J'ai trouvé un homme qui connaît cette chanson.	5. Je cherche un poste qui soit intéressant.
3. Je veux acheter une blouse qui m'aille bien.	6. J'ai un poste qui est intéressant.

309.

1. sache	3. puisse	5. puisse
2. veuille	4. lit	

310.

1. aie	3. connaisse	5. comprenne
2. veuille	4. existe	

311.

1. ayez	5. soient	8. agisse
2. soyez	6. dise	9. parle
3. fasse	7. sois	10. vienne, vienne
4. allions		

312. 1. Il se dépêche afin d'arriver à l'heure.

    2. Il est content d'être ici.

3. Il ordonne à son fils de partir.
4. Il permet à l'avocat de parler.
5. J'attends son arrivée.
6. Nous ferons cela avant notre départ.

313.
1. alliez
2. plaise
3. vient (viendra)
4. revenions
5. peut (pourra)
6. boive
7. puisse
8. parte
9. sait
10. connaisse
11. fassions
12. dit (dira)
13. pleuve
14. soyons
15. ayez
16. arriver

314. Answers will vary. Verbs in answers to numbers 1, 3, 4, 5, 6, 9, 10, 11, 13 and 16 will be in the subjunctive. Verbs in answers to numbers 2, 8, 12 and 14 will be in the indicative. The verb in the answer to numbers 7 and 15 will be in the infinitive. Following are some possibilities.

1. Je regrette que cet incident soit arrivé.
2. Je pense qu'il m'aidera.
3. J'irai au cinéma à moins que je ne finisse pas mes devoirs.
4. Je suis content(e) que vous puissiez venir avec moi.
5. Je suis désolé(e) que tu partes.
6. Il est étonnant qu'il puisse faire du patinage cet hiver.
7. J'étudierai tous les jours afin de réussir aux examens.
8. Il est sûr qu'il réussira.
9. C'est le plus beau poème (la plus belle peinture) que je connaisse.
10. Il n'y a personne qui puisse le faire.
11. Je veux que vous fassiez les devoirs.
12. Je connais quelqu'un qui sait parler cinq langues.
13. Je doute qu'il dise la vérité.
14. Il est certain que le train arrivera à l'heure.
15. Je suis heureux de les aider.
16. Que mon professeur revienne l'année prochaine!

315.
1. sois arrivé(e)
2. ayons dit
3. aient reconnu(e)(s)(es)
4. soit venue
5. soyez resté(e)(s)(es)
6. ait souffert
7. aient fait
8. ait étudié
9. se soit amusée
10. se soient couchés

316.
1. Elle doute que nous ayons compris.
2. Je regrette que tu sois arrivé(e).
3. Il est possible que vous ayez fini à l'heure.
4. Je ne crois pas qu'elles soient venues.
5. Je doute qu'elle ait fait le travail.
6. Pensez-vous qu'il se soit rasé?

317.
1. Il doute que nous ayons reconnu cet homme.
2. Je ne crois pas qu'ils soient partis.
3. Il est important que vous ayez fait vos devoirs.
4. Il se peut qu'elle soit revenue de bonne heure.
5. Je doute qu'il ait su la réponse.

318.
1. C'est dommage qu'il ait plu le jour du pique-nique.
2. Il est bon que vous ayez (nous ayons) apporté des parapluies.
3. Je suis heureux (heureuse) que tu aies trouvé un emploi d'été.
4. Il est bon que vous ayez (nous ayons) réussi à vos (nos) examens.
5. C'est dommage qu'il soit tombé malade le jour de son anniversaire.

6. Je suis heureux (heureuse) qu'elle ait gagné à la loterie.
7. Je suis surpris(e) que notre (votre) équipe ait perdu le match.
8. Je suis désolé(e) qu'il se soit fait mal au pied.
(Impersonal expressions may vary as long as they are logical.)

319.

1. vînt	5. fussions	9. vinssiez
2. pût	6. sussiez	10. rentrassent
3. fût	7. fissions	11. devinsses
4. finissent	8. écrivît	12. se couchassent

320.
1. Il voulait que nous venions.
2. J'étais heureux qu'elles soient (aient été) à l'heure.
3. Il fallait qu'elle le fasse.
4. Elle était trop fatiguée pour que la soirée soit agréable.
5. Je cherchais quelqu'un qui puisse le faire.
6. Je craignais que l'équipe ne gagne pas le prix.

321.

1. eût été	5. eût écrit	9. fussent revenus
2. fussent, venues	6. eusses réussi	10. eût, fini
3. eussiez su	7. eussent su	11. cussions fait
4. fût parti	8. eusse eu	12. nous fussions débrouillé(e)s

322.
1. Je regrettais qu'elle ne soit pas venue à l'heure.
2. Bien qu'elles aient déjà compris, ils continuaient à leur expliquer.
3. J'étais contente qu'il ait connu mon ami.
4. Il fallait que vous ayez dit cela.
5. Il semblait que nous ayons fait des efforts.
6. Il avait peur que le pain ne soit devenu trop dur.

323.
1. S'il eût eu assez d'argent, il fût allé au cinéma.
2. Si vous fussiez venu, vous eussiez vu Paul.
3. S'il eût été prêt, il fût parti.
4. Si vous fussiez venu, vous eussiez appris la nouvelle.
5. S'il eût fait beau, nous fussions partis.
6. Si elle fût revenue, elle fût venue nous revoir.

324.
1. Le nez de Cléopâtre s'il avait été plus court, toute la face de la terre aurait changé.
2. Si elle avait eu assez d'argent, elle serait venue nous voir.
3. Si nous avions su cela, nous l'aurions dit.
4. S'il avait fait beau, elle serait partie.
5. S'il avait plu, elles ne seraient pas venues.
6. Si j'avais su cela, je ne vous aurais pas répondu.

325.
1. André dit qu'il ne peut pas le faire.
   André a dit qu'il ne pouvait pas le faire.
2. Marie dit qu'elle n'a jamais vu rien de si beau.
   Marie a dit qu'elle n'avait jamais vu rien de si beau.
3. Jean promet qu'il fera tout pour nous aider.
   Jean a promis qu'il ferait tout pour nous aider.
4. Ils disent qu'ils pourront aider la nouvelle étudiante.
   Ils ont dit qu'ils pourraient aider la nouvelle étudiante.
5. Mes parents me promettent qu'ils me donneront une auto si je reçois de meilleures notes.
   Mes parents m'ont promis qu'ils me donneraient une auto si je recevais de meilleures notes.

6. Monsieur Leblanc dit qu'ils iront en Afrique cet été.
   Monsieur Leblanc a dit qu'ils iraient en Afrique cet été.
7. Claire répond qu'elle a déjà lu ce livre. Claire a répondu qu'elle avait déjà lu ce livre.
8. Anne dit qu'elle aimerait voir ce film. Anne a dit qu'elle aurait aimé voir ce film.
9. Pierre dit qu'il faisait beau hier.
   Pierre a dit qu'il faisait beau hier.
10. Roger dit qu'elle aura fini à trois heures.
    Roger a dit qu'elle aurait fini à trois heures.
11. Marie demande s'ils ont gagné le match.
    Marie a demandé s'ils avaient gagné le match.
12. Le professeur demande si nous serons à la réunion.
    Le professeur a demandé si nous serions à la réunion.

326. L'avocat lui a demandé où elle était à deux heures du matin le 8 octobre.
Mme Leclerc a répondu qu'elle était dans la cuisine.
L'avocat lui a demandé si elle avait l'habitude d'être dans la cuisine si tard. Mme Leclerc a répondu que non, mais que ce soir-là elle ne pouvait pas dormir et donc, elle était descendue dans la cuisine pour chercher un verre de lait.
L'avocat lui a demandé si elle avait entendu ou vu quelque chose d'étrange.
Mme Leclerc lui a répondu que oui, qu'elle avait entendu des cris dans la maison de sa voisine et qu'elle avait vu un homme attaquer sa voisine avec un couteau.
L'avocat lui a demandé si elle pourrait identifier cet homme.
Mme Leclerc lui a répondu que oui, qu'elle pourrait l'identifier clairement, car la lumière était allumée dans sa maison.
L'avocat lui a demandé si cet homme était dans la salle.
Mme Leclerc a répondu que oui, que c'était l'accusé.
L'avocat l'a remerciée et lui a dit qu'elle pouvait quitter la barre des témoins.

327. 1. Je lui parlerai avant de manger.
Je lui parlerai avant de chanter.
Je lui parlerai avant de danser.
Je lui parlerai avant de décider.
Je lui parlerai avant de revenir.
Je lui parlerai avant de finir.
Je lui parlerai avant de commencer.
2. Que faut-il faire afin de venir?
Que faut-il faire afin de réussir?
Que faut-il faire afin de finir à l'heure?
Que faut-il faire afin de savoir la leçon?

3. Il part sans manger.
Il part sans attendre.
Il part sans faire ses devoirs.
Il part sans parler.
4. Après avoir parlé, il est parti.
Après avoir fini, il est parti.
Après avoir mangé, il est parti.
Après avoir dit au revoir, il est parti.
5. Après être rentré, il est venu me voir.
Après être entré, il est venu me voir.
Après être retourné, il est venu me voir.
Après être descendu, il est venu me voir.

328. 1. Avant de partir, il a mangé.
Après avoir mangé, il est parti.
2. Avant d'aller au musée, nous avons déjeuné.
Après avoir déjeuné, nous sommes allés au musée.
3. Avant de jouer au tennis, nous avons fait le ménage.
Après avoir fait le ménage, nous avons joué au tennis.
4. Avant de lire le journal, elle s'est habillée.
Après s'être habillée, elle a lu le journal.

329. 1. avant d'arriver
2. après être arrivé(e)(s)(es)
3. en arrivant
4. en mangeant
5. après avoir mangé
6. avant de manger
7. Ne pas traduire.
8. Battre trois œufs.
9. Que faire?
10. Oh! être riche!

330. Answers will vary. Following are some possibilities.

1. Avant de me coucher, je me brosse les dents.
2. Afin de réussir aux examens de français, j'étudie beaucoup.
3. Après m'être réveillé(e) samedi matin, j'ai pris le petit déjeuner.
4. Oui, j'écoute de la musique (Non, je n'écoute pas de musique) en faisant mes devoirs.
5. Avant de prendre mes repas, je me lave les mains, etc.

331. Answers will vary. Following are some possibilities.

1. Après m'être réveillé(e), je me lave la figure.
2. Avant de prendre le petit déjeuner, je fais de la gymnastique.
3. Après m'être habillé(e), je lis le journal.
4. Avant de sortir, je fais la vaisselle.
5. Après avoir mangé, je parle au téléphone avec mes ami(e)s.
6. Avant de me coucher, je regarde les nouvelles à la télévision.

332.
1. Elle fait faire les dessins à l'architecte.
2. Elle fait peindre les murs au peintre.
3. Elle fait installer les salles de bains au plombier.
4. Elle fait poser des fils électriques aux électriciens.
5. Elle fait bâtir les étagères à livres au charpentier.

333.
1. Le professeur a fait écrire le devoir par la classe.
2. Elle fait chanter la chanson par les garçons.
3. Nous faisons écrire une lettre par notre ami.
4. Je fais jouer du piano par l'enfant.

334.
1. Le professeur les fera réciter.
2. La fille l'a fait faire.
3. Nous les ferons faire.
4. Il la fera construire.
5. Vous l'avez fait venir.
6. Elle se les a fait laver.
7. Fais-les entrer.
8. Faites-le venir.

335.
1. Non, ils ont fait repeindre la maison par le peintre.
   Ils la lui ont fait repeindre.
2. Non, ils ont fait redécorer les chambres par le décorateur.
   Ils les lui ont fait redécorer.
3. Non, ils ont fait remplacer les tuyaux par le plombier.
   Ils les lui ont fait remplacer.
4. Non, ils ont fait planter les fleurs par les jardinières.
   Ils les leur ont fait planter.
5. Non, il ont fait laver les fenêtres par le laveur de vitres.
   Ils les lui ont fait laver.
6. Non, ils ont fait réparer le toit par le couvreur.
   Ils le lui ont fait réparer.
7. Non, ils ont fait construire la nouvelle cuisine par les ouvriers.
   Ils la leur ont fait construire.
8. Non, ils ont fait mettre l'électricité par l'électricien.
   Ils la lui ont fait mettre.

336.
1. Il la lui fera écrire.
2. Elle se l'est fait faire.
3. Il le leur fait écrire.
4. Il la lui fera faire.
5. Il les lui fait apprendre.
6. On le leur a fait jouer.
7. Fais-le-lui réparer.
8. Faites-la-leur chanter.

337. Answers will vary. Following are some possibilities.

1. Le clown me fait rire.
2. Une histoire triste me fait pleurer.
3. Le tonnerre me fait courir.
4. La victoire me fait crier.
5. Le bébé me fait sourire.

338.
1. J'ai vu Marie marcher sur le boulevard.
2. Je la vois arriver.
3. Je laisse (J'ai laissé) partir Pierre.
4. Je le laisse jouer. (Je l'ai laissé jouer.)
5. J'ai entendu pleurer le bébé.
6. Je les ai entendues chanter.
7. Je les écoute chanter.
8. Il regarde les peintres peindre.

339. Answers will vary. Following are some possibilities.

1. J'ai laissé le bébé dormir.
2. J'ai vu les soldats marcher sur les Champs-Élysées.
3. J'ai entendu Céline Dion chanter des chansons.
4. Je laisse les enfants jouer dans le parc.

340.
1. à
2. de
3. de
4. de
5. —
6. à
7. —
8. de
9. de
10. —
11. de
12. —
13. à
14. —
15. —
16. de
17. à
18. —
19. —
20. de
21. de
22. d'
23. —
24. —

341. Answers will vary. Use the preposition **à** in numbers 2, 3, 4, 7, and 12 and the preposition **de** in numbers 1, 5, 6, 8, 9, 10, and 11. Following are some possibilities.

1. Je rêve de devenir riche.
2. J'apprends à parler français.
3. Je passé du temps à lire un roman.
4. Je songe à aider mon ami(e) malade.
5. Je crains de ne pas réussir à l'examen.
6. J'essaie d'aider mes parents.
7. Je m'amuse à faire des dessins.
8. Je me permets de ne pas étudier le samedi.
9. Mes parents m'empêchent d'aller à la discothèque.
10. Mon professeur me conseille d'étudier pour mon examen.
11. J'écris à mes parents de venir me voir.
12. Mon ami(e) m'invite à aller au cinéma avec lui (elle).

342.
1. Balzac a écrit le roman.
2. Les Romains ont construit ce monument.
3. Céline Dion a chanté la chanson.
4. Cézanne a peint cette peinture.
5. Un grand architecte construira cette maison.
6. On m'a aimé.
7. On a fini le travail.
8. On a détruit cette ville pendant la guerre.

343.
1. Le français se parle au Québec.
2. Ce mot ne s'écrit pas sans *s*.
3. Le plus beau monument se verra au centre de la ville.
4. Autrefois, cela se faisait à la main.
5. La ville s'est modernisée.
6. Les portes s'ouvriront à huit heures.
7. Ces autos se fabriquaient dans cette usine.
8. Cela ne se dit pas.

Chapter 6

1. 1. Marie travaille bien, n'est-ce pas?
Est-ce que Marie travaille bien?
2. Il fait ses devoirs chaque soir, n'est-ce pas?
Est-ce qu'il fait ses devoirs chaque soir?
3. Pierre se couche de bonne heure, n'est-ce pas?
Est-ce que Pierre se couche de bonne heure?
4. Elle s'habillait bien tous les jours, n'est-ce pas?
Est-ce qu'elle s'habillait bien tous les jours?
5. Ils viendront à l'école à l'heure, n'est-ce pas?
Est-ce qu'ils viendront à l'école à l'heure?
6. Ils sont allés au cinéma hier soir, n'est-ce pas?
Est-ce qu'ils sont allés au cinéma hier soir?
7. Ces étudiants ont lu ce livre, n'est-ce pas?
Est-ce que ces étudiants ont lu ce livre?
8. Pierre s'est reposé hier soir, n'est-ce pas?
Est-ce que Pierre s'est reposé hier soir?

2. 1. Regardes-tu la peinture?
2. Allez-vous à Paris?
3. Savons-nous la réponse?
4. Écoutent-ils la radio?
5. Court-elle?
6. Te dépêches-tu?
7. Nous lèverons-nous de bonne heure?
8. Se couchent-elles à dix heures?
9. Suis-je amusant?
10. Puis-je le faire?

3. 1. Pleure-t-elle beaucoup?
2. Ouvre-t-il la porte pour les gens âgés?
3. Rencontre-t-elle des amis au café?
4. Se dépêche-t-il toujours?
5. Se lève-t-elle de bonne heure?
6. S'amuse-t-elle bien le samedi?

4. 1. Hélène et Pierre, feront-ils les décorations?
2. Marie, fera-t-elle les sandwichs?
3. Anne et Gisèle, apporteront-elles les CD?
4. André, préparera-t-il les boissons?
5. Nicole, mettra-t-elle la table?
6. Les amis, se reposeront-ils l'après-midi?
7. Le soir, tout le monde, se retrouvera-t-il chez Marie?
8. Les amis, s'amuseront-ils à la fête?

5. 1. Avons-nous fait nos devoirs?
2. A-t-elle dit la vérité?
3. Louise, est-elle vite montée?
4. Sommes-nous arrivés à l'heure?
5. Se sont-ils couchés?
6. Se sont-elles moquées de vous?
7. Nous sommes-nous dépêchées?
8. Hélène, s'est-elle lavée?

6. 1. Hélène et Pierre, ont-ils fait les décorations?
2. Marie, a-t-elle fait les sandwichs?
3. Anne et Gisèle, ont-elles apporté les CD?
4. André, a-t-il préparé les boissons?
5. Nicole, a-t-elle mis la table?
6. Les amis, se sont-ils reposés l'après-midi?
7. Le soir, tout le monde, s'est-il retrouvé chez Marie?
8. Les amis, se sont-ils amusés à la fête?

7. 1. Quand
2. Combien
3. Où
4. Comment
5. À quelle heure (Quand)
6. Pourquoi
7. Quand
8. Où
9. Combien
10. Comment

8. 1. Où habites-tu en France?
2. Quand es-tu arrivé ici?
3. Comment es-tu arrivé ici?
4. Pourquoi es-tu venu à cette université?
5. Combien de temps vas-tu rester ici?
6. Combien de cours as-tu?
7. À quelle heure se termine ton dernier cours?

9.
1. Qui
   Qui est-ce qui
2. Qu'est-ce qui
3. Qui est-ce que
   Qui

4. Qui est-ce qu'
   Qui
5. Qu'est-ce qu'
   Que

6. Qu'est-ce qu'
   Qu'
7. qui
8. quoi

10.
1. Qui parle? (Qui est-ce qui parle?)
2. De qui est-elle la sœur?
3. Qu'est-ce qu'il a vu? (Qu'a-t-il vu?)
4. Sur quoi est-ce qu'il écrit (écrit-il) sa composition?
5. Qu'est-ce qui a fermé la porte?
6. À qui est-ce qu'il parle (parle-t-il)?
7. Qu'est-ce qui se passe? (Que se passe-t-il?)
8. De quoi est-ce qu'elle parle? (De quoi parle-t-elle?)
9. Qui est-ce qu'il regarde? (Qui regarde-t-il?)
10. Qu'est-ce qu'il fait? (Que fait-il?)
11. À qui sont ces livres?
12. De qui est-elle la fille?
13. Qui va à la bibliothèque? (Qui est-ce qui va à la bibliothèque?)
14. Qu'est-ce qui fait ce bruit?

11.
1. À qui sont ces peintures?
2. De qui est-il le fils?
3. À qui sont ces livres?

4. De qui est-elle la mère?
5. Quoi de neuf (nouveau)?

12.
1. Qu'est-ce que c'est que le Louvre?
2. Qu'est-ce que c'est que le Tour de France?

3. Qu'est-ce que c'est qu'un symbole?
4. Qu'est-ce que c'est que la Sorbonne?

13.
1. —Quels restaurants aimes-tu?
   —J'aime les restaurants français.
2. —Quels films aimes-tu?
   —J'aime les films d'aventure.
3. —Quelles peintures sont bonnes?
   —Les peintures impressionnistes sont bonnes.

4. —Quel livre est intéressant?
   —Ce livre de photos est intéressant.
5. —Quelle robe est jolie?
   —Cette robe bleue est jolie.

14.
1. Quelle
2. Quels (Qui)
3. Qui
4. Quels
5. Quelle
6. Quelles

15.
1. Quel paysage!
2. Quelle girafe!
3. Quel arbre!
4. Quels éléphants!

16.
1. Lequel
2. Laquelle
3. Lesquels
4. Lesquelles

17.
1. À laquelle
2. Auquel
3. Auxquelles
4. Auxquels

18.
1. Duquel
2. De laquelle
3. Desquelles
4. Desquels

19.
1. Auxquelles
2. Combien
3. Lequel
4. Qui (Qui est-ce qui)
5. De qui
6. laquelle
7. Quel
8. De qui
9. De quoi
10. Quand
11. Qu'est-ce que c'est que
12. Que
13. À qui
14. À quelle heure (Quand)
15. Pourquoi
16. Qu'est-ce qui
17. Lesquels
18. Où

20.
1. Comment t'appelles-tu?
2. Quel âge as-tu?
3. Quand es-tu né(e)?
4. Où es-tu né(e)?
5. Pourquoi as-tu déménagé?
6. Combien de frères et de sœurs as-tu?
7. À quelle heure pars-tu pour l'école?
8. Avec qui sors-tu?
9. Avec quoi viens-tu en classe?
10. Quels sports aimes-tu?
11. Quelle sorte de musique aimes-tu?
12. Que fais-tu pour t'amuser?
13. Où vas-tu pendant les vacances d'été?
14. Où es-tu allé(e) l'été dernier?

Chapter 7

1.
1. Il ne va pas au théâtre.
2. Vous ne lirez pas le roman.
3. Je ne crains pas cet homme.
4. Je n'écoute pas le professeur.
5. Tu n'habitais pas à Paris en ce temps-là.
6. Vous n'arriveriez pas en retard.
7. Je ne me reposerai pas dimanche.
8. Elles ne se couchaient pas à onze heures tous les soirs.
9. Vous ne vous retrouverez pas à la gare.
10. Ils ne se moquent pas de lui.
11. Nous ne nous débrouillons pas bien.
12. Il ne s'habille pas bien.

2.
1. Nous ne voulons pas partir.
2. Elle n'aime pas chanter.
3. Elle ne veut pas se lever.
4. Tu ne vas pas t'habiller.

3.
1. Je n'ai pas acheté la robe.
2. Vous n'aviez pas compris la situation.
3. Ils n'ont pas écrit leurs devoirs.
4. Nous ne sommes pas restés ici.
5. Elle n'est pas tombée du cheval.
6. Ils ne seront pas venus à l'heure.
7. Elle ne s'est pas bien reposée.
8. Nous ne nous serons pas dépêchées.
9. Elles ne se sont pas plaintes de tout.
10. Vous ne vous êtes pas levés de bonne heure.

4.
1. Non, je n'ai pas (nous n'avons pas) reçu la lettre.
2. Non, il n'a pas lu l'histoire.
3. Non, je ne suis pas allée au cinéma hier.
4. Non, elles ne sont pas parties de bonne heure
5. Non, je ne me suis pas levé de bonne heure.
6. Non, elle ne s'est pas endormie.

5.
1. Est-ce que Georges ne vous parlera pas?
2. Ne lit-il pas le livre?
3. N'ouvre-t-elle pas la fenêtre?
4. Ne se dépêche-t-il pas?
5. Ne vous réveillez-vous pas?
6. N'avez-vous pas fini?
7. N'ont-elles pas craint cet homme?
8. Ne sont-elles pas rentrées de bonne heure?
9. Ne se sont-ils pas couchés?
10. Ne t'es-tu pas blessé?

6.
1. Ne vis-tu pas bien ici?
2. Ne saura-t-il pas la vérité?
3. Ne nous dépêchons-nous pas?
4. Ne vous levez-vous pas de bonne heure?
5. N'a-t-elle pas cru l'histoire?
6. Ne sont-elles pas revenues de bonne heure?
7. Ne s'est-il pas rasé?
8. Ne vous êtes-vous pas bien débrouillé?

7.
1. Oui, je parle (nous parlons) français.
2. Si, je parle (nous parlons) français.
3. Oui, ils viendront à l'heure.
4. Si, ils viendront à l'heure.
5. Oui, il a fini.
6. Si, il a fini.
7. Oui, elle se réveille.
8. Si, elle se réveille.

8.
1. Oui, il vit bien ici.
2. Si, ils sont venus.
3. Si, elle prendra le déjeuner ici.
4. Oui, il a lu ce roman.
5. Si, ils ont craint le criminel.

9.
1. Il ne sait le réparer.
2. Il ne cesse de pleuvoir.

3. Elle n'ose le dire.
4. Elle ne peut le faire.

10.
1. Il vous dit de ne pas avoir peur.
2. Elle vous demande de ne pas venir.
3. Elle vous dit de ne pas être heureux.
4. Je vous demande de ne pas leur parler.

5. Elle vous dit de ne pas le faire.
6. Elle affirme ne pas avoir vu ce film.
   (Elle affirme n'avoir pas vu ce film.)

11.
1. Elle ne dit jamais la même chose.
2. Jamais, elle ne le fait.
3. Elle n'a jamais chanté.
4. Je n'ai aucun espoir.
5. Marie ne trouve rien.
6. Marie n'a rien perdu.
7. Rien n'est dans la cuisine.
8. Rien ne s'est passé.
9. Il n'y a personne dans la boutique.

10. Il n'a vu personne.
11. Personne ne frappe à la porte.
12. Personne n'est arrivé.
13. Je n'ai ni crayon ni stylo.
14. Il ne parle ni à son père ni à sa mère.
15. Elle ne veut ni pain ni beurre.
16. Ni l'un ni l'autre n'est parti.
17. Pierre ne parle jamais de rien à personne.
18. Il ne va nulle part.

12.
1. Je n'ai jamais vu ce film.
2. Nous n'avons pas du tout dansé.
3. Il n'oubliera jamais cette leçon.
4. Il ne prend guère de vin.
5. Est-ce qu'il va jamais étudier?
6. Il n'a plus aucun CD.

7. Elle n'a ni amis ni ennemis.
8. Il n'a écrit que des poèmes.
9. Il n'a guère de temps.
10. Elle n'a que deux frères.
11. Elle ne chante plus de chansons.

13.
1. Non, il n'y a rien d'intéressant à faire.
2. Non, elle ne va jamais travailler.
3. Non, il n'y a personne ici.
4. Personne n'est venu.

5. Non, il n'a aucun livre.
6. Non, il n'a ni livres ni journaux.
7. Non, je n'ai guère le temps de le faire.
8. Non, elle n'est pas du tout riche.

14.
1. Il n'est pas riche non plus.
2. Ni elles non plus, elles n'ont pas beaucoup d'argent.
3. Marie ne le sait pas non plus.
4. Ni moi non plus, je ne viens pas.

5. Ni lui non plus, il ne la verra pas.
6. Elles ne mangent pas ici non plus.
7. Il ne l'a pas fait non plus.

15.
1. Jean ne mange pas d'épinards.
2. Jean n'aime pas jouer au tennis.
3. Jean ne sait (pas) quoi faire.
4. Jean ne se lève jamais de bonne heure.
5. Jean n'est pas allé au cinéma hier.
6. Jean ne s'est pas couché de bonne heure hier soir.

7. Jean n'a ni auto ni bicyclette.
8. Jean n'a acheté aucune chemise hier.
9. Jean n'achète jamais rien quand il est en vacances.
10. Jean ne parle à personne.

16. Answers will vary. Following are the possibilities:
1. Je joue souvent (quelquefois) au baseball.
   Je ne joue jamais (plus) au baseball.
   J'ai joué (Je n'ai pas joué) au baseball l'année dernière.
2. Je joue souvent (quelquefois) du piano.
   Je ne joue jamais (plus) du piano.
   J'ai joué (Je n'ai pas joué) du piano l'année dernière.

3. Je vais souvent (quelquefois) au cinéma.
Je ne vais jamais (plus) au cinéma.
Je suis allé(e) (Je ne suis pas allé[e]) au cinéma l'année dernière.
4. Je fais souvent (quelquefois) des voyages.
Je ne fais jamais (plus) de voyages.
J'ai fait un voyage (Je n'ai pas fait de voyage) l'année dernière.
5. Je dîne souvent (quelquefois) au restaurant.
Je ne dîne jamais (plus) au restaurant.
J'ai dîné (Je n'ai pas dîné) au restaurant l'année dernière.

17. Answers will vary. Following are some possibilities.
1. Je ne bois pas la bière. Je ne mange pas d'épinards.
2. Je n'aime ni la couleur orange ni la couleur noir.
3. Je n'ai aucune idée.
4. Aucun tapis (Aucune décoration) ne me plaît.
5. Je ne fais jamais de fautes.
6. Personne ne viendra vous voir ce soir. (Personne n'est d'accord avec vous.)
7. Rien ne lui plaît.
8. Je n'ai jamais fait de ski.
9. Je n'ose dire la vérité.

Chapter 8

1.
1. Elle parle français.
2. Il chante bien.
3. Ils jouent de la guitare.
4. Elles étudient à la Faculté de Médecine.
5. Ils vont en vacances.
6. Ils sont intéressants.
7. Elles sont belles.
8. Ils jouent dans le jardin.

2.
1. Êtes-vous content, Monsieur?
2. Es-tu malheureuse, Marie?
3. Êtes-vous paresseux, Jean et Georges?
4. Es-tu fatigué, Jean?
5. Êtes-vous contents, Monsieur et Madame Leblanc?

3.
1. On va au cinéma.
2. On mange une pizza.
3. On discute politique.
4. On écoute des chansons.
5. On est content(s).
6. On s'amuse bien.

4.
1. la
2. les
3. le
4. les
5. les
6. l'
7. les
8. l'
9. le
10. la

5.
1. Pierre les résout.
2. Je l'écris.
3. Anne le lit.
4. Ils les font chaque soir.
5. Nous les aimons.
6. Tu la comprends.
7. Vous les aidez.
8. Tu l'étudies cinq fois par semaine.
9. Anne et Marie les préparent bien.
10. Elles le reçoivent.

6.
1. Oui, je le pense.
2. Non, je ne le crois pas.
3. Oui, je le pense.
4. Non, je ne le crois pas.
5. Oui, je le sais.

7.   1. l'   3. l'   4. le
         2. le

8.   1. Oui, Paul me parle.
         2. Oui, Jean m'écoute.
         3. Oui, il vous (te) dit bonjour.
         4. Oui, il t'invite (vous invite).
         5. Oui, elle vous (nous) voit.
         6. Oui, elle vous (nous) appelle.
         7. Oui, elle me répond.
         8. Oui, il m'écoute.
         9. Oui, ils nous regardent.
        10. Oui, ils nous écrivent.

9.   1. Il m'apporte des fleurs.
         2. Il nous invite à dîner.
         3. Il vous aide.
         4. Il te donne des cadeaux.
         5. Il nous respecte.
         6. Il me téléphone souvent.
         7. Il vous prête ses outils.
         8. Il t'écoute toujours.

10. 1. Elle lui donne un livre.
         2. Elle leur donne des photos.
         3. Elle lui donne un collier.
         4. Elle leur donne des cravates.
         5. Elle lui donne un bracelet.
         6. Elle lui donne des livres.

11. 1. la   4. les   6. lui
         2. lui   5. leur   7. la, lui
         3. le

12. 1. Il y va.   3. Elle y sera.   5. Il y répond.
         2. Le livre y est.   4. Il y montera.   6. Il y obéit.

13. 1. Oui, j'y réponds.
         2. Oui, je leur obéis.
         3. Oui, j'y obéis.
         4. Oui, je lui réponds.
         5. Oui, j'y réfléchis.

14. 1. Nous en sortons.
         2. Elle en vient.
         3. Ils en sortiront.
         4. Il en a.
         5. Elle en choisit.
         6. Elle en achète.
         7. Il en parle.
         8. Il en est fier.
         9. Elles en ont beaucoup.
        10. Il en a un peu.
        11. Elle en achète une douzaine.
        12. Il en prend quatre.
        13. Il en a plusieurs.
        14. Elle en a quelques-uns.
        15. Il en a quelques-unes.

15. 1. Nous y allons.
         2. Il leur répond.
         3. Nous en avons besoin.
         4. Les valises y sont.
         5. Elle y répond.
         6. J'en ai plusieurs.
         7. Il lui parle.
         8. Elle en a quelques-unes.
         9. Il y en a beaucoup ici.

16. 1. Elle me les montre.
         2. Il nous le sert.
         3. Elle te l'envoie.
         4. Il nous la dit.
         5. Il vous l'apporte.
         6. Il le lui envoie.
         7. Elle les leur donne.
         8. Elle t'en donne.
         9. Il vous en pose.
        10. Il lui en donne plusieurs.
        11. Il m'en apporte.
        12. Elle m'y attend.
        13. Il nous y rencontre.
        14. Il y a en a quatre.

17.
1. Elle se la rappelle.
2. Il se les brosse.
3. Vous vous la lavez.
4. Elles se les lavent.
5. Elle s'en souvient.
6. Il se la fait faire.

18.
1. Le médecin m'en donne chaque semaine.
2. Le vendeur l'y rencontre.
3. Le professeur la leur explique.
4. Le banquier lui en prête.
5. Le bijoutier te le vend.
6. Le garçon leur en apporte trois.
7. L'avocat les leur donne.
8. Le biologiste y en fait.
9. Le facteur nous l'apporte chaque matin.
10. Le pharmacien le lui donne.
11. L'épicier vous en vend.
12. Le marchand de fruits les lui vend.
13. Le chauffeur de taxi les y rencontre.
14. Le conducteur les leur vend.

19.
1. Il ne le fait pas.
2. Les y cherchez-vous?
3. Ne l'entend-il pas?
4. Ne l'y mange pas!
5. Les voilà.
6. Elle me l'expliquera.
7. Il ne nous la répète pas.
8. Je lui en avais donné.
9. Ne l'y a-t-elle pas attendu?
10. Elle leur en écrivait.
11. Il ne l'aurait pas lu.
12. Il l'a crue.
13. Les as-tu écrits?
14. Elles les y ont prises.
15. Elle la lui aura dite.
16. Il l'a écouté chanter.
17. Je l'ai fait venir.

20.
1. Je voudrais l'acheter.
2. Je voudrais le lui donner.
3. Je vais leur parler.
4. Je vais les y mettre.
5. Elle va en avoir honte.
6. Il me dit de ne pas l'acheter.
7. Il me demande de ne pas lui en parler.

21.
1. Je la regarde jouer du piano.
2. Je l'ai entendu pleurer.
3. Je le regarde le préparer.
4. Je la laisse le finir.
5. Je l'ai laissée le finir.
6. Je l'ai entendu la chanter.
7. Il le fait faire.
8. Il l'a fait construire.
9. Il la lui a fait construire.

22.
1. Parlez-moi!
2. Lisez-la!
3. Donne-le-lui!
4. Parle-lui-en!
5. Allez-y!
6. Achète-le-toi!

23.
1. D'accord, lisez-la!
2. D'accord, parlez-nous-en (parlez-m'en)!
3. D'accord, écrivez-les-lui!
4. D'accord, répondez-y!
5. D'accord, allez-y!
6. D'accord, parlez-leur-en!
7. D'accord, donnez-nous-en (donnez-m'en)!

24.
1. Il ne lui obéit pas.
2. Il en a trop.
3. Elle y est allée.
4. Elle les y a mis.
5. Il ne la leur dit pas.
6. Elle n'y répond pas.
7. Ne l'écoute pas!
8. Il se le rappelle.
9. Il y en a beaucoup.
10. Elle y en a mis douze.
11. Donnez-m'en!
12. Lui en parlez-vous?
13. Je vais les lui donner.
14. Donnez-les-leur.
15. La lui as-tu donnée?
16. Ne lui en parle-t-elle pas?

25.
1. Pierre ne les a pas lavées.
Il ne les lave pas maintenant.
Il va les laver plus tard.
2. Anne ne la lui a pas écrite.
Elle ne la lui écrit pas maintenant.
Elle va la lui écrire plus tard.
3. M. Leblanc ne l'a pas peinte.
Il ne la peint pas maintenant.
Il va la peindre plus tard.
4. M. et Mme Leblanc n'y en ont pas acheté.
Ils n'y en achètent pas maintenant.
Ils vont y en acheter plus tard.

5. Anne et Pierre ne l'y ont pas rangée.
Ils ne l'y rangent pas maintenant.
Ils vont l'y ranger plus tard.
6. Mme Leblanc ne les y a pas jetées.
Elle ne les y jette pas maintenant.
Elle va les y jeter plus tard.
7. Marie ne leur en a pas donné.
Elle ne leur en donne pas maintenant.
Elle va leur en donner plus tard.
8. Mme Leblanc ne les y a pas plantées.
Elle ne les y plante pas maintenant.
Elle va les y planter plus tard.

26. Answers will vary. Following are the possibilities.
1. Oui, je leur en écris.
Non, je ne leur en écris pas.
2. Oui, je leur en ai écrit une cette semaine.
Non, je ne leur en ai pas écrit une cette semaine.
3. Oui, je les y ai achetés.
Non, je ne les y ai pas achetés.
4. Oui, j'y vais souvent.
Non, je n'y vais pas souvent.
5. Oui, j'y suis allé(e) hier.
Non, je n'y suis pas allé(e) hier.
6. Oui, j'y en achète.
Non, je n'y en achète pas.
7. Oui, je lui en ai donné un.
Non, je ne lui en ai pas donné un.
8. Oui, je les aime.
Non, je ne les aime pas.

9. Oui, il (elle) m'en donne beaucoup.
Non, il (elle) ne m'en donne pas beaucoup.
10. Oui, je me la rappelle.
Non, je ne me la rappelle pas.
11. Oui, je la leur dis.
Non, je ne la leur dis pas.
12. Oui, j'y habiterai l'année prochaine.
Non, je n'y habiterai pas l'année prochaine.
13. Oui, j'y réfléchis.
Non, je n'y réfléchis pas.
14. Oui, j'en achèterai plusieurs samedi prochain.
Non, je n'en achèterai pas plusieurs samedi prochain.
15. Oui, je vais le faire ce week-end.
Non, je ne vais pas le faire ce week-end.

27.
1. m'
2. nous
3. te
4. se
5. se
6. vous
7. me
8. nous
9. s'
10. t'

28.
1. Moi
2. toi
3. Lui
4. moi
5. lui
6. eux
7. vous
8. elles

29.
1. C'est moi qui ai envoyé les invitations.
Moi, j'ai envoyé les invitations.
2. C'est nous qui avons acheté le cadeau.
Elle et moi, nous avons acheté le cadeau.
3. Ce sont elles qui s'occupent de la musique.
Elles, elles s'occupent de la musique.
4. Ce sont eux qui préparent les sandwichs.
Eux, ils préparent les sandwichs.

5. C'est lui qui va faire le gâteau.
Lui, il va faire le gâteau.
6. C'est vous qui allez chercher les boissons.
Lui et toi, vous allez chercher les boissons.
7. C'est elle qui va faire les décorations.
Elle, elle va faire les décorations.
8. C'est toi qui vas faire la présentation du cadeau.
Toi, tu vas faire la présentation du cadeau.

30.
1. Je le ferai moi-même.
2. Il le fera lui-même.
3. Les garçons le feront eux-mêmes.
4. Nous le ferons nous-mêmes.
5. Chacun pour soi.

31.
1. Oui, j'y pense (nous y pensons).
2. Oui, j'ai (nous avons) peur de lui.
3. Oui, je partirai (nous partirons) sans eux.
4. Oui, j'en ai (nous en avons) honte.
5. Oui, je pense (nous pensons) à elle.
6. Oui, j'y vais (nous y allons).
7. Oui, c'est elles (ce sont elles) qui parlent.
8. Oui, ils vont chez elle.
9. Oui, elle va avec lui.
10. Oui, j'en ai (nous en avons) besoin.
11. Je me présente à lui.

32.
1. Ce sont les miens. Où sont les tiens?
2. Je n'aime pas la mienne. Aimez-vous la vôtre?
3. Il a pensé aux siens et elles ont pensé aux leurs.
4. J'ai besoin des miens et vous avez besoin des vôtres.
5. La nôtre est plus petite que la tienne.
6. Nous avons les nôtres. Avez-vous les vôtres?
7. Il a parlé de la sienne et tu as parlé de la tienne.
8. J'ai besoin de la leur.
9. Pierre va chercher les siennes et les miennes.
10. Vous mettez le vôtre et je mets le mien.
11. Nous sommes fiers du nôtre et ils sont fiers du leur.
12. Elle préfère les nôtres aux vôtres.
13. Il a cherché le sien et les filles ont cherché le leur.
14. Le tien est meilleur que le mien.
15. Il a téléphoné à la sienne et nous avons téléphoné à la nôtre.

33.
1. Ce sont les vôtres.
2. C'est le mien.
3. C'est la tienne.
4. C'est la nôtre.
5. C'est la sienne.
6. C'est le sien.
7. Ce sont les miennes.
8. Ce sont les leurs.

34. Answers will vary. Following are some possibilities.
1. Mon professeur de français est vieux. Le tien (Le sien, Le vôtre, Le leur) est jeune.
2. Ton ordinateur marche bien. Le mien (Le sien, Le leur, Le nôtre) marche mal.
3. Mes amis sont intelligents. Les tiens (Les siens, Les leurs, Les vôtres) sont stupides.
4. Ma sœur est grande. La tienne (La sienne, La leur, La vôtre) est petite.
    Mon frère est petit. Le tien (Le sien, Le leur, Le vôtre) est grand.
5. Ton frère est brun. Le mien (Le sien, Le leur, Le vôtre) est blond.
    Ta sœur est blonde. La mienne (La sienne, La leur, La nôtre) est brune.
6. Mes amies sont fortes. Les tiennes (Les siennes, Les leurs, Les vôtres) sont faibles.

35.
1. Non, c'est celle de ma sœur.
2. Non, c'est celui de mon ami.
3. Non, ce sont ceux de mon frère.
4. Non, ce sont celles de ma mère.
5. Non, c'est celui de mon amie.
6. Non, c'est celle de mon oncle.

36.
1. Celles-ci, celles-là
2. Celui-ci, celui-là
3. Celles-ci, celles-là
4. Celui-ci, celui-là
5. Celle-ci, celle-là
6. Ceux-ci, ceux-là
7. Celui-ci, celui-là
8. Celle-ci, celle-là

37.
1. Il
2. c'
3. Elle
4. C'
5. C'
6. Ce

38.   1. Ceci   4. ce   6. Cela (Ça)
        2. Cela   5. Cela (Ça)   7. ceci (cela)
        3. C'

39.   1. qui   4. qui   7. qu'
        2. que   5. que   8. qui
        3. qu'   6. qui

40.   1. Voilà un garçon qui est sportif.
        2. La dame qui entre est la femme de mon professeur.
        3. L'église qui est au centre de la ville est grande.
        4. La jeune fille qui danse est très intelligente.
        5. Je connais cette femme qui donne de bons discours.

41.   1. Voilà le restaurant que Pierre préfère.   4. Le film que nous avons vu est américain.
        2. Le journal que je lis est parisien.   5. C'est un médecin que je connais.
        3. La robe qu'elle a achetée est très chère.

42.   Answers will vary. Following are some possibilities.
        1. J'aime les restaurants qui servent les mets italiens.
        2. Je connais quelqu'un qui pourra vous aider.
        3. J'aime les films qui traitent de sujets comiques.
        4. _____ est un acteur que j'admire.
        5. _____ est une actrice que j'aime bien.
        6. J'aime les gens qui sont honnêtes.

43.   1. ce qu'   3. ce qui   5. ce qui
        2. ce qui   4. ce que   6. ce qu'

44.   1. Dis-moi ce qui t'intéresse.   4. Dis-moi ce que tu fais les samedis.
        2. Dis-moi ce que tu trouves amusant.   5. Dis-moi ce que tu penses des politiciens.
        3. Dis-moi ce qui te fait peur.   6. Dis-moi ce qui te rend heureux (heureuse).

45.   1. qui   4. lequel   6. lesquels
        2. qui   5. lesquelles   7. lesquels
        3. laquelle

46.   1. Voilà le garçon avec qui je suis sorti.
        2. Voilà la maison dans laquelle j'ai habité.
        3. Les hommes à qui j'ai écrit sont mes anciens professeurs.
        4. C'est le pinceau avec lequel l'artiste travaille.
        5. Voilà un morceau de papier sur lequel il a dessiné.
        6. Le restaurant dans lequel Paul entre est très petit.
        7. La fille chez qui nous allons est gentille.
        8. Voilà les tables sur lesquelles Marie a mis des fleurs.
        9. Le musée devant lequel il attend son ami est formidable.
       10. Le théâtre auquel nous sommes allés est très vieux.
       11. La conférence à laquelle elle a assisté était intéressante.
       12. Les lettres auxquelles il a répondu étaient urgentes.
       13. Les hommes à qui il a écrit sont avocats.
       14. Les musées auxquels je suis allée sont grands.

47.   1. L'appartement où j'habite est très petit.
        2. La boulangerie où j'entre est bonne.

3. Le bureau où je vais se trouve au centre de la ville.

4. Les restaurants où nous dînons ne sont pas chers.

5. Les églises où nous allons sont vieilles.

48.
1. Le garçon dont le père est mort est mon ami.

2. Le musée dont le nom m'échappe est célèbre.

3. La dame dont nous cherchons le chien est une amie de ma mère.

4. L'homme dont les usines sont à Lyon habite à Paris.

5. J'aime ce jardin dont les fleurs l'embellissent.

6. Le crayon dont vous vous servez n'est pas bon.

7. Les livres dont vous m'avez parlé sont intéressants.

8. La peinture dont vous avez envie est très chère.

49.
1. Voilà une fille dont le père est médecin.

2. Voilà le mannequin dont les robes sont jolies.

3. Voilà les garçons dont vous connaissez la sœur.

4. Voilà un professeur dont la fille est chimiste.

5. Voilà un garçon dont le père est mort.

6. Voilà une femme dont j'admire la beauté.

7. Voilà un peintre dont le tableau est cher.

8. C'est un beau tableau dont nous avons parlé.

9. C'est un livre dont vous avez envie.

10. As-tu étudié le poème dont il a parlé?

11. C'est un livre dont j'ai besoin.

12. J'ai vu la jeune fille dont ils ont parlé.

13. C'est un beau poème dont nous avons lu quelques passages.

50.
1. C'est la fille à la mère de laquelle j'ai parlé.

2. C'est un homme avec la fille duquel je suis sorti.

3. Il y a une boutique ici près de laquelle se trouve un bureau de tabac.

4. Il a fait un discours à cause duquel j'ai pleuré.

5. Voilà les jeunes filles avec le frère desquelles je suis sortie.

51.
1. ce dont	3. à quoi	5. ce dont
2. quoi	4. quoi	

52.
1. Ce que	6. dont	11. quoi
2. qui	7. ce qui	12. qui
3. dont	8. ce qu'	13. avec qui
4. où (dans laquelle)	9. duquel	14. avec lesquelles
5. que	10. dont (de qui)	

53.
1. Je connais un homme qui parle arabe.

2. Je connais une femme que tout le monde admire.

3. Je connais un garçon dont la mère est médecin.

4. Je sais de quoi il s'agit.

5. Je comprends ce que vous dites.

6. Nous arrivons à la ville où Pierre habite.

7. Les étudiants auxquels nous parlons sont intelligents.

54.

1. N'importe qui
2. Quelqu'un
3. Tout le monde (Chacun)
4. On
5. quelque chose
6. tout
7. Les autres
8. tous
9. quelques-uns
10. l'une et l'autre
11. ni l'un(e) ni l'autre
12. Certaines
13. n'importe quoi
14. autre chose
15. Tout ce que
16. plusieurs
17. quelques-unes
18. Chacune
19. Quelqu'un d'autre
20. Les un(e)s, les autres
21. l'un à l'autre
22. l'une ou l'autre
23. N'importe qui
24. la même
25. Aucune
26. Personne (Nul)
27. Tout
28. Rien
29. M. un tel
30. Quiconque
31. autrui
32. autre chose

Chapter 9

1.
1. Il va en voiture.
2. Il ira loin.
3. Je vais mal.
4. Il va mieux aujourd'hui.
5. Ce chapeau vous (te) va bien.
6. Comment allez-vous? (Comment vas-tu? Comment ça va? Ça va?)
7. Je vais bien.
8. Il va à la pêche.

2.
1. J'ai soif.
2. J'ai faim.
3. J'ai sommeil.
4. J'ai froid.
5. J'ai chaud.
6. J'ai mal à la tête.
7. J'ai mal aux dents.
8. J'ai tort. (J'ai honte.)
9. J'ai raison.
10. J'ai tort.

3.
1. J'avais beau venir. Personne n'était la.
2. Elle a peur de cet homme.
3. Il a honte de son travail.
4. Nous avions raison.
5. J'ai mal à la tête.
6. Les filles ont l'air fatiguées.
7. Pierre a de la chance.
8. Le train a une demi-heure de retard.
9. L'avion a dix minutes d'avance.
10. Il a l'occasion d'aller à la Martinique.
11. Qu'avez-vous? (Qu'as-tu?)
12. Quel âge avez-vous? (Quel âge as-tu?)
13. Il a cinquante ans.
14. Elle a besoin du livre.
15. La maison a vingt mètres de hauteur.
16. Nous avons chaud.
17. Les enfants ont sommeil.

4.
1. Elle est en train d'étudier.
2. Les garçons sont de Paris.
3. Cela m'est égal.
4. Nous serons de retour demain.
5. Ces livres sont à elle.
6. Ça y est.

5.
1. fait des économies.
2. faisons attention.
3. fait le ménage.
4. fais une promenade.
5. fais fortune.
6. font les courses.
7. fais des économies.
8. fait les devoirs.
9. fait la vaisselle.
10. font un voyage.
11. fais le ménage.

6.
1. Il fait chaud.
2. Il fait frais.
3. Il fait du soleil.
4. Il fait du brouillard.
5. Il fait nuit.
6. Il fait de son mieux.
7. Ce médicament vous (te) fera du bien.
8. Je me suis fait mal au bras.
9. Nous avons fait la queue pendant une heure.
10. Je l'ai fait exprès.
11. Ça ne fait rien.
12. Ils ont fait semblant de ne pas entendre.

7.
1. Je dois cinq dollars à Marie.
2. Il doit venir.
3. Elle devait partir pour New York.
4. Il doit être malade.
5. Vous auriez (Tu aurais) dû venir.
6. Il devrait étudier.
7. Je peux le faire.
8. Nous n'avons pas pu finir.
9. J'aurais pu vous aider (t'aider).
10. Il a pu le faire.
11. Nous avons su la vérité.
12. Elle a voulu ouvrir la porte.
13. Il n'a pas voulu y aller.

8.
1. vit
2. demeurons
3. vit
4. demeurez
5. vivent

9.
1. Elle habite Paris.
2. Ils habitent la Suisse.
3. Vous habitez New York.
4. Nous habitons le Mexique.

10.
1. joue
2. jouons du
3. jouent aux
4. jouez de
5. jouent
6. jouez au

11.
1. manque
2. manque à
3. manquez de
4. manquent
5. manquent à

12.
1. Il a manqué le train.
2. Elle me manque.
3. Je lui manque.
4. Ils manquent de patience.

13.
1. du
2. à
3. de
4. aux
5. à

14.
1. Je pense à elle.
2. Qu'en pense-t-il?
3. Elle pense à lui.
4. Que pense-t-elle de lui?
5. Nous y pensons.
6. Que pensent-elles d'eux?

15.
1. sort
2. s'en va
3. laisse
4. m'en vais
5. quitte
6. sort
7. pars

16.
1. a passé
2. s'est passé
3. nous sommes passé(e)s de
4. se sont passées
5. a passé
6. s'est passé
7. s'est passé de

17.
1. Le film me plaît.
2. Les peintures modernes lui plaisent.
3. Le cinéma lui plaît.
4. La pièce leur plaît.
5. Le livre te plaît.

18.
1. Je me souviens de cette occasion.
2. Je me souviens de cette fille.
3. Ils se souviennent de cette soirée.
4. Vous vous souvenez de la guerre.
5. Nous nous en souvenons.

19.
1. sert
2. se sert d'
3. sert
4. sert
5. se sert de

20.
1. savons
2. connaît
3. sais
4. Savez
5. connaissent
6. sait
7. connaissez
8. Connais, sais

21.
1. Il a su la vérité.
2. Il a connu cette femme.
3. Elle savait la vérité.
4. Elle connaissait ces enfants.

22.
1. viens de
2. viennent de
3. venez d'
4. venons de
5. viens de
6. vient d'

23.
1. Je venais de chanter cette chanson.
2. Elles venaient de sortir.
3. Vous veniez d'arriver.
4. Nous venions de rentrer d'Espagne.
5. Tu venais de manger.
6. Il venait d'entrer.

Verb Charts

REGULAR VERBS

Infinitive *(Infinitif)*	**parler**	**finir**	**répondre**
Present participle *(Participe présent)*	parlant	finissant	répondant
Past participle *(Participe passé)*	parlé	fini	répondu
Present *(Présent)*	je parle	je finis	je réponds
	tu parles	tu finis	tu réponds
	il parle	il finit	il répond
	nous parlons	nous finissons	nous répondons
	vous parlez	vous finissez	vous répondez
	ils parlent	ils finissent	ils répondent
Present subjunctive *(Présent du subjonctif)*	je parle	je finisse	je réponde
	tu parles	tu finisses	tu répondes
	il parle	il finisse	il réponde
	nous parlions	nous finissions	nous répondions
	vous parliez	vous finissiez	vous répondiez
	ils parlent	ils finissent	ils répondent
Imperfect *(Imparfait)*	je parlais	je finissais	je répondais
	tu parlais	tu finissais	tu répondais
	il parlait	il finissait	il répondait
	nous parlions	nous finissions	nous répondions
	vous parliez	vous finissiez	vous répondiez
	ils parlaient	ils finissaient	ils répondaient
Future *(Futur)*	je parlerai	je finirai	je répondrai
	tu parleras	tu finiras	tu répondras
	il parlera	il finira	il répondra
	nous parlerons	nous finirons	nous répondrons
	vous parlerez	vous finirez	vous répondrez
	ils parleront	ils finiront	ils répondront

Conditional (*Conditionnel*)	je parlerais	je finirais	je répondrais
	tu parlerais	tu finirais	tu répondrais
	il parlerait	il finirait	il répondrait
	nous parlerions	nous finirions	nous répondrions
	vous parleriez	vous finiriez	vous répondriez
	ils parleraient	ils finiraient	ils répondraient
Imperative (*Impératif*)	parle	finis	réponds
	parlons	finissons	répondons
	parlez	finissez	répondez
Conversational past (*Passé composé*)	j'ai parlé	j'ai fini	j'ai répondu
	tu as parlé	tu as fini	tu as répondu
	il a parlé	il a fini	il a répondu
	nous avons parlé	nous avons fini	nous avons répondu
	vous avez parlé	vous avez fini	vous avez répondu
	ils ont parlé	ils ont fini	ils ont répondu
Pluperfect (*Plus-que-parfait*)	j'avais parlé	j'avais fini	j'avais répondu
	tu avais parlé	tu avais fini	tu avais répondu
	il avait parlé	il avait fini	il avait répondu
	nous avions parlé	nous avions fini	nous avions répondu
	vous aviez parlé	vous aviez fini	vous aviez répondu
	ils avaient parlé	ils avaient fini	ils avaient répondu
Future perfect (*Futur antérieur*)	j'aurai parlé	j'aurai fini	j'aurai répondu
	tu auras parlé	tu auras fini	tu auras répondu
	il aura parlé	il aura fini	il aura répondu
	nous aurons parlé	nous aurons fini	nous aurons répondu
	vous aurez parlé	vous aurez fini	vous aurez répondu
	ils auront parlé	ils auront fini	ils auront répondu
Past conditional (*Passé du conditionnel*)	j'aurais parlé	j'aurais fini	j'aurais répondu
	tu aurais parlé	tu aurais fini	tu aurais répondu
	il aurait parlé	il aurait fini	il aurait répondu
	nous aurions parlé	nous aurions fini	nous aurions répondu
	vous auriez parlé	vous auriez fini	vous auriez répondu
	ils auraient parlé	ils auraient fini	ils auraient répondu
Past subjunctive (*Passé du subjonctif*)	j'aie parlé	j'aie fini	j'aie répondu
	tu aies parlé	tu aies fini	tu aies répondu
	il ait parlé	il ait fini	il ait répondu
	nous ayons parlé	nous ayons fini	nous ayons répondu
	vous ayez parlé	vous ayez fini	vous ayez répondu
	ils aient parlé	ils aient fini	ils aient répondu
Literary past (*Passé simple*)	je parlai	je finis	je répondis
	tu parlas	tu finis	tu répondis
	il parla	il finit	il répondit
	nous parlâmes	nous finîmes	nous répondîmes
	vous parlâtes	vous finîtes	vous répondîtes
	ils parlèrent	ils finirent	ils répondirent

Imperfect subjunctive (*Imparfait du subjonctif*)	je parlasse	je finisse	je répondisse
	tu parlasses	tu finisses	tu répondisses
	il parlât	il finît	il répondît
	nous parlassions	nous finissions	nous répondissions
	vous parlassiez	vous finissiez	vous répondissiez
	ils parlassent	ils finissent	ils répondissent
Past anterior (*Passé antérieur*)	j'eus parlé	j'eus fini	j'eus répondu
	tu eus parlé	tu eus fini	tu eus répondu
	il eut parlé	il eut fini	il eut répondu
	nous eûmes parlé	vous eûmes fini	nous eûmes répondu
	vous eûtes parlé	vous eûtes fini	vous eûtes répondu
	ils eurent parlé	ils eurent fini	ils eurent répondu
Pluperfect subjunctive (*Plus-que-parfait du subjonctif*)	j'eusse parlé	j'eusse fini	j'eusse répondu
	tu eusses parlé	tu eusses fini	tu eusses répondu
	il eût parlé	il eût fini	il eût répondu
	nous eussions parlé	nous eussions fini	nous eussions répondu
	vous eussiez parlé	vous eussiez fini	vous eussiez répondu
	ils eussent parlé	ils eussent fini	ils eussent répondu
Passé surcomposé	j'ai eu parlé	j'ai eu fini	j'ai eu répondu
	tu as eu parlé	tu as eu fini	tu as eu répondu
	il a eu parlé	il a eu fini	il a eu répondu
	nous avons eu parlé	nous avons eu fini	nous avons eu répondu
	vous avez eu parlé	vous avez eu fini	vous avez eu répondu
	ils ont eu parlé	ils ont eu fini	ils ont eu répondu

VERBS WITH SPELLING CHANGES

acheter

Present	j'achète, tu achètes, il achète, nous achetons, vous achetez, ils achètent
Present subjunctive	j'achète, tu achètes, il achète, nous achetions, vous achetiez, ils achètent
Future	il achètera, nous achèterons, ils achèteront

appeler

Present	j'appelle, tu appelles, il appelle, nous appelons, vous appelez, ils appellent
Present subjunctive	j'appelle, tu appelles, il appelle, nous appelions, vous appeliez, ils appellent
Future	il appellera, nous appellerons, ils appelleront

commencer (and all verbs ending in **-cer**)

Present	je commence, tu commences, il commence, nous commençons, vous commencez, ils commencent
Imperfect	il commençait, nous commencions, ils commençaient
Literary past	il commença, nous commençâmes, ils commencèrent

espérer (**préférer, répéter, protéger,** etc.)

Present	j'espère, tu espères, il espère, nous espérons, vous espérez, ils espèrent
Present subjunctive	j'espère, tu espères, il espère, nous espérions, vous espériez, ils espèrent

essayer (and all verbs ending in **-ayer, oyer, uyer**)
(Note also alternate forms: **j'essaye, j'essayerai,** etc., for verbs ending in **-ayer.**)

Present	j'essaie, tu essaies, il essaie, nous essayons, vous essayez, ils essaient
Present subjunctive	j'essaie, tu essaies, il essaie, nous essayions, vous essayiez, ils essaient
Future	il essaiera, nous essaierons, ils essaieront

jeter

Present	je jette, tu jettes, il jette, nous jetons, vous jetez, ils jettent
Present subjunctive	je jette, tu jettes, il jette, nous jetions, vous jetiez, ils jettent
Future	il jettera, nous jetterons, ils jetteront

lever (**mener, emmener, geler,** etc.)

Present	je lève, tu lèves, il lève, nous levons, vous levez, ils lèvent
Present subjunctive	je lève, tu lèves, il lève, nous levions, vous leviez, ils lèvent
Future	il lèvera, nous lèverons, ils lèveront

manger (and other verbs ending in **-ger**)

Present	je mange, tu manges, il mange, nous mangeons, vous mangez, ils mangent
Present subjunctive	je mange, tu manges, il mange, nous mangions, vous mangiez, ils mangent
Imperfect	il mangeait, nous mangions, ils mangeaient
Literary past	il mangea, nous mangeâmes, ils mangèrent

In this list, the number at the right of each verb corresponds to the number of the verb, or of a similarly conjugated verb, in the table which follows. An asterisk (*) indicates that **être** is used as the auxiliary verb in the compound tenses. A dash plus an asterisk (—*) indicates that the verb is conjugated with **avoir** or **être** in compound tenses.

accueillir	12	croire	11	offrir	25	revoir	41
acquérir	1	cueillir	12	ouvrir	25	rire	32
admettre	22	découvrir	25	—*paraître	8	rompre	33
*aller	2	décrire	15	parcourir	9	savoir	34
*s'en aller	2	détruire	7	*partir	26	secourir	9
apercevoir	31	*devenir	39	*parvenir	39	sentir	26
—*apparaître	8	devoir	13	peindre	10	*se sentir	26
appartenir	39	dire	14	permettre	22	servir	26
apprendre	30	—*disparaître	8	plaindre	10	*se servir de	26
*s'asseoir	3	dormir	26	*se plaindre	10	*sortir	26
atteindre	10	écrire	15	plaire	27	souffrir	25
avoir	4	élire	21	pleuvoir	28	soumettre	22
battre	5	*s'endormir	26	poursuivre	36	sourire	32
*se battre	5	envoyer	16	pouvoir	29	*se souvenir de	39
boire	6	être	17	prendre	30	suffire	35
combattre	5	faire	18	prévoir	41	suivre	36
comprendre	30	falloir	19	produire	7	surprendre	30
conduire	7	interdire	14	promettre	22	survivre	40
connaître	8	interrompre	33	recevoir	31	*se taire	27
conquérir	1	haïr	20	reconnaître	8	tenir	39
construire	7	joindre	10	reconstruire	7	traduire	7
contenir	39	lire	21	recouvrir	25	transmettre	22
convaincre	37	maintenir	39	*redevenir	39	vaincre	37
convenir	39	mentir	26	rejoindre	10	valoir	38
corrompre	33	mettre	22	remettre	22	*venir	39
courir	9	*mourir	23	reprendre	30	vivre	40
couvrir	25	*naître	24	retenir	39	voir	41
craindre	10	obtenir	39	*revenir	39	vouloir	42

IRREGULAR VERBS

Note: Only irregular forms are given for the following verbs. The conditional is always formed by adding the regular endings to the future stem. An asterisk (*) indicates that the verb is conjugated with **être** in auxiliary tenses.

[1]acquérir

Past participle	acquis
Present	j'acquiers, tu acquiers, il acquiert, nous acquérons, vous acquérez, ils acquièrent
Present subjunctive	j'acquière, tu acquières, il acquière, nous acquérions, vous acquériez, ils acquièrent
Future	il acquerra
Literary past	il acquit, ils acquirent

[2]*aller

Present	je vais, tu vas, il va, nous allons, vous allez, ils vont
Present subjunctive	j'aille, tu ailles, il aille, nous allions, vous alliez, ils aillent
Future	il ira
Imperative	va, allons, allez

[3]*s'asseoir

(There is another, less used conjugation for this verb: **je m'assois, nous nous assoyons, il s'assoira,** etc.)

Past participle	assis
Present	je m'assieds, tu t'assieds, il s'assied, nous nous asseyons, vous vous asseyez, ils s'asseyent
Present subjunctive	je m'asseye, tu t'asseyes, il s'asseye, nous nous asseyions, vous vous asseyiez, ils s'asseyent
Future	il s'assiéra
Imperative	assieds-toi, asseyons-nous, asseyez-vous
Literary past	il s'assit, ils s'assirent

[4]avoir

Present participle	ayant
Past participle	eu
Present	j'ai, tu as, il a, nous avons, vous avez, ils ont
Present subjunctive	j'aie, tu aies, il ait, nous ayons, vous ayez, ils aient
Future	il aura
Imperative	aie, ayons, ayez
Literary past	il eut, ils eurent

[5]battre

Present	je bats, tu bats, il bat, nous battons, vous battez, ils battent

[6]boire

Past participle	bu
Present	je bois, tu bois, il boit, nous buvons, vous buvez, ils boivent
Present subjunctive	je boive, tu boives, il boive, nous buvions, vous buviez, ils boivent
Literary past	il but, ils burent

[7]conduire

Past participle	conduit
Present	je conduis, tu conduis, il conduit, nous conduisons, vous conduisez, ils conduisent
Literary past	il conduisit, ils conduisirent

[8]connaître

Past participle	connu
Present	je connais, tu connais, il connaît, nous connaissons, vous connaissez, ils connaissent
Literary past	il connut, ils connurent

[9]courir

Past participle	couru
Present	je cours, tu cours, il court, nous courons, vous courez, ils courent
Future	il courra
Literary past	il courut, ils coururent

[10]craindre (and other verbs ending in -indre)

Past participle	craint
Present	je crains, tu crains, il craint, nous craignons, vous craignez, ils craignent
Literary past	il craignit, ils craignirent

[11]croire

Past participle	cru
Present	je crois, tu crois, il croit, nous croyons, vous croyez, ils croient
Present subjunctive	je croie, tu croies, il croie, nous croyions, vous croyiez, ils croient
Literary past	il crut, ils crurent

[12]cueillir

Present	je cueille, tu cueilles, il cueille, nous cueillons, vous cueillez, ils cueillent
Future	il cueillera

[13]devoir

Past participle	dû (*fem.* due)
Present	je dois, tu dois, il doit, nous devons, vous devez, ils doivent
Present subjunctive	je doive, tu doives, il doive, nous devions, vous deviez, ils doivent
Future	il devra
Literary past	il dut, ils durent

[14]dire

Past participle	dit
Present	je dis, tu dis, il dit, nous disons, vous dites, ils disent
Literary past	il dit, ils dirent

[15]écrire

Past participle	écrit
Present	j'écris, tu écris, il écrit, nous écrivons, vous écrivez, ils écrivent
Literary past	il écrivit, ils écrivirent

[16] envoyer

Present	j'envoie, tu envoies, il envoie, nous envoyons, vous envoyez, ils envoient
Present subjunctive	j'envoie, tu envoies, il envoie, nous envoyions, vous envoyiez, ils envoient
Future	il enverra

[17] être

Present participle	étant
Past participle	été
Present	je suis, tu es, il est, nous sommes, vous êtes, ils sont
Present subjunctive	je sois, tu sois, il soit, nous soyons, vous soyez, ils soient
Imperfect	il était
Future	il sera
Imperative	sois, soyons, soyez
Literary past	il fut, ils furent

[18] faire

Past participle	fait
Present	je fais, tu fais, il fait, nous faisons, vous faites, ils font
Present subjunctive	je fasse, tu fasses, il fasse, nous fassions, vous fassiez, ils fassent
Future	il fera
Literary past	il fit, ils firent

[19] falloir

Past participle	fallu
Present	il faut
Present subjunctive	il faille
Future	il faudra
Literary past	il fallut

[20] haïr

Past participle	haï
Present	je hais, tu hais, il hait, nous haïssons, vous haïssez, ils haïssent
Literary past	il haït, ils haïrent

[21] lire

Past participle	lu
Present	je lis, tu lis, il lit, nous lisons, vous lisez, ils lisent
Literary past	il lut, ils lurent

[22] mettre

Past participle	mis
Present	je mets, tu mets, il met, nous mettons, vous mettez, ils mettent
Literary past	il mit, ils mirent

[23] *mourir

Past participle	mort
Present	je meurs, tu meurs, il meurt, nous mourons, vous mourez, ils meurent
Present subjunctive	je meure, tu meures, il meure, nous mourions, vous mouriez, ils meurent
Future	il mourra
Literary past	il mourut, ils moururent

24*naître

Past participle	né
Present	je nais, tu nais, il naît, nous naissons, vous naissez, ils naissent
Literary past	il naquit, ils naquirent

25ouvrir

Past participle	ouvert
Present	j'ouvre, tu ouvres, il ouvre, nous ouvrons, vous ouvrez, ils ouvrent

26*partir

Present	je pars, tu pars, il part, nous partons, vous partez, ils partent
Literary past	il partit, ils partirent

27plaire (se taire: present, il se tait)

Past participle	plu
Present	je plais, tu plais, il plaît, nous plaisons, vous plaisez, ils plaisent
Literary past	il plut, ils plurent

28pleuvoir

Present participle	pleuvant
Past participle	plu
Present	il pleut
Present subjunctive	il pleuve
Future	il pleuvra
Literary past	il plut

29pouvoir

Past participle	pu
Present	je peux, tu peux, il peut, nous pouvons, vous pouvez, ils peuvent
Present subjunctive	je puisse, tu puisses, il puisse, nous puissions, vous puissiez, ils puissent
Future	il pourra
Literary past	il put, ils purent

30prendre

Past participle	pris
Present	je prends, tu prends, il prend, nous prenons, vous prenez, ils prennent
Present subjunctive	je prenne, tu prennes, il prenne, nous prenions, vous preniez, ils prennent
Literary past	il prit, ils prirent

31recevoir

Past participle	reçu
Present	je reçois, tu reçois, il reçoit, nous recevons, vous recevez, ils reçoivent
Present subjunctive	je reçoive, tu reçoives, il reçoive, nous recevions, vous receviez, ils reçoivent
Future	il recevra
Literary past	il reçut, ils reçurent

32rire

Past participle	ri
Present	je ris, tu ris, il rit, nous rions, vous riez, ils rient
Literary past	il rit, ils rirent

[33]rompre

Present	je romps, tu romps, il rompt, nous rompons, vous rompez, ils rompent
Literary past	il rompit, ils rompirent

[34]savoir

Present participle	sachant
Past participle	su
Present	je sais, tu sais, il sait, nous savons, vous savez, ils savent
Present subjunctive	je sache, tu saches, il sache, nous sachions, vous sachiez, ils sachent
Future	il saura
Imperative	sache, sachons, sachez
Literary past	il sut, ils surent

[35]suffire

Past participle	suffi
Present	je suffis, tu suffis, il suffit, nous suffisons, vous suffisez, ils suffisent
Literary past	il suffit, ils suffirent

[36]suivre

Past participle	suivi
Present	je suis, tu suis, il suit, nous suivons, vous suivez, ils suivent
Literary past	il suivit, ils suivirent

[37]vaincre

Present	je vaincs, tu vaincs, il vainc, nous vainquons, vous vainquez, ils vainquent
Literary past	il vainquit, ils vainquirent

[38]valoir

Past participle	valu
Present	je vaux, tu vaux, il vaut, nous valons, vous valez, ils valent
Present subjunctive	je vaille, tu vailles, il vaille, nous valions, vous valiez, ils vaillent
Future	il vaudra
Literary past	il valut, ils valurent

[39]*venir

Past participle	venu
Present	je viens, tu viens, il vient, nous venons, vous venez, ils viennent
Present subjunctive	je vienne, tu viennes, il vienne, nous venions, vous veniez, ils viennent
Future	il viendra
Literary past	il vint, ils vinrent

[40]vivre

Past participle	vécu
Present	je vis, tu vis, il vit, nous vivons, vous vivez, ils vivent
Literary past	il vécut, ils vécurent

[41]voir

Past participle	vu
Present	je vois, tu vois, il voit, nous voyons, vous voyez, ils voient
Present subjunctive	je voie, tu voies, il voie, nous voyions, vous voyiez, ils voient

Future	il verra
Literary past	il vit, ils virent

[42]vouloir

Past participle	voulu
Present	je veux, tu veux, il veut, nous voulons, vous voulez, ils veulent
Present subjunctive	je veuille, tu veuilles, il veuille, nous voulions, vous vouliez, ils veuillent
Future	il voudra
Imperative	veuille, veuillons, veuillez
Literary past	il voulut, ils voulurent

French Typographical Rules

	French	English
.	**le point**	*period*
?	**le point d'interrogation**	*question mark*
!	**le point d'exclamation**	*exclamation mark*
,	**la virgule**	*comma*
:	**le deux-points**	*colon*
;	**le point-virgule**	*semicolon*
'	**l'apostrophe**	*apostrophe*
*	**l'astérisque**	*asterisk*
( )	**les parenthèses**	*parentheses*
{ }	**les brochets**	*brackets*
/	**la barre oblique**	*oblique/slash*
—	**le tiret**	*em dash*
« »	**les guillemets**	*French quotation marks*
" "		*quotation marks*
…	**les points de suspension**	*French points of ellipses*
…		*points of ellipses*

As you can see in the preceding chart, almost all punctuation marks are the same as in English except for quotation marks.

French	English
« Comment ça va ? »	"How are you?"

La virgule *(comma)*

In French there is never a comma before a conjunction in a series whereas in English the comma is optional.

Il mange du bifeck, des haricots verts, des pommes de terre et de la salade pour le dîner.

He eats steak, green beans, potatoes, and salad for dinner.

The big difference in punctuation between French and English is in spacing. In English, there is no space between the word preceding the punctuation mark and the punctuation mark whereas in French, there is a thin space before the punctuation mark if it is composed of two parts. This space is not a normal word space. It is smaller than the English word space. It is called **une espace insécable** (a non-binding space). In many cases there is also a space after the punctuation mark.

This is the case for exclamation marks (!), question marks (?), colons (:), semicolons (;). the percentage mark (%), currency symbols ($, €), the number sign (#), and the **guillemets** (« »).

Faites attention !	*Pay attention!*
Comment va ta sœur ?	*How is your sister?*

Points of ellipses in English are separated by a space whereas in French, they are placed tightly together and join the preceding word.

French	English
...	. . .
Elle a acheté des pommes...	*She bought apples . . .*
pour le dîner.	*for dinner.*

Guillemets

If guillemets and punctuation marks appear together, the guillemet precedes the punctuation mark. Note that there is a thin space before and after the guillemets.

Il crie : « Au secours » !	*He shouts: "Help!"*

The **guillemets** are used at the beginning and end of a dialogue. Em dashes (**tirets**) are used in between.

French

«Bonjour, Marie ! Comment vas-to ?

— Salut Jean ! dit Marie.

— Es-tu alleé au concert samedi soir ?

— Non, jai étudié pour l'examen répond Marie.

— C'est dommage ».

English

"Hello Mary! How are you?"

"Hi John," said Mary.

"Did you go to the concert Saturday night?" asked John.

"No, I studied for an exam," Mary answered.

See Chapter 3 for use of periods and commas in numbers and dates.

As is the case for this book, if there is a mixture of French and English, then many times the French spacing rules are not applied.

Following is a chart that summarizes when to use a thin space before and after puntuation marks.

PUNCTUATION MARK	BEFORE	AFTER
l'astérisque devant un mot *asterisk before a word*	1 space	no space
l'astérisque après un mot *asterisk after a word*	no space	1 space
le deux-points *colon*	1 space	1 space
le point-virgule *semicolon*	1 space	1 space
la virgule *comma*	no space	1 space
le tiret *em dash*	1 space	1 space
les points de suspension au début d'une phrase *points of ellipsis at the beginning of a sentence*	no space	1 space
les points de suspension au milieu ou à la fin d'une phrase *points of suspension in the middle or at the end of a sentence*	no space	1 space
le point d'exclamation *exclamation mark*	1 space	1 space
la barre oblique *oblique*	no space	no space
les parenthèses/bracket (ouverture) *parenthesis/bracket (opening)*	1 space	no space

FRENCH TYPOGRAPHICAL RULES

PUNCTUATION MARK	BEFORE	AFTER
les parenthèses/bracket (fermeture) *parenthesis/bracket (closing)*	no space	1 space
le point *period*	no space	1 space
le point d'interrogation *Question mark*	1 space	1 space
les guillemets (ouverture) *Quotation marks (opening)*	1 space	1 space
les guillemets (fermeture) *Quotation marks (closing)*	1 space	1 space

The following spacing rules are different in Canada from those used in France.

	BEFORE	AFTER
le point d'exclamation *exclamation mark*	no space	1 space
le point d'interrogation *question mark*	no space	1 space
le point-virgule *semicolon*	no space	1 space

Index

à:
  in adverbial clauses of manner, 81
  with geographical names, 73–74
  before an infinitive, 82–83, 227
  to join two nouns, 79
  to mean *with*, 71, 79 80
  with modes of transportation, 76–77
  with place names, 71
  with time expressions, 77
adjectives:
  agreement problems, 33–35
  of color, 34–35
  comparison of, 47–48
    irregular comparatives, 50–52
    useful phrases with comparatives, 54
  compound, 35
  demonstrative, 58–59
  feminine of, 24–31
  indefinite, 59–64
  plural of, 31–33
  position of, 36–46
  possessive, 54–57
    with indefinite pronouns, 55
  superlative of, 49–52
    irregular superlatives, 50–52
    without superlative or comparative forms, 53
    useful phrases with superlatives, 54
adverbs:
  comparison of, 47–48
    irregular comparatives, 50–52
  formation of, 41–45
  interrogative, 235
  position of, 46
  superlative of, 49–52
    irregular superlatives, 50–52
agreement of the past participle, 154–157
aller:
  s'en aller versus *partir, sortir, laisser, quitter,* 294
  expressions with, 285
  present tense of, 126
  with an infinitive, 173
après, 78
  with the past infinitive, 222

arithmetical operations, 93
article:
  definite, 1–4
    contractions of, 14–15
    omission of, 14
    partitive versus, 19
    plural forms of, 4–8
    singular forms of, 1–3
    uses of, 9–14
      with days of the week, seasons, time
        expressions and dates, 11
      with general or abstract nouns, 9
      with languages and academic subjects, 11
      with names of continents, countries,
        provinces, regions, islands, mountains
        and rivers, 13
      with parts of the body or clothing, 14
      as a possessive, 55–56
      with titles, 10
      with weights and measures, 13
  indefinite, 16
    omission of, 16–18
    partitive versus, 19
s'asseoir, 135
avant, 78
avec, 70–71, 81
avoir:
  agreement of the past participle of verbs
    conjugated with, 154–155
  versus *être* as an auxiliary verb, 158
  expressions with, 286
  present tense of, 124

beau, forms of, 30

ça, 271
ça faisait... que and the imperfect tense, 147–148
ça fait... que and the present tense, 129–130
cardinal numbers, 88–89
causative construction with *faire,* 223–224, 262–263
ce, 271
ce dont, 278
ce que, 274

ce qui, 274
ceci, 271–272
cela, 271
chez, 72–73
collective numbers, 91–92
comparative:
  of adjectives and adverbs, 47–49
  followed by a noun, 49
  irregular, 50–52
compound tenses, 186–192
  interrogative of, 234
  negation of, 243
conditional tense:
  formation of, 182
  past conditional, 190
  uses of, 183–185
    after certain conjunctions, 184
    to express the idea *would*, 183
    to express probability or unsure action, 185
    in indirect discourse, 185
    to soften a request, command or desire, 184
conjunctions:
  conditional tense after, 184
  future tense after, 177–178
  requiring the subjunctive, 207–209
connaître versus *savoir*, 296
conversational past tense (*see passé composé*)

dans:
  with geographical names, 75
  with modes of transportation, 77
  with place names, 72
  with time expressions, 78
dates, 94
de:
  in adverbial clauses of manner, 81
  with geographical names, 75–76
  after indefinite pronouns, 80
  before an infinitive, 227–228
  to indicate relationship of cause, 80
  to introduce the material from which an object
    is made, 80
  to join two nouns, 79
  to mean *with*, 71, 80
  with place names and locations, 71–72
definite article:
  contractions of, 14–15
  omission of, 14
  partitive versus, 19
  plural forms of, 4–8
  singular forms of, 1–3
  uses of, 9–14
    with days of the week, seasons, time
      expressions and dates, 11
    with general or abstract nouns, 9
    with languages and academic subjects, 11

definite article, uses of (*cont.*):
    with names of continents, countries, provinces,
      regions, islands, mountains and rivers, 13
    with parts of the body or clothing, 14
    as a possessive, 55–56
    with titles, 10
    with weights and measures, 13
demeurer versus *habiter* and *vivre*, 292
demonstrative adjectives, 58–59
demonstrative pronouns, 270
  indefinite, 271–272
depuis:
  and the imperfect tense, 147–148
  and the present tense, 129–130
descendre with *être* and *avoir* in the *passé composé*,
  158
devoir, special uses of, 289–290
dimensions, 93
direct and indirect discourse, 218–220
direct object pronouns, 253–254
  le, la, l', les, 253–254
  me, te, nous, vous, 255–256
  special use of *le*, 255
(*see also* pronouns)
disjunctive pronouns, 266–267
dont, 276–277

en:
  with geographical names, 74
  to introduce the material from which an object is
    made, 80
  with modes of transportation, 76–77
  with place names, 74
  pronoun, 258
  with the present participle, 140–141
  with time expressions, 78
entendre with the infinitive, 226
entrer with *être* and *avoir* in the *passé composé*, 158
-*er* verbs:
  passé composé of, 148
  passé simple of, 168
  present tense of, 99–100
être:
  as an auxiliary verb, 156–159
  versus *avoir* as an auxiliary verb, 158
  expressions with, 287–288
  imperfect tense of, 143
  with the passive voice, 230
  present tense of, 125
  verbs conjugated with, 156–159

faire:
  in causative construction, 223–224, 262–263
  expressions with, 288–289
  present tense of, 127
falloir, 128

first conjugation verbs, 148
  (*see also -er* verbs)
fractions, 92
futur antérieur, 188–189
future perfect tense, 188–189
future tense:
  formation of, 174–176
  uses of, 177–180
    after certain conjunctions, 177–178
    in indirect discourse, 179
    after *penser que, savoir que, espérer que, ne pas
      savoir si*, 179
    to express probability, 180

gender:
  feminine, 1–4
  identification by word endings, 2
  masculine, 1
  nouns indicating occupations, nationalities,
    relationships and domestic animals, 3
  words with different meanings in the masculine
    and feminine forms, 4

habiter versus *demeurer* and *vivre*, 292

il y a... que and the present tense, 129
il y avait... que and the imperfect tense, 147–148
imperative: 137–139
  affirmative, 131–134
  negative, 139
  position of object pronouns with, 263
  subjunctive as an, 209–210
imperfect subjunctive:
  formation of, 215–216
  uses of, 216
imperfect tense:
  formation of, 142–143
  versus the *passé composé*, 161–165
  si and, 147
  uses of, 144–148
indefinite adjectives, 59–64
indefinite article, 16
  omission of, 16–18
  partitive versus, 19
indefinite pronouns, 279–283
  with possessive adjectives, 56
  with possessive pronouns, 269
  prepositions after, 80
indirect discourse, 218–220
  and the conditional tense, 185
  and the future tense, 179
indirect object pronouns, 255–256
infinitive:
  with *faire*, 223
  following a noun or adjective, 82–83
  with *laisser* and verbs of perception, 226, 262–263
  negation of, 245–246

infinitive (*cont*.):
  position of object pronouns with, 261
  preceded by *à*, 227
  preceded by *de*, 227–228
  after prepositions, 221–222
  of reflexive verbs, 137
  uses of, 221–222
interrogation (*see* interrogative)
interrogative:
  with *est-ce que*, 232
  by inversion, 233–234
  lequel, 239–240
  negative, 244
  with *n'est-ce pas*, 232
  quel, 238–239
interrogative adverbs and adverbial expressions, 235
interrogative pronouns, 236–237, 239–240
inversion, 220, 233–234
-ir verbs:
  passé composé of, 149
  passé simple of, 169
  present tense of, 107–108
irregular verbs (*see* Verb Charts, pages 373–378)

jouer, jouer à, jouer de, 292

laisser:
  with the infinitive, 226, 262
  versus *partir, s'en aller, sortir, quitter*, 294
lequel:
  versus *dont*, 276–277
  interrogative pronoun, 239–240
  relative pronoun, 275–277
literary past tense (*see passé simple*)

manquer, manquer à, manquer de, 292–293
mood, 98
monter with *être* and *avoir* in the *passé composé*, 158

ne:
  in negative sentences, 242–244
  with the subjunctive, 208
negation (*see* negative)
negative:
  of compound tenses, 243
  imperative, 139
  infinitive, 245–246
  interrogative, 244
  omission of *pas*, 245
  si in answer to a negative question, 245
  of simple tenses, 242
  words and phrases, 246–249
nouns:
  compound, 8–9
  feminine, 1–3
  gender of, 1–4
  masculine, 1–3

nouns (*cont.*):
  occupations, nationalities, relationships and
    domestic animals, 3
  plural forms of, 4–7
  singular or plural, 8
nouveau, forms of, 30
numbers:
  arithmetical operations and dimensions, 93
  cardinal, 88–90
  collective, 91–92
  fractions, 92–93
  ordinal, 90–91

on, 56, 100, 252–253, 266, 269, 281
ordinal numbers, 90–91
où:
  interrogative adverb, 230
  as a relative pronoun, 276

participle, past:
  agreement of:
    with reflexive pronouns, 159
    with verbs conjugated with *avoir*, 154–155
    with verbs conjugated with *être*, 157–158
  irregular, 150–154
  regular, 148–150
participle, present, 140–141
  after prepositions, 140–141
partir versus *sortir*, *s'en aller*, *laisser*,
  quitter, 294
partitive, 18–21
  versus the definite and indefinite
    articles, 19
  exceptions to the rule for
    using, 19–20
  replacement with *de*, 20–21
pas, omission of, 245
passé antérieur, 191–192
passé composé:
  of -*er* verbs, 148
  formation of, 148–154
  versus the imperfect, 161–165
  of -*ir* verbs, 149
  of irregular verbs, 150–154
    (*see also* Verb Charts, pages 373–378)
  of -*re* verbs, 150
  of reflexive verbs, 159
  uses of, 160–161
  of verbs conjugated with *être*, 156–158
passé du conditionnel (*see* conditional, past)
passé simple:
  of -*er* verbs, 168
  formation of, 168–172
  of -*ir* and -*re* verbs, 169
  of irregular verbs, 169–172
    (*see also* Verb Charts, pages 373–378)
passé surcomposé, 191

passer:
  with *être* and *avoir* in the *passé
    composé*, 158
  passer, *se passer*, *se passer de*, 294–295
passive voice, 230–231
  with *être*, 230
  forms of, 230
  with *se*, 231
past anterior (*see passé antérieur*)
past participle:
  agreement of:
    with reflexive pronouns, 157–159
    with verbs conjugated with
      avoir, 154–155
    with verbs conjugated with *être*, 157
  irregular, 150–154
  regular, 148–150
penser à versus *penser de*, 293
plaire, 295
pluperfect subjunctive:
  formation of, 217
  uses of, 217
pluperfect tense, 186–187
plus-que-parfait, 186–187
possessive adjectives, 54–57
possessive pronouns, 268–269
pouvoir, special uses of, 290
prepositions, 70–85
  in adverbial clauses of manner, 81
  of cause, 80
  with geographical names, 73–74
  after indefinite pronouns, 80
  before an infinitive, 82–83, 227–228
  followed by an infinitive, 221–222
  to introduce the material from which an object is
    made, 80
  to join two nouns, 79
  to mean *with*, 79–80
  with modes of transportation, 76–77
  with place names and locations, 71–73
  with the present participle, 140–141
  with time expressions, 77–78
present participle, 140–141
  after prepositions, 140–141
present perfect, 160
present tense, 99–130
  of -*er* verbs, 99–100
  of first conjugation verbs, 99–100
  formation of, 99–128
  of -*ir* verbs, 107–108
  of irregular verbs, 110–128
    (*see also* Verb Charts, pages 373–378)
  of -*re* verbs, 109
  of reflexive verbs, 133
  of second conjugation verbs, 107–108
  of spelling-change verbs, 103–107
  of third conjugation verbs, 109

present tense (*cont.*):
  uses of, 129–130
  of verbs beginning with a vowel, 102
pronouns:
  demonstrative, 270
    indefinite, 271–272
  direct object, 253–256
    le, la, l', les, 253–254
    me, te, nous, vous, 255–256
    special uses of *le,* 255
  disjunctive, 266–267
  double object, 259
  en, 258
  indefinite, 279–283
  indirect object, 255–256
    lui, leur, 256–257
    me, te, nous, vous, 255–256
  interrogative, 236–237
    le, 255
  object:
    direct, 253–256
    double, 259
    indirect, 255–256
    position of, 260–263
      with affirmative commands, 263
      with causative *faire,* 262–263
      with conjugated verbs, 260–261
      with an infinitive, 261
  possessive, 268–269
  reflexive, 265
  relative, 272–278
  stress, 267, 293
  subject, 99, 252–253
  y, 257

que:
  interrogative pronoun, 236
  relative pronoun, 273
quel, interrogative adjective, 238
qu'est-ce que, 236, 238
qu'est-ce que c'est, 236, 238
qu'est-ce qui, 236
qui:
  interrogative pronoun, 236–237
  relative pronoun, 272–273, 275
qui est-ce que, 236
qui est-ce qui, 236
quitter, versus *partir, sortir, s'en aller, laisser,* 294
quoi:
  interrogative pronoun, 236–237
  relative pronoun, 278

se rappeler versus *se souvenir de,* 295
-re verbs:
  passé composé of, 150
  passé simple of, 169
  present tense of, 109

reflexive pronouns, 265
reflexive verbs, 132–137
  imperative of, 139
  negative imperative of, 139
  in the infinitive, 137
  negative of, 242
  versus non-reflexive verbs, 136
  with parts of the body, 136
  passé composé of, 159
  present tense of, 133
relative pronouns, 272–278
rentrer with *être* and *avoir* in the *passé composé,* 158

savoir:
  versus *connaître,* 296
  present tense of, 127
  special uses of, 290–291
seasons, 95
second conjugation verbs, 109, 150, 169
  (*see also -ir* verbs)
sequence of tenses, 218–220
servir versus *se servir de,* 296
si:
  in answer to a negative question, 245
  and the imperfect tense, 147
si clauses, 193
  in the subjunctive, 218
sortir:
  with *être* and *avoir* in the *passé composé,* 158
  versus *partir, s'en aller, laisser, quitter,* 294
se souvenir de versus *se rappeler,* 295
spelling-change verbs, 103–107
subject personal pronouns 99
subjunctive:
  avoiding the, 212
  imperfect:
    formation of, 215–216
    uses of, 216
  past, 213–214
  pluperfect:
    formation of, 217
    uses of, 217
  present, formation of, 195–200
  uses of:
    after an affirmation, 210
    with expressions of doubt, 206
    as an imperative, 209–210
    with impersonal expressions, 204–205
    after indefinite words, 211–212
    in noun clauses, 200–212
    after *quelque... que,* 211–212
    in relative clauses, 210
    after *rien, personne, quelqu'un,* 211
    after *si... que, quelque... que, quel... que, qui que...,* etc., 211–212
    with subordinate conjunctions, 207–209
    after a superlative, 211

superlative of adjectives and adverbs, 49–52

third conjugation verbs, 109, 149–150, 169
  (*see also -re* verbs)
time, 95–96
typographical rules, 379

valoir, 128
venir de, 297
  and the imperfect tense, 148
  and the present tense, 130
verbs:
  compound tenses, 186–192
  conditional past tense, 190
  conditional tense, 182
  future perfect tense, 188–189
  future tense, 174–180
  imperative, 137–139
  imperfect tense, 137–139
  irregular (*see* Verb Charts, pages 373–378)
  mood, 98–99
  passé antérieur, 191–192
  passé composé, 148–163
    of *-er* verbs, 148
    versus the imperfect, 161–165
    of *-ir* verbs, 149–150
    of irregular verbs, 150–154
    of *-re* verbs, 150
    of reflexive verbs, 159
    uses of, 160–161
    of verbs conjugated with *être*, 156–158
  passé simple, 168–172
    of *-er* verbs, 168
    of *-ir* and *-re* verbs, 169
    of irregular verbs, 169–172

verbs (*cont.*):
  passé surcomposé, 191
  passive voice, 230–231
  pluperfect tense, 186–187
  present perfect, 160
  present tense, 99–130
    of *-er* verbs, 99–100
    of *-ir* verbs, 107–108
    of irregular verbs, 110–128
    of *-re* verbs, 109
    of reflexive verbs, 133
    of spelling-change verbs, 103–107
    uses of, 129–130
    of verbs beginning with a vowel, 102
    (*see also* Verb Charts, pages 369–378)
  reflexive, 122–137
  regular (*see* Verb Charts, pages 369–372)
  with spelling changes, 103–107
    (*see also* Verb Charts, pages 371–372)
  subjunctive, 195–218
    imperfect, 215–216
    past, 213–214
    pluperfect, 217
    present, 195–200
    uses of, 200–214
  (*see also* individual verb tenses)
vieux, forms of, 30
vivre versus *habiter* and *demeurer*, 292
voilà... que:
  and the imperfect tense, 147–148
  and the present tense, 129–130
voir, with the infinitive, 226
vouloir, special uses of, 291

y, 257

Companion Audio Recording

A companion audio recording that features selected answers from the answer key is available online. (Please see the inside ad to find directions.) Spoken by native French speakers, the audio provides a convenient way to improve your French pronunciation and listening comprehension as you check your answers.

For any question that includes more than one possible answer, only the first word or phrase from the answer key is included.

Below is a list of selected exercises:

Introduction

Track 1   About this recording

Chapter 1

Track 2   Exercises 14, 20, 25
Track 3   Exercises 31, 35, 36

Chapter 2

Track 4   Exercises 17, 18, 27, 28
Track 5   Exercises 29, 30, 31, 33
Track 6   Exercises 35, 44, 54, 57

Chapter 3

Track 7   Exercise 3

Chapter 4

Track 8   Exercises 6, 9, 11, 12, 13

Chapter 5

Track 9   Exercises 28, 87, 119, 123
Track 10   Exercises 124, 138, 139, 149, 151
Track 11   Exercises 157, 160, 173, 181, 182
Track 12   Exercises 188, 191, 196
Track 13   Exercises 202, 203, 204, 207, 208
Track 14   Exercises 209, 210, 211, 213, 217
Track 15   Exercises 219, 231, 235, 243
Track 16   Exercises 245, 253, 255
Track 17   Exercises 261, 268, 270, 271, 272
Track 18   Exercises 274, 275, 278, 279
Track 19   Exercises 298, 299
Track 20   Exercises 301, 320, 322
Track 21   Exercises 326, 328, 330
Track 22   Exercises 331, 332, 339, 341

Chapter 6

Track 23   Exercise 1

Chapter 7

Track 24   Exercise 17

Chapter 8

Track 25   Exercises 40, 46, 47, 48
Track 26   Exercises 49, 50, 53